THE COMPLETE GUIDE TO

DECORATING YOUR HOME

THE COMPLETE GUIDE TO

DECORATING YOUR HOME

How To Become
Your Own Interior Designer

RIMA KAMEN

BETTERWAY BOOKS
Cincinnati, Ohio

Cover and cover photograph by Susan Riley
Typography by East Coast Typography, Inc.

96 95 94 93 92   5 4

Library of Congress Cataloging-in-Publication Data

Kamen, Rima
   The complete guide to decorating your home
   Includes index.
   1. Interior decoration—Handbooks, manuals, etc.　I. Title
NK2115.K26　1989　　747　　88-34950
ISBN: 1-55870-117-6

To Harvey, for his love, patience, encouragement, and support.

Contents

Introduction

You're about to change your life. Inside this book you'll find everything you've ever needed to know about decorating but were afraid to ask. It's all there for you: the most current trends, money-saving ideas, and tricks of the trade. You'll find out the secrets of how professionals turn out magazine-quality rooms; even learn "designer lingo." Most important, I promise you'll never make another decorating mistake again.

I bet you're thinking this is a gimmick, too good to be true. You're probably asking yourself, "Why would a professional interior designer give away the benefit of all her years of training and experience?" The answer is, I'm tired. I've been in one too many homes where the owners have attempted to decorate themselves. Usually the proportion and scale are wrong and the choices of furniture, fabric, and wall coverings are less than mediocre. It's disturbing. You work too hard for your money to throw it away. There's no reason for you to make horrendous decorating mistakes you'll be forced to live with. Why bother to decorate your house if you're not going to decorate it right? Right?

I confess, I've never quite gotten over the reality that clients are willing to pay me $100 an hour just to come over and give them some decorating ideas. Perhaps I suffer from the "imposter" syndrome. I tend to take for granted the education and experience I've chalked up over the years which label me a professional. After all, I ask myself, what's

the big deal about having developed a sharp eye, good taste, and a keen color sense? Can't anyone develop these skills? I believe the answer is a definite "yes." You *can* do it.

How? I'm going to teach you everything I know about interior design. In order to justify the 1,000 hours I put into compiling and writing this book, I couldn't resist multiplying those 1,000 hours by the $100 per hour fee I charge. Being a great rationalizer, I feel compelled to tell you that you are getting $100,000 worth of my consultation services for the mere price of this book. It's a great trade. You're getting one of the greatest bargains of your life, and I'm getting the pleasure of seeing you happier and more successful.

I'm a firm believer that one's environment has a profound influence on one's feelings of self esteem and self worth. People who take pride in their homes also take pride in their health, their physical looks, their work, their families, and their friends. Over the years, I've seen clients go through personal metamorphoses after having their homes redecorated.

One client in particular, a rather depressed, lonely new divorcé, asked me to come over to discuss redecorating his home. He answered the door wearing an old wrinkled gray shirt that hung out of a pair of ill-fitting jeans. Over a glass of wine, he confessed, "I need something to perk up my life." I looked around the living room, experiencing the gloominess of its decor, despite the magnificent ocean view that seemed incongruous with the "downer" aura of the house. The old, sagging sofas and chairs were covered in an old, worn-out brown fabric. The flat, gray carpeting was soiled and stained. The only accessories were odds and ends of cheap knick-knacks that had survived his divorce. There wasn't a plant in sight, and the lighting made both of us look like we had risen from the dead.

"This place needs a bulldozer! Gut it! Throw it out, throw it all out!" I blurted. (I was never known for my great tact.)

He looked at me, horrified by my audacity. I'm sure he thought I was crazy. "You've got to be kidding," he said, looking sadly around the hopeless room, I suspect reminiscing about how he and his ex-wife had loved the furniture when they first bought it.

I jumped up and began one of my best performances. I was selling him the concept of bringing the beauty of the ocean view into the interior of the house. "White," I said, "Everything's going to be white!" We would add hand-painted fabrics to match the colors of that beautiful sunset and pastel-colored neon lighting to give the home drama at night.

He listened skeptically, potential dollar signs inflaming his eyes. I thought at any moment he'd escort my body out the door.

"And the fireplace, it's ugly. We'll paint it white, and have the sunset colors washed over it in a subtle, flowing pattern."

His eyes began to light up. "How much is all of this going to cost me?"

"Don't worry about it," I said evasively, hoping we could deal with that aspect later.

"Easy for you to say," he answered, pulling himself out of the old sofa with a new spirit and energy. "How much money do you need up front?" he asked, pulling his checkbook from a drawer. He seemed so happy and excited as we said good night to each other.

Months passed as the once-dowdy house was magically transformed into the bright, cheerful home of a "winner." I watched my client come alive before my very eyes. His new wardrobe reflected the colors and style of his new home, as he proudly showed off the dramatic rooms to his friends and neighbors. He exuded a new air of confidence and energy. One of the most rewarding moments in my career was when he said, "Thank you so much. You've changed my life."

I'm a firm believer that decorating should be fun and enjoyable. After all, you've worked hard and decorating your home is a luxury you well deserve. Be enthusiastic. You'll get out of your home all the love and care you put into it. If the thought of decorating your home is drudgery and a chore, take the time to read this book. DECORATING IS FUN!

1
First Things First

"Hmmm," you say, scratching your head with a puzzled look on your face. "Where do I start? What do I have done first?" Stop! Don't do anything yet! Before you run around in circles, wasting time and energy, and accomplishing nothing, let's start at the beginning and take a trial run. This sneak preview will ease your trepidations about the task ahead. Follow me through a guided tour that will make each stage of your decorating project easy and fun. At the end of the tour you'll get a present . . . beauty and success in your home.

The Mental Project

MAKE A DECISION

You're either going to decorate your home or you're not going to decorate your home. If you elect to do it, do it right. Often, I find that people try to skimp or take shortcuts that don't work. If you change one thing in a room, it's bound to affect the appearance of the other things in the room. An old, worn-out sofa will look even worse against brand-new draperies. And vice versa: tattered and faded draperies will become more of an eyesore against a brand-new sofa.

"What do you think I am, rich?" I can hear you screaming at me. Of course not. If you were, you wouldn't be reading this book, you'd be jetting off to the south of France while a famous designer decorated your two million dollar estate. Because I understand that you're probably working with a limited budget, I plan to tell you how to "go for it" without spending any more money than you had originally planned to spend.

If you can't afford to do your entire house "right" with one swift imprint of your credit card, don't despair. It's perfectly okay to decorate one room at a time, as long as you've pre-planned later stages. Don't decorate only one room without knowing exactly what you're going to do with the rest of the house later. It won't work; your house will look choppy and end up a hodgepodge.

If you're starting from scratch, pre-plan the entire design project before you open your wallet. If your budget is limited, don't try to do the whole house at once. It's better to leave empty spaces than to clutter them with compromises you're sure to despise by next year. Your walls, flooring, counter tops, and lighting should be planned first. If your backgrounds are wrong, everything else you put in the room will look wrong. If you can't afford the treatments you'd really like to have eventually, choose neutrals. There's nothing wrong with using white, beige, or gray; they're safe. Later, it'll be easier to make changes or add detailing.

Buy the most important, necessary pieces first. Beds, living room sofas, and dining table and chairs are a must. If you've pre-planned the total look, you'll know exactly what pieces to buy now and what pieces you plan to add later. For example, if you're planning an eclectic look, you might want to buy one or two high quality white overscaled sofas for your living room and have puddled draperies made in a soft, subtle print. Of course, you've ordered enough extra fabric to make throw pillows and a skirted table. Six months from now you'll buy that twelve-paneled Oriental screen you've had your heart set on to put behind the sofa. Maybe you're feeling plush enough to purchase that stunning glass and silver leaf coffee table you fell in love with last year. The next year, you get a big promotion and raise and you're ready to splurge on that antique Oriental rug and a few fine pieces of artwork. You even manage to squeeze into the budget a few large indoor plants and trees. The rest of your rooms will fall into place in much the same way if you plan ahead.

If you're only giving your home a "facelift," you'll still need to pre-plan the entire project. Be brutally honest about your rooms. Try analyzing the rooms through the eyes of an impartial stranger. Decide which pieces can be freshened up and updated by reupholstering or slipcovering. Which table and chairs would look great with a new finish and which ones would look better in the garbage can? Will your old carpeting look even older next to fresh fabrics and finishes? Will a new area rug make the room look fresh and new? Are you willing to part with those cheap posters and knick-knacks? Have your window coverings lost their life? You'll find plenty of easy, money-saving ideas within the pages of this book.

Okay, you've made the decision, you're committed. What's next?

LEARN THE BASICS OF GOOD DESIGN

I bet you thought I was going to say "money." All the money in the world can't buy the knowledge of good design and good taste. Some of the worst design jobs I've seen in my life were done by amateur decorators with unlimited funds, but a deficit of basic design knowledge and good taste.

Before you spend a dime, read Chapter 2: The Basics of Good Design. You'll have a clearer understanding of how line and shape dictate the quality of an object and affect the emotional impact and feeling of your rooms. You'll see how using texture and pattern correctly adds character to your rooms. You'll learn how to create unity, variety, harmony, emphasis, and balance to give your rooms that professional look. You'll become more aware of correct proportion and scale.

Know what you're after before you bother going after it. Your home should be functional and comfortable as well as beautiful. In Chapter 2 you'll also find out how to plan your life space to satisfy your needs and please your tastes.

LEARN WHAT'S AVAILABLE

Your materials are your tools. You can't make a silk purse out of a sow's ear if you don't know what a sow's ear is. Read through the basic materials described in Chapter 3, and use a little creative thinking to see how you can use these materials, either alone or in combination, to create new and unique decorating ideas.

Look through the source books and trade magazines I've suggested in Chapter 6: Stretching Your Decorating Dollar to find new products on the market. Try to visualize how you can use those materials in interesting and unique ways. Look at photographs of rooms done by professional interior designers. What materials did they use to make that room different and exciting? Walk through furniture stores and showrooms and notice how they're using new materials. Don't forget to examine retail store displays. Most display artists use subtle tricks to create drama by using easily obtainable, inexpensive materials and props. There's a wealth of ideas just waiting out there for you to notice.

If you're lazy and would rather settle for the mundane because it's easier, your home will reflect your attitude. Learn the materials, how to use them, how to mix and blend them, and where to find them.

DEFINE YOUR PERSONAL STYLE

Get in touch with your own particular tastes and adapt them to the architecture of your home. Now isn't the time to be wishy-washy. If you're not sure exactly what style you want or what style your home is crying out for, why not take a personal inventory? In Chapter 4: Selecting Your Style, you'll find a self-test that will help you know yourself and end your confusion.

Please, don't buy anything until you've thoroughly analyzed your tastes and lifestyle. Make a commitment to a style you love and feel confident you can live with for a long time. It's not a wonderful feeling to spend a great deal of money and energy decorating your home in "California casual," only to find yourself wishing that you'd done the whole project in "opulent traditional." Buyer's remorse hurts.

PREPARE A FURNITURE PLAN

Chapter 5: Preparing a Furniture Plan will tell you exactly how you can make a floor plan with ease. Before you even think about buying one piece of furniture, you must make sure it will fit in correctly with your home and complement the overall scheme. This step is crucial to successful decorating. If you skip it, you're sure to make mistakes that can't be corrected easily.

A furniture plan will also help you visualize and create more exciting floor plans. You'll have fun playing around with sizes, shapes, and angles of furniture before you buy it. Attempting to rearrange furniture that doesn't fit after it's made and delivered will only aggravate your bad back and give you a headache.

PREPARE A REALISTIC BUDGET

Okay, now we're ready to talk about money.

Chapter 6: Stretching Your Decorating Dollar will show you how to make an estimated budget and revise it until it works for you. I've even included a worksheet you can use by just filling in the amounts.

Chances are that you haven't got a clue yet how much your lavish decorating fantasies are going to cost you. No matter how expensive you estimate this little decorating project to be, I warn you, the final tally might throw you into a coma.

Assuming you only have a certain amount of money you're able to spend right now, Chapter 6 will show you how to use it wisely and effectively. If you skip preparing a budget, you'll end up halfway through the project with bare windows and an empty checkbook.

Throughout this book you'll find an abundance of unique money-saving ideas you've never dreamed of before. Use the dollar-stretching ideas that are right for you and your home, and you'll find your dollars will go further than you'd ever imagined.

DEVELOP A GOOD COLOR SENSE

Chapter 8: Understanding Color will teach you everything you'll need to know about color. You'll find out how to identify different hues, values, and intensities. You'll be astonished at how different colors will make you feel. Most important, you'll learn how to develop the right color schemes for your home. I'll even give you inside information about the latest color trends and tell you what color schemes are yesterday's news.

START SHOPPING

The good news is . . . it's time to go furniture shopping. The bad news is . . . don't buy anything yet. Learn to say "just looking" to sales people.

Find out what's available, what you like, what you don't like. Make sure that what you do like works with the overall decor of your home. Just gather ideas for now. When you fall in love with a piece of furniture, take home a picture. Most stores and showrooms will gladly give you a tearsheet or snap a Polaroid shot for you. Make sure you have the dimensions of each piece you select, and draw them on your furniture plan to confirm that the pieces will work in your room.

If you can't find exactly what you're looking for, it's time to consider having some pieces custom made. You'll find instructions on how to draw elevations of built-ins and custom-made pieces in Chapter 6. You might even want to copy a piece that's stolen your heart, but you can't afford.

If you can't find the right chairs in the exact finish you want, shop the unfinished furniture stores. You'll be able to find the frame you want and have it custom finished and upholstered.

If you can't find the exact sofa or loveseat you want, try a custom upholsterer. Show the upholsterer a drawing or photograph of the piece, complete with exact dimensions, and have him give you a bid.

Once you've done your shopping and most of your pieces are selected, or you've gotten bids on having them custom made, fill in the prices on your budget and move on. Ready to shop for your wall coverings and fabrics now? Once you've read Chapters 11 and 12, this should be a breeze. Take home as many samples as you'd like, play with them, live with them for a while. Give yourself time to change your mind. Try to visualize how a wallpaper will look in a particular room. Imagine how a fabric will look on a sofa or chair.

Make sure you know the exact yardage you will need for each upholstered piece and the exact number of rolls of wallpaper you will need for each room. Once you have this information, you can go ahead and add the prices to your budget. Flooring comes next. After you've selected your furniture, wallpaper, and fabrics, you'll begin to "feel" what colors and textures will look right on your floors. Bring all of your samples to the store or showroom and hold them up to any potential flooring. Take the flooring samples you choose home with you, live with them for a while, see how they match your

other fabric, wall covering, and finish samples in both natural and artificial lighting.

If you're using area rugs, you might want to select them prior to choosing fabrics and wall coverings, especially if they contain hard-to-match colors. If you're using custom-made area rugs, don't worry, they can easily be matched to most of your fabric and wall covering choices. Now add the flooring prices to your budget.

DRESS UP YOUR WINDOWS

Go ahead, design and get bids for your window coverings now. The decision will be a lot easier now that you know most everything else that's going on in the room. Read Chapter 15: Choosing Your Window Coverings to give you some great dollar-stretching ideas. You'll even learn the art of communicating with the person who will be making your window coverings. Just get the prices and the correct amount of yardage you'll need for now, pencilling those amounts in on your budget.

TIME TO PAINT

I bet you thought we'd never get to selecting your paint. How could you possibly have known what color paint to use until you had everything else selected? You might even want to consider using painting textures and techniques that will pull together everything else you've chosen. You'll find some exciting ideas and new trends in Chapter 9: Miracles with Paint.

Start interviewing painters and getting bids now. When you're convinced you've selected the right painter and the right painting textures and techniques, it's time to set up a date. Most good painters are booked months in advance. And don't forget to add this cost to your budget.

LIGHTING'S NEXT

Once you've read Chapter 10: Effective Lighting, you'll be better informed and ready to make the right decisions. If there's still any element of doubt in your mind, don't rule out paying a professional lighting consultant to give you advice.

If you'll need an electrician to install your lighting, now's the time to call and get a bid for the work. Most electricians work by the hour, so it's difficult to know exactly what the total cost for installation will be. Have him estimate his hours as realistically as possible.

Check the delivery time for all the lighting fixtures you plan to order. Make a date with your electrician at least three weeks after that date, because you can bet that's how late the fixtures will be. If they're in stock, just schedule your electrician for the week before the painter is due to arrive. If your lighting isn't in by the time the painter begins, you stand a good chance of having holes cut in walls that have been freshly painted. Again, be sure to add lighting and installation costs to your budget.

ADD UP THE BUDGET

By now you've got some reasonably exact figures on what each item is going to cost. Time to tally up your budget. If you've added in the extra expenses I've suggested in Chapter 6 at the end of your budget and still haven't had a nervous breakdown, it's time to order! Make sure you've left an adequate allowance for the inevitable artwork, accessories, and plants; they'll come later. If you're cursing yourself for not having listened to your mother's advice to marry someone very rich, and you'll have to eat tuna casserole for the next ten years in order to pay for this little project, it's time to cut some corners. Don't fret, by the time you've finished reading this book, you'll be dancing with optimism.

READY TO ORDER?

Be prepared to watch your checkbook deflate rapidly. Make sure you're 100% positive about the items you're about to commit yourself to; they're rarely returnable.

It's a good idea to make a purchase order for each item you buy. If it's a piece of upholstered furniture, staple a sample of the fabric to be used on the purchase order that you give the showroom or store. If it's a piece of furniture that's to be finished, make sure you specify the exact finish you want.

You'll find more details about the mechanics of ordering everything in each individual chapter. Make sure you read these guidelines thoroughly. *Most decorating mistakes take place at the time a piece is ordered.*

The Physical Project

Congratulations! Now that you've selected and ordered everything for your house, it's time to see how everything is going to look. This is the fun part. Your home will be transformed into a bustling hub of workmen and deliveries. The project will run smoothly if you know how to coordinate and supervise the work correctly.

• Start with a naked space. Strip the room or rooms to be decorated. Old furniture that will no longer be used should be sold or given away. A great time-saving idea is to call in a used furniture company who will buy everything you don't want for one blanket price. Or donate everything to a charity; they'll come by and pick it all up. If you've got the patience and time, sell the furniture piece by piece by placing an ad in the local newspaper. Take down old window coverings and get rid of any artwork, accessories, and plants that will no longer work.

• Now's the time to make any structural or architectural changes. If the task is simple, like pulling off an old door and widening the opening or enlarging a window, a good handyman can usually do the job. If the work is more complex, find a good general contractor to handle the work. Be sure to draw the changes to be made, complete with accurate dimensions, before you begin. Watch over each stage of the work being done to make sure your plans are being followed correctly.

• Once your windows are the right size and in the right place, you can call your drapery workroom to measure. Make sure you supply an accurate drawing, with detailing of course, and order the correct amount of fabric to be sent directly to the drapery workroom. You'll most likely need to give a deposit to get the work rolling.

• Rip out all old, unwanted moldings, baseboards, and trim now.

• Rip out all old, unwanted flooring next.

• Replace what needs replacing or make any additions, such as new crown molding or chair rails. Have your general contractor take care of this for you or hire an experienced and licensed carpenter to do the work. Watch over the work as it is being done to make sure it is being executed neatly and correctly.

• Heating, air conditioning, or ventilation changes or additions should be made now. Have your general contractor do this for you, or hire a licensed specialty contractor to do the work. Make sure you plan vents so that they don't interfere with your furniture placement.

• Your electrician should come by now to put in any additional electrical outlets you'll need and prepare any wiring for the new lighting or lighting changes you're planning. He should come back after the room is painted and dry to install the actual lighting fixtures. Either have your general contractor use his electrician or hire a licensed electrician who will usually work by the hour.

• If you're adding any decorative facings to walls, columns, fireplaces, or ceilings, now's the time to do it. Again, have your general contractor do it, or use a licensed carpenter. Watch over every stage of the work to make sure it is being done correctly.

• If you'll be refinishing existing hardwood floors, now's the time to have them stripped and sanded; it's too messy to do later. Cover the newly stripped floor with plastic or a drop cloth so that it doesn't get damaged or stained by the workmen coming and going through the room.

• Begin calling every store and showroom from which you ordered furniture, fabrics, and wall coverings. Make sure your orders are being processed and the goods will arrive in time for your specific deadline date. Be relentless. Don't ever assume that because you ordered something, paid for it, and gave the salesperson the date you needed it by, that you'll have it by that date. It rarely happens. You must follow through with nagging calls constantly, making yourself such a nuisance that they'll rush through your order just to shut you up.

• Your painter can begin now. Insist he use drop cloths to protect anything left in the room that could be damaged by paint. Watch over his preparation techniques. A good painter will prepare the walls by first filling in all cracks, chips, and irregularities, letting them dry, then sanding them. Woodwork seams and flaws should be filled in, dried, then sanded thoroughly. Primer coats should be used on all woodwork and walls that will be hard to cover. The painter should remove all door and window hardware as well as all electrical plates before painting. He should mask off moldings, windowpanes, and all edges where paint might bleed through to an area where it is not intended to be.

Provide your painter with the name and number of the paint you have selected for each room. Have him buy the smallest size of each color of paint and apply a three foot by three foot sample of those colors in the areas where they are to be used. Let the paint dry thoroughly to see how it looks before allowing him to continue. If need be, now's the time to make any color changes. When you're convinced you've selected the right colors, let the painter buy the paint in larger amounts and get on with the job.

• Installing your flooring is a Catch-22. If you put down the flooring before the painter paints, he's liable to damage the flooring. If you paint before the flooring's laid, the installers are bound to damage the walls and molding. I generally put in hard flooring before paint, making sure the floor is thoroughly covered and protected. I always put in carpeting after painting and assume I will have to have the painter come back and touch up the damage the carpet installers have done with their rubber heels against the walls. Make sure your painter saves enough paint for touch-ups and agrees to come back at the end of the job to do touch-up work.

• Once the walls are painted, your electrician can come back and attach the lighting fixtures and add any dimmer switches you'll need.

• By now your window coverings should be ready. Once your flooring is down, arrange to have them installed any time.

• Assuming you were smart, ordered all your furniture before you started the actual work, and used my special nagging techniques, it's all ready to be delivered. Feel free to scream and yell at upholsterers and finishers who give you excuses for your pieces not being finished. I usually use a guilt-giving technique to speed up their work. Try making up an impending disaster that will happen if the pieces aren't ready on the exact day you want them. Feign a nervous breakdown or threaten a lawsuit if you must.

• Time to call a professional delivery service to arrange pick up and delivery of all of your pieces. Retail stores usually arrange delivery for you. If you're buying from wholesale showrooms, it's up to you. Find a reliable service through referrals, your source books, or the Business-to-Business Yellow Pages. Most delivery services charge by the hour, although you can find some services that charge a flat fee determined by the number of pieces and the amount of driving time it will take to pick up and deliver the items. Take the time to compare prices and services. Most services will set up and align all your furniture for you, even assemble furniture, attach furniture to walls if need

be, and hang pictures. Other services are not as accommodating. Make sure you ask what the service will and will not do. Of utmost importance, ask if the delivery service carries insurance for any items they might damage. *Don't use a service that doesn't carry insurance.*

• Delivery day! This is the exciting day you've been anxiously awaiting. Get up early in the morning and call everyone to confirm that the pieces are ready, and let them know approximately what time each piece will be picked up by the delivery service. Be prepared to hear excuses like, "The piece was ready, but when we were putting it on the loading dock, one of our workmen dropped it. It'll be fixed by next month." Relax, this is normal. I've never done an installation where at least two or three different horror stories didn't happen at the last minute. I've compared notes with many other designers and they report the exact same phenomenon. Experience has taught me not to panic; all problems can be worked out with patience and endurance.

If you've done your homework well, worked from a furniture plan, checked and double checked the progress of each piece for correct construction, fabric, and finishes as it was being made, chances are the number of delivery day catastrophes will be minimal.

Be there to coordinate and supervise the delivery. As each piece is brought in, direct the delivery man to the exact spot where the piece is to be placed. A professional service will be patient with you as you make sure the piece is placed within a fraction of an inch of perfection. They'll even fluff pillows, remove any spots of dirt that happened during delivery, and clean the glass and mirror surfaces for you.

Now, that wasn't too difficult, was it? Your personal decorating project will flow just as smoothly as this trial run if you follow the ideas, suggestions, and guidelines found throughout the remainder of this book. Enjoy!

2
The Basics of Good Design

A natural flair, good taste, and a discerning eye are great assets for an interior designer. But, yes, you can improve and perfect your decorating skills just by reading this chapter and putting forth a little practice and effort. Most important, you should try to be as observant as possible from now on. Make it a habit to constantly look around your environment, not merely seeing objects as they appear, but analyzing them. What do they consist of? How are they made? What is their size? Their texture? Their lines? Be observant! It's the key to developing your creativity and learning good design techniques.

What Is Design?

Webster's Dictionary defines design as (noun) "a mental project or scheme in which means to an end are laid down." As a verb, design is "to conceive and plan out in the mind" and "to devise for a specific function or end." Thus, design is a conscious process. It's the act of using the materials available to us to perform a function, whether it be utilitarian, aesthetic, or both. You do have the inborn ability to design your own environment in a way that is satisfying and right for your own life.

The purest form of design is to create something that has never existed before, a figment of your imagination, a dream. The most perfect example of design in nature is the egg. If a bird can be creative, so can you.

My first assignment when I entered the School of Interior Design at U.C.L.A. was to make a portfolio of photographs which were to describe pictorially a number of words we were given: whirling, powerful, meek, sad, and exhilarating. I set out one morning, armed with a cheap camera and rolls of film, trying to find subject matter to photograph that would portray these words. Dumbfounded, I scoured the city for objects that might work, cursing my teacher for subjecting me to this ridiculous project. I was literally being forced to see things in the world around me that had never been apparent before. Months later I successfully completed the project and handed in the carefully cut and pasted pictures, resenting the exorbitant amount of money I had spent on film and developing hundreds of pictures, only to use a select few. I only recently realized how valuable that first lesson was. I learned to be observant; to see things that most other people don't see. It was the foundation of my successful design career.

What Are the Elements of Design?

LINE

Line is one of the basic elements of all design, a close cousin to shape and space. When one of these three elements exists, you can safely bet the other two are hovering nearby.

Line in nature. The human body is a prime example of the basic natural lines found in nature; so is a leaf, a cloud, a horizon line, a mountain. As you hurry to work in the morning or rush to McDonald's for lunch, take time to slow yourself down, really see the line, form, and shape of the world around you. Notice the jagged lines that form a range of mountains; the curved lines that form the pebbles on the beach; the square and rectangular lines that form the skyscraper; the radiating lines that make up the vein of a leaf; and the variety of lines that give a drawing or painting its meaning. These are your sources of inspiration.

Abstract lines are implied but don't really exist. Hard to visualize, I know. Picture the line the headlights of a car make on the freeway, or the lines made by the whirling rotors of a helicopter.

Symbolic lines are symbols with meanings attached. Oriental writing is a good example. The character that means "house" actually looks like a house.

Contour lines trace the outline or overall shape of an object. Line may not only imply form, but actually is form. For example, a bicycle is a combination of complex lines that produce a form; that form serves a particular function.

Lines that create texture and pattern are either lines drawn closely together or similar lines repeated in some type of overall composition. Placed together, they form a definite pattern or texture. Line usually directs your eye and creates an emphasis. You'll respond emotionally to the quality of that line. Horizontal lines will make you feel restful, stable, and calm. Just visualize the tranquility of lying on the beach, basking in the warmth of the sunshine, waves gently flowing. Feel the soothing effect of the horizon line.

Vertical lines appear to defy gravity. They'll give you an uplifted feeling and create a pleasing balance next to horizontal lines. Diagonal lines are dynamic, full of energy. They'll demand your attention and wake you up with drama and animation. Curving lines can make you feel an inner turbulence. Huge, upward curves will make you

feel inspired. Horizontal curves will make you feel gentle and relaxed. Large, downward curves will make you feel serious or sad. Small ones will make you feel playful and humorous. Think of a child's room, filled with marbles, balls, and checkers.

If you really work on experiencing these feelings, you'll see that line, all by itself, can dictate your mood.

The direction of a line also has an impact on your emotions and feelings. Horizontal lines, along with making you feel rested and peaceful, create an informal setting. A room with low ceilings and elongated furniture is a good example. Vertical lines, like those of high ceilings and tall doors and windows, give you a sense of arrogance and pride. Diagonal lines, like those in sloped ceilings, walls, and furniture, generate a feeling of activity.

SPACE

Space is a key word in designer lingo. To be able to visualize space will be your greatest asset in decorating your home. *Actual space* is the space that really exists. *Pictorial space* is an illusion, like that created in a two- or three-dimensional drawing, painting, or sculpture. When you erect walls, you enclose and define space. When you add a roof, you divide two segments of space: the space of the inside structure and the space of the outside environment.

Implied space can be easily understood if you visualize a drawing that has its forms sharply cut off at the edges of the picture, leaving some of the lines incomplete. The artist has "implied" a larger space. *Spatial illusions* fool your eyes by deliberate manipulation of line and shape. Your eyes will automatically have a strange reaction to certain combinations of line, shape, light, and color.

When a designer tells you he is designing a "space," he means he is seeing the design project as the problem, and the design of the space as the solution. A space planner is a trained draftsperson who is skilled at making a space work efficiently for the particular uses and functions his clients have requested. Basically, this is what you will do for your home when you get to Chapter 6: Preparing Your Furniture Plan. (In a simple and easy way, of course.)

SHAPE

Shape is the general outline of an object. Two-dimensional shape relates to the contour of an object. The word "form" means shape, but also includes an object's mass and volume. Let's divide shape into four main categories.

Geometric shapes. All geometric shapes are variations of straight lines, angles, or curves. Every shape contains one or more of the basic elements of a circle, square, or triangle. Squares and rectangles will affect your emotions differently depending upon not only their size and placement, but their color and direction. Angular shapes, like a dramatically angled ceiling, will add life, spirit, and a note of drama to your room. Triangles can be varied to suit any of your moods. The diagonal lines of a triangle seem to visually increase the size of an object. Angular shapes stir up motion and will attract and hold your attention. Circles make you experience motion, as your mind automatically relates them to easily movable balls and wheels. They create a natural focal point and unity because each point on the circle's edge is an equal distance from its center.

When you combine any of these geometric shapes to balance each other, you create form. The form creates unity, which is one of the major principles of design.

Natural shapes, obviously, are the shapes you see every day in the natural world around you. We're all familiar with the shapes of leaves, flowers, insects, birds, and animals. *Abstract shapes* are distorted shapes; ones that have been changed into something different. While you still know the source of the shape it's been simplified by omitting many of its unnecessary elements. *Non-objective shapes* don't even relate to anything you'd recog-

nize in the natural world. They're shapes you can't really name or identify.

TEXTURE

Texture is the quality of a surface. It's the way that surface feels when you touch it. Use a variety of textures in decorating your home to create interest and variety. Let's use a little creative imagination here. Close your eyes and visualize a room with four completely different textures. First, run your fingers over the smooth surface of the walls and the highly polished furniture. Now feel the rougher textures of the used-brick fireplace and the stone planters. Next, experience the soft plushness of the velvet carpeting. And last, gently touch the delicate and lightly textured ferns and flower petals. These are called tactile textures, ones that you can feel. Visual textures are illusions or simulations of tactile textures.

Textures affect your emotions in many ways. You get an immediate impression of everything you touch. Did you ever play the game in school or art class where different objects were placed in separate paper bags? One paper bag would contain a cotton ball; another a rock; the next, a feather; and the last, an egg. You were blindfolded and asked to feel the secret object inside the bag and describe how it felt.

If a texture is too hard or coarse, it can irritate you. If it's too sleek, it will make you feel cold and slippery. Very smooth materials like metals, lacquers, glass, and satin reflect light strongly, attracting your attention and making colors seem stronger and clearer. Moderately rough surfaces like brick fireplaces absorb light unevenly, making colors seem less vibrant. Extremely rough surfaces create energetic patterns of light and dark.

Texture, when used and combined correctly in your home, creates a special beauty and character. It plays an important role in the feeling, the aura of your rooms.

PATTERN

Pattern goes hand in hand with texture. Pattern means a motif is being repeated over and over again; it is repetitive. You'll soon be analyzing and considering the decorative qualities of the patterns of the fabrics and wall coverings you want in your home. We'll talk more about pattern when we get into each individual chapter. What's important now is to see how pattern can create texture and texture create pattern.

COLOR

Color is the most magic ingredient in decorating your home. It is one of the most important concepts you'll need to understand in order to create an exciting decor. Since its importance cannot be overlooked, I've dedicated the entirety of Chapter 8 to the subject. So hold tight, you'll soon learn everything you need to know about making color work for you and your home.

What Are the Principles of Good Design?

UNITY

Unity is the designer's concept and the honesty used to make that concept a reality. It means carrying through one single motivating idea through repetition and similarity.

When you design your home, all of the objects and colors should relate to each other in some way. This means using repetition of color, pattern, line, and shape in order to create unity. However, try not to get stuck on this concept without using a little creative thinking. Unity without a little variety can be very monotonous.

VARIETY

Variety means that you should vary colors, shapes, patterns, and themes within the rooms of your home, without sacrificing unity, of course.

You'll achieve harmony when you combine variety and unity correctly.

EMPHASIS

Emphasis means giving appropriate significance to each part of your room. Call more attention to the most important parts and less attention to the least important parts. Aim to create focal points, or centers of interest, set against less important backgrounds.

The overall look you'll want to achieve is contingent on which elements you downplay. For example, your home might have a fabulous panoramic view that is the natural and obvious focal point of your living room. This will become the emphatic level of the room's design. Now, maybe you have an important painting that you love and want to hang on your twenty foot high fireplace. Great! This now becomes the dominant level of emphasis. Next, you've chosen some simple and elegant upholstered pieces that blend subtly with your living room. These pieces now become your sub-dominant level of emphasis. And of course, you've decided to keep your floors, walls, ceilings, and other accessories rather neutral. These become your subordinate level of emphasis. In order to determine what you should emphasize, take a good look at the natural conditions that exist in the room. They will lead you to the right solutions.

RHYTHM

Rhythm is continuity. Your home will feel alive with the movement and direction rhythm implies. The main ways of achieving rhythm are by using repetition and progression. You can repeat or alternate shapes, colors, or textures. I usually repeat the forms, colors, and textures that make up the basic character of a home, avoiding repetition of ordinary and commonplace things. To avoid monotony. relieve repetition with a contrast of some type.

Progression means a sequence or transition. You can increase or decrease one or more qualities of a room by making successive changes that create motion directed toward an overall goal. This can be more powerful and exciting than plain old repetition. Visualize the pattern formed by the flames of a fire and the intriguing hypnotic rhythm it creates.

BALANCE

Balance is equilibrium. Since we all strive to achieve well-balanced lives, shouldn't our living environments also be well balanced? Your rooms should make you feel at peace and relaxed. Did you ever walk into a room that made you feel uneasy, on edge? Something just didn't feel right? It's probably because that room was not well balanced.

There are three basic types of balance. *Symmetrical balance*, the simplest and most common, is achieved when one side of something is exactly the same as the other side. It's easy and we're used to it; our bodies were created with symmetrical balance. However, sometimes symmetrical balance is dull and boring. Sometimes it's downright impractical and inconvenient. For instance: you're building a home and you put a door in the center of the wall in the name of symmetry, but the door really isn't in a logical place. You've made the room difficult to furnish because the two walls on each side of the door are exactly the same size.

Asymmetrical balance is when two sides are equivalent in weight and mass, but not identical. As you decorate your home, you'll learn to use asymmetrical balance to create informality, flexibility, and spaciousness. Its use also creates movement, spontaneity, beauty, and individuality.

Radial balance has a circular movement out from, toward, or around a focal point. A good example of radial balance is the light thrown from a circular lighting fixture or the patterns found on a circular bowl.

To create a pleasing balance in your rooms, you should pay attention to the relative heights of every object in the rooms. All too often, I've visited homes where the would-be decorator has filled a room with all very low furniture, unrelieved by varying heights. It's very disturbing to have your eyes forced downward. Personally, I get a kind of "Jack and the Beanstalk" feeling when I'm in such a room.

To remedy this unsettling condition easily, add some tall indoor plants or trees, a large painting placed over a low sofa, a few tall torcheres, or perhaps a sculpture on a pedestal. In reverse, if everything in the room is too high, add balance with interesting objects placed below eye level, such as two great urns placed on either side of a fireplace or large floor baskets filled with wood, flowers, or plants.

PROPORTION AND SCALE

Proportion and scale go hand in hand. Proportion is the relationship of one object to another object, or to the whole. Scale is the relationship of the size of an object to another object. So that you won't confuse the two terms, let's say that proportion can be either pleasing or not pleasing, while scale can either be large or small.

Many professional interior designers use an oversized scale to produce dramatic and overstated rooms. The use of oversized sofas, pillows, chairs, and enormous trees is very popular right now. These designers, however, know the basic rules of scale and proportion and are skilled at breaking them. It's important to have a clear understanding of the basic architecture of the house and the rooms, as well as to consider the ceiling heights, the angles, and the lighting.

Some homes and/or people demand a grand scale. Others beg to be decorated on a more conventional scale. The character of your home and its occupants should be a major consideration when you select the right scale to use. Knowing when, where, and how to use an oversized scale as opposed to using smaller pieces is a gut reaction of feeling, intuition, and appropriateness.

One of the cutest "eye openers" I've encountered as an interior designer was the day I walked into some new clients' home. They asked me to stop by to give them some ideas and suggestions on redoing their family room and kitchen. I immediately noticed a magnificent mountain view that appeared to be cut in half by windows that were too low and suggested they start the project by replacing the windows with larger, higher windows. They stared at me with puzzled looks, "What are you talking about, we can see the view perfectly?!" I quickly noticed that I was looking down upon two people who were very short; she was about 4'10" tall and he was about 5'5". I'm 5'9" tall barefooted and was wearing high-heeled shoes that took me well over the 6' mark. I laughed as I bent down to the eye level from which they were seeing the view. They were right, it was perfect. "Oh well," I told them, "Short people do have some advantages. I might get more fabric for my money when I buy clothes, but you just saved a fortune by not having to put in new windows."

The lesson I learned is the importance of taking human scale into consideration. Your home is where you live, and the size of the rooms and furnishings should fit you and your family. This tiny couple would feel ridiculous and lost sitting on the huge, overstuffed sofas I have in my living room. I would feel like Papa Bear sleeping in their small double bed (which they refused to replace with a king size).

Creating good proportion and scale in a room is a matter of learning to see how objects relate to each other in size. Most amateurishly decorated homes I've seen have a multitude of elements that are grossly out of scale. Most people tend to hang small pictures over huge pieces of furniture and place tiny tables next to large sofas. As you read through this book, you'll learn more about developing a keen eye for correct proportion and scale.

COMPOSITION

Composition is the sum total of everything you've learned so far. It's the grouping of different parts of your decorating scheme to achieve a unified look. It's your basic yearning to create order in your life. Composition applies to your furniture, wallpaper, fabric, accessories, pictures, you name it. It's how you put everything together. When you get dressed, presumably you put yourself together so that everything you wear blends well together, flatters your body, feels right, and presents a total look that is pleasing. You've put your best foot forward, and other people just naturally gravitate to you. Just apply the same techniques to decorating your home and your success will be assured.

The composition of the interior of your home should relate to the exterior environment. Ideally, the exterior should flow into the interior. For example, I recently designed a home on a bluff overlooking the beach and used the colors and patterns of the ocean, sand, and adjacent mountains to create a composition that was in harmony with the environment. I'm currently working on a condominium for a bachelor living in a large city high rise. The lines and colors of the interior relate to the view of the city lights and the sharp angles of the buildings that can be seen from every window. If I were doing a home surrounded by dense trees in the mountains, I would make every effort to bring that environment inside by repeating the dense foliage in the interior. Thus, composition is not only the way you arrange things, but the way you relate everything to the entirety of your environment.

Creating Your Life Space

Basically, your house is just a shelter to protect you from the elements. But, let's face it, you're way past the caveman stage and want more from your home. The concept of territoriality goes way back in time, and refers to the basic feelings that your territory is that portion of the universe which belongs to you. Your special place creates feelings of belonging, safety, comfort, and familiarity. You even put monograms on your towels and pajamas to make a statement about your ownership and individuality. Your home is an extension of you, your family, and your friends. Your home is your personality, your unique and special identity. There are many considerations to be made in determining how you will choose to decorate your home.

CLIMATE

Climate will often dictate your choice of materials. If you live in a cold, damp climate, you would naturally opt to create a feeling of warmth and snugness. Just visualize sitting in front of a roaring fireplace in a room filled with plush carpeting and rich woods. On the other hand, if you live in a warm or hot climate, you would want to use ''cool'' materials and pastel colors. If you use light colors and plan large areas of uncluttered space, you'll actually feel cooler.

LOCATION

Location is another factor to consider when you decorate. You would certainly choose different materials for your high rise condominium with a panoramic view than you would for your country home nestled in trees by the lake, wouldn't you?

MOBILITY

Mobility is another consideration. Nowadays, many people change their homes almost as often as they change their underwear. Whether it is the popularity of the mobile home, job relocation, divorce, a quick profit in a booming real estate market, or merely the quest for bigger and better, we all seem to be moving on. So, if you're not sure you're there to stay and you can't afford to redecorate every year, remember the word, ''versatility.'' Plan your furnishings so that they can move and grow with you.

HOUSEHOLD

The number and ages of the people in your household is a primary factor in planning your life space. The needs of each individual and the needs of the family as a whole must be met. Remember to consider the amount of both privacy and interaction with other family members each person needs. Everyone in your family should have their own private space where they can express individual needs and personality.

LIFESTYLE

Lifestyle is another major consideration in decorating your home. Are you single, spending most of your time working and traveling, regarding your home as a pit stop for sleeping and eating? Or are you a family who likes to spend a lot of time at home, enjoying family meals, games, hobbies and other amusements together? Do you enjoy entertaining at home? Do you give small, intimate dinner parties or large, elaborate cocktail parties? Do you work out of your home?

PSYCHOLOGY

Psychology also plays a major role in home decorating. Some people are claustrophobic and feel physically confined and anxious when put in rooms that are too small. Other people are agoraphobic and feel an overwhelming insecurity when put in rooms that are too large and open. The agoraphobic person needs the psychological protection of a snug nest, while the claustrophobic needs wide open spaces. Ideally, a home should include a good compromise. Group spaces should be more wide open, have higher ceilings and an easy flow between areas, while private spaces should be smaller and have lower ceilings and fewer windows.

Your personal taste plays an important role in designing your life space. We'll get more into this in Chapter 4: Selecting Your Style.

What Are the Goals of Design?

UTILITY

Utility should be the first goal. It means the space you design works effectively and serves the purpose that it was meant to serve. Utility is the primary purpose. Your rooms should be planned for usefulness, comfort, and efficiency. However, please refrain from being too practical. A "too" efficiently planned home can be very boring and cold. Be flexible. Use utility as a goal, but not the only goal.

ECONOMY

Economy is the second goal, and refers not only to your budget, but to the human, material, and environmental resources available. For example, economy of human resources can mean an efficiently designed kitchen for a person who is a gourmet cook, or choosing low maintenance kitchen materials for a person who doesn't have the time or inclination for housekeeping.

Material resources refers to the use of objects you already have. Often, the repair or adaptation of something you already own will suffice or even work better than something new you rush out to buy. Monetary resources refers to your budget, which we'll discuss more in Chapter 6: Stretching Your Decorating Dollar. *Just remember: it's foolish to buy haphazardly without having your overall plan in mind.* Trust me, you'll end up with a lot of mistakes and unneeded items.

Conservation of natural resources is also a consideration in the goal of economy, not only for the sake of ecology but for the budget. For instance, wooden objects have a long life, can be refinished many times, and when they are no longer useful can be absorbed into the environment. Always consider the possibilities of giving old objects new life and new purposes. A little imagination is all that is necessary.

BEAUTY

Beauty is the third goal of decorating. We think of beauty as that which pleases the senses and lifts the spirits of a particular person. It is subjective. Beauty directly relates to taste, which I'll talk more about more in Chapter 4.

CHARACTER

Character is the fourth goal of decorating. How you personalize your space has to do with how much time, money, and effort you are willing or can afford to spend. You can completely remodel your home, gutting it and rebuilding it to your own specifications; you can merely slap some paint on what's existing and throw in your own furniture, or anything in between. It's up to you.

Personalizing your space is a natural tendency. Think about the nights you've spent in hotel rooms, how you arranged your toiletries on the bathroom counter or laid out your clothes for the next day. Your ability to create character in your home in the same way will come through naturally.

3
Your Materials

Materials are your tools; your creativity, the power behind you. A basic understanding of the materials available to you is essential to the foundation of your creativity. Let's go through the list, so you'll know what you have to work with.

Wood

Wood is abundant in nature and has been used as a basic material for many centuries. New and innovative ways of using wood and simulating wood are rapidly being introduced into the marketplace. It is an extremely strong material, can be shaped easily, retains its shape under pressure, can't be easily broken, and holds up well when bent or pulled. Because wood is so resilient, it is an excellent choice for floors and furniture. Wood is also a great insulator and doesn't transmit heat or cold. On the other hand, wood can burn, rot, or decay. Insects can attack it. It may swell, shrink, or warp with changes in humidity. We'll discuss more details about wood in Chapter 16: Choosing Your Furniture.

Masonry

Masonry is any material such as stone, brick, or tiles that is put together with mortar. The term also includes plaster and concrete. Masonry is derived from the earth's surface and is usually hard, dense, and heavy. It doesn't rot, decay, or invite insects or rodents. Materials are long lasting, require very little maintenance, and retain their shape under great pressure. Textures range from very smooth to very rough. They can be shaped, curved, or used in their natural state. Of course, there are negatives. Masonry can be costly, plaster and stucco tend to crack, concrete blocks tend to chip, and softer stones often disintegrate. These problems are difficult to repair. Masonry is not as strong in tension as wood or metal, and is a poor insulator against coldness and dampness. Most types of masonry reflect noise rather than absorbing it.

Marble is limestone which has crystallized. It ranges from granular to compact in texture and takes kindly to a high polish. *Granite* is a very hard igneous rock formation of visibly crystalline texture formed essentially of quartz and orthoclase or microcline. Both of these materials come in a wide variety of colors and textures. They make beautiful counter tops, table tops, table bases, and flooring. It is currently popular (and expensive) to use granite for the entire counter top of your kitchen. It's important to understand that marble and granite are natural materials and will contain some, if not many, flaws. This is considered to be part of the natural beauty of the material. If your city has a marble yard, take the time to wander through it. You'll be amazed at the variety of different types of marble and granite available, as well as discovering other types of materials such as stones containing fossils. The possibilities of creative use in decorating are endless.

Glass Blocks

Glass blocks have made a great comeback recently. They are hollow blocks set together with mortar and available in a variety of shapes and sizes. All glass blocks admit light, but give a degree of privacy while still providing insulation against heat and cold. They can even be used to construct an entire supporting wall. The way glass blocks diffuse light and create abstract patterns from objects can be very exciting. Recently I was in a restaurant that had glass blocks inset in a unique and interesting pattern on some of its interior walls. The designer had installed colored neon lights in strategic places to reflect through the glass blocks. It created a mesmerizing effect. Why not use this idea in your home?

Concrete

Concrete is a mixture of cement and sand with gravel or other aggregates. Generally thought of as an exterior material, it also is an ingredient in terrazzo, which is concrete made with stone chips and then polished to an irregular mosaic-like pattern. But forget terrazzo, it's passé.

Concrete is now being used in some new and exciting ways. There are special stains and dyes that can be applied. Besides being an economical way of flooring a large space, it's a new and professional look. With these new finishing techniques available, the possibilities for concrete as a material to be used in the interior of your home are endless.

Plaster

Plaster is a thick, pasty mixture of treated gypsum and water, combined with materials such as sand and lime. (Stucco refers to weather-resist-

ant plaster, most often used on exteriors.) It will hold any shape it's given before it hardens. It takes kindly to texturing, coloring, and painting, can be covered with wallpaper or fabric. Heavy textured plain white walls are very "hot" right now. However, plaster does crack and chip, show fingerprints and soot, and scratch easily.

Ceramics

Ceramics are objects made of clay and then hardened. The clays used for ceramics differ. Colors range from white through red, tan, gray, brown, and black. Textures vary: coarse, irregular, fine, even, and dense.

Earthenware is a coarse clay fired at a low temperature. It's thick, porous, fragile, and opaque. It can be glazed or left unglazed.

Porcelain is a high grade white ware fired at extremely high temperatures. It resists breakage and has an extremely hard glaze.

China is a white vitrified ware that is thin and translucent. Fired at a slightly lower temperature than porcelain, it sometimes looks just like porcelain. English china or bone china has a brilliant glaze and contains a percentage of animal bone.

Glass

Glass dates back 4,000 years. It is made by melting and fusing silicates, alkalis, and lime, along with other materials that give it various qualities, at very high temperatures. Crystal, the finest glass, contains lead. The color comes from the minerals gold, copper, cobalt, cadmium, and uranium. Use cut glass, engraved glass, etched glass, enameled and gilded glass, sandblasted glass, leaded glass, and stained glass to create limitless unusual effects in your home.

Mirror

Mirror is glass with a metal backing. It can expand the size of a room, spread light throughout a room, glorify a view, heighten a ceiling, and bring sparkle to a dark and dreary corner. Mirror comes in clear, smoked, bronze, black, and even peach finishes.

Fiberglass

Fiberglass is glass spun into fibers. Foam glass is made by adding a gas-producing agent into the molten glass. Glass fibers provide excellent insulation against extreme temperatures and sound. Because fiberglass is very lightweight, it's commonly used in molded furniture for public seating and inexpensive household chairs. Fiberglass is now being used as the base material for faux stone (fake stone surfaces) because it is less expensive and lighter than wood. Any piece of furniture can be made to look like stone and can be finished in a variety of colors and textures. Mixing faux stone with other materials such as glass, metal, lacquer, or bleached wood can create some exciting new furniture ideas. You can even install neon lights in faux stone pieces for exciting drama.

Metal

Metal does not burn, rot, or decay. But most metals do rust or corrode when exposed to moisture or air. Metal has a great tensile strength and a great capacity to transmit heat, cold, and electricity.

Many laminate companies make a variety of metal laminates. Use them to create interesting walls, ceilings, fireplaces, columns, and range top hoods. Because these laminates can be curved easily, use them for table bases or even curved metal walls.

Aluminum is a whitish, lightweight metal that doesn't deteriorate. It can be polished, brushed, or anodized to a satiny surface and comes in a wide range of metallic hues.

Chromium is a blue-white metal that holds a high polish. It's most commonly used in lighting fixtures and furniture. Chromium is hard, cold, and resists corrosion.

Copper has a lustrous orange finish that will oxidize to a dull greenish brown or blue green. It is soft, easily shaped, and a great conductor of electricity. Use copper for wonderful fireplaces. range top hoods, and even front doors. For easier maintenance, have copper coated to prevent oxidation. Copper alloyed with tin becomes bronze. Copper alloyed with zinc becomes brass.

Steel is iron that has been hardened with chemically-dissolved carbon. Steel rusts like iron, so it should only be used if painted or enameled.

Stainless steel is a blue-gray metal that has chromium added to resist rust and stains. It's hard, durable, and reasonably inexpensive.

Silver is the whitest and softest of all the metals. It reflects twice as much light as stainless steel. Silver is usually hardened with copper. Often, silver is plated over an alloy base. Its application in decorating is limited because of its high cost.

Plastics

Plastics can be molded into shapes and perform jobs no other material can. Wood, coal, milk, petroleum, natural gas, and many other substances are turned into different types of plastic. There are numerous techniques for forming plastics. The materials can be compressed into molds; extruded through dies to form continuous sheets, rods, filaments, or tubes; injected into cavities of complex outline; drawn into molds by vacuum methods; blown full of gas or air to make them rigid, semi-rigid, or flexible; or sprayed over foams. In laminating such materials as Formica, Laminart, Wilsonart, and Nevamar, layers of cloth, paper, wood, or glass fibers are impregnated with uncured resin or alternated with uncured plastic film, then pressed into a single sheet.

Acrylics include such trade names as Plexiglas and Lucite. They are glamorous, glass-like, strong, and rigid. Acrylics are lightweight, can be clear or tinted, patterned or plain. They do scratch easily, but can be buffed smooth with a buffing compound. The newest trends in acrylic include everything from picture frames to Z-shaped barstools, coffee tables, four-poster beds, and even domed skylights.

FRP (Fiberglass Reinforced Plastics) range from stiff to flexible, hard to soft, and come in any color. They have a high resistance to chemicals and weather and can be molded easily into exciting furniture forms.

Nylon is usually opaque and comes in many colors. It is resistant to abrasion, rigid, and has a high tensile strength. However, the hard glossy surface can be scratched easily and stained by coffee, tea, and other foods.

Melamines are widely used for counter tops and table tops. They're extremely durable and hard. Melamines don't scratch or chip easily. They resist water, food, heat, and stain damage. Colors don't fade or lose their brilliance. The surface can be a high gloss, satin, or mat finish.

Polyethylenes are flexible or semi-flexible and have a wax-like surface. You'll see them used often for common squeeze bottles, but they can be used for molded, non-upholstered chair shells.

Polystyrenes have a lustrous finish and come in a limitless range of opaque and translucent colors. They're hard, rigid, tasteless, odorless, and resistant to most household chemicals and foods. However, polystyrenes don't hold up very well when they're bent or struck with any force. They're frequently used in modular furniture systems.

Vinyls are tough, strong, lightweight, and relatively inexpensive. They're versatile, can be rigid or non-rigid, and either transparent or opaque. Various effects can be achieved with the processes of embedding, embossing, or printing. Although vinyls withstand food and chemicals, they do stiffen in cold weather. Vinyls are used most often in flooring because they are durable, easily maintainable, resilient, act as an insulator, and control sound. Vinyl flooring comes in a wide assortment of colors, sizes, and designs. I'll talk

more about vinyl flooring in Chapter 14: Choosing Your Flooring.

Most plastics are tough, durable, absorb no moisture, and don't rot or mildew. But before using plastics in your home, be sure to ask about flammability. Many plastics are rated slow burning or self-extinguishing, but a few types have been found not only to burn, but to melt or break down molecularly, giving off lethal and even explosive gases. Be careful.

Now that you know the basics of good design, understand how to create a life space, and have a comprehensive understanding of the basic materials available to you, you've grown closer to seeing how professional interior designers get their ideas. More aware now of the goals, elements, and principles of design, you can relate those concepts to your composition and use the materials available. You're on your way to stimulating your own creativity and opening up possibilities of new and innovative ideas.

It's essential to learn to visualize your home or room as a "space" and that space as the "problem." Once you've defined the problem, you can use the information you've just learned, along with what you're about to learn, to find the right solution to fill that space.

Professional interior designers are constantly keeping abreast of the current trends and new materials by reading trade magazines and scouring the showrooms for new ideas. You should do this, too. It's important to know what's available to you before you begin decorating your home. In Chapter 7, you'll find more ideas on how to find the right sources.

Be observant! Professional interior designers get their ideas from everything they see and experience throughout the day, turning a trite observation into a new design concept. It takes practice, but it's fun, rewarding, and you can do it, too. I've spent many sleepless nights tossing and turning, mentally designing a new project. That's probably when I get my best, most original ideas.

I know, you're probably asking, "What good is a great concept if I haven't the foggiest idea how to execute it?" Where do you find that fabulous piece of furniture you conjured up in your head at three o'clock this morning? Where do you find that knockout fabric you designed in your dreams last night? Be patient, you'll find all the answers you need as you read through this book.

Of course, I suspect you're also asking, "Sure, now I understand the basics of good design and the materials available, but it looks like the professionals are breaking the rules all the time. How do I break the rules without making a mess?" Unfortunately, it's hit and miss. It takes a lot of experience and mistakes to learn how to break the rules effectively. I've created a design concept on a wish and a promise, crossing my fingers and holding my breath nervously as I watched my eccentric ideas come to life.

Remember the project for the bachelor that I mentioned in the introduction? I insisted we paint out his used-brick fireplace with white and then hire an artist to paint over the white brick in the same celadon and pink striations that I had hand-painted on the tussah silk pillows thrown on the sofas. I'd never seen this done before and knew it was virtually impossible to get the white paint off the used brick once it was painted. I confess I was panicked, but I hung in there insisting it would "make the room." Fortunately, it did, and my client thought I was brilliant. I confess, the fabulous effect was only the result of a gutsy guess.

For those of you who are less daring and confident, I suggest you get your ideas from magazines and showrooms; it's a lot safer. Adapt a concept or idea that you've seen so that it's just different enough to become your own creation. Be open minded. Experiment with size, scale, and color, but use similar professional photographs as your guidelines.

4
Selecting Your Style

Now that you know the basics of good design, it's time to apply everything you've learned to help you define and select your individual style. I suspect you've thumbed through hundreds of interior design magazines over a period of years, meticulously saving the stacks of pictures you adore. If you haven't been so industrious, it might be a good idea to make up for lost time now. Search as many decorating magazines as you can for pictures you love and can relate to; tear them out and keep them in a file. As you go through that file with all the pictures you so laboriously cut out, saved, and filed, you probably won't be able to remember why you originally tore out each photograph. You probably won't even see a particular relationship between one picture and another. There's just something about that room that strikes your fancy.

Recently, since you've been contemplating decorating your home, perhaps you've been walking through furniture stores or even traipsing through your city's design center to see what's happening and to get some fresh ideas. If not, now's the time to do some extensive window shopping. You might even be recalling different friends' homes you've visited over the years and thinking you want your home to look just like theirs. But the truth is, you're confused and not 100% sure what style you really want. You scream, "Help!" Relax, I'm here.

Let's break down this task into easy segments that will be easier for you to digest. First, put a check mark next to the words that best describe your particular style of living.

- ☐ Formal
- ☐ Conventional
- ☐ Modern
- ☐ Serene
- ☐ Dignified
- ☐ Simple
- ☐ Graceful
- ☐ Quaint
- ☐ Informal
- ☐ Unconventional
- ☐ Traditional
- ☐ Exhilarating
- ☐ Casual
- ☐ Cluttered
- ☐ Plain
- ☐ Sophisticated

Now that you've checked off one or more of the words that best describes your personal style and that of your family, go back through the stacks of photographs you've pulled from magazines, and begin eliminating, one by one, the pictures that don't relate to your personal style.

Next, go through the following list and check off any words that describe what type of "feeling" you ideally would want your room or rooms to evoke.

☐ Elegant
☐ Conservative
☐ Flamboyant
☐ Ordinary
☐ Dull
☐ Youthful
☐ Playful
☐ Luxurious
☐ Amusing
☐ Grandiose
☐ Strong
☐ Bold
☐ Graceful
☐ Offbeat
☐ Plain
☐ Ostentatious
☐ Amusing
☐ Sedate
☐ Dramatic
☐ Common
☐ Whimsical
☐ Opulent
☐ Powerful
☐ Dramatic

Which mood or combination of moods did you choose as those that would give you the greatest pleasure? Now, go back through the remaining stack of pictures and pull out the ones that exemplify the moods you chose. You've probably narrowed down your selection to only a few of the original photographs and have made a major step forward in selecting your style.

Although I rarely perform the same test on my new clients, I do make it my business to carefully observe them and their families from the onset of the job. I watch them in action, analyzing their preferences, noting what objects they love and refuse to part with, how they dress, how they speak, how they relate to one another. Keen observance gives me a true feeling for their tastes, needs, and desires, even if they themselves are oblivious to the style they really want.

One of the most fruitful exercises I do with clients before I begin their design project is to take them for a quick but thorough tour through the design center. I don't allow them to select anything and guard them from falling in love with any particular piece of furniture. I just ask them to point out what general styles they like and what colors or color combinations excite them. They're also asked to comment on which styles and colors they hate. This practice has saved me enormous amounts of energy and time in the long run. By the time we've finished our quick window shopping session, I've usually pinpointed their specific tastes. There's no reason why you can't do this for yourself. Just think of it as an enjoyable preliminary exercise that will save you from making expensive and irritating mistakes in the long run.

What Are the Basic Looks?

THE COUNTRY LOOK

If your tastes tend toward the casual country look, this section is for you. Chances are your fantasies include romantic rides through the English countryside or a cozy breakfast in bed in a small inn in France. You probably love little calico prints, chintz, lace, simple wood furniture, ladder-back chairs, crude wooden bowls, copper cooking utensils, and delicately hand-painted kitchen tiles. You're a hopeless romantic. You love to spend winter evenings snuggled under a patchwork quilt in front of a roaring fire. You look forward to summer days, picking strawberries and flowers from your garden and arranging them in cute little baskets.

You can call it rustic, or farmhouse, or even provincial. The mood of these rooms is fresh, informal, and simple. They have unpretentious charm. Country rooms are comfortable and comforting. Strong, undiluted colors are part of this look; red and blue with grass green, yellow, and blue, fresh pinks and greens. Your choice of fabrics ranges from linens, cottons, plain woven wools, chintzes, and calicos, to tweeds.

The furniture can be early American pine, maple, or cherry. Or blend collections of country furniture from around the world. Much of the fun is in collecting fascinating accessories like old weather vanes, baskets, pickle jars, wooden decoys, or anything you happen upon in the antique shops you visit.

The country look has warmth. It can be extremely primitive or more sophisticated; it can even be modern. I've seen old barns and buildings converted into homes, their expansive wall space and high exposed beams making a fabulous backdrop for country colors, textures, and accessories.

A word of warning . . . please don't try to decorate the interior of your home in the country look if the exterior or interior architecture doesn't call for it . . . no matter how much you love this look. There's nothing sillier looking than an architecturally modern house with twenty foot windows and ceilings decorated in this way.

Although I've stereotyped the country look, there are many sub-categories to consider.

Country French rooms usually include authentic or reproduction furniture originating in France. The fabrics might be little French cotton prints and fine laces. Of course, accessories and artwork should have a French influence. Baskets of lacy spring flowers add freshness to crisp, chintz-covered little round tables. The look is relaxed, delicate, and romantic.

Country English rooms are more serious and dignified. The furniture should have simpler lines and fewer curves than country French. The fabrics would be straightforward; more plaids and fewer flowers. Accessories and artwork include casual English themes such as hunting scenes and duck decoys. This decor is wintry and comfortable, reeking of the crisp green grass and pure air of the English countryside.

American Indian rooms are making a come-

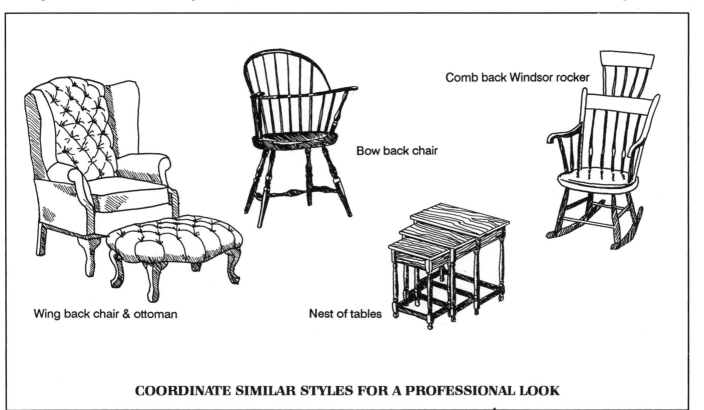

Comb back Windsor rocker

Bow back chair

Wing back chair & ottoman

Nest of tables

COORDINATE SIMILAR STYLES FOR A PROFESSIONAL LOOK

USE WICKER AND RATTAN PIECES FOR "THE GARDEN LOOK"

back. The furniture is crude and functional, but comfortable. Authentic Indian rugs in bold geometric patterns are scattered about. In one corner, resting against a wall, there might be a handmade ladder purely for decoration. Indian arts and crafts can be displayed boldly against heavily-textured white walls. Arrangements of exotic cactus look fabulous with this motif. Indian folk art stores are popping up everywhere, specializing in exciting handmade feathered headdresses, drums, and silver and turquoise jewelry.

Early American is a style you might want to forget. The look is identified with cheap maple furniture reproductions from the discount furniture store, mixed with cute little curtains and milk glass knick-knacks from the five and dime store. Erase this look from your memory and go on to replace your nostalgia with:

Country Pine is a more "in" way of getting that early America look. A country pine room is usually filled with either authentic or reproduction light pine furniture. The fabrics and wall coverings are fresh and patterned. You might want to use down-to-earth ginghams and calico prints mixed and matched with care, then add a thick, colorful rag rug to make the room even cozier. Accessories can be scattered baskets filled with skeins of yarn, firewood, or fresh strawberries. The kitchen could have copper pots and pans hanging from a wood or wrought iron rack. The dining room might have a bleached pine hutch displaying a collection of antique plates resting behind a plate rail. The bedroom would be feminine and delicate, full of crisp white wicker and cotton eyelet. This decor can be charming and inviting. In the winter, throw some hand-crocheted blankets on the sofa and snuggle up in front of the fireplace. In the summer, open the windows, add some crisp white tablecloths topped with baskets of fresh flowers, and bask in the cooling breeze.

The *Cottage Look* is definitely informal and homey. Large, comfortable upholstered pieces and soft wall coverings and window coverings accented with floral prints make up this type of decor. You can use lots of natural cane and wicker pieces along with textured scatter rugs and small antique accessories. Again, baskets and flowers add a charming finishing touch to these rooms.

The *Farmhouse Look* is an interesting slant on basic "country." We automatically visualize the exterior as a red-painted wood barn sporting a large weather vane, but owning an old barn is not essential to creating this look. Make use of white walls, high ceilings, and exposed crude beams to create an authentic converted farmhouse look. A loft would be divine. Why not build one if you don't have one? Although more crudely-made wood furniture looks right in farmhouse rooms, don't negate an eclectic feel. The massive white walls are perfect for huge modern paintings. You might even want to mix modern, over-sized white sofas and glass coffee tables with rag rugs and smaller antique accessories. The farmhouse look is definitely a funky, eccentric look for sophisticated city slickers who have a compelling desire to be more earthy.

The *Garden Look* is a sunny, cheerful summer look. White painted or natural wicker, rattan, and bamboo furniture creates the light, airy feel of this room. Lots of bright, open windows and the frothiest, greenest plants you can find make this type of room just like a cozy greenhouse. Fabrics are crisp florals in vibrant garden colors.

The *Rustic Look* is a "back-to-basics" country look. Visitors would suspect you even chop your own wood for the fireplace. Wood surfaces are crude and roughly sawn. Walls are heavily textured with brick, stone, and wood. Floors are wood, stone, or brick, scattered with thick, heavily textured rugs. The kitchen might even have a stone or brick fireplace and rustic-looking table and chairs. The master bedroom might have a crudely-made four poster bed and a patchwork quilt. Twig furniture, available commercially, looks great in these rooms.

The *Southwestern Look* is the hottest look going these days. Adapted from the motif of Santa Fe, New Mexico, these rooms capture the casual atmosphere of the region. Floors are light bleached

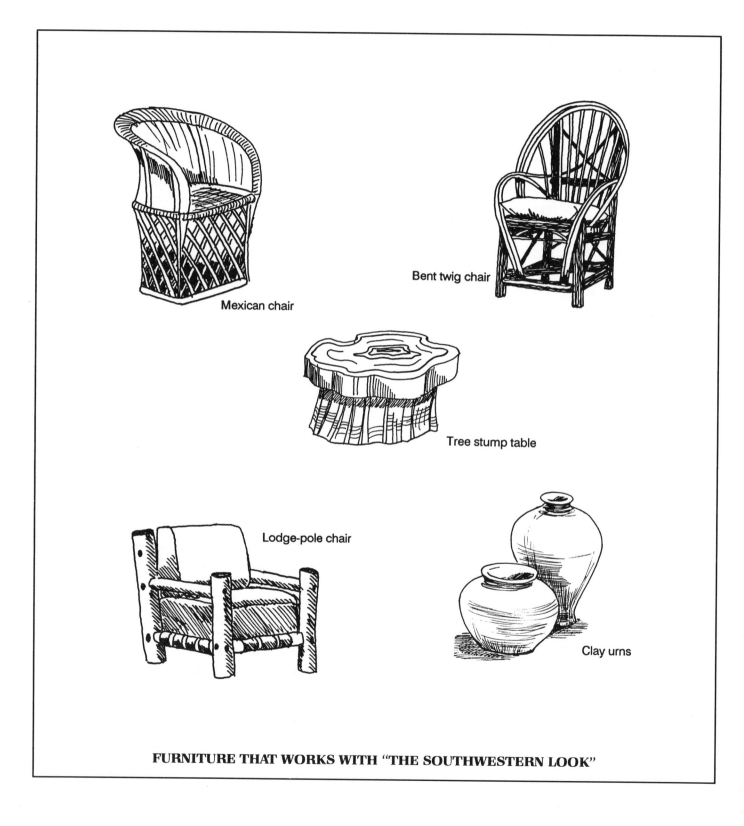

Mexican chair

Bent twig chair

Tree stump table

Lodge-pole chair

Clay urns

FURNITURE THAT WORKS WITH "THE SOUTHWESTERN LOOK"

wood covered with cotton Dhurrie rugs. Walls can be textured and white or covered with a neutral "raffia weave." Craig Milne of Design Team International in Los Angeles suggests placing straw in your plaster for that professional touch. The furniture can be a mixture of lodge-pole, bleached wood, and crude-looking faux stone. Fabrics are simple white and beige textures, accented with colorful hand-woven pillows and throws. Accessories might include hand-tied ladders, drums, and authentic Southwestern art. It's a great look for a warm climate.

Eclectic Country can be a mixture of one or more of the above looks. A well done eclectic country room will gracefully blend woods, textures, patterns, and colors that relate well together. If you're choosing an authentic look, such as "Santa Fe" or "American Indian," stay within the authentic theme. You can add some well chosen, simple modern pieces, but mixing various other country looks won't work. Other country looks can be mixed together or combined with modern if you use your instincts and knowledge of the basics of design to mix and match pieces that relate to one another in some way.

THE GRACIOUS LOOK

You're bound to choose this look if you're prim and proper, neat as a pin. You go to work dressed in an immaculately pressed suit, put your pinky out when you sip tea, and never ever put your elbows on the table. You love to entertain. You serve your drinks from delicate crystal decanters with brass tags, and put out petit fours or tiny mints on silver trays. You love Agatha Christie novels and dream of adventures on the Orient Express, taking along your trunks of elegant clothing, of course. You love fine bone china, Lalique crystal, and the paintings of the great masters. No cheap knick-knacks for you. If your towels are scalloped and monogrammed, there's no question in my mind that you're a prime candidate for the gracious look.

You fall into the gracious look category if you

can relate to the above, whether you love modern, traditional, or eclectic decors. The range of possibilities is endless. You love elegant fabrics of satin, damask, silk, chintz, linen, and cotton. The fabrics you choose will be simple, elegant, and expensive. If you choose patterns, they'll be subtle and classic. Nothing too bright or loud for you. You'll shy away from cute and whimsical accessories and select only the finest paintings. If you choose the gracious look, you might want to go over the following list of styles to find the one that best suits your personality.

Contemporary is a clean, safe look that's never in style and never out of style. Flooring is usually wall-to-wall carpeting with areas of tile. Walls are usually painted white or beige; some might be wallpapered with subtle, neutral patterns. Furniture is functional; high-grained and polished. Fabrics are simple and practical. Accessories are classic, perhaps a collection of hand-blown glass. Artwork is serene and serious, framed in fine wood. The contemporary look has no frills.

Modern is a more dramatic, elegant look. A casual modern room might have shiny wood or tile floors covered with Oriental rugs. Walls might be painted white or covered in suede. Furniture is classic and simple in design, often combining glass, chrome, and leather. Fabrics are sleek and neutral. Accessories are sparse; one "important" thick acrylic square might sit alone on the coffee table. Artwork might include one immense, museum-quality abstract canvas and a breathtaking marble sculpture resting on a lacquered pedestal.

A more formal modern room might have white silk upholstered walls, sofas, and chairs; a dash of color added by splashes of satin throw pillows. Furniture will be impeccably crafted, smooth and shiny, perhaps made of high quality lacquer and glass. Floors might be white marble covered with elegantly carved area rugs. Fine modern crystal adorns the thick, built-in shelving behind the lacquered bar. Artwork is serious and expensive, maybe even an authentic Miro framed in thick Lucite.

The *Scandinavian Look* is again simple and sleek. Furniture is highly polished teak with fine graining and straight lines. Fabrics are plain, neutral textures. Walls are white and bare, maybe one large woven rug hangs dramatically on a massive wall. Floors are made of highly polished wood covered with neutral woven area rugs. Accessories might include finely crafted stainless steel bowls and candlesticks.

The *Traditional Look* refers to any style that's not modern, whether it is the "antique look" or the "period look." It's for those of you who cling to your heritage and find comfort in past history. The traditional look is always in style, not a passing trend. If you tend to resist change and hate to redecorate, it's a look that's here forever.

The *Antique Look* can cover many periods and countries, either done authentically or mixed and matched. The gracious look pulls together furniture that is more finely made than the country look. Wood furniture is smoother, more highly polished. Fabrics are more elegant, simple, and tailored. Walls are either painted plainly or wallpapered in traditional patterns, framed with interesting crown moldings. Flooring is darker stained hardwood, finished and buffed to a high gloss, and covered with antique rugs. Accessories are fine old crystal decanters or collections of tiny antique silver frames. The artwork might be originals or replicas of the old masters.

The *Period Look* can include any period, such as Georgian, Victorian, or Colonial. Be careful: period looks should relate to the architecture of your home and are almost impossible to mix. Read over Chapter 16: Choosing Your Furniture before selecting any "period" furnishings. To be effective, this look must be done with careful research and attention to authenticity.

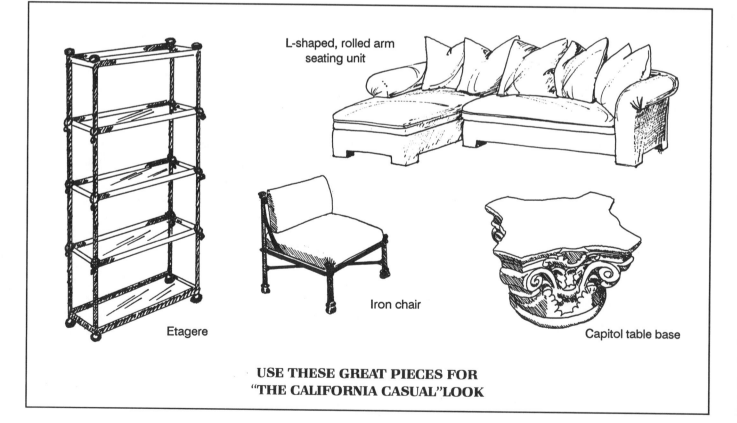

L-shaped, rolled arm seating unit

Etagere

Iron chair

Capitol table base

USE THESE GREAT PIECES FOR "THE CALIFORNIA CASUAL" LOOK

THE SOPHISTICATED LOOK

Do you like to travel to far off places and bring back works of art? Do you dare to be different and unique, to defy the conventional rules? Are you an artist at heart and yearn to express yourself through your environment? Are you willing to risk the chance of being thought offbeat, unconventional? Do you live your life in daydreams and fantasies? Then the sophisticated look is yours. You're the kind of person who searches endlessly through small boutiques tucked in alleys for that one special scarf, who can go through a thrift shop and put together an entire outfit that will make you look like you just stepped out of *Vogue*. You wouldn't dare be caught wearing something that is average and normal. You'll go to the ends of the earth to express yourself through your unique collection of one-of-a-kind costume jewelry and handmade boots. You're a true artist at heart, and you want your home to express your soul.

The sophisticated look is youthful and spirited. You have a disregard for the conventions and blend modern and traditional with elegant fabrics, displaying a true confidence in your taste. Sophisticated rooms are full of exotic forms of furniture and accessories that show your independence. You'll mix a handmade Oriental rug, Moroccan armoire, and a handcarved ivory cigarette table with a glass and chrome dining table and leather and chrome swivel chairs. Your walls will be plain or textured and your floors well polished to receive the shine of your high tech track lighting. If you fancy yourself a sophisticate, dare to be different, read on to find the right niche for you.

California Casual has been popular on the West Coast for some time now. Some designers say its passé, others swear by it, insisting it's here to stay. It's a look exemplified by the interesting stone pieces designed by Michael Taylor and the large canvas sofas popularized by Kreiss.

A California casual room has high, white ceilings sporting theatrical track lighting. The walls are white or beige, smooth or textured; perhaps covered in a textured material such as raffia weave. The floors are bleached wood, often wide planks placed on the diagonal. Mixing wood and stone on the floor also works well with this look as do large off-white or beige clay tiles set in a wide grout. Pastel-colored Dhurrie rugs look great placed over these floors, or wall-to-wall Berber carpeting can be used instead. Large modern windows are covered in bleached or painted four-inch wide shutters or white Verosol shades. Furniture is large, but light. Oversized sofas and pillows made of off-white tussah silk, Haitian cotton, or hand-painted canvas work well. Faux stone coffee tables, console tables, and end tables add interest. Tall floor lamps made of faux stone or bleached wood, topped with large, natural shades pull it all together. Accessories are huge Greek olive jars and interesting hand-painted urns and bowls. Artwork is abstract: usually a pastel collage placed inside a large acrylic box. This is a casual but elegant look that lends itself to warmer climates.

The *City Slick Look* is the most sophisticated of all the modern looks. It's sleek, serious, and functional. I also call it the "penthouse look" because I associate it with well-to-do bachelors who entertain their lady friends with glasses of champagne sipped from fine crystal while admiring the lights overlooking the city.

The furniture is black lacquer and glass. The wall-to-wall carpeting is a low cut velvet pile, perhaps gray, even black. Walls are smooth, covered in suede, patent leather, lizard, or just painted varying shades of gray. The bathroom walls might be covered in dark, smoked glass and sparsely lit. Sofas and chairs are modern, streamlined, covered in flannels and leathers. Dining room chairs are black and chrome. A wall of built-in shelving displays a huge television screen and a fortune's worth of stereo equipment. The coffee table is bare, except for the one fine art book. One major Andy Warhol painting captures your eye. This is definitely the style for a sophisticated bachelor who's "been around."

The *New York Look* is newer, hotter. It's the "in" look for the jet set. Anything goes; you can get as bizarre as you like. No naked walls; they're covered in paint textures such as sponging, marbling, spattering, or tortoiseshell. High ceilings are covered with smoked mirror, then framed with huge, exotically-finished crown moldings. Baseboards can be shiny lacquer, brass, or chrome. In other places, soffits are dramatized by free form neon lighting.

Furniture is large, functional, and modern. An enormous inlaid Moroccan armoire holds the television set and stereo equipment. A mink throw is tossed across the red douppioni silk sofa, balanced by a huge, pickled bergere chair covered in zebra skin. Windows are draped with yards and yards of fabric tied ingeniously over rods, then left to flow and puddle luxuriously upon the floor.

Artwork is major. Important, enormous canvases are left resting against the walls. Exotic indoor trees invite your eyes to venture onto the dramatically decorated balcony. Accessories are scattered about, remnants of so many trips abroad. This is not a look for the shy, meek, or conventional. It is a powerful look that makes a definite statement.

The *High Tech Look* is an open, almost office-like look. It exemplifies simplicity in design and materials. The high tech room should be exclusively high tech, no mixing. Lines are square or rectangular, no curves. Walls are smooth and flat, covered in ordinary paint or high gloss enamel. Flooring is rubber sheeting, plain square tiles set in narrow grout, or a neutral shade of commercial carpeting. Lighting is a combination of black or chrome track lighting and streamlined Italian torcheres. One important halogen quartz pendant hangs over the dining room table. Windows are covered with metal blinds, vertical or horizontal. Furniture is low and compact: black rubber "spaghetti chairs," a thick piece of glass floating on a black lacquered triangle, or a modular sofa upholstered in gray parachute cloth. Accessories are red, black, white, and gray; lots of grids and black rubber. Artwork is bright, bold, and modern. This is a great

look for an efficiency expert, but not recommended for a traditionalist.

The *Oriental Look* refers to an authentic Oriental motif, although mixing Oriental art and accessories with modern or eclectic rooms is a newer, more "in" trend.

In a modern room, an Oriental mix would include combinations of sleek, shiny black lacquered tables and wall units with modern versions of Oriental chairs finished in red or black lacquer. Fabrics would be plain or patterned Oriental silks in traditional colors. Wall coverings would be simple to set off the intricacy of the fine Oriental artwork and accessories. One important piece might be a breathtaking twelve-panel Oriental screen set behind a white silk sofa, raised to ceiling height and lit from behind. Two exquisite Oriental urns displayed on black lacquered pedestals on either side of a metal fireplace and collections of Oriental ivory and jade carvings displayed on a plain glass coffee table would complete this look.

A more traditional Oriental mix would take the same fine artwork and accessories and blend them with dark wood furniture with an Oriental flavor. Perhaps one would add a large Oriental tapestry on one wall and cover the floor with a large Oriental rug that pulled the colors of the room together.

Art Deco might also fit into the category of the period look. It emerged in the later 1920s and lasted through most of the 1930s. The look is best known for its shiny metals, glossy lacquered woods, polished stone, glass, and the new plastics that were being developed at that time. A true Art Deco room is ornate, decorated with etched glass, gold plate, chrome, and checkerboard tiles. This look re-emerged with fervor about five or six years ago, but the trend has faded. It's extremely difficult to recreate an Art Deco room authentically, and reproduction pieces tend to look like they came off a production line. Art Deco is difficult to mix with other styles and periods, and doesn't work well with most types of architecture.

Art Nouveau can also be classified as a period look, and dates back to the 1890s. An Art Nouveau

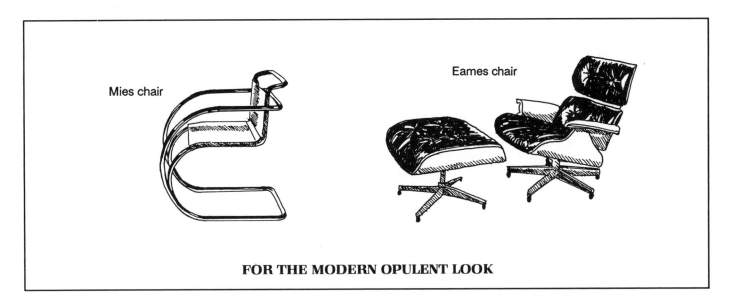

Mies chair

Eames chair

FOR THE MODERN OPULENT LOOK

room would have walls, windows, doors, and ceilings with curved and flowing lines. Furniture will be more straight-backed and rectangular. Iron would be used for supporting columns and railings in swirling, intricate designs. Stained glass windows and Tiffany lamps are part of this era, as are inlaid floor mosaics and ornate wood moldings. Again, this is an extremely difficult style to recreate authentically. However, you might want to borrow some of the more desirable elements, like stained glass and inlaid floor mosaics, to mix with other looks.

The *Junk Look* is the bargain hunter's ultimate eclectic look. If you've become frightened of the costs involved in some of the other looks, but still consider yourself a true sophisticate, there's no reason why you can't get away with this look. You'll have fun shopping the garage sales and rummaging through your friends' attics. The junk look can be any combination of items that works together. Old trunks can be painted or enameled, then stencilled to become interesting coffee tables. Your aunt's old, discarded sofa can be slipcovered with new patterned sheets. Just throw a sheet over it and tie with decorative cording. Drape matching sheets over your windows, attaching them to rods with bows

made out of a contrasting fabric. Make your own throw pillows from remnants of fabric you've found on sale at the local fabric store. Have lamps made out of the vases you couldn't resist buying at the rummage sale. Paint an old, worn-out rocking chair bright red and add a new cushion.

The junk look can be one of the greatest looks of all. No need to make excuses to your friends; after all, your pinched budget gives you the challenge of pushing your creativity to its limit. If you've decorated your home this way without compromising the basics of good design, you can smile with pride.

THE OPULENT LOOK

Do you fantasize about what it would be like to be President or First Lady? Do you love to dine in elegant restaurants, seated in booths of hand-rubbed leather and served on fine china and crystal while your chauffeur and limousine wait outside for you? Do you refuse to wear anything unless it bears the label of a famous European designer? No hanging around the house in sweats for you. Your basic at-home wear is an elegant silk robe, as you wander about rearranging tiny silver frames filled with impressive family portraits of your ancestors.

You yearn for grandeur and dream of the grand style.

Yes, you belong to the opulent look. You love marble and marquetry, bronze, brocades, silks, tapestries, and fine velvets. You'd kill to own an original sixteen-panel Chinese screen. Even if your tastes lie in the more modern, you'll insist on big sofas upholstered with quilted fabrics, deep pile carpeting, lavishly tufted chairs, and enormous lamps.

And, as you luxuriate in your fine porcelain bathtub, soaking in only the finest perfumes from France, dusting with expensive talc, and admiring your fine collection of crystal perfume bottles, you worry frantically about your checking account. Cheap copies of this look are easily detected and can be gauche. So make sure you have the taste and bank account to go with your grandiose dreams. If you've got it, flaunt it, but I suggest you hire an interior designer.

The *Modern Opulent Look* is similar to the New York look. The major difference is that everything is authentic. No fake finishes for you. A modern opulent room has thick, lustrous marble floors and walls. Area rugs are expensive furs and antique Orientals. The furniture is the real thing: Charles Eames and Ludwig Mies van der Rohe. Fabrics are only the finest of leathers and silks. Artwork is rotated as you lend parts of your collection to the Museum of Modern Art for special exhibits. Plants are exotic species worth thousands of dollars each. Accessories are limited editions and signed pieces from famous crystal makers. Need I go on?

The *Traditional Opulent Look* is a period look, perhaps duplicating the lifestyle of a famous prince

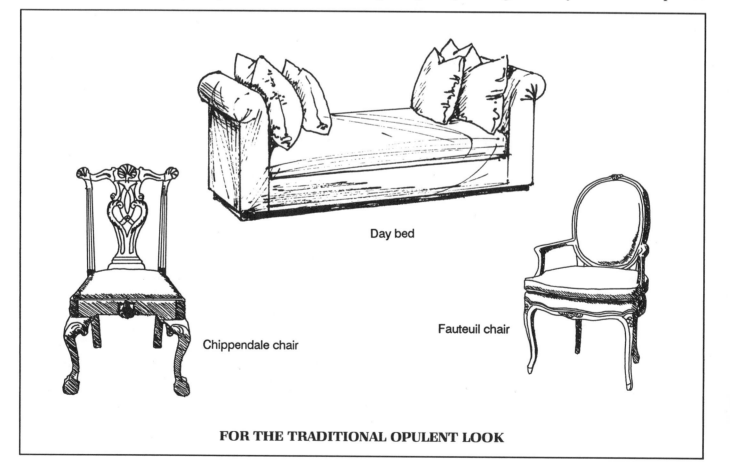

Day bed

Chippendale chair

Fauteuil chair

FOR THE TRADITIONAL OPULENT LOOK

or princess, a count or duchess. If you just happen to own a castle, this look works well. The traditional opulent room is filled with expensive heirlooms: tapestries, crystal, china, silver, original Van Goghs, antique furniture with a fascinating story behind each piece. Velvets, silks, damasks, and brocades cover the down-filled sofas and chairs. Other pieces of furniture are finished in fine gold or silver leaf. Windows are draped with elegant fabric, falling in flowing cascades upon the marble floors. Don't bother reading Chapter 6: Stretching Your Decorating Dollar; you can bet it won't stretch this far.

The *Eclectic Opulent Look* is a mixture of the above two looks. I suggest you invest in a well-seasoned interior designer to help create this special look for you.

By now you should have a good idea of what look and style will make you and your family feel comfortable. Keep on browsing through magazines to confirm your tastes. By the time you've finished this book, you'll be well equipped to achieve the look you want with ease.

HINT:

Just remember! Decorating fashion follows clothing fashion.

Opulence is in.

5
Preparing a Furniture Plan

Just as a house can't be built without blueprints, a room can't be furnished without a furniture plan. Careful planning and preparation are "musts" for a successful design project. In order to save time and money in the long run, as well as avoid potential catastrophic mistakes, know what furniture and other pieces you want to put in your space and where you will place them before purchasing anything. Arranging your furniture on paper is called making a furniture plan or floor plan.

Analyzing Your Space

The first step in preparing a furniture plan is analyzing the space you have to work with and deciding what purpose and feeling you want to achieve within that space. Wander around the room and study it from every angle to get the feel of the room. Ask yourself:

- Are there any architectural changes you would like to make?
- Would the room be better if you moved a wall, added a built-in bar, built-in bookcases, recessed lighting?
- Are the windows right? Do they provide adequate natural lighting? Are they placed correctly? If not, what changes should be made?
- Look at the door or doors. Are they boring? Would the room be enhanced if you removed the door? Widened the doorway? Replaced or resurfaced the door?

- Look at the ceiling. Is it too high or too low? Now's the time to decide whether you should correct a too high or too low ceiling with structural changes or with color and materials.
- Look at the woodwork, the baseboards, the molding. Should they be replaced or removed? How can they be enhanced? Can they become an interesting element of the room?
- Take a good look at the flooring. Are you planning wall-to-wall carpeting, tile, or perhaps bleached wood floors and area rugs? You'll need to know this now so that you can plan the size of the area rug to coordinate correctly with the furniture and the room.
- Analyze both the natural and artificial lighting. What changes need to be made? What type of lighting needs to be added to enhance the room?
- Let your mind wander and fantasize. What, if any, architectural features could be added to the room to make it more dramatic? Should the fireplace be re-faced in marble and brass? Should you add decorative columns on the walls? Now's the time to decide, as any changes you make will affect the dimensions of the room. A new fireplace will mean a new hearth. A column on the wall will mean new wall dimensions and a different layout for furniture.

Be original. Visualize your furniture placed at surprising angles. Add unique accent pieces to create interest. Tear your thoughts away from the conventional seating layouts you always see and try to formulate new, more unusual ideas for furniture placement. Two seven-foot sofas across from each other with a coffee table between them usually works, but the arrangement is common and boring. Create other alternatives.

Determining Your Needs

Next, make a list of all the activities that will take place in the room and what pieces of furniture and equipment those activities will require.

• If the room is a group space such as a living room, family room, or den, is it to be broken up into several different areas? The major "conversation center" will become the primary seating group. This center can also be used for watching television, listening to music, reading, buffet dinner parties, or games. Studies show that people like to sit opposite each other at a slight angle. If there is too much space between them, they'll opt to sit side by side. Successful conversational groupings are somewhat circular in shape and have a maximum distance between people of eight to ten feet. Make sure there is enough circulation for people to get in and out of the furniture grouping easily.

In larger rooms, a secondary reading or conversational area should be added. This might be a game table and chairs, a window seat, a large lounge chair and small table, or yet another full-sized conversational seating area.

• Home entertainment areas are becoming more and more popular with the advent of huge television screens and home video equipment. I usually make it a point to discuss with my clients any future plans they have for updated and larger equipment. I try to convince them to have this equipment built into a wall or to build a custom cabinet that can be closed when not in use to hold all the equipment. Electrical equipment isn't particularly attractive unless it's planned and placed with utmost care. There is nothing more unattractive than a television set sitting on top of an old television cart, its back and protruding cords ex-

posed. Make plans for attractive housing for any equipment you now own and any future purchases you might make.

• Pianos can be large and impressive. Open, they are beautifully crafted pieces of furniture that deserve a place of prominence in your room. The curved side of a grand piano should face into the room for proper sound. Pianos should also be placed away from windows and heating vents, as changes in temperature can affect them adversely.

• Dining areas can be arranged in a multitude of ways. Most commonly: a rectangular table in the center of a room; a round table in the center of a room; a rectangular table with one short side placed against a wall; and a table placed for built-in seating along two sides. However, there are ways to create dining spaces that are much more exciting. For instance, I have a huge square glass-top table on a faux stone base placed on an angle in my dining room. Along two sides I have upholstered seating, while the other two sides each have two pull-up black lacquered Queen Anne arm chairs.

Angle your dining table or create interest with irregular shapes and sizes. If you have a large dining room, consider the concept of "double dining," which is the use of two, usually round, dining tables side by side. This look can be very elegant.

• Bedroom "sets" are out. Your bedroom should be functional, of course, but there's no reason why it can't be dramatic, too. Most people tend to place their beds against a solid wall with nightstands on either side and a set of drawers on the opposite wall. This arrangement is hotel-like and boring. Why not play around with angling your bed in a corner? Use a triangle behind it to display a huge vase lit from behind. Why not use a large armoire against a wall to house your bedroom television and stereo equipment? Or build equipment right into the wall? Why not use interesting accent pieces instead of conventional nightstands? Add a chaise longue and cigarette table or two pull-up chairs at the end or side of the bed. If your bedroom is large enough, why not have a separate conversational and television viewing area? And, if you like to write letters or do a little work in the bedroom, why not have a desk and pull-up chair?

• Children's rooms usually need to be more functional and space saving, but that doesn't mean they have to be boring. Typical furniture arrangements include one large bed placed at a right angle to the wall; one single bed set parallel to the wall; two single beds placed against adjacent walls at right angles to each other; and don't forget trundle beds and bunk beds. As you learn to develop a furniture plan, you'll have a chance to create clever and new ideas for placement of furniture in children's rooms. You'll learn the space-saving qualities of built-ins and inexpensive ways of creating storage space.

Drawing Your Furniture Plan

As an interior designer, I always prepare a furniture plan before doing anything else. This becomes the blueprint of the room or rooms to be furnished. I use it to make a list of all the furniture, accessories, lighting, and plants that need to be selected. I even use the furniture plan to prepare my clients' budgets, listing each piece that will be required to make up the complete project.

It's easy. First, Plan A. I try to locate the original blueprints of the home from the architect or builder. This step can eliminate the work of measuring the entire house. Unfortunately, the original blueprints are not always easily available. If I do obtain the blueprints, I examine them carefully to determine whether any changes have been made to the original structure of the house. If you can't get your hands on a copy of the original plans, we'll go to Plan B — making your own plan from scratch.

It'll be easiest for you to measure and draw each room separately. For larger projects, I do reconstruct the entire house on one drawing, but this technique is a little difficult for the beginner. All you'll need is:

A large metal carpenter's tape measure
A sharp pencil

An eighteen-inch metal straight edge ruler and/or a plastic architectural scale

A pad of treated vellum tracing paper printed with a grid. You can either buy paper with grids of ¼" or purchase a pad that's divided into one inch squares and then subdivided into eighths of an inch.

All of the above supplies can be purchased readily at any art supply store or stationery store. No need to waste money on any costly plastic templates. You'll find a complete set of furniture templates here in this chapter.

Next, tools already gathered, make an accurate drawing of each room to be furnished. One-fourth inch on your ruler will equal one foot. If you are using an architectural scale, this is already done for you on the side that reads ¼". Make sure you don't use the side that reads "¼" size"; they're two different measurements.

Measure the total width and length of the room. Draw this major outline in ¼" scale on the grid paper.

Measure the sizes of any alcoves or other room irregularities and carefully draw them on the plan.

Measure the location of the windows and doors and their sizes; draw them on the plan.

Measure radiators, fireplaces, or any architectural details that need to be on the plan. Make sure you take overall dimensions of the fireplace as well as its hearth, the width of the mantle and the mantle top, and the width and length of wall space over the mantle.

Measure the ceiling height, the width of the baseboards, and the width of the trim on the windows and doors.

Make a diagram of the door paneling, the windows, the distance from the top of the window to the ceiling and the height of the window from the floor. Make sketches of any unusual features. These notes will come in handy later.

Now you have your basic room plan. You'll be using it to create your furniture plan and keep important notes which will prevent you from making mistakes, such as buying a sofa whose back protrudes up over the window sill behind it.

Don't cut out the templates on pages 51–55; they're there for your reference. Instead carefully remove pages 265–272 and cut out any furniture templates that you will need. Slide the cutout pieces around your basic plan. Have fun moving the furniture around the plan easily, playing quickly with different ideas for placement. Once you're relatively satisfied with the arrangement, use the template to trace each piece of furniture exactly where you want it. You don't have to redraw the entire furniture plan if you change your mind. Just use another piece of tracing paper right over the original plan and retrace the furniture any way you'd like. You'll have a permanent record of each concept you tried.

Play around with the templates until you reach the perfect solution for the room. Make sure that televisions don't have strong lighting from a window reflecting into them. Pretend you're sitting on the sofa you drew on the plan. Notice what your view will be. Be sure that you've included enough walk space and open space between furniture. Convinced you've created the perfect furniture layout for the room? Then go on to the next step.

Consider lighting. If you're including any table or floor lamps, draw them on the plan as circles, in scale to the actual dimension of the lamp you plan to use, of course. Place an X inside the circle to indicate that it's a lamp.

Visualizing the room, indicate the length and width of any large pictures and paintings that need to be purchased. You'll know exactly what size to look for by including them on your plan. For instance, if your plan shows an eight foot sofa with large 12″ rolled arms, the picture above the sofa should be approximately six feet wide, or the distance between the two areas.

Draw any plants or large trees where you plan to place them. Use the plant templates provided on pages 265–269.

Voilà! You now have a "plan view," or furniture plan, of your new room.

Rules of Thumb

Let's double check your furniture plan to make sure you've left enough clearances. Some of the standard rules of thumb are:

- For major traffic paths, leave four to six feet.
- For minor traffic paths, leave one foot, four inches to four feet.
- For foot room between seating area and the edge of the coffee table, leave at least one foot.
- For foot and leg room in front of a chair or sofa, leave one foot, six inches to two feet, six inches.
- For chair or bench space in front of a piano, leave three feet.
- Allow two feet per person for occupied chairs.
- Leave one foot, ten inches to three feet as space to get into chairs.
- Leave one foot, six inches to two feet as a traffic path around the table and occupied chairs.
- Leave one foot, six inches to two feet as space for making a bed.
- Leave one foot, six inches to two feet, four inches as space between twin beds.
- Leave at least three feet of walk space in front of dressers.

Drawing Your Elevations

Now that the furniture plan is finished and you've thoroughly checked to make sure you have enough walk space, are there any built-ins or cabinets that need to be custom made? If the answer is yes, it's time to discuss elevations.

Elevations are drawings of built-ins and furniture that show their exact dimensions. Dimensioning an elevation means indicating on a drawing the accurate measurements for each and every detail of a piece. Carpenters and upholsterers rely solely on your drawings, elevations, and measurements to build your furniture.

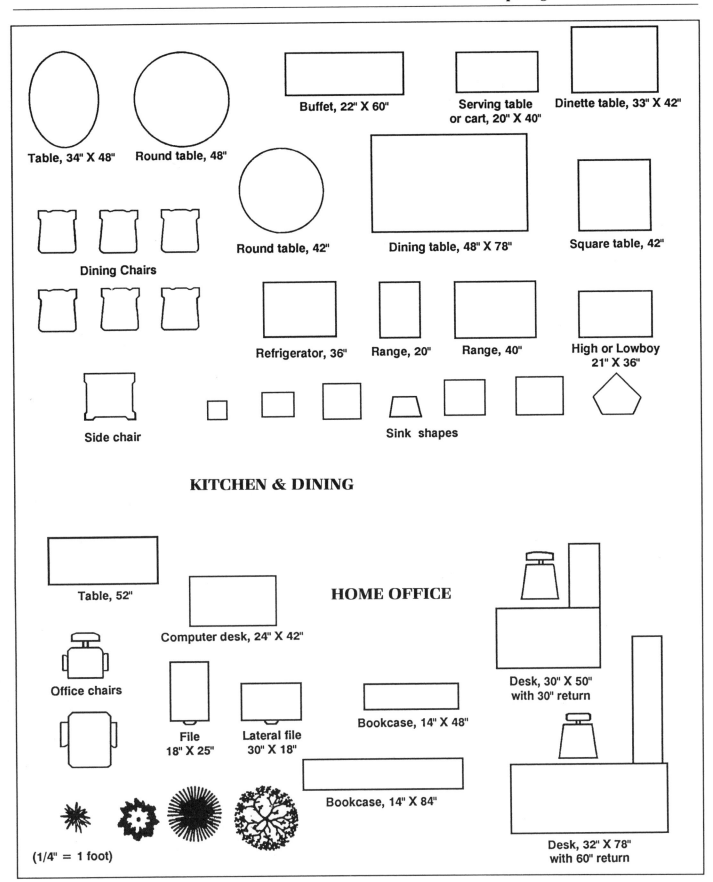

Table, 34" X 48"   Round table, 48"

Buffet, 22" X 60"

Serving table
or cart, 20" X 40"

Dinette table, 33" X 42"

Dining Chairs

Round table, 42"

Dining table, 48" X 78"

Square table, 42"

Refrigerator, 36"   Range, 20"   Range, 40"

High or Lowboy
21" X 36"

Side chair

Sink shapes

KITCHEN & DINING

Table, 52"

Computer desk, 24" X 42"

HOME OFFICE

Office chairs

File
18" X 25"

Lateral file
30" X 18"

Bookcase, 14" X 48"

Desk, 30" X 50"
with 30" return

Bookcase, 14" X 84"

(1/4" = 1 foot)

Desk, 32" X 78"
with 60" return

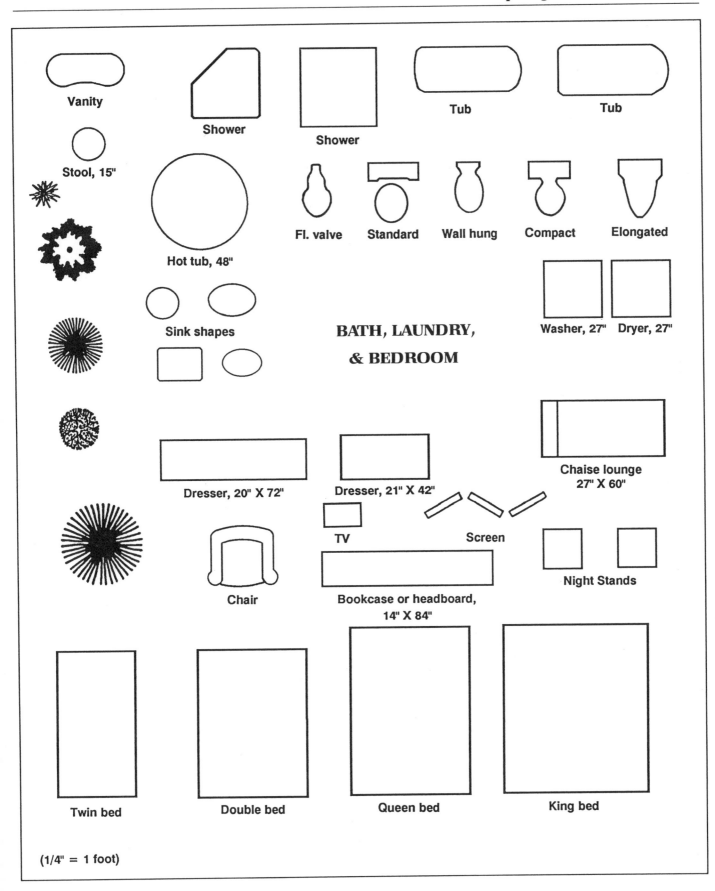

Vanity

Shower

Shower

Tub

Tub

Stool, 15"

Fl. valve   Standard   Wall hung   Compact   Elongated

Hot tub, 48"

Washer, 27"   Dryer, 27"

Sink shapes

BATH, LAUNDRY,

& BEDROOM

Chaise lounge
27" X 60"

Dresser, 20" X 72"

Dresser, 21" X 42"

TV

Screen

Night Stands

Chair

Bookcase or headboard,
14" X 84"

Twin bed

Double bed

Queen bed

King bed

(1/4" = 1 foot)

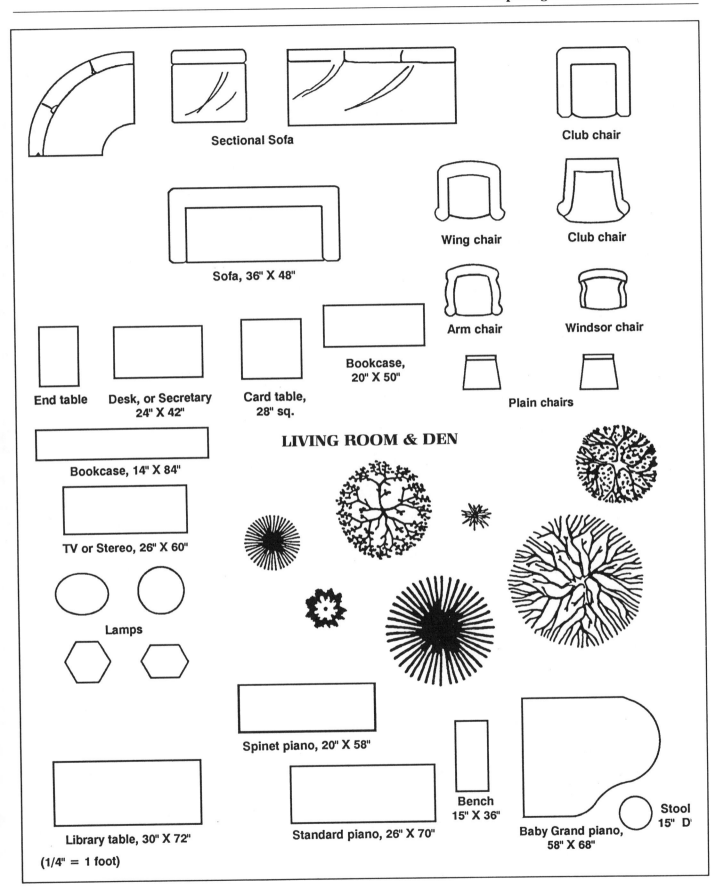

Sectional Sofa

Club chair

Wing chair

Club chair

Sofa, 36" X 48"

Arm chair

Windsor chair

End table

Desk, or Secretary
24" X 42"

Card table,
28" sq.

Bookcase,
20" X 50"

Plain chairs

Bookcase, 14" X 84"

LIVING ROOM & DEN

TV or Stereo, 26" X 60"

Lamps

Spinet piano, 20" X 58"

Library table, 30" X 72"

Standard piano, 26" X 70"

Bench
15" X 36"

Baby Grand piano,
58" X 68"

Stool
15" D'

(1/4" = 1 foot)

> **Hint:** Always have your carpenter double check your overall dimensions for all built-ins. A 1/16″ mistake could be catastrophic.

It's always a safe practice to provide your carpenter or upholsterer with drawings and dimensions of both front and side views of a piece. Often, even a top view or "plan view" is necessary to show every detail.

Draw the overall dimensions of the piece: height and width. An elevation is usually drawn in ½″ scale. Double check these dimensions from the furniture plan to be sure they're accurate.

Add any shelving, noting the thickness of the wood or any other material to be used. Don't forget to allow for the thickness of laminates over wood.

Add any drawers or cabinet doors, noting measurements, and specifying whether they are recessed, flush mount, etc. Specify the exact type of hinges and hardware you want.

If you'd like to add a television swivel or storage for videotapes, discs, and cassettes, draw each detail. Measure radio and stereo equipment, drawing appropriate spaces for each piece. Again, don't forget to allow space for the thickness of the wood.

A "kick" is usually necessary at the bottom of a piece in order to avoid bumping toes and damage from vacuum cleaners. Specify the height and depth of the kick.

Now do a side view of the piece, showing not only the height of the piece but the depth. Show any details and dimensions that appear from the side.

When you're finished with both views, go back and note any additional details that you might want. Specify types of hinges, how doors are to be mounted, type of hardware, pulls, knobs, touch latches, etc., material to be used, finish to be used on interior and exterior, and other information necessary to make the piece.

Study the drawings that follow. Once you realize how simple furniture plans and elevations are to make, a whole new world of design will open up to you. Learn to create on paper and the sky's the limit!

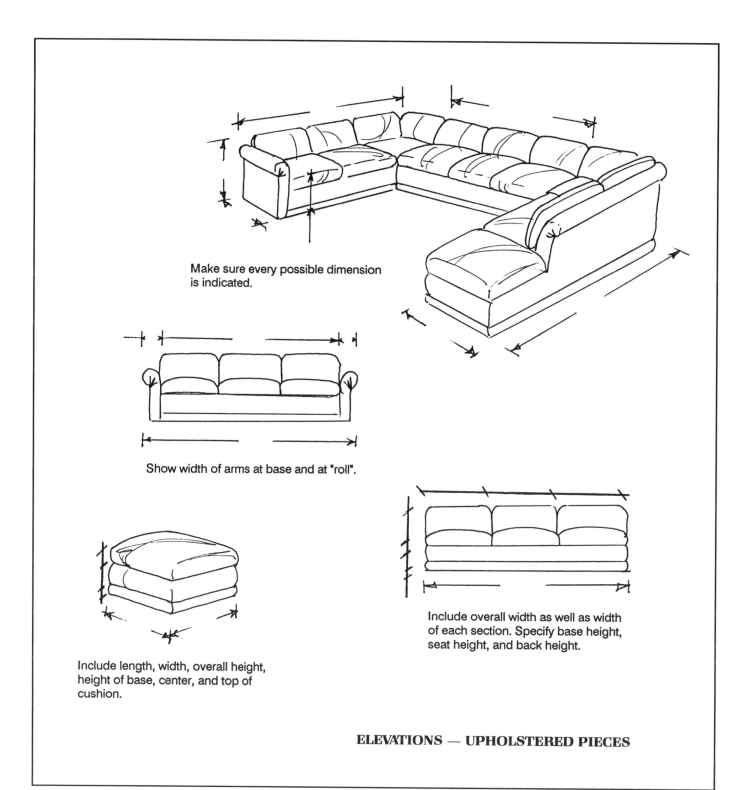

Make sure every possible dimension is indicated.

Show width of arms at base and at "roll".

Include length, width, overall height, height of base, center, and top of cushion.

Include overall width as well as width of each section. Specify base height, seat height, and back height.

ELEVATIONS — UPHOLSTERED PIECES

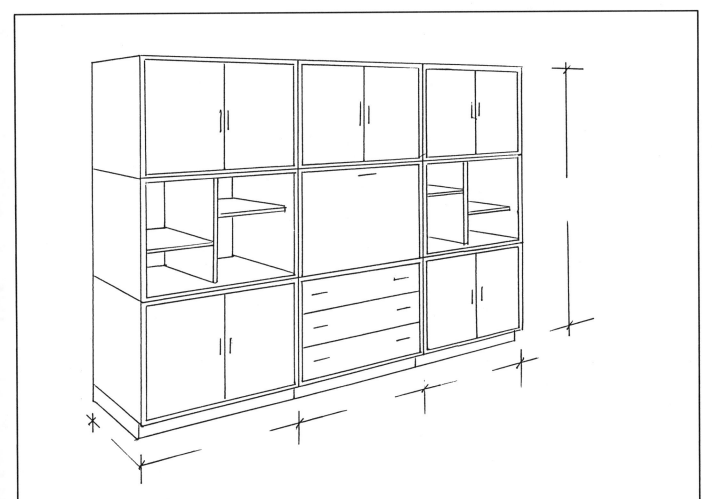

FILL-IN ALL OVERALL DIMENSIONS. ADD NOTES FOR:

Thickness of wood

Types of hinges

Hardware for adjustable shelves

Type of pulls or knobs

Any interior detailing

Interior & exterior finishes

ELEVATIONS — BUILT-IN OR FREESTANDING UNITS

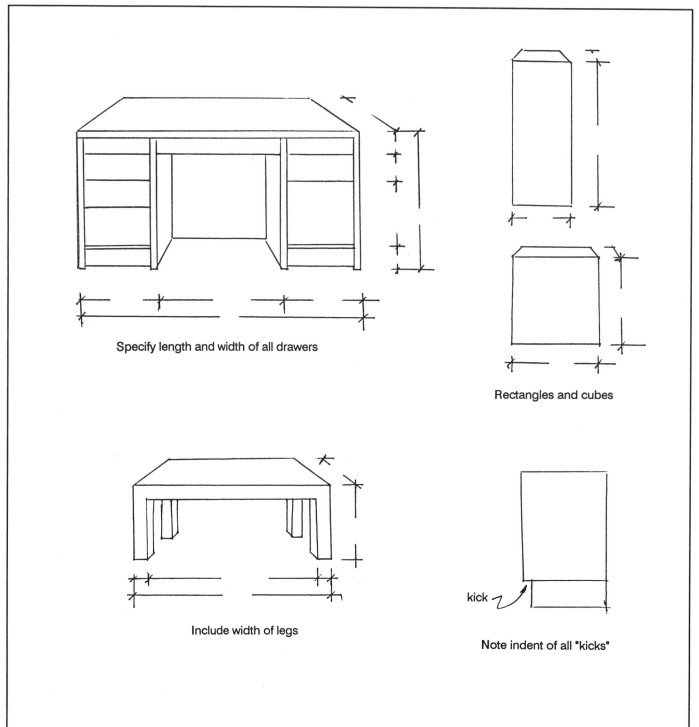

Specify length and width of all drawers

Rectangles and cubes

Include width of legs

kick

Note indent of all "kicks"

ELEVATIONS — DESKS, TABLES, PEDESTALS

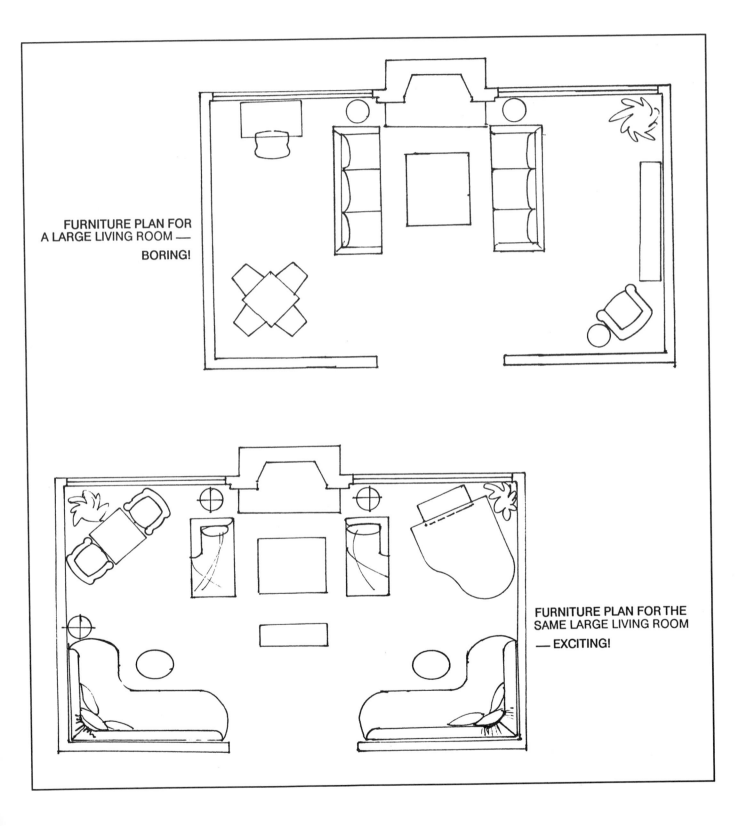

FURNITURE PLAN FOR
A LARGE LIVING ROOM —
BORING!

FURNITURE PLAN FOR THE
SAME LARGE LIVING ROOM
— EXCITING!

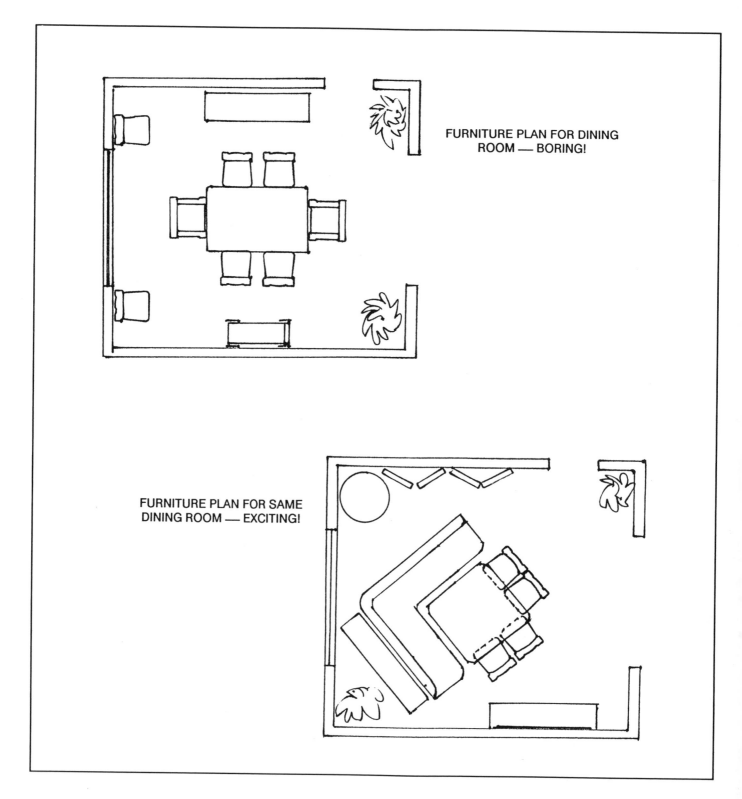

FURNITURE PLAN FOR DINING
ROOM — BORING!

FURNITURE PLAN FOR SAME
DINING ROOM — EXCITING!

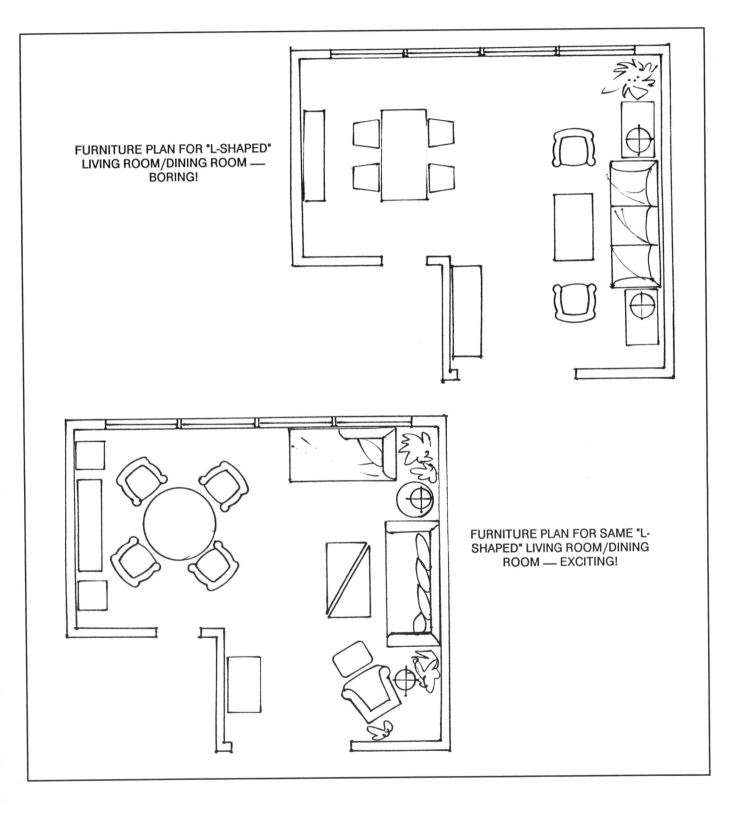

FURNITURE PLAN FOR "L-SHAPED" LIVING ROOM/DINING ROOM — BORING!

FURNITURE PLAN FOR SAME "L-SHAPED" LIVING ROOM/DINING ROOM — EXCITING!

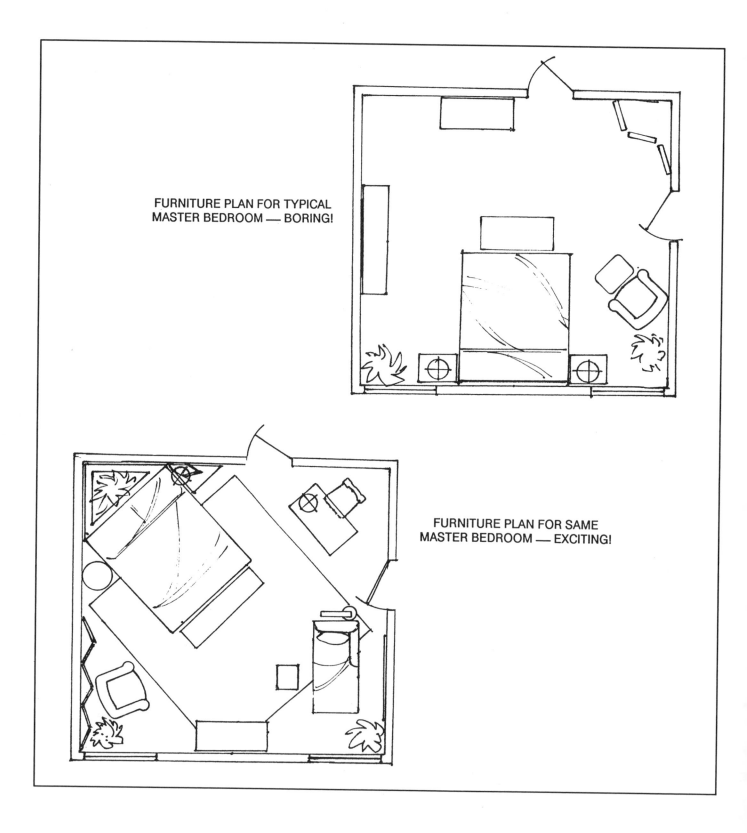

FURNITURE PLAN FOR TYPICAL
MASTER BEDROOM — BORING!

FURNITURE PLAN FOR SAME
MASTER BEDROOM — EXCITING!

6
Stretching Your Decorating Dollar

Maybe you've scrimped and saved for twenty years for this day, diligently counting pennies, cutting out pictures from magazines and filing them away. Perhaps you've just gotten that big job promotion, closed that big deal, received a large income tax refund, or have finally taken a second mortgage on your house. Possibly, you've just received a huge inheritance, or even won the state lottery. But let's face it, every dollar counts, whether you've just bought a new home or are renovating your old one. My clients, no matter how wealthy they are, are always appalled at how much decorating really costs.

Preparing a Realistic Budget

Realistic is what you can afford and what you are willing to spend. How much pleasure will the money you spend bring over the course of time? Would you rather invest the money in the stock market, vacations, or a new Ferrari? Only you know the answers to these questions.

If we were filthy rich, of course, we'd say "I want it all" and hire a team of famous interior designers to decorate each one of our estates and villas. But for most of us, no such luck.

Many of the professionally designed rooms we admire in *Architectural Digest* and other design magazines cost upwards of $70,000, not including the original artwork. Don't despair, great rooms can be put together effectively for a few thousand dollars with creativity, hard work, and a good pair of walking shoes. Obviously, your tastes, the size and number of rooms to be decorated, and the extent of the project need to be taken into consideration.

Since you've already prepared a furniture plan for your project, the next step is to work on your estimated budget. Let's go room by room. It's easier to think and plan by breaking down the project into smaller, less overwhelming segments.

The format I use to prepare a budget for my clients begins on the following page. Just estimate the amounts for now and fill them in with a pencil. You'll revise it with the accurate amounts later.

Once you've estimated these amounts and tallied them up, it's time to start analyzing the budget and fine tuning the amounts.

If the budget is acceptable, great! Let's get going. But if you're still in shock over the exorbitant total, here's what you should sit down and ask yourself:

- Do I want what I want now and am I unwilling to make compromises?
- Does that mean that I will only be able to do one or two rooms of the house now?
- Am I willing to wait until have more money to complete the house?
- Do I insist that I do the whole house at once?
- What am I willing to give up? Quality? Workmanship? Quantity? Time? Energy?
- Am I willing to do some of the labor myself to save money?

• Am I willing to take the time and energy to find less expensive sources, substitutes, and alternatives?

Can Hiring an Interior Designer Save You Money?

Sometimes, yes. It depends on who you hire and what financial arrangements you make with that person. Many interior designers have sources and money-saving ideas that will work to your benefit.

Interior designers have different fee structures. Some of the most common ways of working with a designer are:

Straight fee for the entire job. Here, designers will quote you a blanket fee, usually based on the estimated number of hours it will take them to do the project.

Hourly rates vary with the region of the country and the experience and popularity of the designer. Paying by the hour is an economical arrangement for clients who need help with some aspects of the job, but are willing and able to do much of the legwork and supervision themselves.

A cost plus arrangement means that you will purchase everything through your designer at his wholesale or net cost, plus a markup, usually 15% to 1/3. If you were planning to purchase everything at retail, this option will allow the opportunity to buy below retail and still have the services of an interior designer. If designers supervise workmen for you, they are entitled to a cost-plus markup on their services as well, so you might want to consider hiring and supervising your own workmen.

A retail-less arrangement means that the interior designer will charge you the retail value less a percentage, usually 10 to 30%. This can be misleading. Assume a designer purchases at a 50% discount; a $1,000 item at retail-less, let's say 30%, will cost you $700. Now compare. That same $1,000 item at cost-plus 30% will cost you $650. At straight retail, it would cost you $1,000.

Straight retail, although a common arrangement, appears to be the most expensive deal you

can make. Another snag arises in that it is difficult to determine the retail value of a custom-made piece.

Design fees include the initial cost of consultation, drawings, shopping, and presentation. Not all designers charge design fees. Shop around for designers to determine which one will best suit your design budget needs.

How Do You Find the Right Interior Designer?

The most obvious and best answer to this question is by referral. If you know people who have had their homes professionally done by interior designers, check them out. Ask them if you can come over and take a look at the house to see if you like their designer's work. Make sure you inquire about the designer's fee structure, honesty, and reliability.

If you don't know anyone who has used an interior designer, don't hesitate to call the local chapter of the ASID (American Society of Interior Designers) for a list of qualified candidates. Trade magazines such as *Architectural Digest* have many designers' work in each issue. Follow the trade magazines and select designers whose work you like. If you opt to call an interior designer who has advertised in a newspaper, magazine, or yellow pages, make sure you check their references thoroughly. Department and furniture stores often offer interior design services. The negatives are that the in-house designers are often not well qualified, and you will be coerced into purchasing furnishings only from that store.

Better yet, use a service called Decorator Previews to help you find the right interior designer. This is a designer-client matchmaking service. Decorator Previews will enable you to review the work of designers and architects in your area, compare fee structures, and help you zero in on your tastes and needs. This concept was developed by Karen Fisher, former decorating editor at *Cosmopolitan*, style editor at *Esquire*, and the executive editor at *American Home*.

Budget

PAINT

_____ gallons of paint @ _____ per gallon $ _____

labor: total bid or _____ hours _____ per hour $ _____

WALLCOVERING

_____ rolls or yards @ _____ per roll or yard $ _____

labor: _____ rolls or yards @ _____ per roll or yard $ _____

additional preparation of walls or blank stock $ _____

LIGHTING

_____ lamps @ _____ per lamp $ _____

_____ chandeliers @ _____ per chandelier $ _____

_____ sconces @ _____ per sconce $ _____

_____ accent lights, down lights, recessd lights, track lights, etc. @ _____ per fixture $ _____

additional parts and bulbs needed $ _____

electrician _____ hours @ _____ per hour $ _____

WINDOWS AND DOORS

_____ new windows @ _____ per window $ _____

_____ new doors @ _____ per door $ _____

_____ skylights @ _____ per skylight $ _____

labor to install $ _____

UPHOLSTERED GOODS: CUSTOM MADE

_____ sofas @ _____ per sofa $ _____

_____ chairs @ _____ per chair $ _____

_____ love seats @ _____ per love seat $ _____

_____ chaise longues @ _____ per chaise longue $ _____

_____ ottomans @ _____ per ottoman $ _____

_____ upholstered beds @ _____ per bed $ _____

_____ pillows @ _____ per pillow $ _____

_____ yards fabric @ _____ per yard $ _____

delivery charges $ _____

fabric protection service $ _____

UPHOLSTERED GOODS: READY MADE

_____ sofas @ _____ per sofa $ _____

_____ chairs @ _____ per chair $ _____

_____ love seats @ _____ per love seat $ _____

_____ chaise longues @ _____ per chaise longue $ _____

(Upholstered Goods: Ready Made, continued)

_____ ottomans @ _____ per ottoman $ _____

_____ upholstered beds @ _____ per bed $ _____

_____ pillows @ _____ per pillow $ _____

delivery charges $ _____

fabric protection service $ _____

REUPHOLSTERING AND SLIPCOVERING

labor for each sofa, chair, etc. $ _____

_____ yards fabric @ _____ per yard $ _____

pick up and delivery charges $ _____

fabric protection service $ _____

HARDGOODS

_____ chair frames @ _____ per frame $ _____

labor to finish _____ chairs @ _____ per chair $ _____

labor to upholster _____ chairs @ _____ per chair $ _____

_____ armoires @ _____ per armoire $ _____

_____ chests @ _____ per chest $ _____

_____ sofa back tables @ _____ per table $ _____

_____ console tables @ _____ per table $ _____

_____ nightstands @ _____ per nightstand $ _____

_____ headboards @ _____ per headboard $ _____

_____ dressers @ _____ per dresser $ _____

_____ end tables @ _____ per end table $ _____

_____ coffee tables @ _____ per coffee table $ _____

_____ dining room tables @ _____ per table $ _____

_____ kitchen tables @ _____ per table $ _____

_____ table bases @ _____ per base $ _____

_____ glass tops @ _____ per top $ _____

_____ pedestals @ _____ per pedestal $ _____

_____ antique pieces @ _____ per piece $ _____

labor to finish or refinish $ _____

delivery charges $ _____

WINDOW COVERINGS

Draperies:

_____ yards fabric @ _____ per yard $ _____

lining: _____ yards fabric @ _____ per yard $ _____

labor and installation $ _____

blackout shades or lining $ _____

(Window Coverings, continued)

      trimming $ _____

      hardware $ _____

Shutters:

      _____ windows @ _____ per window $ _____

      labor and installation $ _____

Mini-blinds, Verticals, or Verosols:

      _____ windows @ _____ per window $ _____

      labor and installation $ _____

Roman Shades:

      _____ shades @ _____ per shade $ _____

      _____yards fabric @ _____ per yard $ _____

      trimming $ _____

      labor and installation $ _____

FLOORING

      _____ sq. ft. tile @ _____ per sq. ft. $ _____

      _____ sq. ft. wood flooring @ _____ per sq. ft. $ _____

      _____ sq. yds. carpeting @ _____ per sq. yd. $ _____

      _____ sq. yds. padding @ _____ per sq. yd. $ _____

      labor to installer per sq. ft. or sq. yd. $ _____

      additional preparation work needed $ _____

      sub-flooring, if needed $ _____

ARTWORK

      _____ paintings @ _____ per painting $ _____

      _____ sculptures @ _____ per sculpture $ _____

ACCESSORIES

      _____ pieces @ _____ per piece $ _____

PLANTS

      _____ large trees @ _____ per tree $ _____

      _____ smaller plants @ _____ per plant $ _____

MIRROR WORK

      _____ sq. ft. mirror @ _____ per sq. ft. $ _____

      labor and installation $ _____

DETAILS

_____ doorknobs @ _____ per doorknob $ _____

_____ plates @ _____ per plate $ _____

_____ pulls or handles @ _____ each $ _____

_____ linear feet of molding @ _____ per ft. $ _____

_____ linear feet of baseboard @ _____ per ft. $ _____

_____ miscellaneous $ _____

BATHROOMS

flooring:

_____ sq. ft. @ _____ per sq. ft. $ _____

_____ sq. yds. @ _____ per sq. yd. $ _____

paint:

_____ gallons @ _____ per gallon $ _____

special effects:

wallcoverings:

_____ rolls @ _____ per roll $ _____

_____ yds. @ _____ per yd. $ _____

tile: _____ sq. ft. tile @ _____ per sq. ft. $ _____

labor to install $ _____

shower stall door $ _____

bathtub $ _____

toilet $ _____

bidet $ _____

sinks $ _____

faucets, drains, handles, etc. $ _____

knobs, pulls, etc. $ _____

mirrors: _____ sq. ft. @ _____ per sq. ft. $ _____

labor to install $ _____

plumbing installation $ _____

cabinets $ _____

KITCHENS

flooring:

_____ sq. ft. @ _____ per sq. ft. $ _____

_____ sq. yds. @ _____ per sq. yd. $ _____

paint: _____ gallons @ _____ per gallon $ _____

special effects:

wall covering:

_____ rolls @ _____ per roll $ _____

_____ yds. @ _____ per yd. $ _____

lighting: _____ fixtures @ _____ per fixture $ _____

(Kitchens, continued)

tile work: _____ sq. ft. tile @ _____ per sq. ft.　　　　$ _____

labor to install　　　　$ _____

counter tops　　　　$ _____

sinks　　　　$ _____

faucets　　　　$ _____

garbage disposal　　　　$ _____

trash compactor　　　　$ _____

refrigerator　　　　$ _____

oven and stove　　　　$ _____

center island　　　　$ _____

plumbing installation　　　　$ _____

electrician　　　　$ _____

cabinets　　　　$ _____

SUB-TOTAL　　　　$ _____

Now add:

sales tax: There is usually no sales tax on services and installation. However, items such as carpeting, draperies, and cabinets that are billed to you including installation are subject to sales tax. Check with your state's Board of Equalization for laws that apply　　　　$ _____

15% freight charges on ready-made pieces from another state　　　　$ _____

10% freight and delivery charges for fabrics and wall coverings　　　　$ _____

15% for mistakes you might make and items you must have, even if they don't fit into your budget　　　　$ _____

TOTAL　　　　$ _____

Currently, there are five offices of Decorator Previews:

LOS ANGELES
8425 West Third Street, #404
Los Angeles, CA 90048
(213) 655-9019 (Bobbie Everts)

SAN FRANCISCO
3025 Fillmore Street
San Francisco, CA 94123
(415) 563-3977 (Barbara Waldman)

CHICAGO
111 East Chestnut
Chicago, IL 60611
(312) 337-1007 (Michael Walsh)

WASHINGTON, DC
1025 Connecticut Avenue, N.W., Suite 1008
Washington, DC 20036
(202) 289-4900 (Cindy Gross)

NEW YORK
36 Gramercy Park East
New York, NY 10003
(212) 777-2966 (Karen Fisher)

No matter what method you choose for selecting an interior designer, make sure you have seen an adequate sampling of their work. Ask to see their portfolios, which should include many photographs of recent work. It's also a good idea to ask the designer if you can visit some recent jobs they've done to see the work in person. Make sure you call at least three of their references to confirm their honesty and reliability.

> **HINT:** Interior designers prefer to be called "interior designers." They cringe when you call them "decorators."

Are You Really Getting a Bargain?

You've decided to go it alone, sans designer. You take a trip to your state's local office of the Board of Equalization and get your resale number. This number is your passport into every wholesale source. That is, assuming you pay sales tax on everything you buy for yourself and others, and until the American Society of Interior Designers (ASID) gets legislation passed to stop unlicensed people from doing design work.

But are wholesale showrooms really giving you a bargain? Sometimes yes, sometimes no. Believe it or not, I've often found that department stores run specials on many items they buy in volume at rock bottom prices. These prices are often less than my wholesale costs. Consider the amount of overhead and rent a showroom must pay in order to survive. They are buying their merchandise from manufacturers directly or paying craftsmen to produce certain items for them. Only when a showroom is representing its own line of manufactured goods are you eliminating the middle man.

Go Straight to the Source

It isn't difficult to find the sources that the showrooms use. Often though, that source has a contract with particular showrooms and will refuse to sell to you directly, as it is unethical and jeopardizes their relationship with those showrooms. In that case, you are forced to buy from the showroom or find an alternative source that can make a similar item. You can often find skilled artisans who can copy pieces for more than one-half of the net or wholesale price. For instance, I have a cabinetmaker and finisher who can duplicate almost any piece of furniture for me, as long as it wasn't originally made from a mold. I also have a woman who hand-paints fabric for me. She can reproduce almost any fabric or pattern in any custom color I might specify at a huge savings off showroom prices.

How Do You Find the Sources?

To find the manufacturer of a specific item, you can always be sneaky and look over the shoulder of the salesperson as she is showing you the manufacturer's catalog. This isn't very nice, but do what you must.

Trade magazines such as *Architectural Digest*, *Designer's West*, and *Interior Design* have advertisements that give the manufacturer's name, address, and telephone number. These magazines also publish pictures of rooms done by well-known designers. Most pictures are also accompanied by credits that list some of the designer's sources. Often, they'll even reveal who made the draperies, the custom upholstered pieces, and who did the custom finishing.

Each of these magazines publishes a yearly buyer's guide or a resource directory. If you subscribe to them, you will receive these source books automatically.

You can find almost anything you want with proper research and a lot of perseverance. The money you save will be well worth it. Don't forget to call your local telephone company and request a copy of the Business-to-Business Yellow Pages. It contains a wealth of sources and information.

Where Are the Key Places to Cut Down on Costs?

If you've exhausted every source to find the items and workmen you really want, but still can't get the budget down to an acceptable amount, it's time to start considering substitutions and alternatives.

Professional labor is expensive. If you feel you are competent and have the time, you'll save a considerable amount of money by doing some of the work yourself. Painting and refinishing some furniture is not all that difficult. Know your limitations. Upholstery, wallpapering, and cabinet work are best left to the professionals. Laying a floor is only for the most ambitious and self confident.

If you can sew there are many dramatic and exciting window coverings you can make that will save you money. For instance, I have a client who bought bolts of $1.00 per yard fabric from a seconds warehouse and draped them over rods in a billowy effect, tied the corners with huge fabric bows, and let the sides flow to the floor. All she did was hem the bottom by hand. The windows looked fabulous and she spent under $100. Another client did the same thing on her four poster bed to create a fairy tale effect with gauze that she dyed pale pink and celadon in the washing machine. A little creativity goes a long way.

I've seen other clients find incredible bargains at garage sales and secondhand shops. One client bought an antique carved table for $35. She hand-painted and stenciled it, and placed it in the entry under a very expensive Venetian mirror. I would have taken it for a $3,000 piece.

Finding bargains and substituting enables you to save your money for the expensive pieces you just can't live without. There are many laminate tables that look like expensive lacquer but at a fraction of the cost. In the case of a sofa back table placed against a wall and behind a sofa, there's no need for an expensive table. You can have a table made with only the top and sides laminated. No one will ever see the unfinished edges.

Eliminate expensive nightstands and end tables. Be creative. Use a corkboard table that comes in standard sizes at your local home improvement center. Cover it with an exciting tablecloth made of hand-painted silk or canvas. Put an inexpensive piece of ¼" glass on top, and voilá. Or use a stripped and bleached tree trunk with a piece of glass placed on top of it. Your local firewood company might have tree trunks, but if not, they can direct you to where you might find one.

One of the most exciting money-saving ideas I've used recently is to layer flagstone. In order to cut a budget for a client, I went to the nearest stone yard and picked out flagstone. I layered the stone in front of his sofa in a free form and added a piece of thick glass. It looked great. Instant coffee table for under $100. (Make sure your floor can support the weight.)

I use boulders and rocks quite often. You can find them at your local building supply company. Take a fabulous tree or plant and surround it with huge rocks or boulders; even hide a few uplights to give the area more drama. This is a great effect for only a few dollars.

Often I go downtown and search factory warehouses for odd lots and seconds of fabric and carpeting. You can find bolts of fabrics for draperies and upholstery at rock bottom prices. Play around with the idea of tie dyeing, airbrushing, or hand-painting the inexpensive fabric. Odd lots and remnants of carpeting can also be money savers if you have only small areas to carpet.

One of the most innovative ideas I've come across is hand-painted corrugated cardboard used as a wall covering. A major wallpaper and fabric showroom sells this item for more than $40 per yard net. I found the source of corrugated cardboard in the Business-to-Business Yellow Pages and had the woman who hand-paints my fabrics airbrush and spatter the cardboard. It cost me less than $2.00 per yard.

Or take an afternoon off to browse through the Oriental section of your city to find a beautiful kimono. Hang it on a large wall, sleeves extended, supported by a rod. I've seen this done a lot, but it always looks dramatic. The bonus here is that when you're tired of looking at the kimono as a wall hanging, you can always wear it.

Saving money on upholstered pieces is often foolhardy. There are many different qualities of frames, foam, springs, and craftsmanship. Consider the wear and tear a piece will have to endure over the years before you decide to cut corners. If the piece is to go in a frequently used room, don't skimp. The inexpensive sofa or chair will lose its shape and wear out quickly. If the sofa or chair is to be in a seldom used room, a less expensive version might be just the right decision.

Pillows are still popular, especially oversized, down-filled ones. But down filling is expensive. A good upholsterer can make pillows filled with polyester that will give the same look at less than half the price. You can always have them redone with down if you change your mind later.

Silk trees and plants have made a great comeback. There are now some very authentic looking, virtually undetectable fakes. Although initially they are more costly than the real thing, you won't be out the money when they wither and die. Consider silk trees and plants for dark spots in your house that hold no promise for successful plant growth. In the long run, they're less expensive.

Now that I've gotten your creative juices flowing with money-saving, innovative ideas, the fun begins. Search unlikely places for ideas, such as marble yards, secondhand shops, garage sales, the used furniture section of your local newspaper, and even auto salvage yards. Yes, you can have a car engine lacquered and use it under a piece of glass for an interesting coffee table. You can even have the rear end of a car sawed off, have it lacquered, and upholster the trunk area to make an exciting sofa. Find an old, inexpensive armoire, and have it lacquered white or black. Add new brass handles and put it in the same room as your new $2,000 sofa. No one will know unless you tell them.

Are You Being Ripped Off?

If you've decided to use an interior designer, insist on seeing copies of all invoices. If the designer refuses, and he might, question his integrity. If he cuts off or whites out the name of the company he purchased the item from, it's okay; most designers are reluctant to reveal their sources.

Make sure any installers you use are state licensed. Call their individual associations for a quote on the standard prices for their services. Get at least three bids from three different installers. Never pay in full before the job is completed. A one-third or one-half deposit is standard. All work must be satisfactorily completed before final payment.

Carpet layers, tile installers, wood flooring installers, painters, electricians, and plumbers vary in the rates they charge. Make sure they won't bill you more at the end of the job because of additional preparation work they didn't notice ahead of time. It is always preferable to get a complete bid for the entire job instead of paying an hourly rate. Workmen who work by the hour tend to dawdle.

Wall covering installers usually charge by the roll or the yard. Removing old wallpaper first is quoted separately. If blank stock is needed to cover bumpy or irregular walls or suggested under very shiny wallpaper, the installer should quote a separate price for that, too.

Fabric costs will always be quoted by the yard. You must pay in full before they will cut the goods for you. Freight and delivery charges will be added later, usually about 5 or 10%. Some showrooms offer custom-colored fabric. They will charge a standard set-up fee for their dyes and will require a minimum yardage order.

Carpeting, if bought at a retail source, will be quoted with a per yard price that includes delivery, installation, and padding. Make sure they intend to use quality padding and inexperienced installers. Wholesale carpet sources quote a price on just carpeting. Padding, installation, and labor must be arranged and paid for separately. If you are buying direct from a carpet mill, they'll charge you an "overage." This is the amount of carpeting that ran over while they were running the carpet through their machines.

Wood flooring varies in cost per square foot, according to the type and quality of wood used, the intricacy of the pattern, the amount of staining and bleaching necessary, and the quality of the workmanship. Make sure the bid includes preparation work and subflooring, if necessary. Repairing old wood floors and piecing are bid separately.

Making cabinets for kitchens and bathrooms is a highly competitive business. If you choose prefabricated cabinets that come in standard sizes, make sure the bid includes delivery, installation, staining, painting, etc. If you're having custom cabinets made, make sure you get at least three bids for the work; prices vary greatly. Make it a point to call the cabinetmaker's references and take the time to examine two or three of their completed jobs.

Tile is usually bid by the square foot. Prices vary according to the intricacy of the tile and its pattern. Stay away from tile layers who charge by the hour. The more detailed the job, the more it will cost.

Upholstery costs vary greatly also. There are many backyard operations that do excellent work, others that do not. Shop around. Be sure to check references and look at finished pieces the upholsterer has done recently. Some upholsterers will charge by the piece, others will charge by the foot. All of them will charge extra for details such as skirts, shirring, and channeling. Most upholsterers can also make bedspreads, comforters, and pillows. Ask. Both prices and quality vary.

Painters should bid the entire job, no matter how long it actually takes them to complete it. Ask if the price includes all supplies. Ask if they know how to mix custom colors and do specialty finishes such as faux marble walls. Expect added costs for these skills.

Plumbers and electricians usually have a standard hourly rate. If you use a contractor, he'll quote you a total price, and if the plumbing or electrical labor runs over, that's his problem, he underbid it.

To avoid being ripped off, make sure:

- All people you hire to do work for you are state licensed.
- You have gotten three separate written bids for each job you are contracting.
- You have personally and thoroughly examined two or three samples of each workman's craftsmanship.
- You have not paid a workman in full until his job is satisfactorily completed.
- All contracts and agreements are in writing.

Revising Your Budget

Now you've gotten all your bids from contractors, workmen, and installers. You've spent endless hours shopping and pulling out magazine pictures. Your desk is coated with catalogs, brochures, samples, and estimates. Your throat is dry from days of telephone calls tracking down valuable sources. It's time to tally up the results.

Sort through all your notes, pictures, and samples, selecting only your first choices. Put everything else aside. Item by item, fill in the blanks on the budget form in pencil, adding any incidentals I might have left out. Follow my formula for adding delivery and freight charges, sales tax, mistakes, and "must haves." Add it up.

You now have a reasonably accurate accounting of what this little project is really going to cost you. If the amount is acceptable to you, great! Time to move on to the next chapter and get started.

If not, don't panic. Ask yourself again the questions that appear earlier in this chapter. Sit down with your budget, and slowly and painfully remove those items that you can live without. Perhaps you can have a wonderful sponged wall in the powder room instead of that $40 per roll wallpaper you love. Maybe you can paint the cabinets in the kids' bathroom instead of putting in new ones. After all, there are some great knobs and pulls available. Maybe they don't need new sinks after all.

Okay, so you can't bear to part with the granite counter top for the kitchen. But maybe you're willing to give up the two matching hand-painted loveseats with down pillows. Wouldn't plain fabric with just hand-painted pillows filled with polyester give the same effect? And who really needs expensive tile in the laundry room, no one sees it anyway. A less expensive vinyl will do just as well. And maybe, just maybe, foam-backed fabric will be just as effective on the dining room walls as the wall upholstery you had your heart set on. It really was too expensive.

Have faith. Keep the train of thought. Revise and rework the budget until it's acceptable. Substitutions and alternatives will flow from your creative mind as you read through the rest of this book. In the long run, you won't even remember those things that you thought you couldn't live without — you'll be too busy enjoying the overall look.

7
Designer Lingo

Every professional field has its own lingo. I remember the first time I ordered fabric at a showroom, the salesperson asked me, "Will that be per forma?" I stuttered, "Uh, er, yeah," not having the foggiest idea what "per forma" meant. If you'd like to decorate like a pro, you might as well sound like a pro. This chapter is full of fun words and phrases designers love to use, as well as the terms essential to communicating with people "in the business."

My introduction to the "in crowd" of the interior design world was my first job as a design assistant to a well-known interior designer who catered to super rich jet setters. My first day was exciting, as he took me with him to an installation he was doing for a popular movie star. I watched him dart around the room nervously as a magnificently lacquered armoire was brought into the living room and set down in place. His eyes lit up and he threw his hands quickly in the air. "IT'S TO DIE FOR!" he exclaimed. "Yeah, it's real nice," I said. He just stood there and stared at me, sincerely hurt by what appeared to be my lack of enthusiasm. I obviously had a lot to learn about the importance of designer lingo.

It's now years later and my design vocabulary, as well as my tact, has somewhat improved. I sat for hours one evening sipping wine with Craig Milne and Judy Brustman of Design Team International in Los Angeles compiling the following words and phrases that are a must for any aspiring decorator to know. It also seems that enthusiasm and an animated expression are a major component in successful decorating.

- *Budget* means there's never enough money to really do exactly what you'd like. I was once working on a 10,000 square foot mansion for a very rich man. He asked me, "Do you think we can fit a large vault into the construction budget?" I replied, "What for? You won't have any money to keep in it when you're done building this house anyway!"
- *Pull it together* means "unity," finding a central theme.
- A *find* means a bargain or special piece that "works."
- *Look* means a unique overall style, decor.
- *Style* not only refers to a type of decor, but to a sixth sense. Some people have style, others don't. Some rooms have style, others don't.
- *Fake it* means if you can't afford the real thing, make it look like you can.
- *New* means a style, a particular piece, a color, a technique, has not been used over and over again; it's fresh. *Newer* refers to decorating materials and techniques that are in vogue. *Newest* refers to decorating materials and techniques that have just been introduced.
- *Hot* means "in." Faux finishes are hot.
- *Passé* is the opposite of hot. It means the same as "out."
- *It's to die for* means it's fabulous, it's marvelous. It's also acceptable to use derivatives, like It's to die from or It's just to die.

- *It's the best in the life* means it's great, there's no better. You can use this expression as a reply of agreement to "it's to die for" or when a recent death in the family makes "it's to die for" a poor choice of words.

- *Divine* means it's perfect, it's "knockout," it's to die for.

- *Go for it* means if you're going to do it, do it right! For example, if you're going to wallpaper, wallpaper the whole room, not just one wall.

- *Go all the way* is a synonym for Go for it. It means all or nothing. This is not a good expression to use in front of your sixteen year old daughter.

- *Tacky* means that the design job is in bad taste, everything's wrong. For more impact, you can wrinkle your nose discreetly as you say it.

- *Old* means something's passé, out of style, and has been used too much; it's seen better days. For example, plastic flowers are "old."

- *Basket case* means there's no hope for a room. Bring in the bulldozer.

- *Too easy* means that it just looks like you went shopping, bought something, and plopped it in a room. Matched bedroom sets are "too easy."

- *Too matchy* means everything in a room matches "too" well. It's like a red-headed woman who buys a red purse, red shoes, and a red belt to match her new red dress. If she tops her outfit off with a new red hat, there are even stronger words than "too matchy" that you can use.

- *Too stark* means too empty or too bare. There's a fine line between carefully thought out minimalism and a plain, almost empty room.

- *Sparse* means minimal. It's a positive connotation of the design concept, "less is more." Good design technique includes knowing when to leave well enough alone.

- *Clutter* means there's too much of everything, usually too much of the wrong thing. Again, less is more.

- *Ditz* means ridiculous looking clutter. For example, a living room filled with collections of old Barbie dolls and bottle caps is filled with "ditz."

- *Too frou-frou* means too prissy, too ruffly, too sweet. Cute little ruffled curtains are "too frou-frou."

- *Clean-lined* means simple elegance. A room or a piece can be elegant because of its simplicity and good design.

- *What is it lacking?* This expression means something's missing, but you just can't put your finger on it. The room needs some other element to make it work.

- *Buff up* means to spruce up a room. For example, to freshen up a room by slipcovering an old sofa, painting old hardwood floors, and adding a few plants.

- *It works* means a particular element of a room blends with and adds to the total look of the room.

- *Interesting* means there's "punch" in a room. There are one or more elements in the room that give it excitement and drama.

- *Funky* means a room has a whimsical feeling. It's unconventional.

- *Important piece* is a piece that "makes" the room. One fabulous antique Oriental screen or one major piece of art.

- *Bold* means that a room or a piece of furniture makes a statement. A bold room makes an impact; you don't forget it.

- *Hunky* means large. The trend in design now is to use "hunky," overscaled upholstered pieces.

- *Opulent* means luxurious, rich looking. Opulent decors are now more "in" than ever.

- *Are you keeping all of this?* This expression is the tactful way of saying to a client, "Everything in your house is ugly and would look better in the garbage can."

- *Get rid of it!* This expression is the less tactful way of saying to a client, "Everything in your house is ugly and would look better in the garbage can."

- *Mistake* means the designer is stuck with a piece. Most designer's homes or garages contain many items that were "mistakes." When you take a tour through a designer's home and comment on any piece, he'll usually say, "Oh, that was a mistake from a project I did five years ago, would you like to see my latest mistake?"

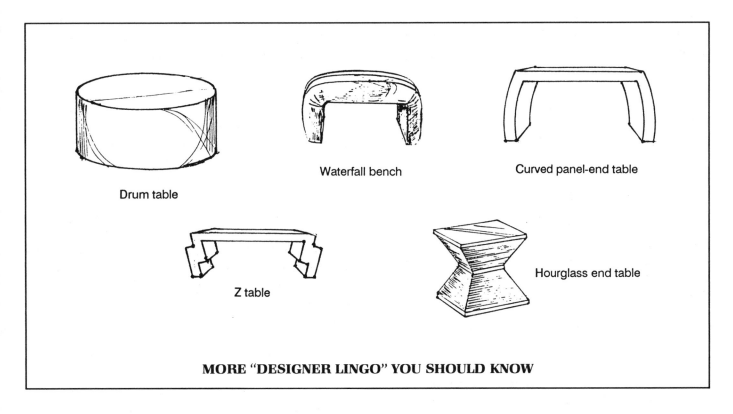

Drum table

Waterfall bench

Curved panel-end table

Z table

Hourglass end table

MORE "DESIGNER LINGO" YOU SHOULD KNOW

Enough lingo, you'll also need to know some terms that are commonly used by designers to communicate with showrooms and workmen:

• *Accessories* are the little elements of a room that give it character and individuality.

• *Adaptation* means that a piece was inspired by an antique.

• *Alloy* is a material composed of two or more metals.

• *Application* is the way in which a material is used.

• *Art Deco* is a design form from the 1920s which attempts to use the design motifs of the industrial machine age decoratively.

• *Art Nouveau*, often called "New Art," arose in the 1890s and had a renaissance in the late 1960s. Its pieces are noted for their sensuous, swirling lines.

• *ASID* is the American Society of Interior Designers, head offices located in New York City.

• *COG* means "customer's own goods." Essentially, this is the same as "COM."

• *COM* means "customer's own material." The price a wholesale showroom quotes you on an upholstered piece does not include any fabric.

• *Contractor* refers to a general contractor you hire to coordinate and supervise workmen. Subcontractors are hired by the contractor to do specific work.

• *Drop* is the distance a tablecloth drops from the edge of a table to the floor or a bedspread drops from the edge of the bed to the floor.

• *Duvet* is a comforter. A duvet cover is a comforter cover. It can be made from two sheets sewn together with a zipper on one side for easy washing.

• *Eclectic* means a mixture of furnishings from different places and periods to create an interesting blend.

• *Faux* means fake.

- *F.O.B.* means "freight on board." This means that the price of a piece of furniture you are ordering from another city or country only includes getting that piece onto its mode of transportation. Once it arrives in your city, all other freight charges are your responsibility and will be added to the cost.

- *Focal point* is the point of major visual interest, such as a view or an important painting.

- *In-house designer* refers to an interior designer who works exclusively for a furniture store, builder, or architect.

- *In the trade* means that you are a professional interior designer who actually makes your living from design work. If you venture through the doors marked "To the Trade," you'll be asked if you're "In the Trade."

- *Installation* is the term used by all designers to describe the major delivery day. An example of the correct usage is: "I'm exhausted. I stayed up all night working on an installation." Most designers prefer to wait until every piece is complete and ready to deliver before scheduling an installation. That way, the client will have the inconvenience of being kept out of his own home by the designer for an entire day, but the excitement of walking into a totally decorated home at the end of the day. Other designers prefer to deliver furniture in a piecemeal fashion. Personally, I feel a piecemeal delivery method should only be used when the client will really be inconvenienced by the lack of certain pieces, such as a bed he might need to sleep on.

- *List* is the design term for "retail."

- *Net* simply means the discounted price a designer will pay for an item.

- *Objet d'art* is a French term used frequently by designers to describe any small art object.

- *Occasional furniture* refers to small pieces that are used only occasionally.

- *On memo* is a term used for artwork and accessories. It means that you can take one or a number of pieces out with you to see how they will look in a room before you actually make the purchase. The standard procedure for taking things

out on memo is to write a check for the full amount to the showroom, instructing them to hold the check for a certain number of days so you can make the decision. Three to five days is standard practice. The salesperson will write you an "On Memo" form, and it's up to you either to return the items within the time limit or call the showroom and inform them you will be keeping the items. If you return the items undamaged within the time limit, they will return the uncashed check to you.

- *Open account* means that you have a charge account with a particular showroom and are able to place orders that will be billed to you later. Open accounts are difficult to get unless you are a prolific interior designer who has built up a reputation with many showrooms and you place many orders frequently.

- *Per forma* means simply that you are not on open account and must pay the full amount for wall coverings and fabrics at the time your order is placed.

- *Project* refers to any design job a designer is working on, no matter how small or large.

- *Quote* means a written confirmation of either the list or net price of a piece of furniture or accessory that a salesperson will write up for you when you ask, "What is the price?" Actually, "May I have a quote?" is the proper way of asking the same question "in the business."

- *Retail* means the suggested price at which an item should be sold to a client or consumer.

- *Sham* is a decorative cover for a bed pillow.

- *Tensile strength* is the greatest stress a substance can bear without tearing apart.

- *Throw* is a small, decorative blanket thrown over a chair, sofa, or bed.

- *To the trade* are the intimidating words you'll see on the doors of wholesale showrooms. These words means that you are only allowed to come in if you have a valid resale number and/or a business card, or are accompanied by your interior designer.

- *Trompe l'oeil* is any decorative treatment that fools the eye.

Shhhh! Trade Secrets:

- *5/10* is a standard discount code used in wholesale fabric and wallpaper showrooms. I'll probably get flogged by many an interior designer for revealing this code but . . . it means you take $5.00 off the first number and ten cents off the second number. For example, if a fabric is coded 19/55, the designer's net is $14.45 per yard.

- *Designer's net* is the discounted price an interior designer will get from a wholesale showroom. It varies from showroom to showroom and item to item. Some showrooms give a 40% discount on all furniture and a 30% discount on all accessories. Other showrooms will give a 50% discount on furniture and 40% on accessories. Each showroom has its own policy.

- *Manufacturer's net* is the discounted price an interior designer or furniture store gets when they buy direct from a manufacturer. Again, discount policies of different manufacturers vary. Some give added discounts for customers who buy often or in large quantities. A large furniture store might get a 50/10 discount, which means they buy their furniture at 50% off, then another 10% is taken off of that amount, or even a 50/10/5 discount, which means another 5% is discounted from the 50/10 amount.

- *Keystone* is another standard design word used in wholesale fabric and wallpaper showrooms. It means the price marked on the wallpaper or fabric sample is list or retail, and the designer's net is 50% less. If a wallpaper sample is marked $30.00 in a showroom that uses keystone, the net price to a designer is $15.00.

You'll find hundreds of additional decorating terms and definitions in the Decorating Dictionary at the end of this book.

8
Understanding Color

Color is a visual language. It's one of the important tools you use to express your individual personality. Learning to see and use color correctly is an art you can easily teach yourself. Color has emotion, style, and meaning. You can't touch or hear color, but you can "feel" it. It's like sound, the transmission of wavelengths. Each hue has a different wavelength and your eye is the receiver. All colors mixed together make white light, the light of daylight and the sun. When you pass white light through raindrops or a prism, you'll see a rainbow, or a full color band. If you were to mix all these colors together you would get gray, not white, because there are impurities in dyes and pigments.

The color an object appears to be is not the color that is absorbed by the pigments in the object, but rather the color that is reflected. For example, if the color of a pillow appears to be red, it's because the dye in the fabric is absorbing all of the wavelengths in white light except the red ones. The type of light that makes the object visible also affects the color the object appears to be. Light is rarely colorless. The color of light varies with its source and whatever it passes through before coming into your eyes. White light such as that from the moon and the sun contains all the hues in the color wheel, balanced and blended so that its effect is that of no color. Light from the moon is bluish, while that from an open fire or an incandescent bulb is yellowish. These color waves move through the air and are received by your eyes as red. But what color red is it? Is it pure red? Does it have yellow or blue in it?

A Basic Color Lesson

In order to understand color, you should know the basic vocabulary. The three most important words are hue, value, and intensity.

HUE

Hue is a word often used synonymously with the word "color," but it is actually the distinguishing difference between colors. Hue is the redness of red, the greenness of green. Hues are pure, undiluted colors. The three primary colors are red, blue, and yellow. They can't be produced by mixing other colors. Mixtures of red, blue, and yellow can produce nearly every other color. The secondary colors are green, violet, and orange.

There are hundreds of different hues and millions of variations of each hue that can be detected by the human eye. The basic six for which there are specific color names are red, yellow, blue, orange, green, and violet. These six colors along with six more intermediate colors, yellow-green, blue-green, blue-violet, red-violet, red-orange, and yellow-orange, make up the color wheel. The intermediate colors lie midway between the primary and

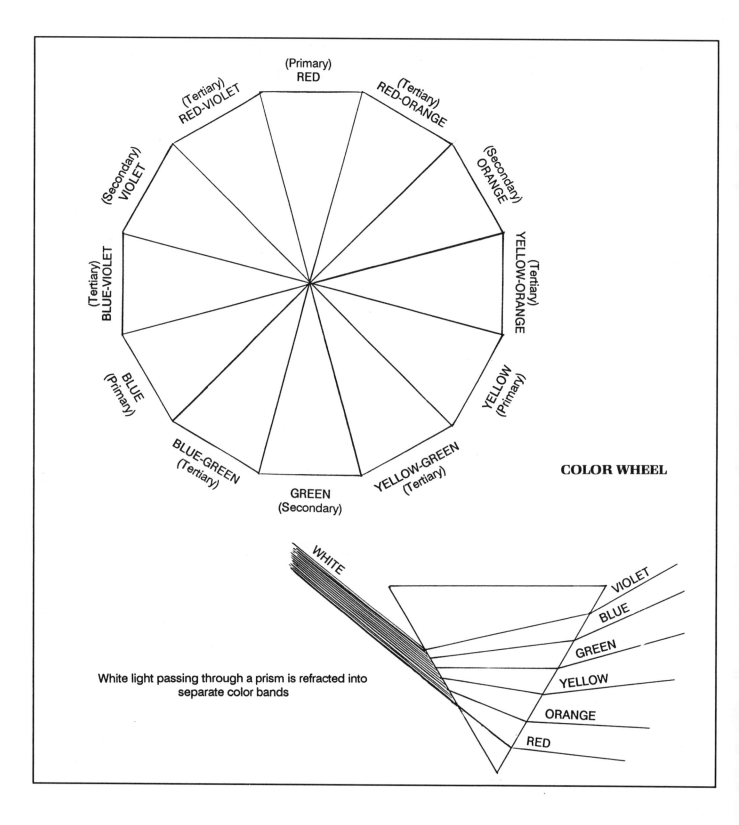

COLOR WHEEL

White light passing through a prism is refracted into separate color bands

secondary colors of which they are products.

Change a hue or create a new one by combining neighboring hues. For instance, blue becomes blue-violet when combined with violet.

Create harmony or contrast with the way you combine hues in a color combination. Use combinations that are next to each other on the color wheel, such as blue, blue-violet, and violet, to create a feeling of harmony and restfulness. Place yellow next to violet to create contrast and excitement. Thus, analogous hues are adjacent to each other on the color wheel, and complementary hues are directly opposite each other on the color wheel. Combine hues in any degree of harmony or contrast.

Use hues to create the effect of the desired temperature in your home. Hues can be either warm or cold. Red, yellow, and orange appear warm and active. They make objects appear closer than they really are, and are called advancing hues. Blue, violet, and green appear cool and restful. They make objects appear small, and are called receding hues.

VALUE

Value is the lightness or darkness of a color. There are many value levels between pure white and black (the absence of light). The neutral, gray, can have any number of values, depending on how much white and black are mixed together. Rooms containing hues of mostly light values will appear to be bright, airy, and cheerful. Rooms containing mostly dark values will tend to be gloomy. Always try to add a few middle values to avoid harshness.

Values range from high-light, normal, to low-dark. Tints are values that are lighter than normal such as pink, which is a tint of red. Shades are values that are darker than normal, such as maroon which is a shade of red. Like hues, values affect each other. Gray appears much darker when seen against a dark surface than it does when seen against a light surface. It's simple to remember: tints are tones with white added, tones are hues with gray added, and shades are hues with black added.

INTENSITY

Intensity, also called chroma, is the strength or degree of a color. A color can be of full intensity, vivid, high, or strong, or it can be low and weak, neutralized.

Increase the intensity of a color by adding more of the dominant hue. Or give the illusion of more intensity by illuminating the object either with the light of that hue or contrasting it with its complementary hue.

Decrease the intensity of a color by adding varying amounts of its complementary hue or mixing a color with black, gray, or white. You can give the illusion of decreased intensity by lighting the object with the light of the complementary hue.

Hue, value, and intensity have a great impact on our emotions and perceptions. Warm hues are stimulating, while cool hues are quieting and relaxing. Warm hues attract more attention than cool hues. Warm hues increase the apparent size of an object, but decrease the apparent size of an overall room. Warm hues bring objects forward, while cool hues tend to make them recede. Warm hues tend to soften outlines more than cool hues, while contrasting hues tend to make outlines more defined than related hues.

Light values are cheerful, while dark values can be restful, gloomy, and depressing. Contrasts demand attention. Extreme values attract attention, but surprising contrasts are even more effective. Light values can increase the apparent size of an object, but a strong contrast with the background can be equally as effective. Light values recede, while dark values advance. Sharp contrast in values can also bring objects forward. Value contrasts are an effective way of emphasizing the contours of objects. High intensities are heartening and strong, while low intensities are peaceful. High intensities definitely attract attention and increase the apparent size of an object, but when used on walls, will decrease the apparent size of the room. High intensities decrease visual distances. Intensity contrasts can emphasize the outline of an object.

Choosing Your Color Scheme

Now that you have a clearer understanding about what color is and can do, it's time to make some decisions about the color scheme or schemes for your home. First, let's define the various types of color schemes.

MONOCHROMATIC

Monochromatic or "one-color" schemes are achieved with tints, shades, and variations of the same hue. Beige to brown schemes and light to dark gray schemes have always been popular. White on white (yes, there are many different tints, tones, and shades of white) are growing increasingly popular. A monochromatic color scheme can be any color, as long as there is only one color in different variations.

The positive of using a monochromatic color scheme is that you'll automatically achieve unity, harmony, spaciousness, and continuity. The effect is almost always quiet and restful. However, be careful not to let the room become boring and monotonous. Add a dash of bright red or yellow somewhere, perhaps a vase of flowers. Make sure you include forms, textures, and spatial relationships to provide some relief.

ANALOGOUS

Analogous color schemes are groups of colors that are related in hue or are neighbors on the color wheel. If all the colors used share one hue, the scheme will have harmony. An analogous color scheme should be made up of three or more hues which contain some degree of one hue. The colors you select should fall within any segment of the color wheel that's less than halfway around it. For example, if the common hue is blue, your color

scheme can include blue, blue-green, blue-violet, or blue-green, blue-violet, and red-violet. You can create interest by introducing variations of lightness, darkness, and saturation.

Analogous color schemes, while still harmonious, create more variety and interest than monochromatic color schemes. Do remember that grayed colors and pure colors tend to neutralize each other. You can create a more pleasing harmony by using light and dark grayed colors or light and dark pure colors.

COMPLEMENTARY

Complementary color schemes are strong and bold. They are developed by using two hues directly opposite each other on the color wheel. Since complementary colors, when used side by side, appear stronger, use this type of color combination with a discerning eye and include variations of value and intensity. To give you a good idea of how powerful these combinations can be, here are a few complementary color combinations: red and green; orange and blue; red and violet; red-orange and blue-green; yellow-orange and blue-violet; yellow-green and red-violet. Ugh! Great for Christmas and football teams, but be careful with these colors in your home.

DOUBLE-COMPLEMENTARY

Double-complementary color schemes are two sets of complements, such as blue and blue-green put together with orange and red-orange. Use double-complementary color schemes with the utmost of discretion.

SPLIT-COMPLEMENTARY

Split-complementary color schemes consist of combining one hue with two hues at each side of its complement, for example, combining yellow with red-violet and blue-violet. This can be a less turbulent and more interesting color scheme than the complementary and double-complementary schemes.

TRIAD

Triad color schemes are made up of three hues that are an equal distance from each other on the color wheel, such as red, yellow, and blue. If used with full intensity, they can be extremely bright and powerful. Triad color schemes can be used more successfully in the home if subdued to combinations such as forest green, saddle brown, and steel gray.

TETRAD

Tetrad color schemes are made up of four hues that are an equal distance from each other on the color wheel. When done correctly and in a subdued manner, this combination can create a pleasing and balanced composition.

Confusing? Still don't know how to choose the right color scheme for your home? Why not get some ideas from Mother Nature? Let's stimulate your creativity with a trip through the basic color schemes found in your natural environment.

First, visualize the colors in the garden; the pinks, blues, yellows, greens, all mixed together in innumerable tints, shades, and values. Now, visualize the colors of the sea; the blues, pale greens, grays, turquoises, deep violets, white froth. Notice how the sunset changes the variations in these combinations. Next, think of the colors in the forest; the greens, gray-greens, black-greens, pale yellows, dark browns. Note how cool they make you feel. Now, move on to the colors of the sun; the reds, red-yellows, oranges, red-oranges, whites, golds. They make you feel warm and content, don't they? Last, feel the colors of the atmosphere; the gray fog, beige smoke, silver evening, mauve shadows. They make you feel alone, a little eerie, suspended in wide open space. You can come back to earth now, this

was just a little exercise in experiencing how colors can "feel."

Now to confess how I develop new and exciting color schemes for clients. First, I ask the client or clients what their favorite color is. The wife will usually answer, "Oh, I guess I like blue a lot, but, of course, I really do like green. And I did see this house that was done in dark purple and I loved it." Then the husband will interject, "Darling, you know how much I love gray and red." The wife, of course, will sneer at her spouse and give me a secretive look implying that I should humor him; she'll be the one making the decisions here. Needless to say, this is a touchy situation and I'm tempted to decorate their house in bright orange just for spite. But in the end, my good taste overrides and I strive to please them both.

First thing the next morning I go fabric shopping for the wishy-washy couple and select several fabrics from which I form the basis of my color scheme. The first fabric I find is blue-green. After all, the wife liked blue and green, didn't she? The second fabric sample I pull is the exact purple the wife said that she loved in the house that she saw. The third fabric is a gray, to please the husband, of course. You can't please all the people all the time, can you? Or maybe you can. Next, I take these fabrics and build one or more exciting color combinations around each one, always keeping in mind the mood and feeling the couple indicated they wanted to achieve. Ninety-nine times out of a hundred this method has produced effective, creative, and exciting color schemes that pleased everyone.

You can use the same method by first having a family meeting to decide which members of the family like what colors. Select a carpet color that goes with all of the colors the family has chosen. If Junior chooses bright fuchsia, you might want to discourage him, perhaps make an appointment for him with a psychiatrist. If your husband says, "Black, I want everything black!" you might want to consider a divorce. But in general, you'll find that there's a way to please everyone by taking the color of their choice and adapting it to the basic color scheme of the house.

Thumb through design magazines and sort through those pictures you've been collecting. Pull out the photographs that have the color combinations you enjoy the most. Paint stores have color fans that include hundreds of their custom paint colors. Buy a color fan and use it to experiment with all the different possibilities. Begin shopping for fabrics and collecting the samples you love, mixing and matching them together. Attach fabric samples or wallpaper samples to your walls for a few weeks to see how the color combinations affect you. Are they growing on you and making you feel comfortable? Are you getting sick of them and feeling the urge to throw them away? Take your time and do these exercises before you make a commitment to a color scheme.

Once you've made a final decision, that color scheme is yours for years to come. Before you make the choice, let's go over some additional considerations to be made before finalizing your color scheme.

Consider the personalities and lifestyles of the entire family. Generally, active, outgoing people prefer very bold, contrasting colors. Quieter, more introverted people will usually want cooler, more neutralized and harmonious schemes.

Take an inventory of the furniture and accessories you already own and don't want to part with. While they can limit a new color scheme, they can also suggest an alternate scheme. It's possible to pull together an odd array of furniture and accessories with a related color scheme. Perhaps a collection of antiques, fine paintings, or accessories might determine your color scheme. If you're lucky enough to be able to start from scratch, use the methods discussed above.

Consider the rooms, windows, doors, fireplaces, floors, and ceilings. Cool hues, light values, and low intensities make small rooms seem larger. Rooms that are too long or narrow will appear shorter and wider when one end wall is warmer, darker, and more intense than the other side walls.

Rooms that are too square or box-like will appear more interesting if one or two of the walls are treated differently than the others, or if one wall and the ceiling or the floor are similar in color. Remember, rooms well lit by either natural or artificial light will make colors look clear. Colors will look darker and duller in rooms with less light. Rooms facing the south and east will get more heat and yellowish light than those rooms that face east or north. Use cool colors in south and west rooms, warm colors in east and north rooms.

Keep the entire house in mind. Make sure the color scheme you choose flows with unity and continuity from one room to another.

Important! Make sure any color you select, whether it is for fabric, wall covering, carpeting, paint, or furniture, is checked and double checked in the room where it will be used. Make sure it's the perfect color in *both* natural and artificial light.

Color Contrasts

Basic to selecting a color scheme is understanding the seven basic types of contrast that affect the character, artistic value, vision, expression, and symbolic effect of your room.

Contrast of hue is exemplified by the triad color scheme of red, yellow, and blue. When these colors are separated by black or white, they emerge more sharply. Contrast of hue is found in folk art such as embroidery, costume, and pottery. Just think of the paintings of Matisse, Mondrian, and Picasso.

Light-dark contrast is like day and night. It is the relationship between black and white. Think of Chinese and Japanese ink drawings for an excellent example of the different gradations between light and dark hue.

Cold-warm contrast identifies a sensation of temperature with the visual realm of color sensation. Tests have proven that people actually feel warmer at the same air temperature in a red-orange room than in a blue-green room. You'll see superb examples of cold-warm contrasts in the paintings of Monet, Pisarro, and Renoir.

Complementary contrast exists when the pigments of two complementary colors are mixed together, making a neutral gray-black. They are opposite; they require each other. When adjacent, they maximize each other's vividness. There can only be one complementary color to a given color, such as yellow and violet, blue and orange, and red and green.

Simultaneous contrast results from the fact that for any given color the eye simultaneously requires the complementary color and generates it spontaneously if it is not already present.

Contrast of saturation is the contrast between pure intense colors and dull, diluted colors. A color may be diluted with white, black, gray, or by using its complementary color.

Contrast of extension relates to the proportion in which you use colors. The force of a color is determined by its brilliance and its extent. For example, yellow is three times as strong as violet. Thus, to be in balance, yellow should be used in only one-third the area as violet. What's important here is to understand that just because you select two, three, or four different colors for a room, it doesn't mean you have to use each color in the same proportion. Since the study of contrast of extension is quite complex, it's important to use your eye to experiment with how much of one color feels right with a different amount of another color.

The way we see color is also affected by how our eyes visualize the way colors are expressed. The effect of luster makes an ordinary color appear to be brighter than bright. Luster is achieved by the way light is reflected and creates an overall impression of subdued light.

An iridescent effect, such as in an opal or mother of pearl, is not due to pigments or dyes, but rather to diffraction brought about the minute structures in the material absorb the rays of light and split them up into their component hues.

What's Hot, What's Not

Black and white contrasts are definitely hot right now. Add a tiny dash of color, perhaps yellow, red, or green.

Navy blue and gray are back.

Mustard yellow is popping up everywhere. Shrimp and turquoise are a definite yes, particularly for Southwestern motifs.

So are sunset colors, like pinks and corals.

Combinations of taupe and black are more popular than ever.

Mix black with cinnamon for an even newer look.

And you can't go wrong with any "luggage" color.

But if you want to be one step ahead of the crowd, go for brighter and bolder colors . . . they're up and coming.

Grayed, dusty colors are on their way out.

Peach has definitely been overdone and is passé.

Combinations of peach and green or pink and green are yesterday's news.

Mauves are out. Pastels are following close behind.

9
Miracles with Paint

Paint is the least expensive, most important tool that you'll use in decorating your home. The color of the paint you select will dictate the mood, the ambience, and the style of the room. Since you've already read Chapter 8, you're now more prepared to choose the right paint colors. But there's more to paint than meets the eye.

What is Paint?

Paint is a blend of four basic types of ingredients. First, pigment, which provides the color. Second, a binder of natural or synthetic resin, which carries the pigment and forms the thin, tough, decorative, and protective film when it dries. Third, a drier, which speeds up the drying of the resin. And fourth, a thinner, referred to as a solvent, which dilutes the paint to a usable consistency. Some paints contain an extender, such as whiting, kaolin, talc, or natural or synthetic silica.

There are thousands of types of custom-made paints for every purpose conceivable. The most common are:

Flat oil paint is the best for interior surfaces because of its consistency, coverage, and finish, but is not widely used because it is hard to find, expensive, and takes a long time to dry.

Latex is a general term used to describe the familiar flat latex paint and the newer mat vinyls used in standard finishes for plaster work. Latex is relatively inexpensive, fast and easy to use, covers well, and has good adhesion. Because latex is water based, it has no odor and allows the surface to breathe, so it can be applied to new plaster. It dries quickly, leaving a washable surface. If it's clean and in good condition, latex can easily be recovered with almost any other finish and will withstand steamy kitchens and bathrooms. Latex generally has more sheen than flat oil paint and can be thinned for use as a color wash.

Undercoat is usually a flat, oil-based paint designed to provide a sound and non-porous ground for other oil-based finishing coats. It isn't meant to be used as a top coat. However, undercoat is widely available and is often used very successfully as a substitute for flat oil paint. It does cover more thinly, so you may need an extra coat. Its powdery texture should be protected by a mat varnish. I suggest buying the best quality if you are using it as a base for a decorative technique, as better qualities dry to a smoother, less absorbent finish. Although the colors are limited, undercoat can easily be tinted.

Eggshell is a hard and smooth oil-based paint with an expensive looking sheen. It's of high quality, durable, but is very expensive. It's great for walls and tints easily. It makes a perfect non-porous ground for various painting techniques. Eggshell is slightly harder to work with than other low-luster finishes and even coverage is difficult to achieve.

Other low-luster finishes are either oil- or water-based. The oil-based paints can be used in much the same way as eggshell. They're easier to work with, but have less covering power and a heavier finished look. When applied in several thinner coats rather than one or two undiluted coats, their appearance is enhanced. Water-based paints are fast drying and create a soft-sheen finish for walls. On woodwork, they're more durable than flat latex and are washable. Water-based paints are more porous and less hard-wearing than oil-based finishes.

Gloss paints are usually based on oil-modified, alkyd media and come in semi-gloss, gloss, and high or hard gloss, all describing the increasing levels of shine. The amount of shine is usually commensurate with the strength of the surface and its water and dirt resistance. Gloss paints are all susceptible to chipping.

Hiring a Professional Painter

If you'll be hiring a professional to do your work, the best way to find a good one is through a reliable referral. Painters can be kids working their way through school or state-licensed contractors. I suggest, if you want a professional and trouble-free job, you select a painter with many years of experience and the proper licensing. Make sure the painter you choose has supplied you with at least three names of satisfied clients. Don't neglect to call those clients to make sure they were happy with the painter. It's also advisable to physically check the painter's work to make sure it is up to your standards. The satisfied client you speak to over the telephone might not be as observant or picky as you are.

I suggest you interview at least three painters before selecting one. Get a price quote from each, making sure the price they quote includes thorough preparation work and the paint and labor for two or more coats of paint as needed to cover a wall. Many painters love to tell you, once they've gotten the job and cashed your check, that they will have to charge extra for preparation work they hadn't planned on, for custom colors you forgot to tell them you were using, and for removing old wallpaper. Be sure you have thoroughly discussed all the above items with the painter and he agrees to include ALL work in his bid.

Have the painter prepare a written contract that spells out exactly what's to be done and exactly what it will cost. If the painter tells you he only works by the hour, politely show him the door. Painters who charge by the hour usually work very slowly. The ultimate cost is sure to be much more than an overall bid for the entire job. You won't be particularly happy when the painter rambles on about his wife's labor pains while the clock is ticking away at an hourly rate.

Don't be surprised if your painter doesn't show up after the first day's work, it's normal. Three days later he'll appear, declaring, "Oh, I'm sorry, but my truck broke down." Or, "Sorry I didn't call you, but my brother-in-law's been in jail and I've just spent the last three days trying to raise the money to bail him out." These are normal excuses. I can't remember the last time I hired a painter whose truck didn't have mechanical problems or who didn't have a close relative in the hospital. The best way to avoid these problems is to include a deadline date in the painting contract. For each day the painter runs over the deadline date, you deduct a specified amount from the final contract price. This should keep him on his toes, his truck running smoothly, his brother-in-law out of jail, and his father-in-law's ticker in tip-top shape.

Never, I repeat, never, pay for an entire job before it's satisfactorily completed! Always pay a deposit, which should only be one-third to one-half of the entire fee, at the onset of the job. The balance due should only be paid upon satisfactory completion of the entire job. An honest and reputable painter will be anxious to please you and willing to come back and go over small details before demanding final payment.

Do-It-Yourselfers

If you are planning to paint your home yourself, here are some of the things you should know before beginning.

Always thin paint before using. If you are using oil-based paint, thin with solvent. If you are using water-based paint, thin with water. Thin paint so it just holds on to the brush. In flat and low-luster paints, the consistency should be similar to light cream. In gloss paints, the consistency should be like ketchup. Undercoats should be applied more thickly, but sparingly. Finishing coats should be thinned more to achieve a fine, smooth surface.

Most large paint companies have a selection of thousands of different colors. These custom colors are derivatives of the basic colors and can be duplicated by the salesperson at the paint store by following the company's proportion formula. I suggest you use the color selection that the paint store offers. If the exact color isn't available, try another store. There are enough companies and colors available on the market that you can find the right color. It's extremely difficult to mix your own custom paint color, let alone duplicate it if you need more or need to retouch a spot next year.

Use a roller for large wall areas. Choose a good quality roller in a manmade fiber that is the right width and pile to suit the job. You might want to get an extension handle for high walls or ceilings. Use a sloping paint tray and never fill it more than one-third full or the roller will get overloaded. Rollers are great for flat paint, but I don't recommend them for applying gloss paints. Roller-painted gloss paints tend to peel off in sheets.

Use the best brushes available for woodwork such as doors, windows, baseboards, and molding. Have a supply of different sizes so you'll be able to do the fine and detailed areas. Make sure you clean brushes and rollers thoroughly. If you've used oil-based paint, first rinse in solvent, then in soap and lukewarm water. Hang to dry. For short breaks, rollers and brushes can be kept from drying out by placing them in plastic bags.

Spray painting is becoming increasingly popular because of its speed. Commercial painters are using compressors and large spray guns to paint apartment buildings and tract houses. Every detail must be masked before spraying, which is time consuming, but the actual spraying time makes up for that time. The positive aspect is that the paint dries quickly and cuts down on drying time between coats. This is a method best left to professional painters who are doing work on large, commercial projects. I suggest you stick with the more conventional and custom methods.

Meticulous preparation is essential for a "primo" paint job, whether you're using a professional painter or doing the work yourself. Make sure you examine every inch of the walls and woodwork for imperfections that can be corrected before painting. Fill in any cracks or holes with spackle, and sand down any bumps or imperfections. Woodwork must be sanded thoroughly and coated with a primer before painting. The salesperson at the paint store will tell you the right product to use for each application. If your preparation work isn't thorough, the paint will peel, chip, and crack. Imperfections will be magnified. Use masking tape on window panes and areas where the paint might bleed to an another surface. Remove all cover plates from electrical outlets, switches, and telephone jacks, replacing them only after the paint is completely dried.

Paint the ceiling first. For a neater job, first paint a twelve inch strip around the sides next to the walls using a brush. Then, using a roller with a long handle, start in a corner and roll away from you into the painted strip. Always paint walls from ceiling to baseboard, working your way to the left. Always paint from dry area to wet area. Be sure to use masking tape to mask off the ceiling, baseboards, and all woodwork. Paint baseboards and woodwork last.

Choosing Your Colors

Now it's time to select your colors. Once you've selected your fabrics, wallpapers, flooring, and furniture, you'll have samples of each from which to match your paint. Always select paint color in the same room that the paint color is going to be used. (You'll find out how lighting affects color in Chapter

10: Effective Lighting.) Have at least three different paint company's complete color fans from which to choose your colors. You should also have, not only the original samples of the fabrics, wallpapers, and flooring that you selected, but the cuttings from the current stock you selected. Remember, dye lots vary, and the "cutting for approval" that was sent to you is the color that you will be matching to the paint.

Now, go through your house, room by room, cutting by cutting of wallpaper, fabric, and flooring, and select the right colors. There might be two, three, or even more colors that might work and four or five different shades of that same color. Which color and shade will be perfect?

First, take the time to examine each color as you hold it up to the wall, to the floor, to the ceiling, to the bright sunlight at the window, to the far dark corner. When you've narrowed down your choices to one or two, take a few days and don't even look at them. When you go back to the color and the room, you'll have a newer and fresher outlook. By Wednesday you might think the color you selected Monday afternoon is horrendous. If you do, start all over again.

If you're convinced you've found the perfect color, buy only the smallest possible container of it. Paint, or have your painter paint, a small sample about three feet by three feet on the wall. Let it dry thoroughly, *then* make your decision. Chances are the color will look completely different than you expected; it will be a little light or a little dark. Keep on repeating this process until you achieve the exact color you want. It's tedious and time consuming, your painter will threaten to walk off the job, but it's the only way I know to avoid costly and irritating mistakes. Trust me, paint is very tricky.

Special Painting Techniques

Paint may not only enliven a room, it can add texture and depth. Let's go on a tour together of the many different finishes and effects you can achieve with paint, ones that might even make you want to forget wallpaper altogether.

BROKEN COLOR

Broken color is the use of one or more colors in relief over a background. Color-textured finishes can hide a multitude of flaws, particularly on older walls and woodwork. Each technique has a different character, adding a unique visual texture and depth. The two basic methods of broken color relate either to adding paint or to subtracting paint.

Use any of the types of paints I've described to achieve these effects. I suggest you use a paint that doesn't dry quickly so you'll have time to complete your work. For grounds, use a water-based glaze or wash over latex and an oil-based glaze over flat oil paint, undercoat, or eggshell. The ground coat must be clean and grease free if the decorative top coat is to spread evenly. For oil-based surfaces, I use a low-luster surface over a suitable undercoat, plus a primer or a sealer on new plaster. Two, three, even four thin coats will always look better than one thick coat. Remember, the ground must be completely dry before you can begin glazing.

Thin the top coat from one-third to one-half the quantity of paint that you would normally need for the room. The thinner the paint or glaze, the lighter and more translucent the effect, but don't thin it so much that it becomes runny. Thin latex paint with water; thin oil-based paint and glaze with solvent.

Tinting is achieved by adding a tiny amount of color to a large can of white paint. Start with a dab of color, mix, then keep on adding until the right shade is achieved. Use mat, semi-gloss, or gloss polyurethane varnish to bring out the color and protect the surface. Thin out semi-gloss or gloss varnish with solvent in about one-third the quantity to avoid streaks and ridges and to make it easier to brush on.

SHADING

Shading is the blending of one color into another on a wall or ceiling. It can be in various tones of the same color or harmonizing tones of different colors. Shading in more than one color generally works best with lighter, pastel colors. Designers use this technique to lift or lower the appearance of a ceiling. Work in narrow bands of color, starting with the lightest and adding a little more of the dark tone to it as you move from band to band. Carefully blend each band of color together with a brush.

COLOR WASHING

Color washing gives a wall a mat finish while achieving a certain luminous, translucent quality. Use a thick wash of salmon pink over cream to give an entire wall a peachy bloom. Or use an almost translucent buff over a white wall to create authentic aging and deliberate damp spots. Use well-thinned flat oil paint or latex paint thinned with water. For a distressed look, leave some areas of ground showing through the first coat, let it dry thoroughly, then apply the second coat so that it covers any previously unpainted parts. This process will enrich the color in the already painted areas. For a more textured look, try criss-crossing brush marks. This look is great in a mat finish, but if you want a little sheen, use a clean, mat polyurethane finish.

STIPPLING

Stippling creates a kind of mottled, orange peel texture. They do make a stippling brush, but you can use a painter's dusting brush, a shoe brush, a soft-bristled hairbrush, or even a broom head. You can even stipple with crunched up rags or with various types of sponges. Usually, stippling is a transparent or semi-transparent glaze over a white or light-colored ground. You can use dark colors over light colors, light colors over dark colors, mat over shiny finishes, or shiny over mat finishes. Use as many colors as you want; the result will be a cloud-like effect. You can stipple both walls and woodwork, but I suggest you choose one or the other to create a pleasing contrast.

SPONGING

Sponging is the easiest of all the broken color methods because it involves putting paint on the ground rather than taking it off. It works best in two colors, with the lighter color on the top. The effect achieved will be contingent upon the colors you select, whether the glaze is opaque, translucent, shiny, or mat, and the type of sponge used. Whatever you use, you'll come up with a rich, mottled surface. Oil-based paint gives a crisper, cleaner texture. A tinted oil glaze will give a translucent, marbled finish. Experiment with bunched-up textured fabrics such as burlap or muslin for different effects. When you sponge new color onto a wet ground, an even softer print will be produced.

RAG ROLLING

Rag rolling can produce a surface that looks like crushed velvet or silk. It's achieved by rolling a bunch of rags that have been crunched up and rolled like a sausage over a wet glaze. The pattern this creates varies with the texture of the fabric you use. This technique generally works with light neutrals or pastels over white. First apply the wet paint, then stipple, then rag roll in different directions, re-bunching the rag so you don't produce too regular a pattern. You can even sponge over the rag rolling to soften the texture, preferably using a lighter color.

SPATTERING

Spattering is the freckling of paint on walls and woodwork to create a texture that's almost three dimensional. A mist effect is created when you choose tones of the same color or same value. A bright, gay, and fresh effect is achieved when you spatter with primary colors or pastels flicked on white. Experiment with different grounds and different spattering colors. Use any type of paint: shiny, low-luster, or mat. Dip the bristles of the brush into paint thinned to a milky consistency, then slide your finger, a knife, or a comb steadily across the bristles to produce a fine spray. If you use more than one color, let each color dry before you apply the next. Protect the final result with varnish, especially if you use water-based paints. Be careful, this can be a very messy process.

DRAGGING AND COMBING

Dragging and combing produce a texture similar to the grain of wood, but more stylized. Drag a wet glaze with a dry brush, revealing some of the "ground" color and get a surface that looks like woven cotton. Add a second glaze color and drag it either vertically or horizontally to produce a texture like raw silk. Drag in vertical and horizontal bands to achieve a plaid effect.

Combing is exactly what it sounds like. Using any type of comb, experiment to produce a much coarser line than dragging. You can comb a shiny glaze in different directions all over a low-luster finish to produce a silk-like surface that light bounces off of in all directions. Use dragging and combing only on walls that are in very good condition, as these techniques magnify irregularities. Use these methods on woodwork, but be sure to follow the grain of the wood, otherwise it will look awkward.

All of the above techniques are easy ones that you can try yourself if you don't mind getting a little messy. There are some more intricate painting techniques that can dramatically transform the surfaces of your home. If you're daring, experiment with these techniques. If you're all thumbs, hire a professional.

GRAINING

Graining is actually "faking" wood surfaces and can be used on almost any surface. For a more realistic look, using tone on tone is preferable. For the more daring, use pale to mid-tone pastels or neutrals over a different colored lighter gray, or beige on off-white. Create exciting effects by using combinations such as black on terra cotta or black on emerald green. Always keep the ground color several tones lighter than the graining color. This is an art best avoided by the novice, as special tools are needed to create the texture, pore marks, mottling, knots, and concentric ovals. Graining, also called "faux boising" is very hot right now.

MARBLING

Marbling can make walls, woodwork, doors, molding, and fireplaces look almost like real marble. I suggest you have this technique done by a painter who is experienced in marbling. The easiest type of marble to simulate is Sicilian marble. It's white with tinges of light greenish gray and yellow with distinctive veins of black and warm gray. Serpentine marble has a black ground mottled with a slightly dusty emerald and streaked with a random criss-crossing or straight, thread-like veins. Multicolored marbles contain some or all the colors of the rainbow. Experiment with your own unique marble finishes to match the interior of your home; the possibilities are endless.

TORTOISE SHELL

Tortoise shell ranges from golden brown, to the tawny tones, to an almost fiery red, through deep browns with near-black markings. The markings are characteristically diagonal. Painted tortoise shell looks great on flat or rounded surfaces, but awkward on carved or paneled surfaces. The look is opulent and shouldn't be used on large areas because it is too overpowering. Use it on the walls of a powder room or a small hall, or on smaller areas of a larger room, such as the doors and moldings. The scale of the patterning should be dictated by the size of the area you are covering. The ground should be a base coat of low-luster oil-based paint in yellow or yellow ocher. The tortoise shell coat is tinted varnish in a dark oak, left undiluted for plaster but thinned for woodwork. This coat is applied in zig-zagging diagonal bands that radiate slightly. The excess paint is blotted with a bunched up rag to purposely blur the markings. A dry brush is gently stroked across the whole surface diagonally to soften the effect. A coat of semi-gloss or gloss polyurethane is added, dried, and the surface polished with warm linseed oil.

PORPHYRY

Porphyry is a rock with a granite-like texture that comes from the minerals embedded in its fine-grained mass. It's a general term describing a whole family of rock types which are found in many different colors. Typical combinations are: brown, veined with near transparent white, and flecked with pink, red, and green; dark green flecked with gold and black; violet, flecked with gold, black, and iron gray; reddish brown flecked with light brown and black; and dark purple flecked with pale pink. The granite-like texture is made by spattering a sequence of watery colors over a plain or sponged ground. The ground should be two coats of a beige-gray flat oil paint. When dry, the ground is spattered with lightened and darkened shades of the same beige-gray. Add three more colors to spatter individually, waiting for each to dry in between. Finish off with two coats of clear varnish, either matt, satin, or gloss, depending on the sheen desired.

ANTIQUING

Antiquing is a technique that gives a surface the look of having been around for a while. It makes a surface age-darkened or sun-faded, a subdued sheen that comes with years of polishing, recesses and crevices that appear darker and dustier without being dirty, and gives angles and curves a worn look that comes with handling and rubbing. Most of the antiquing processes rely on the techniques we've already discussed. The general rule for antiquing is that the top colors should be duller and darker than the ground.

Antiqued walls can tend to look dark and dingy. Instead, use methods of color washing or glazing. Antiquing is more suited to woodwork. Aim to make the color look like it has been naturally faded by sunlight or worn away in the center panels and on the high points of moldings. Use spattering to achieve subtle shading, such as the light and dark specks that often freckle old woodwork. Antique surfaces should be subtle. Use several thinner coats of clear, satin, or mat finish polyurethane varnish, tinting it if you want an even mellower tone. You'll find many excellent antique finishing kits available on the market.

The Finishing Touches

There are many ways to add finishing touches to plaster and woodwork. These are the little details that can pull a whole room together and confirm that it is finished.

LINING

Lining is a series of lines painted on an area of wall to divide it into panels, making the wall seem taller or shorter, wider or narrower, or to define areas of color, marbling, or tortoise shell. Use lining to emphasize the straight and curved relief on wood or plaster molding. The color of the lining shouldn't shout at you, but rather blend with the colors of the wall or woodwork.

FAKE PANELING

Fake paneling can be added on doors and moldings to create interest and contrast. Add dark and light shadings on different parts of the moldings. Moldings should blend subtly with the tones of the wall color and not appear to be a separate element of the room. If the moldings have carving, you might want to use a method called "picking out." The molding is painted a lighter color and the background is filled in with a darker color. Another method is to paint the molding first with an oil-based paint; when dry, paint or oil glaze a slightly deeper tone. The glaze is then stippled down to even it out before wiping it with a rag moistened with solvent, removing the glaze from raised areas, thus leaving it nestling in the crevices.

STENCILING

Stenciling is an excellent way of introducing small or large areas of individual design to just about any interior surface. Panels and borders are relatively quick and easy to apply. Liven up a plaster or wood surface or break up large expanses of wall into smaller panels. Pattern a plain wood floor with a stenciled border or even create a rug-like effect with an overall simple pattern repeat. Bolder and stronger contrasts look better when done in plain, simple shades. More complex designs need delicate coloring and subtle contrasts. Keep it simple. Either buy ready-made stencils, widely available in both traditional and modern designs, or make your own stencils from one of the pattern books that are available. Why not repeat a pattern you've used in a fabric or wall covering for your stenciling?

STAINS

Most paint companies offer only a limited selection of standard stains, but with a little research you'll find stains can be found in a variety of colors and types. Blend together different colors to make your own custom colors or make your own stains by mixing textile dyes. Some paint stores will even make custom stains to order.

Water stains are inexpensive and fade less than other types, but tend to raise the grain of wood and dry in streaks because of uneven absorption. It's best to use water stains on light, close-grained woods rather than on porous, open-grained woods.

Spirit stains will only raise the grain of the wood slightly. They penetrate the wood and dry quickly, making it difficult to avoid patchiness. They must be applied rapidly and care must be taken not to go over the same area twice in order to avoid darker streaks.

Oil stains are the easiest to apply because they dry more slowly and give a more even color. They are particularly suitable for wood floors, but sometimes it takes as long as two days for oil stains to dry.

Always apply stains to clean, untreated wood. The wood surface should be scrubbed, sanded, and rubbed with a solvent to cut any remaining grease. Always sand in the same direction as the grain.

Achieve different colors, depths, and patterns on a single surface with decorative staining. Outline areas with fine, dark lines of oil-based paint to keep different stain colors separated. Or leave the whole area its natural color or stain it a very light color, varnishing only the areas you want to keep in that color. Then stain with a deeper shade and varnish the part you want to keep in that shade. Continue this sequence up to the darkest stain. If you want the varnished areas to look embossed, leave the varnish. If you want a flatter finish, remove the varnish with a solvent before applying a coat of polyurethane varnish.

Bleaching wood is popular right now. Either bleach wood to get it to its natural color, then stain it in a lighter color than it would be naturally, or give it a faded look. I suggest you have this done professionally, but you can do it yourself with alkaline plus peroxide bleach available from most building supply stores. Be prepared for hours of sanding and reapplying in order to achieve the look you want.

GLAZING

Glazing is the application of any transparent or semi-transparent color over another to enrich, intensify, or subdue it. In interior design, the term "glaze" is used to describe an oil-based transparent color. Glaze differs from varnish in that it is purely decorative, while varnish is used for protection and shine.

Oil-based glazes can be glossy, satin, or flat. They are slicker and more transparent than water-based glazes. Designers use them to create a feeling of softness, richness, and depth on surfaces. Glazes that are darker than the ground will add warmth. Glazes that are a slightly lighter tone of a bright color will add brilliance. A glaze in a dark, cool color over a warm ground will add richness and depth. Glazes in a much lighter color than a dark ground will give it a cooler tone. Ready-made glazes can be bought in a variety of colors, or buy a clear glaze and tint it yourself with artists' oil colors. Glazes will usually dry overnight, but take up to three days to harden completely.

Paint glazes contain opaque pigment and thus give a softer effect and are particularly good for distressing. They dry to a slight sheen and give a flatter finish than transparent oil glazes. For a really flat glaze, use flat oil paint or undercoat well thinned with solvent.

Varnish glazes are tinted varnishes used to give woodwork both a decorative and protective finish.

VARNISHES

Varnishes are meant to enhance and protect a surface. There are almost as many varieties of varnishes as there are types of paint.

Polyurethane varnishes are the easiest, most economical, and most versatile. They give maximum protection and durability and come in clear, wood tone, and colored finishes. Tint varnish yourself by dissolving artists' oil color in solvent and adding varnish to it a little at a time, stirring well.

Polyurethane varnishes come in three finishes: mat, satin, and gloss. A gloss finish will show up every imperfection and speck of dust on a surface. Several thin coats make a smoother, more even surface than one thick coat. Varnishes are usually dry to the touch within a few hours and can be recoated in five to six hours. Varnishing works best in a clean, warm, and dry environment. They do not adhere well to greasy surfaces. Varnishes can show brush strokes, so use care and good technique when applying them.

SHELLACS

Shellacs are varnishes made from an insect-derived resin dissolved in methylated spirits. They must be used in warm, dry conditions. Shellacs are best known for their use in French polishing and are very tricky to work with.

LACQUERS

Lacquers originated with the fine Oriental lacquer work that was made with the sap of the lap tree by skilled craftsmen who prepared and rubbed down surfaces several dozen times. Nowadays, similar surfaces that almost look as good as the Oriental originals can be created with paint and shellac. The finishes are smooth as satin, hard as glass, and brilliant; they create the illusion that you are looking into or through them rather than at them. Because lacquers have an extremely high sheen surface, they do tend to chip and show any damage easily. The quality and durability of lacquer finishes will differ greatly with the integrity and patience of the craftsmen who create them.

Walls can be made to look just like lacquer by applying many coats of tinted glaze, then finishing with clear or tinted varnish. The most nondescript piece of wood can be completely transformed by applying a lacquer finish.

Your Painting Questions Answered

Now that you know what types of paints are available and what techniques you have to choose from, I'm sure you have a million questions. Where to use what? Where should one color end and another begin? The following is a list of the most frequently asked questions and, of course, the answers.

Should we paint the ceiling the same color as the walls, a lighter color, or a darker color?

If you paint your ceiling white or a lighter color than the walls, your room will look higher. If you paint the ceiling a darker color, the ceiling will look lower.

Hint: When you paint your ceiling white, add a dash of the wall color to the white paint to develop a rapport between the two surfaces.

What color should we paint the cornice?

If the cornice is in an old house with high ceilings and fine woodwork, paint the cornice the same color as the ceiling.

We're decorating our basement to be a game room, but the ceiling has pipes and flues exposed. What color can we paint them?

If you paint them black, they'll seem to disappear. However, it's becoming increasingly popular to "up play" ceilings in high tech decors by painting pipes in brightly colored enamels to match or contrast the room. The once unsightly pipes become an interesting and decorative architectural asset. It's your decision and depends on the effect you want to achieve.

What color should we paint the woodwork?

Woodwork should be painted to match the walls if it is plain and uninteresting. If the woodwork is special and you want to accent its beauty, it's perfectly acceptable to paint it a contrasting color.

What color do we paint the doors?

Generally, I like to make dull, uninteresting doors disappear by painting them the same color as the walls. But if the doors are more interesting and finely made, it's okay to paint them a contrasting color if you continue the same technique throughout the entire house.

If adjoining rooms have two different wall colors, what color do we paint the door between the two rooms?

Each face of the door should match the color of the corresponding room. The edges of the door should be painted to match the walls of the room the door swings into. The door jamb should be painted to match the edge of the door which rests against it when it's closed.

Should we paint our paneled doors one color or accentuate the panels with a contrasting color?

It's not popular these days to paint frames and panels in contrasting colors. Paint the door one color . . . please.

What color should we paint our window frames?

Window frames may match or contrast the walls, depending on the degree of accent you want to give them. You can also paint them black or white. I often like to paint window frames, as well as doors, a darker shade of the wall color. For example, if I'm painting the walls a light steel gray, I'll paint the window frames either white for extreme contrast or a darker steel gray for less contrast and a newer look.

What color should we paint the inside of closets?

Closets should be painted as though they were part of the room.

Should we paint the fireplace?

Sometimes, yes. Sometimes, no. If the fireplace is an ugly brick, you can paint it black or white. If the fireplace is made of wood, you can paint it a solid color or consider many of the other techniques we've discussed in this chapter. The mantle can either match or contrast with the woodwork. We'll discuss creating more exciting fireplaces in Chapter 18: Remembering the Details.

Should we paint the wood floors?

Only as an inexpensive alternative to either a fine refinishing job or in a small area that gets very little foot traffic. Painted wood floors chip easily and don't look fresh for very long. We'll talk more about painting wood floors in Chapter 14: Choosing Your Flooring.

What type of paint should we use for interior walls and ceilings?

Unless one of the special effects is desired, use a flat latex paint. They're easy to apply and dry quickly.

What type of paint should we use for woodwork, kitchens, and bathrooms?

Use a semi-gloss alkyd-based enamel on woodwork and in kitchens and bathrooms because this enamel is resistant to water damage.

The above is my general advice, but don't take it too literally. Be creative. Using the ideas and techniques described in this chapter, the type of paint you select and the method you choose to apply it can make the difference between average-looking surfaces and interesting, exciting surfaces.

If you're using a professional painter, make sure he understands the look you want to achieve and that you approve samples of colors and tech-

niques before painting an entire room or house. Your painter should be qualified to select the right types of paints and buying the right quantities for each area.

If you're painting your home yourself, develop a good rapport with the salespeople at the paint store. They'll work with you to select the right types of paint you'll need. They'll figure out how much paint you'll need if you can give them an accurate accounting of the square footage you want to cover. For a ceiling area, multiply the length of the room by the width. For walls, multiply around the room by the height from floor to ceiling without subtracting for windows and doors. For woodwork, window frames, chair rails, and baseboards, allow one pint of paint for every one hundred running (linear) feet.

Hints:

Paint the metal frames of your sliding glass doors a mat color to match the walls.

Use faux boising to update your old molding, or use it to make your old plaster beams look like wood.

Old brown doors are out; paint them to match your moldings.

Give your old outside deck a facelift; paint each plank separately, perhaps in stripes of robin's egg blue and white.

10
Effective Lighting

Without light there can be no vision. How any object appears to us is greatly affected by how light strikes it. When light hits an object, it is either reflected, absorbed, or allowed to pass through. Light can be either natural or artificial. The type and source of lighting you select greatly affects how your colors will appear.

Professional interior designers see lighting as a "problem." The first question they ask is, "What is to be illuminated?" The second question is, "How can it be illuminated?" The third, "Which fixture is capable of doing it?"

Light Sources

The amount of illumination needed for everyday activities is measured in footcandles. A footcandle is the standard measure of the amount of light falling on a surface. You'll need about twenty footcandles of light for casual activities, everyday living, and moving about space. You'll need about fifty footcandles of light for activities such as grooming, reading, and preparing food. You might need up to two hundred footcandles of light for close work, such as sewing.

The number of watts necessary to obtain the number of footcandles you will need varies because of space, equipment, and reflection. Light meters such as the ones used for photography are widely available and will measure the illumination accurately. For small spaces less than 150 square feet, use about two hundred incandescent watts or one hundred fluorescent watts. For average spaces up to 250 square feet, use about three hundred incandescent watts or 150 fluorescent watts. For larger spaces that are more than 250 square feet, use one incandescent watt or ½ fluorescent watt per square foot of space.

If a room contains one activity at a fixed location, light that activity first, then light the rest of the room as needed. Areas used for relaxation should be lit softly, while areas used for vigorous activity should be lit brightly. Outdoor living spaces should be lit for safety and security.

Electric light sources can be divided into several categories: incandescent, the kind we find in normal table lamps; and fluorescent, like the tubes in office ceiling fixtures. There are also high intensity lights which include mercury, the bluish street lights; metal halide, the cool-looking industrial lights; and high pressure sodium, the highway lights which appear yellow.

Incandescent light is a warm color, somewhat yellowish. It's the most flattering to all skin tones. The advantages of incandescent light are that the bulbs and fixtures are relatively inexpensive, there's no flicker or hum, and textures and forms are emphasized because the light comes from a relatively small source.

Fluorescent light is cool and somewhat bluish.

A glass tube with an inside coating of fluorescent powder is filled with vaporized mercury and argon, then the ends are sealed with two cathodes. When electrical currents activate the gases, invisible ultraviolet rays cause the fluorescent coating to produce visible light. There are many different types of fluorescent bulbs available now that can create a warmer color that's more compatible with incandescent light. The advantages of fluorescent lighting are that the tubes last about ten times longer than incandescent bulbs; they produce about three or four times more light for the amount of current used; there is almost no heat produced; and the light source is considerably larger, which spreads the light more and produces less glare. Tubes are available in a number of white colors, from the blue cast of daylight to the pink of natural white. In your home, use only fluorescent sources that produce a warm color light.

Metal halide is usually icy blue, but color corrected versions are warmer. It costs less to operate than other sources and is acceptable for home usage in lower wattages.

Neon, or cold cathode, has a color that is dependent upon the gas and color of its glass tube. It comes in a vast array of colors. Although it's not sufficient for detailed visual tasks, it makes wonderful accent lighting for your home.

GENERAL LIGHTING

General lighting lights an entire room, allowing you to see into every corner. It brings attention to the design and color of the whole space. It can be direct lighting, in which light shines fully on objects to be lit, such as lights concealed in coves that illuminate the ceiling, wall washers, or an entire section of the ceiling can throw light through translucent plastic or glass. Indirect lighting is when light is thrown against a ceiling or wall surface from which some of it is reflected. You'll soon learn how to combine both direct and indirect lighting correctly.

LOCAL LIGHTING

Local lighting can create moods, emphasize important objects, and create variety and rhythm. It provides the right amount of illumination necessary for specific places and activities such as reading, cooking, and sewing. We usually think of local lighting as movable floor or table lamps, but the term can include fixtures attached to the walls, ceiling, or placed in major pieces of furniture. In kitchens and bathrooms, local lighting is usually synonymous with general lighting.

The brightness of the lighting you use has an important effect on what emotions it evokes. Bright light is very stimulating and will make you feel more energetic, but it can be dull and boring as well as expensive in money and energy. Lower levels of brightness seem to make people feel more relaxed and restful, even romantic. Some low levels of brightness might make you feel depressed or frightened. Moderately bright light tends to generate an overall feeling of well being. Appropriately distributed light will contribute to good balance, rhythm, and emphasis.

Glare is irritating. It is usually produced by exposed sources of bright light, too much light from one direction, or incorrectly placed lighting fixtures. Glare almost always creates eye fatigue and a feeling of gloom. Blandness of light, especially when equal throughout a room, can also be fatiguing and depressing.

The location and direction in which light fixtures are placed are extremely important to the overall lighting effect. Lighting placed high in a room can either be revealing and "too efficient" or can be serene and create architectural interest. Light below eye level will make you feel friendly and gravitate into a group. It's also very practical for watching television. Lighting coming from the floor or near the floor can be very flattering to people and creates a wonderful complement to conventional lighting. Lighting from a number of sources around the room spreads interest through the area. It's undemanding and makes a room seem luminous rather than merely lit. Strongly directed lighting, such as from spotlights, can be dramatic as long as it's not too harsh. Lighting to work by should illuminate the entire task space and not form shadows or shine in the workers' eyes.

Wide sources of light, such as a skylight or an illuminated ceiling, give glareless light excellent for vision, but can be monotonous. Smaller light sources that diffuse light broadly through lenses or translucent shades have about the same effect.

The color of the light you choose affects the overall feel of the room. For example, white light shows color as it is and creates no emotional effect other than a general feeling of well being. Warm light is very flattering, brightens warm colors, but deadens blues and purples. Cool light makes rooms seem more spacious and separates objects from each other, but it can tend to make people look like they've just been embalmed. Ideally, careful planning will create a balanced combination of warm and cool lighting.

Lighting Guidelines

How many times have you walked or driven past a lighting store and noticed the many different types of lighting fixtures either hanging from the ceilings or attached to the walls? Selecting the right lighting fixture is one of the most difficult tasks in decorating your own home. However, now that you have a basic knowledge of the types of lighting available and what effects they achieve, the task becomes a little easier. Go back to your furniture plan and pencil in the correct lighting you'll need before setting foot into that confusing lighting store. Let's go room by room to assess what types of lighting you'll need.

ENTRANCE AREAS

The entrance areas to your home should be inviting and create a warm welcome. Diffused lighting from the ceiling or from wall sconces will create a soft, balanced effect. You might want to be more

daring and use neon, maybe even have it installed in a piece of furniture such as a console table. Or perhaps you want to greet guests with a display of your favorite sculptures sitting upon lit pedestals.

LIVING ROOMS AND FAMILY ROOMS

Living rooms and family rooms need a combination of both direct and indirect lighting. Good overall lighting is important for rooms where people will be reading, sewing, or playing games. This lighting should be put on a dimmer switch so when a different level of lighting is needed, it's available. After you've fulfilled the overall lighting needs of these rooms, add other accent lights, such as lamps, torcheres, and sconces.

A few years ago I designed a living room that was lit by placing faux stone columns in several strategic places. I had the lights installed in the columns so the illumination was directed at the ceiling, casting interesting and intriguing shadows throughout the room.

DINING SPACES

Dining spaces should be lit to emphasize the table and what surrounds it. The light should enhance the sparkle of the crystal, china, and silverware. Diffused light lessens glare and is more flattering to the diners' faces.

KITCHENS

Work centers should be extremely well lit with ceiling lighting. The rest of the kitchen area should have a fairly high level of illumination. Try using bands of lighting hidden underneath the bottoms of the cabinets to light the tops of counters.

BATHROOMS

Bathrooms need good overall general lighting from a ceiling fixture. Strip lighting placed along the sides or top of mirrors seems to work the best

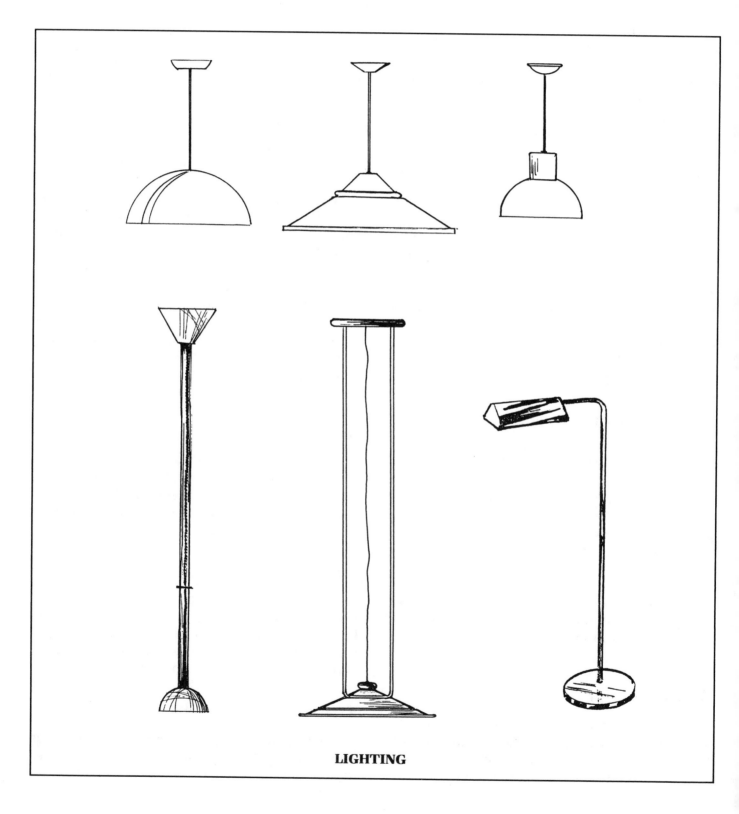

LIGHTING

to provide shadowless illumination to the face. Remember, any lighting you put in the bathroom should be carefully placed so it doesn't glare back at you in the mirrors. Fluorescent lighting gives wonderful overall lighting for a bathroom, but it's not the most flattering type of light to your face.

BEDROOMS

Bedrooms need some general overall lighting. I've found most builders have omitted any type of ceiling fixtures in new homes. I always suggest my clients install track lighting on a dimmer switch. The room can be lit to full brightness or dimmed to any level of light for more intimate evenings. Direct the track lighting away from the bed so it doesn't glare in your eyes. Shine it on artwork, plants, and use it for overall wall washing. Provide reading light with nightstand lamps, use a wall-hung fixture behind the bed or a floor lamp extending from behind or from the side of the bed.

HALLS

Halls need some overall lighting, but are more inviting when you use glare-free ceiling or wall fixtures. Lighting placed near the floor is an effective and interesting way to augment overall lighting. Decorative fixtures also have their place when chosen appropriately.

STAIRWAYS

Stairways should have light that clearly shows the treads from the risers. Use ceiling or wall fixtures that direct the light downward. Be careful of spotty or distracting light that could be dangerous.

EXTERIOR LIGHTING

Exterior lighting should be bright enough to illuminate the entrance. You should be able to find the keyhole to the door easily, and visitors should easily see your address. Terraces, patios, and gardens should be lit for safety as well as for effect. An effectively lit exterior that can be seen from the interior becomes part of the general overall decorating scheme. Use spotlights and floodlights hidden in trees and shrubbery to create a low glow. Make sure all outdoor fixtures you choose are weatherproof.

Choosing the Right Fixture

Now that we've discussed the general lighting for each area of your home, let's get more specific. In this section, you'll discover what fixtures are available to you and where to use each type.

CHANDELIERS

I suggest chandeliers only be used centered over dining tables. In the sixties everyone loved to swag chandeliers in strange corners and off center over bathroom counters. This is out of style. Ornate chandeliers have their place in either traditional or eclectic decors. The new Italian high tech fixtures look wonderful in more modern or high tech rooms.

I remember my first tiny apartment years ago. A cheap white globe hung in the dining area, its bright light glaring annoyingly. Was it ugly! Unfortunately, the design of lighting fixtures hasn't greatly improved since then. As a matter of fact, most moderately priced chandeliers are production made and mediocre in style and quality.

However, there are some fabulous chandeliers to be found if you can afford them. Iron chandeliers with crusty, off-white finishes work well with a variety of decors, including California casual. Chandeliers made from stags' horns are hot and complement the Southwestern look. A high quality crystal chandelier works wonders in traditional and eclectic dining rooms, although I've seen many interior designers effectively mix crystal chandeliers in very modern rooms. The trick is selecting the right chandelier. One magnificent crystal chandelier reflecting into a smoked mirror can be breathtaking.

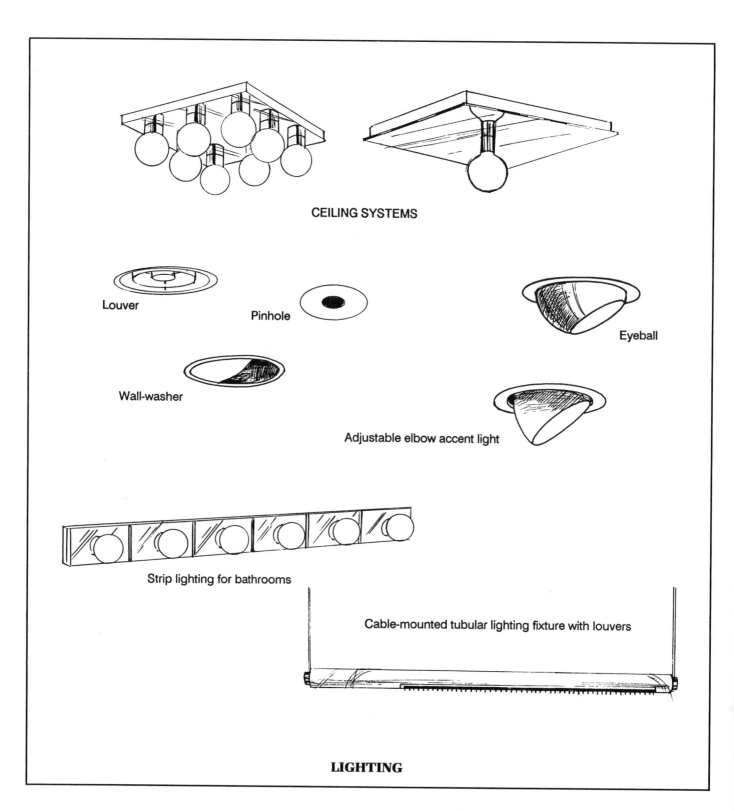

CEILING SYSTEMS

Louver

Pinhole

Eyeball

Wall-washer

Adjustable elbow accent light

Strip lighting for bathrooms

Cable-mounted tubular lighting fixture with louvers

LIGHTING

The size of your chandelier should relate to the size and scale of your room and table. Here are the rules of thumb for selecting the right size chandelier:

A chandelier should be in inches what the diagonal of the room is in feet. For example, if a room is sixteen feet on the diagonal, the lighting fixture should be sixteen inches in diameter.

A chandelier should be about twelve inches smaller than the diameter of the table; small enough so people avoid bumping their heads when they get up.

For rectangular tables, the diameter of the fixture should not exceed two-thirds the length of the table.

A chandelier should be hung two feet, six inches above the table.

Some chandeliers project light up, some project light down, others do both. The reflected light these fixtures throw can be dramatic, but often overpowering.

WALL FIXTURES

Wall fixtures can be used almost anywhere to create additional mood lighting. Choose your wall fixtures according to the size, scale, and style of the room, its furniture, and the amount of space you have to work with. All wall fixtures are most effective when hung at eye level. They can be either uplights, downlights, or a combination of both. For modern rooms, keep them simple.

Some of the best looking wall fixtures on the market are made of a plain white plaster and come in many shapes and sizes. The bulb is hidden inside the fixture and projects light either up or down, creating a fan-like effect. Sconces are more ornate and should be used in elegant settings, almost always in matched pairs. Crystal and iron sconces mix well in eclectic rooms.

PENDANTS

Pendants are similar to chandeliers, only they are simpler and don't have branches. Pendants must also relate to the size and scale of the space. They come in various sizes and shapes such as domes, drops, lanterns, shades, and globes. Use the same rules of thumb for hanging pendants as you would chandeliers.

Some of the new Italian halogen quartz pendants are just the touch a modern, streamlined interior needs. They're smaller in scale than chandeliers and create a halo of light over a table.

LIGHT BULBS

Light bulbs come in many shapes and sizes. Some of the most common names are standard household, teardrop, cone, bent candle, flame, globe, straight sides, tubular, and chimney. If you must use a fixture with exposed light bulbs, and professionally I suggest you don't, experiment with different types to see which are the most pleasing and effective. Choose a clear light bulb when the bulb can be seen and a coated bulb when it can't. Keep clear bulbs down to fifteen watts or less to avoid glare.

LAMPS

Lamps are limited by the length of their cords. They can only be used on or near furniture. Different lamps and shades produce different types of light, but the light they produce is not always the right type needed in the right place. If you do feel a lamp is needed, select it according to the type of light required as well as for its aesthetics.

Most lamps either confine light, as those with opaque shades, or spread light broadly, such as a table lamp with a white silk shade. The wider the opening of the shade, the wider the light will spread. A lamp with a shade above eye level should be placed behind or at the side corner of a seating area. Have all your lamp shades at the same height. If the lamp is to be used for reading, the closer the light bulb is to the bottom of the shade, the more light will reach the reading material.

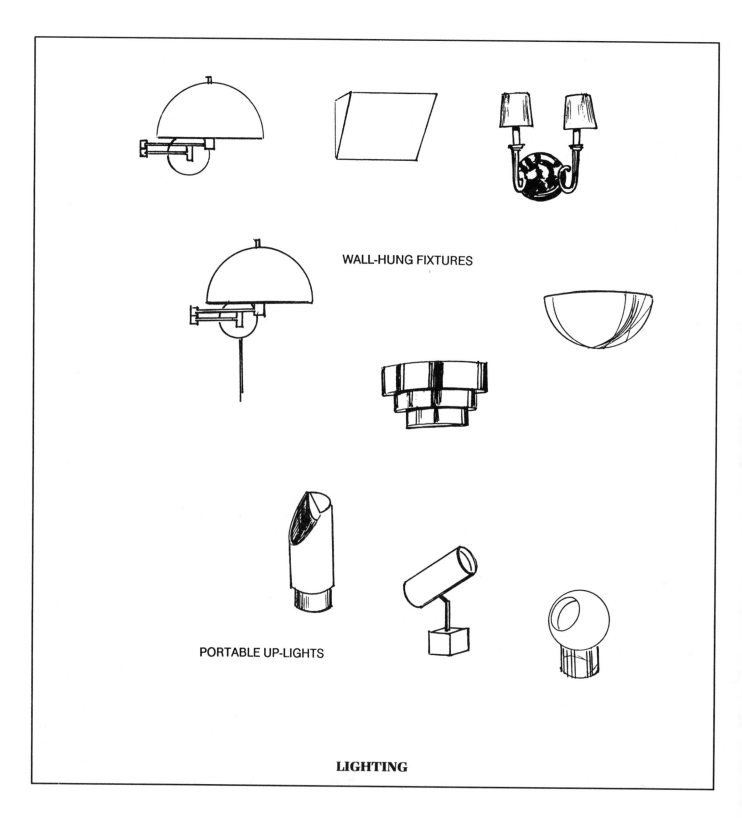

WALL-HUNG FIXTURES

PORTABLE UP-LIGHTS

LIGHTING

For general illumination in a room with deep colored walls or wood paneling, the shade should indicate no more than fifty footcandles on the meter. For general illumination with pale-colored walls, the shade should be no more than 150 footcandles. For illumination to perform specific visual activities, the shade should indicate between 250 and 400 footcandles.

Never have only one lamp on in a space unless that space is extremely small. Never read or perform activities with only one lamp on. Additional light reduces glare, contrast, and shadows. Never position a lamp so that a shadow falls on the activity. A lamp should be placed so that it casts its light directly on the surface of the activity.

WALL WASHERS

Wall washers wash a wall with light, revealing the details and colors of how that wall is covered. Light reflected on the walls works to complement other sources of lighting and tends to flatter people. To achieve wall washing, position the fixture one foot away from the wall and aim it so that it covers the wall thoroughly and evenly.

Wall grazing is similar and is used to reveal textured walls and wall coverings, brick, stone, and other rough surfaces. To graze a wall, position the fixture six to eight inches away from the wall. The light will create shadows under any surface change, bump, or depression.

Don't use wall washing or grazing on walls when:

- Walls are imperfect and have flaws, bumps, or nicks, or if you have any other reason not to call attention to that wall.
- When the interior space is narrow and the lighting along one side makes the room appear lopsided.
- If the wall is mirror or covered with any other shiny surface.
- When the ceiling is sloped along the special wall.

- When the wall opposite is a large and undraped wall that exposes windows or glass doors.
- When the wall is divided into small segments with windows and doors.

Do use wall washing and grazing when:
- The wall is finished differently from the other walls.
- When you want to spread a small amount of light a long way.
- When you want to make a small room appear larger.
- When the wall is uninterrupted or totally covered in draperies.
- When you want to shorten an interior space, such as the end of a long hallway.
- When you want to balance the other lighting in the room.

You can achieve wall washing or wall grazing with either recessed incandescent wall washers, built-in fluorescent cornice lights, or track lighting. If you are a renter and don't want to spend a lot of money installing lighting that's difficult to move, portable wall washers are available. They're usually canister shaped and should be placed on the floor. The negative is that you must turn each canister on and off individually.

DOWNLIGHTS

Downlights can define a space and make it sparkle. A room can be expanded by light, but several fixtures are needed to spread the light uniformly. Each downlight you install should produce the same amount of light and be spaced evenly. The manufacturer's catalog will give you the specifications for the spacing ratios. Downlights are used for emphasis, such as lighting up your favorite collection displayed on the coffee table.

There are many manufacturers of these types of fixtures. Their catalogs can be complicated and confusing, even to a professional interior designer. Work with the salesperson to determine your exact needs. There are various types of external features.

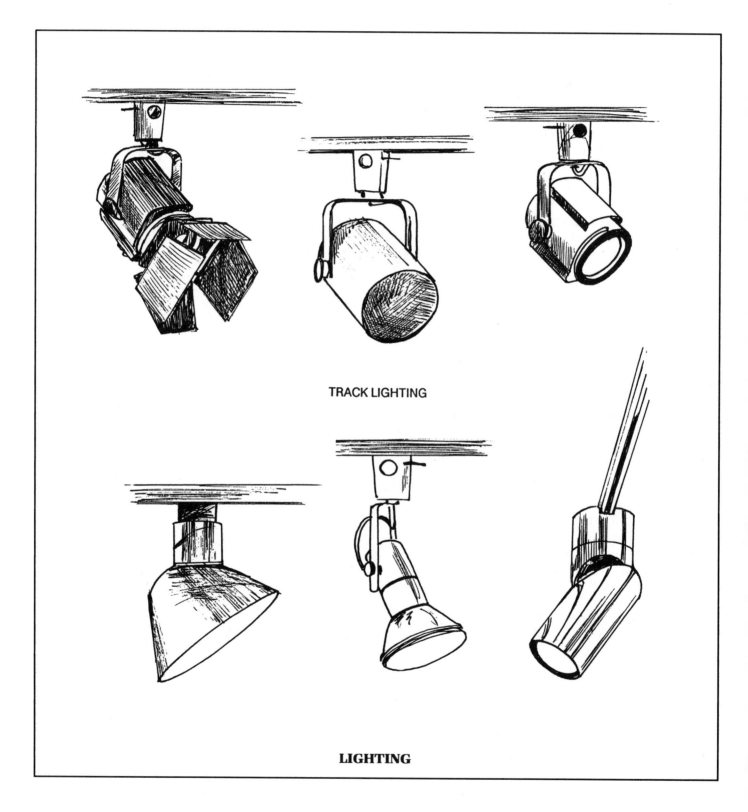

TRACK LIGHTING

LIGHTING

Lenses cover the opening of the fixture and bend the light in some way. Diffusers obscure the light bulb and scatter the light. Baffles are black grooves in the surface of the fixture's opening. Louvers are the metalwork over the opening. Both of the latter reduce brightness and direct the light. Never put downlights over a mirror or glass top table, as it will reflect the light from the downlight bulb.

TRACK LIGHTING

Track lighting is my favorite; I use it everywhere, it's so dramatic and versatile. The track itself is an electrified holder that comes in standard widths of two, four, eight, and twelve feet, but can be cut to any size on the job. The track fixtures come in many different styles, shapes, sizes, and finishes. Purchase both the track and the fixtures from the same manufacturer; parts are rarely interchangeable.

Low voltage fixtures need transformers to reduce the regular line voltage. The transformers are usually built into the fixture. You must use low voltage bulbs: either a parabolic reflector (PAR), a multi-faceted reflector, or a standard small reflector. Again, make sure you work hand in hand with the lighting salesperson to determine your needs, and use a licensed electrician to install the lighting.

The size of the lit area is determined by the beam width, the fixture's distance from the object it is shining on, the aiming angle, and the amount of other light in the room. Once you've installed your track lighting, play around with angles to achieve the right effect. I often use track lighting even over dining tables a lot because I feel that it creates a more modern look and can be positioned so it doesn't glare in the diners' eyes.

Special Problems

LIGHTING GLOOMY ROOMS

If you can't see the sky clearly from any window of your room or there isn't enough daylight to perform most tasks, you are the owner of a gloomy room.

First, try rearranging the furniture so that any light that does come in through the windows is shining on the surfaces that need illuminating. Second, if rearranging the furniture doesn't help all that much, consider adding more windows and/or enlarging the existing window openings. Third, if the room has access to the roof, seriously consider putting in a skylight. Skylights are usually made of clear or non-clear plastic or glass and are used to gather all the light possible. Some are domed, some are flat. Fourth, if you don't have access to the roof, consider installing glass doors to replace existing wood doors to the outside.

The least expensive solution is to repaint the room. Gloomy rooms need to be painted in colors that reflect as much light as possible. Pale colors with large amounts of white reflect as much as 85% of the light, while dark colors absorb light and only reflect about 10% of the light.

The wall opposite and furthest away from the window should be highly reflective. To increase light, use pale colors and mirrors or anything shiny to create reflected light. Keep the ceiling and floors as light in color as possible.

Sometimes a gloomy room is caused by exterior obstructions, such as a roof overhang or a dense tree. Alter, remove, or replace anything on the exterior that's obstructing the light coming into the room.

TOO MUCH SUNLIGHT

Too much sunlight can be annoying and produce unwanted heat as well as fade draperies, carpeting, and wall coverings. The amount of sunlight coming into a room is a result of how your house is oriented, the height of your house, the exterior obstructions, the angle of the sun, and the time the sun sets and rises.

The number of windows in a space and where they're located is important. West windows receive the sunlight in the afternoon in a decreasing angle until sunset. East windows receive direct light in the morning at a very low angle. South windows receive sunlight between 10:00 a.m. and 2:00 p.m. North windows never receive direct sunlight; any light coming in from a north window is reflected from somewhere else.

There are really only three methods of obscuring the sun: window treatments, architectural devices, and landscape materials. Window treatments should be adjustable — able to direct, scatter, and soften the light. The most commonly used window treatments are draperies, shades, shutters, and blinds. We'll discuss the pros and cons of each of these treatments in Chapter 15. You might want to consider architectural devices to obscure the sun such as awnings, balconies, fences, walls, courtyards, patterned glass, latticework, louvers, porch or deck roofs, recessed windows, bay windows, shutters, or trellises. Landscaping can also solve your problem. Trees, shrubs, vines, and hanging plants can block or scatter direct sunlight. The broader the landscape material the wider the area it shades.

Of course, you can always try rearranging the furniture. Work surfaces, table tops, and desks should not be next to windows that receive direct sunlight. Sofas and chairs shouldn't face bright, glaring windows. Eating areas should be adjusted so the seating doesn't face the strong lighting during eating hours. Repainting is another option. Use the opposite of the rules for a gloomy room to determine the right colors to use on the walls, floors, and ceiling.

Tricks of the Trade

• Place three uplight floor canisters behind your sofa. Use three different colored bulbs to create exotic "wall art" with light.

• Use commercial theatrical spotlights with "gels" (pieces of colored cellophane) covering the bulbs.

• Simply place inexpensive uplights behind your plants to enhance drama.

11
Choosing Your Fabrics

It's exhausting and confusing to shop the fabric showrooms, searching through the wings, lugging around bags full of samples. And yet, the fabric showroom is the first place you're compelled to head for when you dive into your decorating project. It starts out fun, looking at the colorful and interesting fabrics, finding patterns, colors, and weaves that you love; mixing and matching them together, trying to visualize how each will look upholstered on your sofas or draped on your windows. But after endless hours, calluses on your feet, a headache from the clang of the metal doors, and tendinitis of the wrist, you're more confused than ever. To add to your frustration, the one perfect fabric you found was marked "Wing Sample. Do Not Take."

You ask the blonde Adonis at the desk, "How can I see how this fabric is going to look in my home if I don't have a sample?" He answers, "I don't know," and ignores you in favor of a personal conversation on the phone. Determined, you cough and tap your fingers on the counter. He finally looks up, annoyed, and says, "Listen, lady, would you like me to mail you a sample?" "Yes," you shout in optimism as he hands you a card to fill in your name and address and begins listing the two hundred fabric samples that you are taking home. Feet aching, you carry the five shopping bags brimming with samples to your car parked three blocks away,

throw the samples in your trunk, and angrily pluck the parking ticket off your windshield.

Once home, you take the fabrics and throw them on the living room floor, dying to sort through and see what you've selected. Your husband's screaming, "I'm starving, when's dinner going to be ready?" Junior is hitting the baby over the head with the platen of his computer printer, which he's just dissected. You whip up a quick gourmet meal of macaroni and cheese for the clan, clean up with the speed of lightning, and dash back to the living floor to play with your fabric samples.

Delighted to be left alone and off your feet, you start emptying the bags, sorting through and arranging the samples into piles according to color. You begin noticing that a fabric you remember selecting in blue is there, but it's in red. Then you see that all the fabrics you really thought were great are nowhere to be found. Oh well, you continue with what you have and are puzzled that these fabrics don't look the same as they did in the showroom. Some of them are just plain ugly, others are the completely wrong color. So, methodically you begin the process of elimination, tossing the rejects back into the bag, knowing they'll have to be returned. In two or three hours, you've narrowed the selection down to two fabrics that "will do." You anxiously rush upstairs to find your husband, who's watching Monday Night Football, and flash the samples in his face. "Won't this look great on the living room sofa?" you ask, anxious for his approval. "You've got to be kidding, that's awful, darling," he snaps, brushing you away because you're blocking his view of a fifty-yard touchdown run. Tears well in your eyes, as you take the fabric sample and begin dusting the furniture with it, wondering if your feet can hold up for one more day of fabric shopping. There's got to be an easier way.

There is. But first, you should know more about fabrics and sources. Before you set out on your next fabric shopping expedition, read on to make sure it'll be productive and successful.

What is Fabric?

Fabric can also be called cloth, material, or textile. It can be machine made or handmade. The performance and appearance of a particular fabric depends on what basic material or blends of materials it's made from, the quality of those materials, the way it's been fabricated, and how it's been finished.

In order to understand fabric, you need a little knowledge of the fibers that were used to construct that fabric. A fiber is a threadlike object or filament that gives a fabric its substance and texture. Natural fibers come from reeds and grasses, flax and jute, the wool and hair of animals, the seeds of plants, and the filaments caterpillars spin for their cocoons. Often, textile mills add various synthetic fibers. Each fabric and fabric blend has its own unique qualities: strength; elasticity; and resistance to abrasion, stains, sun, moisture, mildew, and fire. Each feels and looks different. Some are more durable and versatile than others. New synthetic fibers are being developed, blended, and modified each day. Processing and finishing methods are constantly being improved.

A fabric can be a combination of two or more fibers spun together in one yarn. Each combination produces its own set of characteristics and each has its advantages and disadvantages. It's extremely difficult to keep up with the pros and cons of all the new blends appearing on the marketplace daily. I make it a practice to give each fabric I'm going to use for a project my own personal test. I suggest you do the same.

First, crumple the fabric in your hands tightly and hold it crunched up for a few minutes. If the fabric comes out looking like a wrinkled prune, toss it in the reject pile and find a more wrinkle-free alternative. If it passes the wrinkle test, next give it the "ketchup, red wine, and water" test. First, pour a little ketchup on the sample. If the ketchup is absorbed and doesn't wipe off with a little soap and water, throw it in the reject pile. Next, pour some red wine on it; grape juice will do, too. Again, if it absorbs and doesn't wipe off, kiss the fabric goodbye. Use water to see if the fabric is water resistant or repellent. The water should bead on the surface and not be absorbed into the fabric. Wait for it to dry to make sure it doesn't water spot. The next test is for frustrated pyromaniacs. Take a lit cigarette and place it on the fabric. If it singes and burns quickly, reject it. Next, use a cigarette lighter or match to light one of the ends of the fabric sample. (It's wise to do this test outside and near a large pail of water.) If it bursts into flames, shop for a more practical alternative. Last, take a plastic comb and a metal fork and run them over the fabric several times to see if the fabric will pierce or fray easily. You never know when someone will have a sharp object in their back pocket when they sit on your sofa. These are rough tests, I know, but they release a little pent-up anger and prevent any future problems. If the fabric passes these tests, you're in business, as long as you've made sure the fabric isn't out of stock or discontinued before you went to all this trouble.

How is Fabric Made?

Natural fibers are cleaned first, drawn out so they are even and parallel, then spun or twisted into yarn. Synthetic fibers are already clean, continuous, and parallel when they are extruded as filaments. They're simply twisted into yarn. Yarns can be used alone or in combination with other yarns.

They vary according to the type of fiber or fibers used in their tightness and twist, in their ply, or the number of strands in the yarn, thus affecting the size and appearance of the finished product. The type and length of the fiber used, along with the tightness of the twist, produce the basic type of yarn.

Cotton yarn will differ according to how the fibers were treated. For instance, "carded" yarns contain all but the shortest fibers, with the remaining ones somewhat straightened. "Combed" yarns are composed entirely of long fibers that are laid parallel before spinning. These yarns are stronger, smoother, and more expensive.

Silk of high quality is derived from long, unbroken filaments. Spun silk is made from the short fibers that can't be unreeled from the cocoons.

Wools are either woolen yarns that are soft, fuzzy, and loosely woven, spun from fibers that are only partially straightened; or worsted yarns that are tightly twisted from long, combed fibers and are usually strong and smooth.

Synthetics are derived from fibers that are continuous, parallel, and relatively smooth strands called filaments. These filaments are generally twisted into ply yarns. The fibers can be cut into short lengths and blown apart, then combined together as a mass. Then they can be twisted into soft yarns which are called "spun" rayon, nylon, etc.

The way the fibers are twisted affects the character of the yarn, and thus the resulting fabric. They can be twisted tightly or loosely, given a right-hand or left-hand twist, or individual strands can be combined to make two, three, four, or multiple ply yarns. Elastic yarns are made by covering elastic cores with fibers. There are also fabrics made by covering metallic wires with fibers. Fabrics can contain one size of yarn or combine several different sizes to create any desired effect.

Once the yarn has been created from the fiber, the fabric is constructed. There are several different methods of fabric construction, each producing its own unique end product.

Felting is the process of matting together fibers to form a web. Conventional felts are made of wool, hair, or fur fibers that have been matted by moisture, pressure, and heat. This process induces shrinkage and produces a dense cloth that is firm, slightly fuzzy, and has a low tensile strength. Needle or needle-punched felts are made by a machine pushing barbed needles through a mat of fibers to entangle them. No heat or pressure is used. The various types of fibers and needles used produce the different weights and strengths that are available.

With the process of bonding, another nonwoven fabric is made. Layers of fibers are bonded together by a binding agent that is set by wet or dry heat or by chemical action. Another process, called melding, involves the use of thermoplastic or heat-softening fibers that are either introduced into the fiber mix or used as a sheath on a fiber with a higher melting point. When subjected to heat, the fibers fuse together.

Films are made by processes that produce sheets instead of filaments. These films are thin plastic sheeting that are used for such items as shower curtains or wall coverings. For upholstery fabrics, they're fused onto a knit or woven backing. These films come in a variety of textures, ranging from a smooth, leather-like finish to a suede-like softness, to three dimensional patterns.

Knitting is produced by blunt rods or needles that are used to interlock a single, continuous yarn into a series of loops. The resulting patterns can be plain, rib, and purl stitches, as well as many variations. Machine knitting is five or six times faster than machine weaving and is becoming more and more popular. Knitted fabrics have a good stretch recovery, are wrinkle resistant, and can be form-fitted easily.

Weaving is the process of interlacing warp yarns, which run lengthwise on the loom and in the fabric, and filling yarns, which run crosswise on the loom and in the fabric to fill and hold together the warp.

A plain weave is simply one filling yarn carried over one warp yarn. Broadcloth is a plain weave

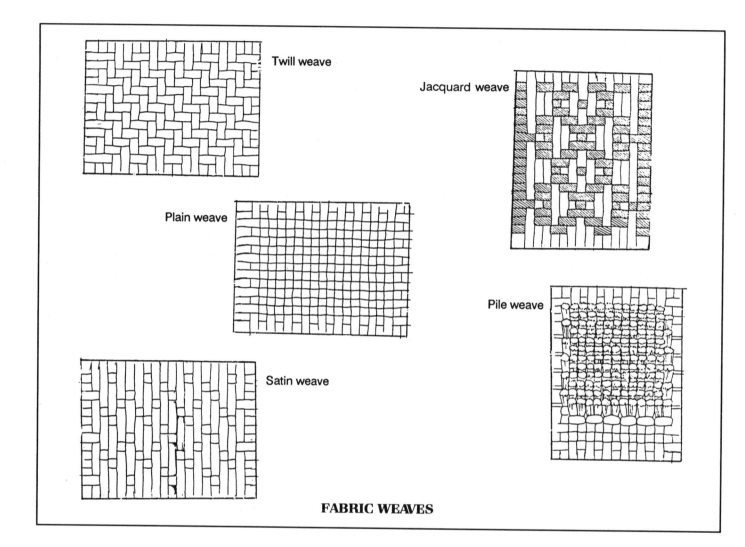

Twill weave

Jacquard weave

Plain weave

Satin weave

Pile weave

FABRIC WEAVES

that gives a smooth surface because the warp and filling are identical in size. Rep is a ribbed texture made by weaving heavy yarns with thinner ones. Basket weaves contain patterns created by crossing two or more filling yarns with two or more warp yarns.

A twill weave will show a diagonal line on the surface of the fabric. This is achieved by having the filling yarns float across a number of warp yarns in a regular pattern. Gabardine and denim are twill weaves. They tend to be soil and wrinkle resistant, soft, and drape well.

Satin weaves are similar to twill weaves in construction, but the filling yarns make longer or more irregular floats over the warp yarn. This minimizes the over-and-under texture and produces a fine, soft, and lustrous surface such as satin, sateen, and damask.

Lace weaves are created when the warp of filling yarns is crossed or twisted at certain points, creating an open, lacy effect.

Pile weaves are a set of yarns that protrude from the background to make a three dimensional fabric. Terrycloth and frieze are made by leaving the loops uncut. Velvet is made by cutting the loops. Patterns can be made by cutting some loops and leaving others uncut, or by using different color yarns.

Jacquard weaves are woven patterns that are produced by a complex machine called a Jacquard loom. Such fabrics as flat damasks, raised brocades, and complex tapestries are made on the Jacquard loom.

COLOR

When does the fabric get its color? Dyes are added at various stages of the construction process. The manufacturer may dye the unspun fibers, the spun yarn, or the woven textiles. In synthetic and plastic fabrics, the dye is mixed with the liquid from which the fiber or film is made. These are generally the most colorfast dyes. Yarns and fibers that have been dyed before fabric construction are the next best choice for color fastness.

The type of dye used greatly affects how colorfast a fabric may be, but all fabrics will fade in varying degrees when exposed to sun, polluted air, or washed or dry cleaned. Try to select fabrics that do not fade or wear out easily, but realize that no fabric is forever. Natural colored fabrics such as beiges, grays, greens, browns, light yellow, and oranges seem to retain their original color and appearance longer than colors of higher intensity. Solid colors will become more listless and faded than will mixtures such as tweeds. Dark colors will lose their richness and depth with even a little fading. If you use textures, their play of light and shade will compensate for loss of color. Patterns will look fresher longer than plain vibrant fabrics.

FINISHING

Once the fabric has come off the loom, it needs finishing to give it its ultimate appearance. Functional finishes affect the basic appearance or performance of a fabric. Luster is given to linens and linen-like fabrics by pounding them with steel and wooden hammers, called beetling. Moiré and crepes are pressed between rollers to give them smooth finishes and tighten the weaves. This process, called calendering, can give the fabric a glazed sheen or emboss it. Crabbing sets and tightens the weave in a wool, while fulling shrinks, compacts, and softens a wool weave. Flannel and fleece textures are produced by gigging and napping. Heat setting will set dyes and pleats permanently. Mercerization, usually applied to cottons, causes the fibers and yarns to swell and contract, increasing the crimp and stretchability of the yarn. Mercerization is done with a solution of sodium hydroxide. If done under tension, the fabric will be stronger, more lustrous, and more receptive to dyes. Shearing and singeing remove surface fibers, fuzz, and lint, and prevent pilling. Shrinking lessens the tendency of most fibers to contract if they are exposed to moisture.

There are many other treatments that will positively affect the versatility and performance of a fabric. Fabrics can be made anti-static and bacteria, mildew, and moth resistant. They can be made crease resistant by impregnating the fibers with resins or agents that either cross-link cellulose molecules to build a "memory" into the fiber, causing it to return to its original shape, or by bonding the fabric to a foam or tricot backing. Fabrics can be made fire and flame resistant with chemical treatments. They can be made elastic by inserting stretch properties during the construction. Fabrics can be made glossy with resins to produce smooth, lustrous surfaces that resist soil and have improved draping qualities. They can be insulated by applying a thin or foamed coating on the back. They can be made soil resistant by coating or impregnating fibers or fabrics with chemicals to make them less absorbent. And, of course, they can be made water repellent by coating or impregnating the fibers with wax or metals. These fabrics hold their shape longer and keep dirt on the surface.

The decorative finish is usually applied to the finished fabric. Roller printing is the most common method. Pigment is applied with copper rollers that have been engraved with the design. One roller is made for each color to be used, but an effect of more colors than rollers can be achieved by engraving different parts of a roller to different depths or by printing one color over another.

Block printing is usually done by hand, although there are now machine methods being used more and more. Wood blocks that are surfaced with metal or linoleum transfer the color to the fabric. Block-printed fabrics will have slight irregularities common to any hand-done process.

Screen printing, also called silk screening, is done by forcing a thick dye through a mesh that has been coated with a moisture repellent in some areas. Color passes through only the untreated areas. A number of screens are used to add or vary the colors. Automatized screen printing is becoming more widely used because the process is very tedious when done by hand.

Batik printing is a resist printing in which parts of the fabric are protected from the dye during each application. A dye-resisting wax or paste is applied to sections of the cloth, preventing dye from being absorbed in those areas. This process is repeated for each color dye used.

Tie dyeing is another resist method in which the fabric is pleated, knotted, and tied, causing portions of the fabric to resist the dye.

Discharge printing is the opposite of resist dyeing. Parts of the fabric are treated with a chemical to remove color.

TYPES OF FABRIC

To make your fabric shopping easier, let's go over some of the most common types of fabrics and their uses. Once you've determined what type of fabric you'll need, just walk into a store or showroom and ask the salesperson to direct you to that type of fabric. You needn't go through every wing in every showroom.

If you're shopping for delicate, thin fabrics to be used for curtains, sheers, or fine tablecloths, browse through the following list.

Bobbinet is a sheer, fine open lace with hexagonal meshes. It's very soft and well suited for tiebacks and ruffles. It comes in whites, creams, and very pale delicate colors.

Dimity is a combed cotton that is fine and tightly twisted. It's a plain weave with a thin cord which makes either a vertical stripe or a plaid. Because it's fine, sheer, and crisp, it's well suited to straight folds or tiebacks. It comes in whites, tints, or patterns.

Filet is a square mesh lace that is knotted at intersecting corners. It comes from fine to coarse, but usually gives a bold, heavy effect. It comes in whites, creams, and plain pastels.

Marquisette is a sheer, open weave. It can be soft and crisp or fine and coarse. It comes in many patterns, prints, and pale solids.

Net refers to any lace with an open mesh. It can be made of almost any fiber.

Ninon is a plain voile-like or novelty weave that is very thin and silky and has a slight sheen. It comes in plain colors, subtle stripes, or shadowy patterns. Sometimes it is embroidered.

Organdy is a plain woven cotton that is sheer and crisp. It's often used for tiebacks and comes in a variety of plain colors as well as printed or embroidered designs.

Point d'esprit is a dotted bobbinet that comes in pale colors.

Dotted Swiss, or *Swiss muslin*, is a plain woven cotton usually embroidered or patterned in dots or figures. It's fine, sheer, and crisp, excellent for informal draping. It comes in white and plain, usually light, colors.

Theatrical gauze is a loose, open, and crisp woven linen or cotton with a shiny texture. It comes in a wide range of plain or two-tone colors.

Voile is plainly woven, open, sheer, and smooth. It comes in a variety of textures and colors, sometimes woven patterns.

Batiste is a plainly woven cotton or Dacron that is delicate and fine. Often it is printed or embroidered, which gives it more body. It comes in most white or pastel shades and is very light and delicate.

Casement cloth is flat and lustrous. It comes in almost any fiber and either a plain or patterned weave.

Fiberglass comes in a variety of weaves and weights, ranging from a sheer marquisette to heavy drapery fabrics. It can be either translucent or opaque, and comes in a wide variety of colors, plain or printed.

Films are usually used for shower curtains, table coverings, upholstery, or wall coverings. They come smooth or textured, plain or printed, thin or thick. They're waterproof and washable.

Muslin is inexpensive, durable, and informal. It's a soft, plainly woven cotton that can be light or heavy, bleached or unbleached, dyed and/or printed.

Osnaburg is a coarse and uneven cotton yarn in an open and plain weave. It usually comes in a natural color, but can be found in a variety of colors and printed patterns. It's an informal fabric that is strong, long lasting, and rough textured.

Pongee is a plain woven wild silk with a broken crossbar texture. It's fairly heavy and comes in a variety of colors. It is often imitated in cotton and synthetics. Variations include *tussah silk, antique taffeta,* and *douppioni,* all extremely popular right now.

Sheeting is a plain, smooth weave that's informal and inexpensive. It comes in medium to heavy weights, whites, colors, and prints.

Silk gauze is a silk weave with slightly irregular threads that make an interesting texture. It hangs beautifully and comes in a wide range of colors.

If you're looking for a light fabric that you can use for draperies as well as bedspreads, pillows, table skirts, screens, wall coverings, table coverings, and slipcovers, take a look at the following list. Many of these fabrics come in heavier weights suitable for upholstery and are available in a wide variety of colors.

Antique satin is a smooth satin with a dull, un-even finish. It's usually heavier than satin and widely used for upholstery and draperies.

Broadcloth varies in fiber and weave. It can be a cotton, synthetic, or silk. It can be a plain or twill weave as well as a spun rayon or wool weave. It's most commonly used for draperies and bedspreads.

Calico is a plain woven cotton printed with tiny figured patterns. It's inexpensive and informal.

Challis is a soft, plain, and firmly woven fabric that can be either wool, synthetic, or cotton. It can be a plain color or a print.

Chambray is a smooth, close, and plainly woven cotton or linen. It has a white-frosted look and comes in a variety of colors.

Chintz is a plain and closely woven cotton that's often glazed. It comes in a huge assortment of colors and prints.

Drill is a cotton with a diagonal twill weave. It's firm, heavy, and durable, but comes in limited colors.

Faille is a plain weave with flat, crosswise ribs. It comes in variations from soft to stiff.

Gingham is a cotton or synthetic plainly woven from colored yarns. It can be light to medium weight and is noted for its checked, striped, and plain patterns.

Homespun is a plain, loose weave whose irregular yarns create a rough and informal texture. It comes in plain colors or is woven of mixed yarns.

India print is an Indian or Persian cotton print with intricate designs in clear or dull colors. It's inexpensive and durable, but fades easily.

Jaspé cloth is a plain weave with varied yarns that create irregular blended stripes. It's firm, hard, and durable and comes in many colors, but is most commonly found in neutrals.

Linen is a plain, firmly woven flax that is cool to touch and has good body, but wrinkles profusely if not treated.

Moiré is a plain, ribbed weave that appears to be watermarked. It comes in a variety of weights and colors and has become extremely popular recently.

Oxford cloth is a plain basket or twill weave that comes in light to heavy weights and in a multitude of colors.

Piqué is a durable, interestingly textured plain weave with narrow raised cords running in one direction or at right angles to each other.

Poplin is a plain weave with fine crosswise ribs; it is firm and durable.

Rep is a plain weave with prominent rounded ribs running either crosswise or lengthwise.

Sateen is usually a mercerized cotton in a satin weave. It's flat and glossy, but has a dull back. It is durable and often used for lining draperies.

Satin is a smooth, delicate fabric with an extremely high sheen. It's durable but slippery.

Seersucker is a durable, plainly woven fabric with crinkly stripes.

Shantung is a plainly woven fabric with elongated irregularities. It comes in a variety of colors.

Stretch fabrics are knitted or woven from cotton, rayon, or other synthetics. They come in either smooth or rough textures.

Taffeta is a close, plainly woven fabric that is slightly cross-ribbed. It's very crisp and has a tendency to crack in strong sunlight. Antique taffeta has unevenly spun threads.

Moving right along, let's go on to a list of medium weight fabrics you can use for heavier draperies and upholstery, bedspreads, pillows, wall coverings, screens, and table coverings.

Bark cloth is a plain, firmly woven cotton with an irregular texture. It comes either plain or printed and is very durable.

Brocade is woven on a Jacquard loom. It has a raised design, usually a multi-colored floral or conventional pattern.

Brocatelle is similar to brocade, but heavier. It's also done on a Jacquard loom.

Burlap has a loose basket weave. It's heavy, coarse, and has an interesting texture. It's inexpensive, but fades easily.

Canvas is a plain, diagonally woven cotton that comes in a variety of weights and colors, as well as stripes and prints. It's inexpensive and is being used more and more now in interior design.

Crash is a rough textured plain weave that's often hand blocked or printed.

Cretonne is a firm, plain cotton weave. It's similar to chintz but heavier, and usually comes in bold, vigorous patterns.

Damask is a combination of two or three basic weaves. It's similar to brocade, but is not in relief. It is firm, lustrous, reversible, and usually comes in a mixture of one or two colors together.

Denim is a heavy cotton with a close twill weave. It's inexpensive, washable, and reasonably sun fast.

Duck is similar to canvas. It's a heavy cotton in a close, plain, or ribbed weave.

Hopsacking is a loose, plain weave that is coarse, heavy, inexpensive, and durable.

Mohair originally came from the hair on Angora goats, but today is usually a blend of cotton and wool. It can be either plain, twill, or have a pile weave or printed design. It ranges from sheer to heavy weight and is resilient and durable.

Monk's cloth is a mixture of cotton with jute, hemp, or flax, or just plain cotton woven in a plain or basket weave. It's coarse and heavy and usually comes in a natural color.

Sailcloth is similar to canvas and duck. It's a plain, heavy, and strong weave most often used on outdoor furniture.

Serge is a twill weave with a pronounced diagonal rib on both its face and back. It has a clear, hard finish.

Terrycloth is usually cotton or linen with a loose, uncut pile weave that loops on one or both sides. It's extremely absorbent but not always colorfast. It makes great bathrobes, but has little use in interior design, other than for towels.

Ticking is a satin or twill weave in cotton or linen. It's strong, closely woven, and durable. It's most commonly used in white with colored stripes for a mattress covering.

Getting tired? We're almost done. I did tell you

that there were endless possibilities for creating different types of fabrics, didn't I?

If you need a heavier fabric for a more durable upholstery, check out the following list.

Bouclé is a plain or twill weave that has a flat, irregular surface. It's woven or knitted from twisted yarns and has small spaced loops on its surface.

Corduroy is a pile weave of cotton or synthetic that has raised cords of varying sizes giving pronounced lines. It's durable, washable, and inexpensive.

Expanded vinyl is a plastic upholstery fabric that has an elastic knit fabric backing and stretches for contour fit.

Felt is a non-woven wool, rayon and wool blend, or synthetic. It's available in intense colors and lends itself to creative table coverings, pillows, and draperies for those who don't like to sew, as it needs no hemming.

Frieze is a heavy pile weave that has cut or uncut loops that form a pattern. Sometimes it contains yarns of different colors or with irregularities. It has a heavy rib and is very durable.

Matelassé is a double woven fabric with a surface that appears puckered or quilted.

Needlepoint is now made on Jacquard looms, but of course you can make your own if you have the time and patience. It comes in a variety of patterns and colors.

Plastic comes in a multitude of textures, colors, and patterns. It is soil resistant and wipes clean, so it's good for some upholstery applications as well as wall covering.

Plush is similar to velvet, but has a longer pile. It can be pressed and brushed to give surface variations or sculptured by having a design clipped or burned out of the pile.

Tapestry is woven on a Jacquard loom. It's heavier and rougher than brocade or damask, and usually has large, pictorial patterns.

Tweed is a plainly woven, soft, irregularly textured fabric. The yarns are dyed before weaving and often several or many colors are combined.

Velour is a weave of short, heavy, stiff cut pile.

It's durable and has a slight luster.

Velvet is a pile weave with loops cut or left uncut. It's luxurious, but shows wear quickly. Velvet comes in a wide array of colors, weights, sheens, and patterns.

Velveteen is a short, close, sheared pile cotton or synthetic fabric. It's strong, durable, and launders well.

Now, won't that blonde Adonis at the fabric showroom be impressed. Just walk right up and tell him, "I need a medium gray tussah silk," or "Please show me your Jacquards." You'll be amazed at how attentive he'll be and how quickly and efficiently you can whiz through the showrooms, locating the perfect fabrics in a matter of minutes. But before you can really feel like a pro, let's have a brief lesson on coordinating fabrics. You'll find out what colors, textures, weights, patterns, weaves, and sheens mix well together and which ones don't.

Mixing and Matching Your Fabrics

Coordinating your fabrics perfectly involves developing a "sixth sense" for color, texture, weight, and sheen. You must be able to visually imagine how the fabrics you select will blend together once they are no longer small samples and become a part of your sofa, windows, bed, etc. The first step in developing this sixth sense is to know what "feel" you want in your room or home. Ideally, your whole house should reflect one basic "feel."

Think of your home in terms of the season of the year it most resembles. A "summer" home would contain light pastels and prints in light colored chintzes, voiles, or Haitian cottons. A "fall" home would have neutral colored velvets, flannels, and brocades. A "winter" home would have darker colored wools, mohairs, and friezes. A "spring" home would have bright canvases, moirés, and sateens. When you've determined the right season for your home, you're one step closer to coordinating your fabrics.

For instance, if your home is definitely a

summer look, you'll choose light and airy fabrics. Combining any kind of heavier fabrics in dark colors would look and feel ridiculous. If your house has a winter look, you'll opt for cozy, warm fabrics with heavy textures and darker colors. Cute little cotton chintz prints would be incongruous. The first secret in selecting and coordinating fabrics correctly is to match the seasonal feel of your home.

Next, match and coordinate your colors so you achieve the contrast or subtle blend you desire. If you've chosen a strong, contrasting color scheme, review Chapter 8 and make sure the scheme you've chosen isn't too overpowering to live with. You might want to consider using subtle variations of the colors instead of the pure forms. Play around with fabric samples of different hues and tones to see which combinations work together in pleasing ways. If you don't have the fabric samples, you can use the color fan from the paint store to select your colors. Always remember that the larger doses of color you plan to use for upholstery and draperies will be stronger and more overpowering than the little samples you're working with now.

If you're planning to use a more subtle and blended color scheme, again, play with different variations of the same color until you come up with the most pleasing combination. Remember that the same color will have a different intensity and look in different fabrics. A bright pink chintz in a summer room will look different than a bright pink flannel in a winter room.

It's tricky to mix and match prints well. If you're a print lover, try not to overdo it. Most prints are light to heavy cottons, and only mix well with other light to heavy cottons. Prints can be mixed effectively if their scales are varied and their colors are matched perfectly. Large prints mixed with other large prints almost never work; they fight each other. It's far more pleasing to mix a large print with a smaller print that is a repeat of the same design in the background of the larger print. You can also mix prints with stripes, pin dots, plaids, and calico as long as none of the fabrics is

too overpowering. If the prints and patterns are too bold and strong, a chaotic effect will result. Don't try mixing cotton prints with heavier textures, it just doesn't work.

Mixing heavier textured or subtly patterned fabrics is easier. When you mix these fabrics, there should be an overall theme, a continuity. Woven shapes, as well as colors, should be repeated and coordinated so that each fabric relates to the other in some way. If you're selecting a mauve heavy texture to upholster your pull-up chairs, and a cream medium texture for your sofas, they should relate in weave and weight. Your fabrics should always be related in some way. Perhaps you might want to choose a third fabric of mauve with cream lines flowing through it for a few throw pillows.

The key to successfully mixing fabrics is to relate them to each other with a peaceful blend of color, texture, and sheen. In most cases, it's preferable to use fabrics together that not only have the same weight, texture, and related colors, but that have the same amount of sheen. You wouldn't mix satin, canvas, and flannel together, would you?

Another consideration in selecting fabrics is the degree of formality or informality that you want to achieve. The general rule of thumb is not to mix casual fabrics with elegant fabrics. However, I've used, and seen many other designers use, incongruous fabrics to create high drama. For example, I've used bright red silk pillows on a gray flannel sofa. I've also been known to mix heavy tussah silks with only a little sheen with small doses of bright metallic fabrics for accent. What can make this look work is using the shinier, brighter fabric for contrast in only very small amounts.

Before you embark on your next fabric shopping expedition, let's talk a little more about versatility. Face reality: if you've got two kids, a two year old and a four year old, you're asking for trouble if you insist on delicate white silk for your sofas. If you, your husband, and three teenagers eat dinner together while watching television in the den, forget fragile, light fabrics. They won't last more than a month under those conditions. Make major considerations for your lifestyle and the wear and tear the fabric you select will receive. You can't expect any fabric to last a lifetime, but you can expect the fabric to look good for many years to come if you choose wisely.

Extremely fragile fabrics like fine silks and laces will deteriorate without your help. Strong or medium sunlight will fade these fabrics easily as well as weaken the fibers, making them prone to tear and rip by merely brushing against them. If you insist on using fragile fabrics in strongly sunlit areas, resign yourself that the fabric is only temporary and will need replacement within a few years.

What's New in Fabric?

Every day more and more exciting and innovative fabrics are being introduced on the market. A browse through a current interior design trade magazine or a walk through a design center will tantalize your creativity. Hand-painted silks are becoming very popular for more elegant, personalized interiors. You'll find patterns ranging from spattered New Year's Eve party designs to intricate hand-painted florals. The grounds will range from heavier tussah silks in whites and creams to shiny douppioni silks in blacks and true whites. The pigments and the paints that the artists use vary from soft pastels that blend and bleed into the fabric to bright party colors and silver and gold metallics that seem to have a three dimensional effect on top of the fabric.

Hand-painted canvas is very hot right now, too. It comes in a variety of weights, colors, textures, and patterns. This look is great for the Southwestern and California casual motifs in pastel colors, but also works well for children's rooms in bright, primary colors. It's definitely a more casual fabric. The negative of canvas is that it's very heavy and doesn't have a lot of give. Upholstered canvas pieces tend to feel stiff when you sit on them. You don't get that sinking in, comfy feeling. If you use canvas for bedspreads, made sure it's lightweight,

or making your bed can become a feat for a weight lifter.

These are the two most popular fabrics that are being used for hand painting. But more and more, we're seeing hand-painted textured cottons and chintzes. These lighter fabrics only look good hand-painted when a wash is used. Stronger colors and patterns seem to sit on top of the fabric awkwardly. Although, several years ago I was in a designer's home who had upholstered his dining room walls with inexpensive black chintz and had an artist paint an Oriental scene on it after it was up on the walls. The effect was striking and dramatic, accented with soft lighting and the crystal and china on the table.

Since hand-painted fabrics are usually quite costly, they're best used for accents like throw pillows and bergere chairs. For the more daring, you might want to try hand-painting your own fabric. Try locating plain silk and canvas from some of the sources discussed in Chapter 6. Then, take a trip to your local artist's supply store and talk to the salesperson about which paints, dyes, and pigments to use. Most important, whether you buy the hand-painted fabric from a showroom or make it yourself, be sure it's heat set. Professional heat setting is done by the rolls with elaborate equipment designed for this purpose. However, small amounts of fabric you paint yourself can be heat set either in the oven or by putting the fabric in the dryer for about half an hour, then ironing it. Again, ask the salesperson at the art supply store to give you heat setting instructions.

Sparkling metallics are also very hot right now, used in small doses, of course. They come in a wide range of colors, weights, and textures. These metallics look great when you update a traditional wood frame chair by lacquering it, then upholstering it in a bright, shiny metallic. It also works well for throw pillows to update an old sofa. Do be careful what fabric you mix metallics with and how much you use. Metallics look awful on large areas or mixed with most prints.

Exciting new textured and patterned fabrics, as well as three dimensional and sculptured fabrics, are appearing on the market more and more. They range from heavy wools to silks to light cotton sculptures, and can add depth to a very simple piece of upholstered furniture. Unless they're extremely lightweight, don't use them for windows, as they will not drape well.

Fabric styles seem to come and go with almost as much frequency as clothing trends. There's a fine line between choosing fabrics that are passé and ones that are classic. There's nothing more disconcerting to me than walking into someone's home who has just recovered all his upholstered pieces and draped his windows with a fabric which was a popular item ten years ago. Some fabrics in particular pop up on the market and take off immediately. Everyone loves them and buys them. These fabrics become outdated too easily. On the other hand, classic fabrics retain their beauty and character forever. Developing a keen eye for classic fabrics and avoiding passing trends comes with keeping up with the trade magazines and being observant.

Ordering Your Fabric

Ordering your fabric is trickier than it sounds. First, you must know how much you will need. There are certain rules of thumb that designers use for estimating yardage, such as allow two yards per foot for a normal sofa. But the rule doesn't always work. Fabrics come in different widths, ranging from forty-five inches wide to fifty-four inches wide, although there are sixty-inch wide fabrics and even 120" wide fabrics used for draperies. If the fabric has a pattern or a print, the tag will give you the exact "repeat." Sometimes, because of the width or pattern of the fabric, the upholsterer may have to "railroad" the fabric, which is using the fabric horizontally instead of vertically.

Before ordering any fabric, always call your upholsterer, drapery workroom, or whoever will be using the fabric and ask exactly how much yardage you will need. Tell them the width of the fabric and whether it's plain or patterned. If it's printed or patterned, give them the dimensions of the repeat. For example, if I need a printed bedspread and pillows made, I call my upholsterer and say, "How much printed fabric, fifty-four inches wide with an eighteen-inch repeat, will I need for a king-size bedspread with a ten inch drop and twenty-inch pillows with jumbo welts?" I rely on him to give me the accurate yardage, then order an extra yard or two for safety's sake.

Next, know the term "dye lot." Fabrics are run by the mill periodically and each run will be a different dye lot. Fabrics from different dye lots can vary from only slightly to drastically. It's important, before ordering, to request a sample of a cutting from the current dye lot to make sure the sample you've chosen isn't completely different than the goods you will be receiving. This is crucial because once you've ordered a fabric and your yardage has been cut, it's not returnable.

There will always be some waste, it can't be avoided. A good upholsterer or drapery workroom will know how to cut the goods for maximum use of the yardage. Also, especially with hand-painted fabrics, a certain amount of shrinkage can be expected. If someone has hand-painted canvas, silk, or cotton for you and painted, let's say seventeen yards, by the time the fabric is heat set you might only have 16½ or sixteen yards left. Always order a little extra. Shrinkage also occurs on washable fabrics that are used for slipcovers, pillows, bedspreads, and tablecloths. Check the label on the sample to make sure it has been preshrunk or ask the salesperson at the showroom to check with the manufacturer to find out how much shrinkage you can expect.

Some showrooms have minimum yardage orders. If you only need a tiny bit of fabric, it's preferable to try to find it in a regular retail fabric shop. Usually, a minimum order is three yards, however, if the fabric is to be custom colored for you, the minimum may be higher. If you do order custom-colored fabric, most showrooms will charge a "set up" fee which covers the price of mixing custom dyes and making a special run of the fabric.

If you like a particular print and would like a plain fabric to go with it, ask the salesperson if you can order the plain ground. Usually, manufacturers will sell you the same fabric in its background color.

When you select or order your fabrics, ask if they are in stock. The salesperson can usually check on the computer and tell you whether the fabric is in stock and available immediately or on back order. Make sure you ask if the current stock is all one dye lot. You can put the amount of yardage you need on reserve, without purchasing it, for a minimum amount of time. This assures that the fabric will be available to you if you decide to use it within, say, the next ten days. If the fabric is on back order, ask when it is due in. If the salesperson tells you two months, assume he means three, four, or even five months.

When you order you will be asked to pay the whole amount. This is standard practice for "cut goods." The showroom may figure out the shipping charges at that time or bill you later. There are many different shipping methods, all of which vary in cost and time. Ask the salesperson to explain these to you. To avoid any later catastrophes, have the fabric shipped directly to you, not to your upholsterer or drapery workroom, where it could get lost among the many bolts lying around. This way, you can check the fabric to make sure it's correct when you receive it, and personally hand it to the upholsterer or drapery workroom along with a swatch stapled to a purchase order to eliminate confusion. I once forgot to do this, and had three different sofas for three different clients being made at the same upholstery shop. Of course, all the fabrics ended up on the wrong sofas. It was a catastrophe.

Assuming all's gone well, and you now have a home full of well upholstered furniture, draperies, bedspreads, and pillows, it's time to look into having your fabric treated for soil resistance. Although many fabrics have tags that say they're pre-treated, my experience has taught me to advise my clients

to call in a fabric protection company such as Fiber-Seal or Permacare. They'll come to your home to give a free estimate. Most services offer a maintenance contract which includes a periodic spray with protective chemicals for your fabrics as well as a hot line to call for immediate advice or service should Fido decide to lift his leg on your favorite couch. It's a rather expensive service, but it's worth it.

Fabric Sources

Of course, the obvious sources for fabrics are the many fabric showrooms in your city's design center. I'll discuss those in a few minutes. But what about those of you without a resale number, a friend with a resale number, or an interior designer? What about those of you with a very limited budget who need to make every penny count?

Comb local retail fabric stores for reasonably priced yardage. Check out their remnant sales for small pieces of fabric that can be used on pull-up chairs and pillows. I've found tremendous selections and good prices on colored canvas, chintz, and silk at the fabric store in my neighborhood. If you need larger amounts, ask the owner if he'll discount if you buy the fabric by the bolt.

Check your Business-to-Business Yellow Pages. You'll find wholesale fabric outlets that specialize in close-outs, seconds, and specialty import items. You'll also find local manufacturers often have warehouses that sell to the public. If your city has a garment industry, take a walk through the garment district. You'll find an incredible assortment of wholesale fabric shops that many clothing manufacturers buy from directly. Use your imagination.

If you decide to use the wholesale fabric showrooms, check the trade source books before shopping. These guides will direct you to the showroom that specializes in the type of fabric you're looking for. You needn't waste time looking through a showroom that specializes in commercial fabrics or one that specializes in country prints when you are looking for a hand-painted tussah silk. Some showrooms carry only their own line of fabrics, while most represent a number of lines. The guides will tell you what fabric lines the showroom represents. Save time when shopping by asking a salesperson to point you to the right collection you are looking for.

Fabric Trend Update

- Function and comfort are in.
- Taffetas that change color with the light are hot.
- Textured silks, silk tweeds, and bright silks are always in.
- Pleated silks are hot for opulent looks.
- Textured wools are back in, especially with modern looks.
- Leathers are hot; printed and embossed leathers are even hotter.
- Stenciled faux furs are really hot; stencil a cowhide to look like leopard or zebra.
- Metallics are in; use lots of shine and iridescence.
- Chenilles are in, but velvets and friezes are out.
- Flannels and men's suiting are definitely out.

California casual living/dining room. A once drab brown and gray space comes alive with off-white and sunset pastels. Interior design by Rima Kamen. Photography by Stewart Hopkins.

A small bedroom goes dramatic with angled bed and hand-painted canvas upholstered walls. Interior design by Rima Kamen. Photography by Stewart Hopkins.

Dining area showing an eclectic Chippendale look. Interior design by Rima Kamen. Photography by Melinda Cogen.

Dramatic foyer blending crystal, wood, and stone for a rich texture. Interior design by Rima Kamen. Photography by Melinda Cogen.

Eclectic master suite. A rich mixture of lacquer, goatskin, and pickled finishes set against eggplant, mauve, and rose. Interior design by Rima Kamen. Photography by Melinda Cogen.

Dining area with updated country look. Interior design by Rima Kamen. Photography by Melinda Cogen.

Eclectic living room takes on a warm glow with a blend of texture, color, and pattern. Interior design by Rima Kamen. Photography by Melinda Cogen.

A cheerful family room — once an old laundry room. Interior design by Rima Kamen. Photography by Melinda Cogen.

FACING PAGE:
A kitchen "facelift" using white cabinets and bleached wood floors to give the illusion of more space.
Interior design by Rima Kamen.
Photography by Stewart Hopkins.

Sensual master bedroom with flannel upholstered bed and "important" Oriental screen. Interior design by Rima Kamen. Photography by Melinda Cogen.

Cozy family room mixing faux stone and Haitian cotton with garden print.
Interior design by Rima Kamen. Photography by Melinda Cogen.

A once useless alcove becomes an "important" entertainment center. Interior design by Rima Kamen. Photography by Stewart Hopkins.

Eclectic California casual bedroom. Interior design by Craig Milne and Judy Brustman of Design Team International. Photography by Fritz Taggart.

California casual dining — bamboo, bleached wood, wicker, and glass. Interior design by Rima Kamen. Photography by Melinda Cogen.

California casual indoor/outdoor dining area with twig chairs and tree stump table. Interior design by Craig Milne and Judy Brustman of Design Team International. Photography by Fritz Taggart.

California casual dining area. Interior design by Design Team International. Photography by Fritz Taggart.

Contemporary seating area created by transforming "old" dining area of L-shaped apartment. Interior design by Rima Kamen. Photography by Stewart Hopkins.

Contemporary living room design with monochromatic color scheme. Interior design by Paolo Giusti. Photography by Kevin White.

12
Choosing Your Wall Coverings

Chances are you've been unable to resist the temptation to flip through the wings of the wallpaper showrooms or the wallpaper books at your local wallpaper store. You've probably even brought home your favorites and taped them proudly on your walls to see how they'll look. Stop and read this chapter before you make any final decisions.

Wall coverings should be simple and uncomplicated. They should serve as a background, not a focal point of the room. Always coordinate all wall covering with fabrics, flooring, and furniture. I recently did a consultation for a couple who were building their own $1.5 million home. The house was palatial, over 10,000 square feet, with winding staircases and twenty-foot ceilings. The woman, who fancied herself an interior designer, pulled out the rolls of wallpaper she had already purchased. She proudly showed me combinations of bold, bright prints and stripes in an array of unrelated and offensive colors for almost every room in the house. Quite frankly, they all looked cheap and gaudy. I asked politely, "What do these wallpapers go with? Have you selected everything else for the house?" She answered, "Oh, they don't go with anything. I just liked them. I thought I'd decorate the house around them." I cringed, appalled that a woman who could afford an estate such as this would lack the sophistication and forethought to either consult an interior designer or learn the basics of interior design first.

Wallpapers

A wall covering can refer to anything used to cover a bare wall. The word "wallpaper" generally pops into our minds automatically. Wallpaper has been around since the Middle Ages in Italy, where marble was imitated with squares of paper called "domino." It can give a room a detailed, finished look. Sometimes it can even make up for a lack of architectural interest. It can also camouflage walls that have irregularities or defects and give warmth and depth to a room. It can enhance a wall's surface texture and tie together the theme of a room.

If your home is modern, use wallpaper sparingly, avoiding all but the simplest prints. Use interesting textures, colors, and finishes to provide a background for your furniture, fabric, accessories, and artwork.

If your home is predominantly traditional, feel free to use conventional prints and patterns. Use the same rules for mixing and matching colors, patterns, and textures of wallpaper as you would fabrics.

Always select your wallpaper to blend and coordinate perfectly with the fabrics and finishes you've chosen. It's always difficult to visualize the way a small wallpaper sample will look once it covers an entire wall or room, especially if the wallpaper has a large repeat. Often, wallpapers have patterns or colors in them that don't even appear on a small showroom sample. Order one sample roll to avoid surprises and costly mistakes.

Wallpaper comes in thousands of designs and patterns. To save time, know what you're looking for before you walk through the door of the wallpaper showroom or store.

PLAIN OR TEXTURED PAPERS

Very plain papers in any color imaginable are available for use instead of paint. I think these papers are "flat" and would rather paint a wall. On the other hand, one-colored textured papers can make exciting and effective background.

Grasscloth is a textured paper that I use with repeated success. It comes in almost any color imaginable and can be coarse and rough or fine and delicate. It works well in almost any decor. I recently used a seafoam green grasscloth in a small apartment overlooking the ocean. Along with the hand-painted fabric in seafoam and muted rose and the natural stone-colored furniture, it created the perfect background for the "beachy look."

Linen is another light airy textured paper. Use it with matching or coordinating linen fabric and light cotton prints to create a fresh, springtime look.

Suede-covered walls look best in deep, dark colors and tend to create warm, cozy rooms with a wintry feel. They also blend well with heavy plaids and other deeply textured fabrics in rooms with rich, dark woods. In more modern rooms, use a suede wall covering as the perfect background for glass, chrome, and leather furniture.

Textured plastic and vinyl wall coverings have made a successful comeback in newer and more interesting forms. Use them for a simple, clean look

in kitchens and bathrooms. Some even have a padded or quilted appearance that gives rooms a finished look while providing efficient sound insulation. Others have a shiny patent leather finish that reflects light dramatically.

New on the market in the last several years are handmade and hand-painted wallpapers. You'll find plain brown wrapping papers that have been crinkled and tie dyed, and corrugated cardboard that's been sprayed one overall color, then hand-painted or spattered. Browse through one of the more innovative and updated wall covering showrooms. You'll discover collections of handmade wallpapers that can be custom ordered to match any color your heart desires.

FLORALS

Florals come in a variety of prints, ranging from bold jungle prints to tiny, fragile flowers. The pattern can encompass the entire paper or be small bouquets loosely scattered. Some are bold and overpowering; others are just plain quaint. I use florals exclusively for traditional homes. Busy gay and bold prints seem out of place and behind the times in modern homes.

Almost every wallpaper showroom and store has a huge assortment of papers printed with lilacs, carnations, violets, sunflowers, mimosa, roses, daisies, anemones, cornflowers, primroses, wisteria, magnolia, camellias, waterlilies, apple blossoms, irises, and tulips. Use them sparingly and in good taste.

FRUITS AND VEGETABLES, LEAF AND VERDURE

Fruits and vegetables such as apples, cherries, strawberries, blackberries, squash, and eggplant are often printed in patterns on wallpaper. I think fruits and vegetables are best left in the refrigerator.

Leaf and verdure prints include a variety of patterns of ivy, pine branches, ferns, palms, bamboo, herbs, maple leaves, and grasses. I think these are best left in the garden. If you like the bamboo look, you'll find fabulous wall coverings made out of *real* bamboo. If you like ferns, buy the real plants.

CHINTZ AND CALICO

Chintz and calico are usually miniature floral prints, but can also be fruits and vegetables or leaf and verdure. They work well in unsophisticated homey rooms with an early American or provincial theme. Mix chintz and calico with light pine furniture, even maple and cherry for a great country look.

BIRDS, INSECTS, FISH, AND ANIMALS

Yes, any animal in the zoo is fair game for this category. You'll find papers printed with zebras, dragonflies, ducks, geese, seagulls, polo ponies, eagles, and even dragons. I remember back many years ago; a friend of mine asked me to select a wallpaper for her son's room. It was my first design job. Unfortunately her son was not blessed with Robert Redford's features. To be honest, he was cute and sweet, but had a simian look. So, in an all out effort to personalize his room, I marched into her home with bags full of wallpapers with whimsical monkeys printed on them. She laughed hysterically, admitting that I had captured the essence of her son's image. The wallpaper was ugly, but quite frankly, so was her son.

You'll find wallpapers with large, overall designs such as zebra stripes or leopard spots. Use these in small, ultra-modern rooms mixed with leather, chrome, and glass furniture to achieve an ultra-dramatic "show-biz" look. But do try to refrain from choosing the traditional bird, fish, insect, and animal scenes; there's nothing worse than walls covered with dangling spiders.

GEOMETRICS

Geometrics can be stripes, plaids, checks, and polka dots, as well as any modern geometric form. Wider, bolder stripes can be used to create a festive effect. Popular right now is a plain natural canvas with wide beige or gray stripes. This paper, with matching fabric, works well with the Southwestern and California casual looks. More subtle, traditional stripes mix well with other prints and patterns if used correctly. A striped wallpaper, stripes running vertically of course, will add visual height to a room, but make it look smaller.

Plaid wallpapers are often used for dens and boys' rooms, rightfully so. They have no place in larger, more open areas, as they give a warm, cozy, but closed-in look. Use plaids cautiously — they are extremely difficult to mix with other patterns and generally look best when mixed with plain fabrics.

Checks are often used in the same types of rooms as calicos and chintzes. They give a cutesy look to kitchens and kids' rooms and mix well with country pine. Checks rarely have a place in a more sophisticated modern or traditional home.

Polka dots can be bold and strong, or tiny and subtle; just a hint of color. Bold dots can be disconcerting and distracting, so I advise against them. Papers with tiny, subtle pin dots can blend as a background and be mixed with other solids, prints, and patterns easily.

Other geometric wallpapers each have their own merits and disadvantages. The huge shiny geometrics that were popular ten years ago are no longer in style. They look out of place in today's interiors. The newer looks in geometrics are smaller-scaled patterns scattered on the wallpaper or geometrics embossed three dimensionally as textured papers.

SCENICS

Scenics are overall patterns that give a feeling of perspective. They come in one-color effects as well as in multicolors. You'll find many English, French, and Oriental scenes as well as murals depicting anything from early scenes of New York to ancient Venice. They're usually sold in sets that make up a complete scene. Oriental scenics and murals have made a major comeback recently, especially those with muted silver backgrounds.

A trompe l'oeil paper, panel, or border is any covering that "fools the eye." These wallpapers look like something they aren't. You can get fake marble tiles, Spanish tiles, moirés, corkboard, louvered shutters, and latticework. There is even a paper that looks like a well-stocked library. Trompe l'oeil wallpapers have come full circle. Considered tacky only a few years ago, they seem to be emerging as the hottest wall covering around these days.

Panels and borders are used as trimmings for plain papers or painted walls or as matching borders for wallpaper, especially for children's rooms. You'll find panels and borders with classic figures, flowers and fruits, fluted columns, cornice moldings, door frames, and wainscoting. These are usually sold in strips by the yard.

CHILDREN'S PAPERS

Children's wallpapers are always bright and cheerful, after all, who wants a depressed kid? They come in a huge variety of patterns and colors to arouse the child's imagination. Many are busy papers, and when mixed with a room full of toys and colorful objects, can become confusing. I suggest using simpler wallpapers for children, such as ones with floating, billowy clouds to create a harmonious and less chaotic background.

Other Wall Coverings

Wallpaper isn't the only show in town. Let's discuss your other wall covering options.

First, there's good old paint. Consider the multitude of colors and finishes discussed in Chapter 9 before you spend unnecessary time and money on wallpaper. And remember, plain pure white walls work best for displaying major pieces of art.

Next, there's fabric. Most any fabric can be backed and/or laminated to be put on your walls. Many wallpaper manufacturers make a wide selection of pre-backed fabrics that are made exclusively as wall coverings. Check your trade source books to

find companies that specialize in backed fabric or services that can back any fabric for you. Remember though, this is more expensive than wallpaper because fabric is more costly and is sold by the yard. Your wallpaper installer will quote you a price based on the number of yards, not rolls. Tightly-woven fabrics work best on walls, as edges tend to fray easily on loosely-woven fabrics.

Wall upholstery is another one of your options. A wall upholsterer can take any fabric and upholster it to your walls using a foam or polyester backing. Fine workmanship is essential, and includes custom welting or double welting on all fabric edges. A good wall upholsterer will be able to match the pattern perfectly at the seams, but there will be a good deal of waste. Generally, the fabric is pre-cut in his shop after he has taken exact measurements on the job. Each piece is sewn together prior to hanging and then stapled to the walls. The welting is added last.

Wall upholstery is an expensive way to cover your walls. The wall upholsterer will quote you a price for the entire job based on the amount of time and labor it will take. The effect is a padded, warm look that adds elegance as well as sound control and insulation to a room. Wall upholstery is most effective in dining rooms, powder rooms, and master bedrooms, although its usage is unlimited. You can even upholster a ceiling.

For those of you who move frequently, use fabric stretched on a wood frame to cover a wall, or attach fabric to your walls with one of the ready-made metal track systems available. These are excellent portable ideas for those of you who move frequently.

Lay your carpeting up the walls to create a soft, sensuous texture and superb sound insulation. Use this idea with modern, built-in platforms for beds and seating.

Don't overlook the decorating possibilities of some of the new laminates on the market. These laminates are made by bonding resin-impregnated layers of paper together with heat and pressure to form a thin, almost rigid sheet of material. The top layer is colored, textured, or printed, then coated with a clear hard film of plastic, such as melamine.

Nowadays there are literally thousands of designs, colors, and textures to choose from. Most come in both shiny and mat finishes. You can get tiny raised pin dots, stripes, embossed checks, or high tech grids. You can even find mirror, chrome, brass, and aluminum finishes as well as laminates that look like linen, cork, burlap, or cane. The newest laminates on the market come in bendable strips that can be used to create or cover a curved surface. Check your source books for the names of the manufacturers. If you write a letter or call, they'll send you a complete set of samples.

Use mirrors on walls to increase light, expand a view, or make a room look larger. Large mirrored panels should be hung professionally, but you can use mirror tiles which come backed with self-adhesive tabs for easy do-it-yourself installation. Experiment with pre-cut mirror strips with beveled edges that come in different lengths and widths. Insert these strips between larger panels of mirror to cover unsightly seams. For accent, use tiny mirror tiles that bend around curves and corners well and come in mosaic form on a cloth backing. Most mirrors come in a variety of colors — clear, smoked, bronze, black, peach.

Use wall tiles for bathrooms and kitchens. Old brick and textured tiles can look new again after they're painted. Thin facings of stone or slate can look real after they're up on the wall. Ceramic tiles are by far the most popular choice for wall tiles. There is a tremendous selection of colors, designs, shapes, and sizes to choose from. Find slick machine-made ceramic Italian tiles for a modern look or handmade clay tiles for a more rustic look. Check your source books for the many manufacturers and showrooms.

What's Hot? What's Not?

I'm often dismayed, sometimes mildly depressed, whenever I walk into a home filled with wall coverings that have long ago become outdated.

Worse yet, the proud owner asks me, "How do you like our new wood paneling? We've just spent a small fortune having it put up." I generally avoid comment and divert the conversation. Please don't spend your hard-earned money on any of the following.

• Avoid cheap wood paneling from your local building supply company, especially if it sports a fake walnut grain finish. It *looks* cheap! If you've covered a wall with rough-sawn light wood placed on an angle, you're one step ahead, but you're still ten years behind. If you love wood paneling, spend the money to have a skilled architectural paneling craftsman put in top quality paneling of rich, well-finished woods with fine professional detailing. Or look through Chapter 18: Remembering the Details for some wonderful effects you can create inexpensively with molding and panels.

• Avoid at all costs mirror squares with gold veining running through them. These squares date back to the days of plastic flowers. Use quality mirror that doesn't distort, in either clear or colored finishes. Spend the money to have it professionally installed. If you can fit it in your budget, have your mirrors finely beveled and/or etched. Fake an expensive look by using pre-cut and pre-beveled strips. Avoid production etching, it looks cheap.

• Avoid the shiny, bright geometric print wallpapers that were popular fifteen or twenty years ago. These are overpowering and impossible to work with no matter where you put them.

• Avoid whimsical little prints with pictures of fruits, vegetables, animals, or fire engines. When I was growing up, my mother wallpapered my bathroom with little caricatures of French poodles. Each poodle was in a different position relieving his bladder and had a cute little saying. That wallpaper was probably a major contributing factor to any neuroses I might have as an adult.

• Flocked wallpaper. No ifs, ands, or buts, get rid of it now! If you're the proud owner of red-flocked wallpaper, go directly to jail. No "get out of jail free" cards for you until you strip that horrible stuff off your walls. Flocked wallpaper went out with flappers, not to mention the goosebumps it gives you if you run your fingers over it.

"If these things are so out, why do they still sell them?" you ask. "Who knows?" I'll answer. "They must still be money makers." But please, I beg you, don't buy them. If you want to decorate your home successfully, spend the time to know and find the latest products.

• Do use hand-painted wall coverings and interesting new textured coverings.

• Open your mind to backed and/or laminated fabrics for your walls; wall upholster if you can afford it.

• Look for the newer versions of grasscloths, vinyls, metal and plastic laminates, and metallics.

• One of the hottest wall coverings right now is "raffia weave," a natural-colored woven wall covering that also comes foam-backed for use on upholstered pieces.

• Experiment with some of the new suedes and patent leathers. Some even look like lizard or crocodile.

• Faux finishes are in. Faux boising, sponging, and marbling are truly hot.

• Trompe l'oeil wall treatments are the rage as are large crown moldings . . . use them anywhere.

• Formal is back, especially moirés and silver murals of Oriental flowers and birds.

Ordering Your Wall Covering

Wallpaper is usually sold in single or double bolts, although some of the more expensive papers are sold by the yard. A single bolt is usually seven yards long and twenty-one inches wide. A double bolt is fourteen yards by twenty-one inches. Measuring a room for wallpaper is tricky because of pattern repeats, windows, and doors. Unless you are a professional and have the utmost confidence in your ability, I suggest you employ professional paper hangers. They will measure your room and tell you how many bolts you'll need to order.

Show the wallpaper hanger the sample of the paper you are going to use. He or she will tell you what wall preparation is necessary, whether you'll need blank stock or not, and be able to figure out allowances for wastage, shrinkage, and pattern repeats. They'll be able to pull off old wallpaper easily and will know the proper type of paste and procedures to use for the particular type of wallpaper you've selected.

Most professional wallpaper hangers will quote a price per roll if the paper is purchased by the roll, or per yard if the paper is purchased by the yard. He or she will quote you separate prices for wall preparation, removing old wallpaper, and applying blank stock. Blank stock is used under bumpy or rough walls or under very shiny and smooth papers to ensure that the imperfections of the wall underneath do not show through the wallpaper.

If you use a professional hanger who is experienced and licensed, he is obligated to take full responsibility for detecting defective wallpaper before it is hung. When the rolls of wallpaper are delivered to you, they'll contain a notice to the hanger that the entire roll must be checked for flaws and defects. If your hanger is conscientious, he or she will do so before hanging. Remember, the wallpaper company will not let you return a defective or flawed run of wallpaper if it's already up on your walls.

Your professional hanger can also hang backed fabrics. Rely on him to give you the correct yardage you'll need before you order. Make sure you allow for the shrinkage that occurs from the process of backing and/or laminating by bringing a sample of the fabric to the company which will process it. They'll know how much shrinkage to expect.

Very few wallpaper hangers can also do wall upholstering. You'll have to find an expert in that field. He'll be able to tell you how much yardage you'll need for the entire job and give you a complete estimate. Make sure you let him know whether you are using a solid or a repeat and how wide the fabric is.

Wall laminate work needs to be done by a professional carpenter. Try to find one who has worked with designers before and understands the look you want to achieve. He'll be able to measure the wall or walls, determine how many sheets of laminate you'll need, and order the materials for you. He'll quote a blanket price that includes labor and materials.

Mirrors should be installed by a licensed mirror and glass company. Get several bids and make sure that the installer is using a top grade of mirror. He'll give you a bid based on the square footage of mirror, any detailing, and labor.

Wall tiles should be installed by a licensed tile installer. He'll be able to measure the area and tell you how many square feet of tile you should order as well as how many trim pieces you'll need. Generally, you order the tile, he supplies the grouting and labor, however, many installers will order tile for you if you ask. Insist on a blanket price rather than an hourly rate. Tile installation is very time consuming. It's wise to order about 10% more tiles than you need to compensate for any measuring errors and any tiles that are defective, discolored, or broken.

Last Minute Pointers

Before you order, let's go over a checklist to make sure you've made the right decision.

- Have you selected the right wall covering? Does the pattern complement other patterns or does it clash?
- Is the wall covering up to date?
- Does it blend with your room and house, not too bold, not too bland?
- Have you matched it perfectly with your fabrics and finishes and made sure it works? Have you double checked the color in both natural and artificial light?
- Are you overusing pattern?
- Is the scale correct? Is it too overpowering or bold?
- Have you included the price of the wall covering, delivery and shipping charge, installation charges, and preparation work in your budget?
- Have you double checked with your installer to make sure you are ordering the right quantity?
- Have you checked with the manufacturer to make sure you'll be receiving the same dye lot as your sample? If not, have you requested a sample from the current dye lot?
- Have you considered any potential problems? Sound, light absorption, heat, moisture, mildew, soot and soil stains, fraying, chipping, peeling, fading?

Trick of the Trade

Save money! Change a room by using a wallpaper border instead of wallpaper or molding.

13
Choosing Your Upholstered Pieces

As I was driving through a busy intersection the other day, my eye was caught by a huge red and white sign that flashed, "SOFA $299 COMPLETE!" I couldn't keep from pulling over and checking out what kind of sofa they could be selling for $299 and still be making a profit. I entered the store pretending to be a naive consumer and browsed through the selection of sofas and chairs with casual interest. To my surprise, the pieces didn't look bad. They were copies of popular, more expensive pieces I was used to seeing displayed in the design center, tagged with fancy prices.

The salesman approached me asking, "Can I help you?"

"Yes," I said, "Can you tell me how this sofa is constructed?"

"Sure," he said and began to give me a dissertation on the frame, springs, padding, and fabric as I plopped myself down on the sofa to sample its comfort.

"Not bad," I said, as the skimpy foam gave in to the weight of my body. I could feel my well-padded bottom sink down to the webbing. I also noticed that the depth of the sofa was shallow, and if I didn't sit up completely straight, there was no cushion to support half of my thighs.

"Isn't it comfortable?" he asked.

"Oh, yes," I replied, as I watched the fabric around me pucker and the cushion next to me pop up. "Can I get this sofa in any other fabrics?" I inquired.

"No," he hedged. "White, it only comes in white."

"Oh, I'm sorry, " I said, pulling myself out of the sofa with great difficulty. "I can't use a white sofa."

By the time I was back on my feet, the salesman was across the room, hovering over a couple who had just walked in. I walked out, noticing that the poor sofa appeared to be permanently imprinted with the indent of my body.

Before you go shopping for a sofa or any upholstered piece, you should know how upholstered pieces are constructed. There are many different grades and qualities that gravely affect not only how that piece looks, but how it will hold up over years of use. Forget fabric, line, color, and design for just a moment and let's take a look at the hidden materials and workmanship that lie beneath the surface.

Custom Upholstery

There are three basic types of upholstered pieces. The first, custom, includes pieces made by

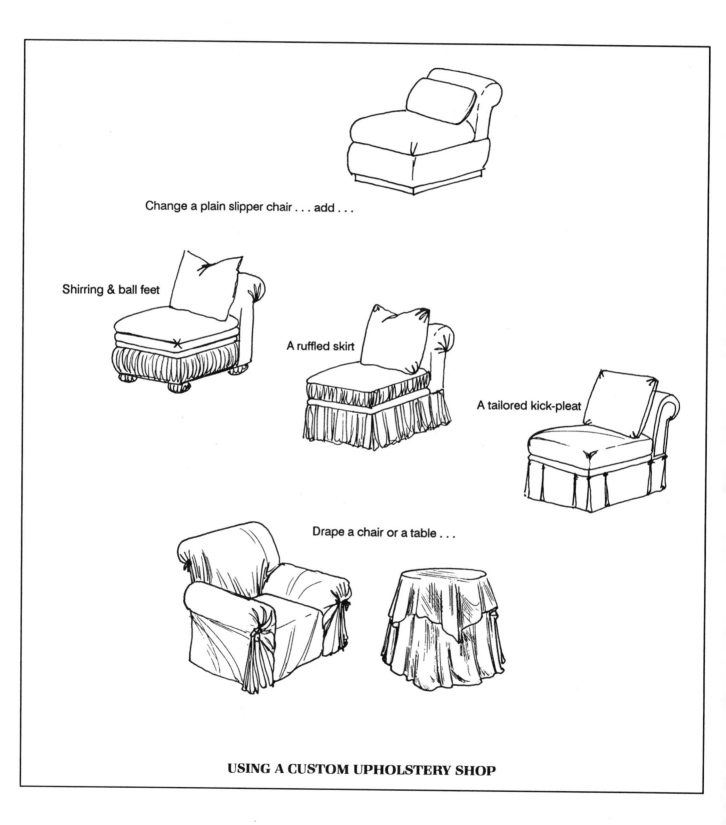

Change a plain slipper chair . . . add . . .

Shirring & ball feet

A ruffled skirt

A tailored kick-pleat

Drape a chair or a table . . .

USING A CUSTOM UPHOLSTERY SHOP

hand and started and completed by one person. The second, semi-custom, have standard parts that are passed along on a production line. Then, custom details such as special legs, arms, skirts, pleats, or ruffles are added to your specifications. Production pieces use only standard parts and are passed along a production line with different operators for each step.

If you select your upholstered pieces from a low to moderately priced retail furniture store, you're usually selecting production run pieces. The store either has their own upholsterer who makes up their pieces for them, or represents one or more larger manufacturers who supply large quantities of pieces to them. The quality of the piece you select depends on the quality control of the upholsterer or manufacturer who supplies that store. The positive of buying from one of these low to middle line stores is that you can purchase reasonably updated upholstered furniture, usually copies of more expensive pieces, for a low price. The negatives are that you are not getting handcrafted workmanship or original style, and you won't have any choice of fabrics and details for the piece.

If you shop in a higher priced retail furniture store, your selection widens. Generally, these stores carry an array of upholstered pieces that they get from major manufacturers. Many of the pieces are semi-custom, which means that the manufacturer will customize the basic sofa for you by adding superficial details such as skirts or pillows, and allow you to select any fabric you want from their own supply of goods.

Usually the fabric they stock is graded according to cost. The salesperson will quote you a price for the sofa based on the grade of the fabric you choose and the extra details you want. Obviously, the positive of this type of shopping is that you can somewhat customize a piece of upholstered furniture to suit your tastes and needs. The negatives are that your choices are limited to what the manufacturer offers, you still don't know the workmanship that lies beneath the finished product, and you

must be prepared to wait six to twelve weeks for delivery unless you decide to buy a floor sample.

For those of you who have access to a trade design center, you'll find many showrooms also carry pieces from large manufacturers. Usually these manufacturers specialize in a higher quality product. Many of the showrooms also have their own upholsterers who make up custom pieces exclusively for that showroom. The furniture you find on the showroom floors will be marked with a code that tells the retail price and the wholesale or net price. If you have a resale number and/or a business card, or are accompanied by an interior designer, ask the salesperson to explain the code to you. The salesperson will quote you a price, followed by either the letters COM or COG. COM means "customer's own material." COG means "customer's own goods." They both mean the same thing . . . that you must supply your own fabric.

Before ordering an upholstered piece from a trade showroom, double check the amount of fabric they've quoted to make the piece. Be sure you've told them the width of the fabric you'll be using and whether it's plain or has a repeat. If the piece is not made locally, you're responsible for all freight charges F.O.B. your city. This cost is usually about 15% of the total cost of the item and means delivery of the piece only to a local warehouse. It's up to you to arrange with your own delivery service to pick it up at the warehouse and deliver it to your home.

Professional delivery services that usually work exclusively with designers charge by the hour, so be sure to figure these costs in your budget. Ask the showroom salesperson to suggest a good delivery service, or find one in either your trade source books or Business-to-Business Yellow Pages.

The positives of buying directly from a trade showroom are that you are getting the net price that interior designers get, you can feel more confident that you're getting a high quality and well-designed piece, and you have more flexibility in customizing your pieces. The negatives are that it's up to you to find your own fabric, make arrangements to get it safely to the manufacturer, make your own separate delivery arrangements; you must wait at least four to twelve weeks for the piece to be made; and costs of freight and delivery are extra.

The next option, and by far the most preferable to most interior designers, is to find your own upholsterer. How? Through referrals, through your interior designer, through the Business-to-Business Yellow Pages, and through your trade source books.

Custom upholsterers range from large, professionally run operations to small, backyard types of businesses. Interview at least three different upholsterers to get a feel for what type of work they do best, how they structure their pricing, what materials they use, the skill of the craftsmen, the care they take in the construction of a piece, and most important, their reliability and integrity.

Custom upholsterers either charge by the piece, by the running feet of a piece, or a combination of both. For example, the upholsterer I use charges a certain amount per each running foot of a sofa, then tacks on additional charges for any detail work such as skirting, shirring, or pleating.

He has standard prices for upholstering chairs which vary according to style: a wood frame chair with a tight seat and tight back is one price, a wood frame chair with loose cushions is another price, a fully upholstered chair is yet another price, as is an ottoman or an upholstered bed. He prices his pillows according to how many inches they are and uses a standard Dacron filling. If I want a down-filled pillow, of course, it's extra money. He also makes bedspreads, comforters, and tablecloths.

Having developed a rapport with my upholsterer over the years, I can call him up and get price quotes on most pieces by describing them accurately over the telephone. If I tell him how wide a fabric is and what the repeat is, he figures out how much yardage I need to order. Other upholsterers charge by the piece only, and must see a picture in order to give you a quote. In any case, it's always a wise idea to give your upholsterer a detailed picture or drawing of the piece you want made up. A purchase order with the price, dimensions of the piece, a description of the fabric to be used, and a small sample of the fabric stapled to it is a must.

The positives of using a custom upholsterer

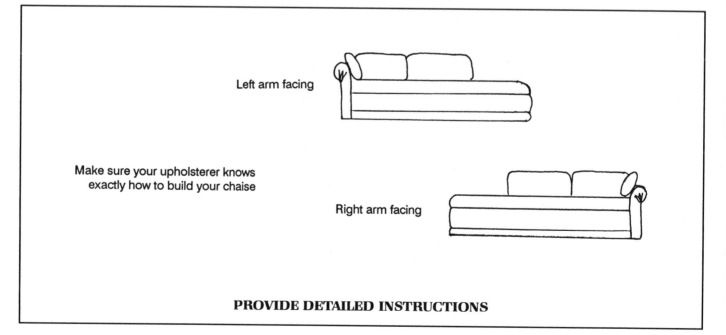

Left arm facing

Make sure your upholsterer knows
exactly how to build your chaise

Right arm facing

PROVIDE DETAILED INSTRUCTIONS

are numerous. First, the price is generally much lower than even the net price you were quoted at the showroom. Second, he'll be able to make up almost any piece as long as you have a picture. This means that you can select any sofa from any source, change it in any way that you like, and have it made in any fabric of your choice. Third, the upholsterer is local, so you can supervise the construction of your sofa while it's being made, making any changes and correcting any errors during construction. Fourth, you save the 15% freight charges that the showroom was adding on or the furniture store had included.

One negative is the possibility that the upholsterer will misread the dimensions on the drawing. He might even flee to Mexico with your 50% deposit and your fabric. Another negative is that you can't sit on a piece to check for comfort before you buy it.

In order to have an upholstered piece duplicated by a custom upholsterer, bring him a detailed picture or make a drawing of the piece. (Complete instructions are in Chapter 5.) Make sure you've provided every detail: length, width, height, back height and thickness, seat height, back and seat cushion thickness, loose cushion size and detailing, throw pillow size and detailing. Specify type of legs desired, casters, welting, pleating, shirring, buttons, quilting, skirting, tassels, channeling. If your fabric is to be used in a certain direction, tell him. Stripes can be upholstered vertically or horizontally. You must let him know ahead of time how you want them.

Custom upholsterers can also reupholster or completely redesign existing pieces. They can make a long sofa into a loveseat or extend a loveseat into a long sofa. They can completely change the look of an outdated sofa or chair by adding or subtracting seat cushions, changing back and seat heights, cutting down or adding to arms, and adding or subtracting surface details. While you still have the same fabric costs, the labor cost for redoing a piece is about one-half the cost of making a new piece. So before you throw out that old sofa or chair, check with your upholsterer first to see if he can revamp it to look like a brand new piece straight out of *Architectural Digest*.

Construction

Since none of us have x-ray eyes, finding out how a particular upholstered piece has been constructed is essential before we spend our hard-earned money. Ask! You'll understand what you're hearing after you've read this section. Be a skeptic. The cost of an upholstered piece should be commensurate with the quality of its construction. Often, unfortunately, the price may be based on the store's cash flow problems.

FRAME

A strong frame is the foundation of any upholstered piece. The frame should be a combination of kiln-dried hardwoods skillfully put together with wood glue and double doweled. All corners should be corner blocked and screwed. Sturdy frames must be made with woods that are tough and durable, and cut and dried so that they will not twist, warp, split, swell, or shrink. The wooden frame must be able to withstand shock and to hold nails and tacks. The most desirable types of wood that should be used are hard maple, birch, poplar, ash, alder, magnolia, mahogany, and oak. Try lifting an upholstered piece to check for weight and sturdiness. Gumwood is used in less expensive pieces because it's easy to work with, but it doesn't hold tacks well. Hickory and pecan are commonly used on upholstered pieces that have some part of the frame exposed because these woods take an excellent finish. A good frame should outlast the rest of the piece.

Frames can be made from metal, such as tubular, square, or flat bars of aluminum or a steel alloy. Each joint and leg should be welded together. The metal becomes an element of the design of the piece and should be bronze, brass, polished chrome plated, or painted a color that will go with your upholstery.

Frames can also be made from cast or molded plastic. They either come as solid frames or component pieces for solid frames. Plastic frames should also have mitered joints that are secured with adhesive and corner blocks.

There are four basic categories of frames. Open frames are usually made of wood, plastic, or metal. They have large cavities in the seat, back, and arm. Solid-based frames have single pieces of shaped wood that are attached to other pieces. Slip frames have a solid base or an open frame that is upholstered separately and attached to the piece. Exposed wood frames have parts of the frame that aren't covered by upholstery. These exposed parts are given a fine finish or painted.

INNER WORKINGS

The inner workings of the piece are done layer by layer and make the heart of the piece. In more expensive pieces each step is done by hand. In less expensive production pieces it is done with machinery at assembly line speed.

First, three- to four-inch jute webbing is woven in a simple basket weave and tacked to the frame. Wooden slat webbing is often used in backs and seats instead of jute, as these wooden slats can eliminate the necessity for very large springs and be set at any height in the cavity. More recently, steel webbing, wires, or sheet webbing made from heavy jute cloth or woven polypropylene is used in production pieces. It is resilient, doesn't stretch out, and can be installed faster than fabric webbing. Rubber webbing can also be used. It becomes firmer and stronger the more it is used. Rubber webbing should be under permanent tension and uniformly stretched for a smooth surface and a comfortable seat.

Next, coiled springs are tied to the webbing and frame close enough to prevent sagging, but separated enough to avoid rubbing against each other. In more expensive pieces, the springs are firmly tied down with thick spring twine with eight knots to each coil. The more knots used, the firmer the piece. Coil springs are wires that are bent in a spiral shape. Conical springs have a smaller circumference at the bottom than at the top. Double helical springs are of equal size at the top and bottom with the center squeezed in. Cylindrical springs are the same width along their entire length.

The firmness of a piece is determined by the size and number of coils used, the overall shape, and the gauge and grade of the wire used. Upholstery springs are made from nine to eleven gauge wire and are the heaviest springs that are used on the seats. Pillow or back springs are made out of a finer wire. Cushion springs are made from even finer wire that is usually placed into inner-spring units for cushions, pillows, inside backs, and some thick inside arms.

Less expensive pieces have "sagless springs" — flat, wavy lines of high-grade steel which look like grill work. They're used in automobile seats and moderately priced furniture with contemporary lines. Sagless springs will give a firm feel rather than a soft, luxurious feel.

Burlap or muslin is then stretched over the springs and tacked to the frame to protect the padding. A good grade of burlap or muslin should be used in more expensive pieces.

Next, stuffing is placed over the burlap or muslin and a layer of white cotton felt is placed over that. An outer muslin cover is put on to insure a smooth outer surface.

Then, an edging should be added to surfaces that are loosely stuffed to retain the stuffing, establish the desired shape, and supply a soft surface under the cover to protect it from wear.

Roll edges are strips of burlap filled with loose stuffing. This holds the burlap tightly to the frame and keeps a roll edge neat and stationary.

Hard edges are stuffing forced forward by rows of stitching through a burlap cover. They're used for spring surfaces where the upholstery comes up 1½ to three inches above the rail.

Spring edges are used when the spring surface is more than three inches above the rail. The springs are covered with loose stuffing sandwiched between two layers of burlap. They are held in place by several rows of stitching that go through the stuffing and the burlap and are anchored to the edge wire.

The stuffing or filling can be horsehair, sponge rubber, or rubberized fibers of various kinds. More expensive pieces are filled with Dacron, urethane foam, cotton felt, feathers, or down. Less expensive pieces might be filled with moss, kapok, or any combination of the above fillings.

Inexpensive loose cushions are made of fine-tempered springs that are wrapped in envelopes of one or a combination of the filler materials named above. More expensive loose cushions will be filled with more expensive material.

Loose stuffings are hairs or fibers that are un-attached and worked into position. They're usually horse and cattle hair, moss, palm fiber, cocoa fiber, sisal tow, excelsior, or tampico.

Compact stuffings are easily cut or bonded together to form a required shape. They're usually polyfoam, foam rubber, or rubberized hair materials in sheets or slabs.

Understuffing is often used for the crown, the raised center of a surface, to build a desired contour. It is usually made from loose stuffing or felted padding. Felted padding is a matted cotton often used as a stuffing for thin, flat surfaces.

Next, the casing goes on. It's usually a muslin layer that envelops the stuffing and holds it in place. This extra muslin layer helps maintain the shape of the piece and reduces the tension on the finish of the fabric.

Then, padding, a felted material of cotton or polyester, is laid over all surfaces to provide a smooth base for the cover and hide any imperfections in the stuffing and shape the surface. It will also dull the sharp edges of the frame and prevent any hairs or fibers from coming through the fabric.

Finally, the fabric you selected goes on. The quality of fine tailoring will be evident in the crisp-ness of the lines, the welting, the way your fabric is seamed and matched, and the fine detail work which will give the piece its finished look.

Upholstery Vocabulary

In order to communicate with your furniture salesperson or your upholsterer, here are some of the terms you should know.

Side chair — A straight dining chair.

Arm chair — A straight dining chair with arms.

Bergere chair — A wood-framed upholstered chair that is usually wide and deep and used as an accent piece or pull up chair.

Slipper chair — A low, armless upholstered chair originally designed for a person to put on his or her shoes.

Slip seat — The removable seat of a side or arm chair. Four screws underneath the seat release it so that it can be recovered easily.

Loose cushion — An upholstered piece that has loose cushions on either the seat and back or both.

Tight seat — An upholstered piece that has tight, contoured upholstering rather than loose cushions.

Tight back — An upholstered piece that has a tightly upholstered back and no loose cushions on its back.

Throw pillow — Separately made pillows that are not part of the piece and are not the cushions.

Pillow — A pad placed on the inside back of a piece.

Cushion — A pad put down on a seat.

Down — The light, fluffy filament that grows from the quills under the feathers of an adult bird. Usually goose feathers are added to strengthen it and help retain its shape.

Foam rubber — Commonly used for cushioning in most upholstered pieces. It should always be wrapped with felted padding. Often, it's mixed with down and innerspring units to make a soft, durable cushion.

Welting — The cording that is covered with fabric and used to finish off the edges of an upholstered piece or a pillow. It comes in many sizes. It can be single welting or double welting.

Single welting — One row of welting, usually ¾" to ½" wide.

Double welting — Two rows of covered cording upholstered together side by side.

Shirred welting — Jumbo welting on which the fabric is gathered onto the welting.

Jumbo welting — Huge, thick welting.

Self-welting — Used for striped fabrics to achieve a perfect alignment of the stripes. It's made a part of the pillow or cushion by turning the top or bottom edges over a filler cord and sewing them into place.

Straight edge, or *knife edge* — The way a pillow is finished. It means the same as it sounds, plain.

Flange edge — A ruffled edge without gathering; usually ½" to 3" wide.

Butterfly corner — Formed by making knots on the inside corners of pillows so that a rounded, gathered corner is achieved.

Rabbit ear — Trade "lingo" referring to the corners of throw pillows that are sewn so that they stand up like rabbit's ears.

Basketball edge — A pillow that is pieced together exactly like a basketball.

Box cushion — Seamed just like a box shape. It may or may not have welting.

Sofa — An upholstered seating piece with arms and back. The minimum size of a sofa is six feet and usually ranges to nine feet, although curved and L-shaped sectionals are longer and can be included in this term.

Loveseat — A shorter sofa, usually four to five feet in length.

Chaise longue — A backless sofa or loveseat that usually has a headrest at one end, sometimes one arm extending from the headrest. It can also be a chair with an ottoman attached to it.

Ottoman — A low upholstered seat with no back or arms. It can be square, rectangular, or circular.

Daybed — An elongated chair, usually a convertible couch, in which the mattress serves as the seating surface.

Banquette — A bench with an upholstered seat and back.

Settee — A seat or bench for two or three people with an upholstered seat and a wood or upholstered back.

Arms — Can be full and extend the entire length of the seat. They can be set back, so that the seat is T-shaped. They can be scooped with an angular or curved notch cut out in front.

Armtops — Can be knife edge, modern square, rounded, scroll, or T-shaped.

Wings — The part of a chair attached to the front or side of a back above the arm. They can be flat, arched, scooped, straight, curved, rounded, square-edged, or knife-edged.

Backs — May be either pad or spring upholstered. The depth of the back is the distance from the front to the back of the seating area. For upright sitting, it should be sixteen to twenty inches deep. For lounging, it should be twenty-one to twenty-five inches deep. The tilt of the back will determine the comfort of the seat. Solid backs are pillowless. Loose pillow or pillow backs have a thin, solid back supporting an upholstered pillow or cushion. An attached pillow back is a solid upholstered back that gives the appearance of a loose pillow back.

Tufting or *buttoning* — Divides a surface into diamond-shaped sections by tying four corners together tightly to form a mound.

Channeling or *fluting* — A decorative finish for back or seats of upholstered pieces. Grooves or channels are built into the stuffing as it is attached to a back or seat. These channels should be uniform in size and width, about three to five inches wide.

Channeled pad — A series of channels built on a base of burlap and tacked into the frame.

Railroading — When the fabric is placed sideways on an upholstered piece in order to avoid visible cuts and seams. This can only be done when the pattern permits.

Decking — Less expensive material used on the seat under a cushion to save money in cover fabric cost. It extends from the back rail to the back of the hard or spring edge and runs across from one side rail to the other.

Sofa bed or *convertible bed* — A sofa or love-seat that opens into a single, double, or queen bed.

Reversible cushions — Loose seat or back cushions which have the same upholstery material on both sides and can be turned over to distribute wear.

Self-covered seat deck — A term used when matching upholstery is used on the surface of the seat on which the cushions are placed. Expensive furniture has self-covered seat decks, while inexpensive furniture has muslin.

Spring edge — The seat springs when they are extended to the front of the seat deck, enabling it to move up and down under pressure. It gives added comfort.

Tailored edge — The term used when springs do not edge the seat platform.

Banding — A narrow piece of fabric that is hand sewn to cover the spring edge of a seat. It shapes the spring edge and reduces the puffiness of the side of the seat.

Border — A strip of fabric, with welting or without, that serves the same function as banding but is installed differently.

Boxing — A thin piece of material that is machine sewn to a cover to accommodate the edges of surfaces and allow a cover to be formfitted.

Panel or *facing* — A strip of material tacked over a piece of shaped board and fastened to the frame.

Ruching — A pleated trimming inserted along an outside edge. It's made from a double thickness of fabric that is box pleated and banded by welting.

Skirts — Usually added to sofas and chairs as decoration. They can be made of the same material or contrasting material, and are usually lined with muslin or sateen. The top edge is usually welted. Skirts can be either flanged, box-pleated, or shirred.

Trims — The finish details of an upholstered piece. They can be buttons, gimps, fringe, double welts, or antique nails.

Gimps — Used on upholstered pieces that have exposed wood surfaces to hide the edges of the cover and the upholstery tacks. They are usually applied with glue.

Furniture "Facelifting"

SLIPCOVERING

Slipcovering is the least expensive way to turn old upholstered pieces into new. The structure of the old piece is left untouched and a new removable cover is made that fits right over the piece. I've seen exciting treatments done on slipper chairs, dining room chairs, and old sofas with flowing slipcovers that are tied at four corners to create a draped effect.

REUPHOLSTERING

Reupholstering can be a good money-saving alternative to buying new furniture. Use only original frames that are of high quality construction. First, go shopping to price new pieces to find out whether reupholstering your old piece is cost effective. Consider the condition of the frame. Is it cracked or warped? Does it need to be cut down or restyled? Does the piece need new cushions or new filling? Do you need to add to existing fillings? Do the springs need to be retied? How much new fabric will you need? Consider the cost of the new fabric, along with pickup and delivery charges and sales tax. If, after shopping, comparing, and getting several bids from reputable upholsterers, you are convinced it's cheaper to reupholster, by all means, go ahead.

RESTYLING

Restyling an old piece will create a completely new piece of furniture. The existing frame can be altered, made longer or shorter, and additional rails and posts can be attached to form a new shape. You can change the depth of a seat, or heighten or lower it, as well as change the type and number of cushions. You can restyle the arms, changing them to any shape you desire. Wings can be added or removed. The back can be heightened or lowered, widened or thickened, or completely reshaped. While upholstery fabric is being changed, you can add tufting, channeling, or quilting. Make sure you select a reputable upholstery shop and provide them with the same drawings and specifications that you would if you were designing a completely new piece.

Making a Final Decision

It's time to choose or revamp the right pieces. Whether you've opted to shop the furniture stores and design centers, brave having custom pieces made, or are reupholstering your existing pieces, the criteria are the same.

• Pull out your furniture plan and make a list of the pieces you will need to buy or redo. Now's the time to make any necessary changes to the plan. Perhaps your reading has prompted you to consider a chaise longue instead of a loveseat, or a bergere chair instead of a large, clumsy upholstered chair. Maybe you want to put a daybed in the guest room instead of two twin beds, or substitute a banquette for some of the chairs in your dining room. Now that new sources and concepts have opened up for you, make sure that the upholstered pieces you've planned are up to date.

• Shop the furniture stores and design center, and examine interior design magazines. Collect pictures and catalogs as you go along. Compare prices and quality. If you like the arms on one sofa, the cushions on another, the back on another, and the quilting on yet another, visualize combining all of these ingredients. Play around with drawing the piece the way you visualize it to see if those elements work well together. Once you're convinced you have a thorough knowledge of what's available

and what's not, you can decide whether to buy the piece directly from a furniture store or showroom or have it custom made. Get several bids from custom upholsterers to see whether having the piece custom made is feasible for your budget. If not, make the compromises you must make and buy the piece that best suits your ideal.

• Comfort is the primary concern in any type of seating. This is a negative aspect to custom-made pieces, as you have no idea how comfortable they will be until they're already made and non-returnable. If you buy a piece from a store or showroom, make sure that you sit in it and get the feel of it. If it feels comfortable, and you're satisfied with the quality of the inner construction, great. When designing your own custom pieces, it's a good idea to find other sofas that are comfortable to you and match the seating dimensions. Seat depths vary and can greatly affect the comfort of a sofa or chair.

• Next, consider scale. Make sure the piece is the right scale and size for the room. You should have the exact measurements that you will need from your furniture plan. If a ready-made sofa, loveseat, chaise longue, upholstered bed, chair, or ottoman is not the exact size you had planned on your furniture plan, don't buy it yet. Get the exact dimensions of the piece and go home and redraw it on the plan to make sure it will fit properly.

• Is the piece the right look for the room? Make sure you aren't breaking the design rules we've gone over by choosing a piece that is incongruous with the feel of your home. Ultra modern sofas look ridiculous in traditional rooms, as do traditional sofas in ultra modern rooms.

• Consider the drama of the piece. Does it provide just the right amount of drama the room needs? Is it overpowering? Too dramatic? Will it blend in or stand out from the rest of your furniture?

• Next, if you're buying a piece from a furniture store, is the fabric you're obliged to live with acceptable and versatile? If you get to choose from the manufacturer's different grades of fabrics, are the choices the right ones for you? If you're having the piece custom made, did you select the right type of fabric for the piece? Very heavy fabrics don't work well for shirring and skirts. Lighter fabrics don't work well on pieces with loose cushions, as they tend to pucker and wrinkle. Make sure you've selected the right fabric for the right piece.

• Does the sofa or loveseat have throw pillows that come with it or do you have to have them made separately? How many throw pillows should you use? What size should they be? Most sofas and loveseats don't come with throw pillows. The number and size of the pillows you select depends on the look that you want to achieve. More traditional pieces generally have fewer and smaller throw pillows. The more modern pieces sport an overabundance of very large pillows.

• The general rule of thumb for more modern sofas is that the pillows should extend a few inches over the top of the back. Make sure the pillows aren't so large that they fall over the back or you can't sit on the sofa because the pillow takes up so much space. Most modern sofas are made deeper nowadays to compensate for the thickness of pillows. Make sure you've allowed for this adjustment in depth on your furniture plan. Make sure you order enough additional yardage for the throw pillows. Most furniture manufacturers will make up extra pillows for you if you order them at the same time you order the piece.

What's Hot? What's Not?

• The "artsy-craftsy" look is in for upholstered pieces.

• For contemporary pieces, channeling and tufting are hot.

• Overscaled upholstered pieces are still a major trend.

• Arm covers are out.

Dollar-Stretching Idea

Update an old sofa; slipcover it by tossing a sheet over, wrap and tie with decorative cording; and/or remove the back cushions and replace with new, large fluffy pillows.

14
Choosing Your Flooring

Now it's time to decide whether you want soft flooring, hard flooring, or a combination of both. Soft floor coverings include wall-to-wall carpeting and area rugs placed over harder surfaces. Ask yourself the following questions to determine your practical needs before you set your heart on a flooring that won't work.

- Where is the flooring to be placed?
- What are your options?
- What are the maintenance problems, if any, of each of your options?
- Will you be covering sub-floors? Poor existing floors?
- Will you be covering or using existing quality flooring?
- How much and what kind of foot traffic will the flooring need to withstand?
- What activities are going to take place in that area?
- Are there any special considerations you should make for very young children, elderly people, handicapped people, or people with allergies?
- Will any pets create problems?
- Should any floorings have special features for specific hobbies or leisure uses?
- What is the comfort level that is important to your and your family?

- What are the soundproofing qualities of the flooring?
- What is the initial purchase cost of the flooring? The continued maintenance costs? The eventual replacement costs?
- Is the material you are selecting durable?
- How long are you going to live in the home?
- Will you be using the home all year round?
- Are there any heat, cold, or moisture problems that will affect the type of flooring you select?
- What aspects will please you aesthetically and go with the interior of your home? Color? Space? Style? Period? Personal taste?

Your decision should be based on how you answered the above questions. Wall-to-wall carpeting and area rugs create warmth and softness in a room as well as adding texture, sound insulation, and intimacy. Hard surface floorings such as wood, tile, and vinyl are more appropriate for higher traffic areas or rooms where there's a good chance of spilling and staining.

Let's examine your flooring options.

Carpeting

Carpeting is a thick and heavy fabric made in long rolls of standard widths. It comes in either

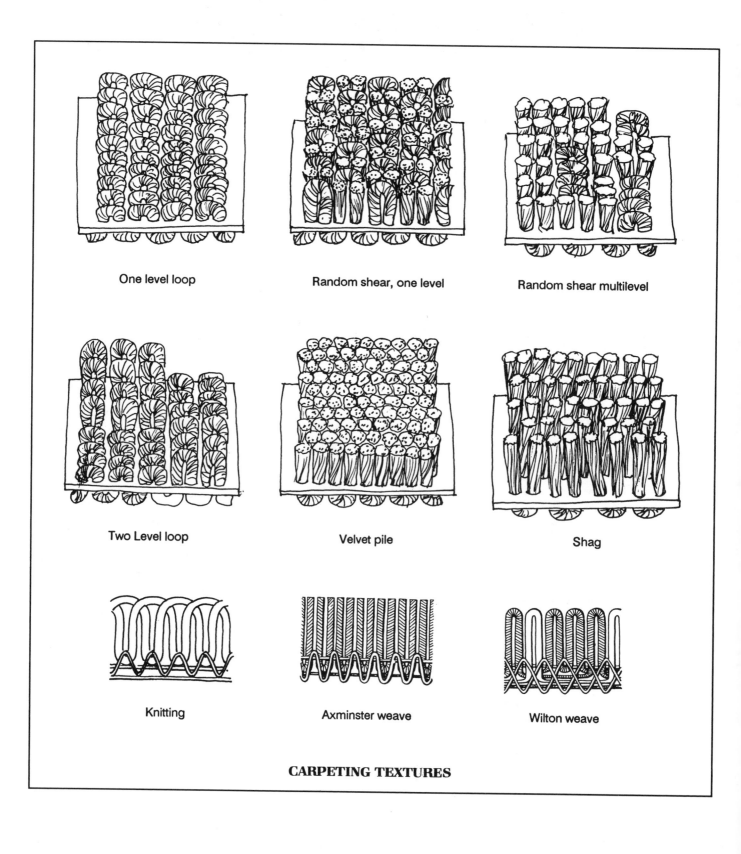

One level loop

Random shear, one level

Random shear multilevel

Two Level loop

Velvet pile

Shag

Knitting

Axminster weave

Wilton weave

CARPETING TEXTURES

natural or manmade fibers and is sold by the yard. Prices vary greatly.

The pile is the surface that's created by making yarn loops and untwisting the yarn to achieve a plush look. Cut pile is made by shearing the loops, then untwisting the yarn. Uncut pile retains the yarn loops, creating a pebble-like, harder texture. Cut and uncut pile combinations use both techniques to achieve interesting textures and patterns. Sculptured pile is made by fastening the yarn loops at different heights to form patterns. A flat pile is a carpeting without any pile and with the same texture on both sides.

CARPET CONSTRUCTION

Carpeting can be woven, knit, tufted, or needle punched. Woven carpeting is made by intertwining the surface pile and the backing together. Most carpeting manufacturers use standard weaves.

Axminster has an even pile height, a heavily-ribbed back, and comes in a limitless array of multi-colored patterns. Care must be taken in installing Axminster so the nap runs in the same direction because it is woven in only one direction.

Chenille has a dense pile and depth. It comes in a variety of designs, colors, and widths. It is very expensive because two loom operations are necessary in order to produce it.

Velvet is a simpler weave that comes in various pile types, heights, and textures. It can be looped or plush and have a cut or uncut pile. It can be a solid color or a mixture of colors.

Wilton weave is made on a Jacquard loom. It is usually a combination of five or six different colors, each being pulled into the loom separately. Wilton weave is a quality carpet with strength and resilience. It can have any pile height: cut, looped, or any combination.

Knit carpeting is knit on machines with three sets of needles which loop the backing, stitching, and pile yarns together simultaneously. The pile can be cut at different levels or left uncut. Many solid colors, tweeds, patterns, and textures are now available on the market.

Tufted carpeting is produced by stitching tufts of carpet fiber through the backing material, then latex is applied to the back to bind the stitches more firmly. The quality of tufted carpeting is determined by the number of tufts per square inch.

Needle punching is done by machine with thousands of needles working together to interlock a fiber core and layers of loose fibers. It's an inexpensive felt-like carpeting generally sold for indoor-outdoor use. Don't confuse it with the extremely expensive custom needle-punched area rugs.

All carpeting has a backing, which is the foundation of the carpeting and supports the pile. It's usually made of jute, cotton, or kraft cord which is a tough yarn derived from wood pulp. Most carpeting has a second backing, which is a material affixed to the underside. These backings improve the stability, make the carpeting lie flat, and prevent stretching, rotting, and mildewing. The material used is matched to the construction of the carpeting. Embossed latex, sponge rubber, solid and foam-type vinyl, polyurethane foam, as well as acetate fibers and knit paper cloth are often used.

TEXTURE

Carpeting comes in a huge variety of textures that vary in popularity from year to year. Select your carpeting for its wear and tear qualities as well as its look.

Velvet cut piles that are all one length are popular and always in good taste. They feel cushiony when you walk on them, but have a tendency to show shadowing and footprints, and they soil easily. They'll also split and show their backing if you wrap them on stairs. Use velvet piles in low traffic areas.

Shags come in different lengths up to six inches. The backing shows when wrapped around stairs and the twisted yarn tends to mat and tangle terribly. Shags used to be very popular in the '60s, but they're a definite no-no now.

Random shears create a sculptured look with a surface of cut and uncut loops at different levels. Most random shears on the market are cheap looking and another definite no-no, especially if they're multi-colored.

Two-level loop piles have a patterned look achieved by cut and uncut loops at different levels and can look even more sculptured than random shears. I'm sorry, but these are a no-no, too.

One-level loop piles are the tightly woven uncut loops you see in commercial carpeting. More and more designers are using this type of carpeting for residential projects because of its modern, high tech look, and the way it stands up in high traffic areas. If your home tends toward modern, this type of carpeting is worth considering.

Berber carpeting is made up of uncut loops, usually in natural colors, although many pastels are appearing on the market. It varies from tight and flat to looser and bulkier. The originals were made exclusively out of 100% wool, but now Berbers are available in a variety of wool and acrylic blends. Berber carpeting is very "hot."

If the carpeting you select isn't wool, then it's obviously a manmade fiber. These fibers fall into four main categories: acrylics, rayon, nylon, and polypropylene. Each manufacturer has its own brand name for these fibers such as Acrilan, Antron, Orlon, Du Pont, and Herculon. There are a multitude of other brand names, all based on the four main categories.

PADDING

Padding protects your carpeting from the impact of footsteps and furniture, provides cushioning, reduces wear, insulates, reduces noise, and protects the backing fibers. Padding is usually made from hair, latex, foam rubber, sponge rubber, or urethane. Jute padding is used for commercial installations in which the carpeting is glued down.

Rubber padding is sold by the ounce and ranges from fifty ounce to a thick, luxurious 110 ounce version. It usually has a waffle-like appearance.

Foam rubber padding is non-allergenic and resists mildew. It comes in thicknesses ranging from 1/16″ to 7/16″. It's a great sound absorber and heat conductor.

Sponge rubber padding is more porous than foam rubber and makes a softer, springier cushion.

Urethane padding resists mildew and insects. It's graded for firmness per cubic inch and comes in grades of 5½ to 8 pounds. It should be at least ⅜″ thick.

Avoid paper-thin pads made of jute, sponge rubber, foam rubber, or shredded urethane as they will cause wear spots in carpeting. Your carpeting salesperson will be able to tell you which type of padding is right for the carpeting you select and your home's individual needs.

PURCHASING YOUR CARPETING

Ready to buy? If you're purchasing your carpeting through a retail or discount store, they'll usually quote you a price per yard which includes the carpeting, padding, delivery, and installation. If you are purchasing carpeting through a wholesale showroom or a carpet mill, they'll usually quote you a price per yard for the carpeting only. You must arrange to have the goods delivered, buy padding separately, and hire a carpet layer to install the carpeting. Usually, the carpet layer will pick up and deliver the carpeting for you as well as sell you the right padding.

Your carpeting supplier should quote you either a "cut price" or a "roll price," depending on the amount of yardage you order. The roll price is a small discount that you get for ordering a larger quantity. Ask.

If you've found the perfect carpeting but it doesn't come in the exact color you want, ask the salesperson if the carpet manufacturer will custom dye for you. Many manufacturers will custom dye for an additional set-up charge, which covers the cost of mixing dyes and setting up the loom. They'll charge a few dollars more per yard and insist upon a minimum order.

Carpeting comes in standard widths of nine feet, twelve feet, fifteen feet, and eighteen feet. I suggest you have the carpet layer of your choice come over and measure for the exact yardage you'll need to order. It's tricky to measure yourself and mistakes lead to major headaches. Remember, manufacturers make carpeting in runs that can be different dye lots, just like fabrics and wallpapers.

For the sake of estimating your budget only, here are the rules of thumb for measuring for carpeting.

1. Measure the length in feet of your room.
2. Measure the width in feet of your room.
3. Multiply the length by the width.
4. Divide that number by nine. You'll now have square yards.
5. For stairs, allow ¾ of a linear yard for each step. Then multiply ¾ yard by the number of stairs.

Please, use this method for estimating how much carpeting you'll need for budget purposes only. Don't order carpeting unless a professional carpet layer has given you the exact amount of yardage.

Now, before you write that salesperson a check, examine the carpeting again. Go over the following checklist to make sure you're buying the right carpeting.

• Check the measurements on your furniture plan with the carpet layer's estimate for yardage to make sure there are no major discrepancies.

• Check the denseness of the carpeting by folding it back and exposing the backing. Make sure the yarn is close together, in even rows, and the backing material is tight.

• The Federal Trade Commission requires the following information to be on the carpet sample label: name of manufacturer or distributor; FTC registration number or manufacturer's name; generic names of all the fibers contained in the carpet; the percentage of each fiber; if imported, the country where it was made. Check the label thoroughly.

• Examine the carpeting you're buying while it's on the floor with a sample of the padding you'll be using under it. Walk on it to make sure it's comfortable.

• Examine the twists of the strands of yarn. If they have a puffed look, the carpeting will not wear well. Multiple, tightly twisted strands of yarn or uncut loops will wear better.

Next, still hold on tight to that check and ask the salesperson, no matter how irritated he is getting, the following questions. (Carpeting is a major purchase and you have every right to know exactly what you're getting.)

• Ask the weight or amount of fiber per square foot if it isn't noted on the label. Weight is directly related to good wear.

• Ask if the carpet has a secondary backing if it's tufted.

• Ask what is included in the purchase price. The padding? The installation? Is there an extra charge for stairs? Will they supply metal stripping for the thresholds? If so, what kind and is there any additional charge?

• Ask if they've included sales tax on materials and labor or materials only. Sales tax laws differ from state to state.

• Ask about the warranty. Are the carpeting and labor guaranteed against stretching and buckling? Most reputable carpet companies will correct stretching and buckling caused by house settling and moving furniture for at least one year after the carpet has been installed.

• Ask about warranty for wear. Most manufacturers offer a standard material warranty for 10% wear within a certain time limit. This is actually ridiculous; how do you determine what "10% wear" consists of? Ask anyway, along with, "Who pays for the labor to replace it?" and "How much of the surrounding area will be replaced?"

• Find out who will install the carpet. Rest assured, the salesperson will tell you his company uses only the most skilled of carpet layers. But

Sculptured edge

All over

Medallion

Border

Random pattern

AREA RUGS

there isn't much you can do when a truckload of inexperienced, ham-handed workers show up at your doorstep instead.

• Ask the salesperson what additional guarantees his store will give you to stand behind its merchandise. He'll probably hem and haw.

• Make sure you ask whether the installers will take up your old carpeting and dispose of it for you. Ask if there are any additional costs for that service.

Now that you've made a total nuisance of yourself and the carpeting salesperson is ready to quit his job, it's time to order. Make sure you purchase a few extra yards in case some areas need to be replaced in the future. When your carpet arrives, check the information on the invoice and on the back of the actual carpeting to make sure it's the same information that was on the back of the original sample. Once in a while a supplier will send out a grade of carpeting different from the one you ordered and paid for.

Rugs

Call them what you please . . . area rugs, throw rugs, scatter rugs . . . there's a vast assortment available from every part of the world. The term "rug" generally applies to a handmade piece, while the term carpet refers to goods made by machine. Buy wall-to-wall carpeting and have it cut to any size, add borders, and have the edges bound. Or select from any number of types and patterns available, either inexpensive copies or valuable collector's items. Let your tastes, needs, and budget direct you.

Ideally, the size of the area rug you select is dictated by the size of your room. A large room with a large area rug should leave about a twelve inch border all around the room. In a small room eight inches is sufficient.

Make sure you draw your area rugs on your furniture plan in the exact spot where they will be placed. You'll know exactly what size you'll need before you begin shopping.

It's wise to deal only with well established, reputable rug dealers. There are many inferior copies on the market. If you plan on buying expensive rugs, take the time to study books on the subject, so you'll know the quality and authenticity of the rugs you're buying.

Oriental rugs are considered objets d'art and can increase in value. Before making this major purchase, know the place of origin and what conditions will affect the supply and demand for the rug. The price will be affected by the rarity of the rug, the quality of the wool that was used, the workmanship, the intricacy of the stitching, the quality of the warp and weft, the color, and any defects, as well as the general overall appearance. Size is not a major determinant in pricing Oriental rugs.

The wool of a fine Oriental rug comes from the shoulder area of an eight to fourteen month old lamb. It should be hand spun, strong, and springy to the touch. Some of the newer Oriental rugs are made with a cotton warp which then becomes the fringe that you can see.

The finest and most expensive of the Oriental rugs are made of silk or a combination of silk and wool. The silk has more knots per square inch and, in quality rugs, should be fine, even, and not woven at an angle.

Determine whether a rug is really handmade by examining the back. If the tension on the yarns is varied it means that more than one weaver worked on the rug by hand.

The color of an Oriental rug is a telltale sign of its authentic age. Types of dyes varied throughout the years and a well-read expert can tell from the type of dye used approximately what year the rug was made.

Rugs are always washed as part of their finishing process. Gold washing bleaches out reds to a silver or gold color and creates a sheen. However, the sheen may disappear and the rug may wear out quickly, which can decrease its value. Antique washing ages a rug artificially, it can usually be detected, and does not affect its price.

Chinese Oriental rugs are noted for their rich

deep pile. They usually have blue or tan designs and circles containing flowers or dragons.

American Oriental rugs look like hand-tied Oriental rugs but are machine made and given their sheen by washing with a chemical solution. They're usually made out of a high quality Axminster, Wilton, or velvet cut pile carpeting.

Persian rugs vary in design and color depending on what region they come from. Saruks, Hamodans, Kashans, and Kirmans, all named for the towns they come from, are known for their floral patterns but often have human or animal figures on them.

Turkish rugs have a longer pile, a coarser construction, and are noted for their simple geometric designs. You'll find Turkish rugs called Koula, Ladik, Bergoma, Milas, or Ghiordes.

Caucasian rugs, often called Shirvan, Kazak, Kabistan, or Karaja, are smaller in size than Turkish rugs and are known for their geometric designs with sharp outlines. They usually come in color combinations of red, blue, and yellow.

Turkoman rugs are known by their rows of octagonal medallions in a center field and their wide, pileless ends. They usually come in greens, reds, whites, and browns. You'll hear them referred to as Beshir, Bokhara, Turkoman, or Samarkand.

Kilim rugs are flatly woven Turkish prayer rugs. They have a tapestry-like appearance and come in bright, bold patterns. You can identify one by the small slits that show in the places where a new color is added to the design. Most are reversible, but rarer Kilims have loose ends on the back. Kilims are becoming increasingly valuable.

Indian rugs are either hand-tied from Punjab province or are Numdahs, which are smaller rugs made from felted goat hair and hand embroidered with the "tree of life" or floral or vine-like patterns. *Druggets* are simpler and more colorfully designed rugs made from the fleece of white-haired sheep.

Dhurries are cotton rugs from India. They come in a huge variety of combinations of light pastels or bright colors. Their patterns are unique and reversible. Dhurries are extremely "hot" right now

and can be found in any size or color you might need. Prices will vary with quality and size.

American Indian rugs are rising in popularity because of the trend in Southwestern decors. The originals were made on the reservations with traditional Navajo designs. A good book on Indian arts and crafts should teach you all you need to know about recognizing these rugs for their collector's value. There are many deceptive imitations on the market, so be careful.

Hand-carved rugs are becoming increasingly popular. Usually, a high quality velvet pile carpeting is cut in various shapes and forms and pieced together to form an overall design. Use any variety of colors or pattern to mix or match with your room's theme. Recently, I had a hand-carved rug made for a client that repeated the exact irises that were hand-painted on the drapery fabric. It's a wonderful but expensive way to pull together a room.

Shop around; there are a multitude of other variations of area rugs that would take an entire book to describe. If you're placing the rug on a hard flooring, be sure you buy a pad for the rug to add to its longevity and reduce slipping. If you buy a valuable rug, make sure you have a signed receipt for your insurance. Check the label for the same information you looked for on the label of the carpeting sample.

Buy only from a rug dealer that you trust implicitly. Ask him to spread out the rug so you can examine it for flaws, uneven edges, irregularities in color, wrinkles, or worn spots. A reputable dealer will tell you the history of the rug and any processes that were used in its construction.

I'm sure the next question you're bound to ask is, "Should I select the carpeting or rugs before I select the fabrics, wall coverings, and furniture?"

My professional advice is, "It depends." If you're using wall-to-wall carpeting, the selection of colors and types of carpeting is vast and you shouldn't have any difficulty matching up your fabrics and wall coverings. However, it's easier to select a carpeting first, especially if you'll be using hard to find colors. But, if worse comes to worst, you can always find a manufacturer who will custom dye your carpeting for you.

If you are going to be using area rugs, I suggest you always select the rugs before selecting the fabrics and wallpapers, as color combinations in the types of rugs and designs you'll want are limited, especially if they're antiques. It's extremely difficult to find a rug in the exact size and colors to match your fabrics and wallpapers. If you'll be using custom-made rugs, you'll have much more leeway.

Hard Flooring

Hard surface flooring, or resilient flooring, is a broad term encompassing a huge variety of materials. Again, let's examine your options and find out the pros and cons of each.

SHEET GOODS, TILE, AND OTHER NON-WOOD MATERIALS

Sheet goods are materials such as vinyl and linoleum that are sold in large rolls ranging from six to fifteen feet wide. A variety of different types and qualities are available.

Vinyl is a mixture of plasticizers, vinyl resin, pigments, and fillers that have been formed under pressure while hot. The more expensive vinyl sheeting comes with filled surfaces in which the pattern runs through the whole material. Vinyl laminate sheeting is even more costly. A laminate of clear vinyl is placed over any backing. You can have any fabric or wallpaper laminated and made into flooring. It's usually about ⅛" thick. Both types of vinyl sheeting will wear well, be resistant to dents and depressions, and the pattern will not wear away. The less expensive vinyl sheeting is unfilled, which means the color and/or pattern is printed or embossed on the surface. This type of vinyl sheeting won't wear as well. The surface will wear out quickly and the pattern will fade.

The positives of vinyl sheet floorings are that they are relatively inexpensive; they come in a wide variety of colors and patterns; they're resistant to most household chemicals, alkalis, denting, and chipping; and they're sound absorbent, resilient, and easy to maintain. These factors make vinyl sheeting a practical and economical choice for basement areas, children's play rooms, kitchens, and bathrooms.

The negatives of vinyl sheet flooring are all aesthetic. Generally, they come in patterns and colors that are outdated and common from the point of view of an interior designer. The usual vinyl sheeting is made to look like brick or tiles; unsuccessfully, in my opinion. Again, if you can afford it and it's practical, always use the real material instead of an imitation.

Vinyl tiles are made the same way as vinyl sheeting but come in boxes of squares, usually 9" by 9" or 12" by 12", although other sizes and shapes are available. Pure vinyl tiles are the most expensive and come in a variety of bright and clear colors. If installed by a professional, they'll be more expensive to install than vinyl sheeting because each piece must be laid separately.

Vinyl asbestos tiles are a combination of vinyl and asbestos. They're more expensive than plain asbestos tile and less expensive than pure vinyl tiles. They're very resistant to moisture, grease, and alkalis. Some come with self-adhesive backing, making them easy to install if you're a do-it-yourselfer.

Asphalt tiles are the least expensive. They come in a limited range of colors and stain easily from grease. They're usually used in very heavy traffic areas in public buildings.

The advantage of vinyl tiles over vinyl sheet flooring is the range of designs you can create with them. Make center designs, overall designs such as checkerboards, or borders to frame contrasting tiles.

The negatives of vinyl tiles over sheet flooring are that seams will be predominant, collect dirt, and the edges often curl if the tiles are not installed properly or if saturated with too much water.

Shop around and see what's new on the market. Updated and more modern vinyl tiles and sheeting are being introduced every day. Consider these options for inexpensive to moderately priced flooring for areas such as basements, kitchens, bathrooms, children's play rooms, and laundry rooms.

Linoleum is made from wood flour, ground cork, pigments, oxidizer oils, and resins, and usually has a burlap or felt backing. It comes standard in 9″ by 9″ tiles or in rolls varying in width from six to fifteen feet. A low cost flooring, the selection of colors and patterns is limited and the colors are not as clear as vinyls. Although linoleum is grease resistant and resilient, it doesn't wear as well as vinyl and will be affected by alkalis when laid directly on a concrete floor. It's relatively easy to keep clean, but will need to be waxed frequently. Considering the labor costs to install flooring, I suggest you don't select linoleum, as its aesthetic value in home decorating is questionable.

Linolite is similar to linoleum, but two and a half times thicker. It was created for maximum wear resistance and is used primarily in commercial jobs.

Asphalt tiles are made from asbestos fibers, fillers, pigments, and resin binders. They usually come in standard 9″ by 9″ squares. The least expensive of all the flooring we've discussed, they're really only suitable for basements and recreation rooms because they stain easily and are hard to maintain, and not very attractive.

Rubber flooring is made from rubber, fillers, and curing chemicals. It comes in a variety of tile sizes ranging from 9″ by 9″ squares to 18″ by 36″ rectangles as well as in sheeting. Its colors tend to be brighter and clearer than vinyl tiles. There are many new high tech designs on the market that look fabulous when first installed. However, rubber flooring can be easily damaged by strong detergents, cleaning fluids, grease, and strong sunlight. It can also be very slippery when wet.

Cork tiles are made from granulated cork that's compressed with resin binders, wax, and cork curlings. They generally come in standard sizes of 9″ by 9″ or 12″ by 12″ squares, as well as some rectangular sizes. They can be used for light traffic areas, but not directly on concrete or below grade floors. The negative of cork tiles is that they must be sealed and finished right after they are installed. When the finish wears off, the cork can become porous and deteriorate. Although they're an excellent sound absorber, they dent easily and absorb dirt.

Brick floors can be used alone in one of the many patterns or mixed with other flooring such as wood, concrete, or railroad ties, especially in areas where you're relating the outdoors to the indoors.

Bricks can be very rough or very smooth and come in a variety of thicknesses ranging from ¼″ to 1½″. In order to lay thicker, heavier bricks you must install a subflooring first. You can find special ¼″ high-fired bricks that have been pre-sealed for indoor use. Other brick flooring needs special waxing or a seal of vinyl to protect and seal it as well as give it a softer, smoother feel and finish. But beware, indoor brick flooring can be cold on the feet and a noise bouncer.

Stone flooring becomes an expensive, permanent architectural feature of your home. Stones come in a wide range of types, colors, and sizes. Again, some of the most exciting floors I've seen are either plain stone floors or stone floors mixed with hardwood. Although easy to maintain by sweeping and mopping, stone does chip and crack easily and is difficult to repair.

Flagstone is a durable stone that comes in irregular shapes and can be sealed or left unsealed. It used to be popular, but it isn't "in" anymore.

Terrazzo is a mixture of marble chips and mortar that either comes in 12″ by 12″ squares or can be custom installed in any size. Like flagstone, it used to be popular, but it's a no-no now.

Slate comes in a variety of colors: charcoal, black, blue-green, green, purple-red. It must be highly waxed as it absorbs and shows stains easily. Once again, it's no longer "in."

Marble has made a great comeback recently. It comes in a variety of sizes ranging from 12" by 12" tiles to any custom size within the realm of the original material. It must be well polished, waxed, and sealed to prevent staining and to show off its excellent patina. Marble comes in a wide assortment of colors and veining, ranging from stark whites and peachy rusts to deep greens. Some are domestic, others are imported from Europe. Qualities vary. If you want an elegant flooring, whether your tastes are traditional or modern, check out what's new in marble; it's a definite "yes."

Cement and concrete floors generally can only be poured in a limited number of colors, but can either be painted or waxed with colored wax to deepen the color and give it a lustrous surface appearance. They're durable, but cracks and chips can happen easily and are difficult to repair. They're also hard and cold on bare feet and bounce noise easily. Generally used in commercial jobs, they're becoming more and more popular in homes if they're colored and waxed effectively and warmed up with area rugs.

Cement tiles are being used more and more as a less expensive alternative to stone, clay, or marble tiles. They can be custom made in any shape or color, or poured and then scored to create patterns that can look like different types of stones. Although cold and hard on bare feet, they're durable and can be used for heavy traffic areas.

Ceramic tiles are made from heat-hardened clay. Floor tiles are made from denser red clays with flecks of minerals or metals in them. Wall tiles are made from less dense white clays. Most tiles are glazed, which seals the clay while it's being fired at a high temperature.

There is an incredibly large assortment of tiles on the market, ranging in size, shape, color, pattern, durability, and quality. Some tiles chip, crack, and fade easily. It's important to buy your tiles from a reputable source who will be honest about the quality of the tiles. Before you buy a tile, ask whether it's appropriate for flooring and if there are specific installation instructions. Some tiles are only to be used on walls and will not withstand foot traffic. Other tiles are too heavy to be placed on walls. Hand-painted tiles usually show wear and fade easily. They're more appropriate for walls and counter tops. When selecting tiles for flooring, make sure they're textured for non-slipping. There's nothing more slippery and dangerous than a slick Italian tile when wet.

Pavers are usually made from clay and either sun dried or kiln dried. They're great for carrying the outdoors into the indoors, but must be sealed properly.

Mexican pavers are still made by hand and dried in open fields and fired in primitive ovens. Characteristically, they're about one inch thick, warped and uneven. They'll cost less than most other tiles, but you'll have to order about 20% more than you need in order to compensate for defective tiles and tiles broken during shipping. When installed and sealed properly, they can give an older home an authentic feel and last a lifetime.

Mexican tiles are now also being made more commercially. These tiles are stronger and less porous and can be purchased pre-stained.

HARDWOOD FLOORS

Hardwood floors have always been popular; they're here to stay. The trend has been towards lighter, bleached wood floors. If your home is older, check underneath old carpeting and flooring to see if the home was originally built with hardwood floors. If so, you're in luck. Old wood floors can be stripped, bleached, sanded, pieced, filled in, and stained to look like brand new floors. If you decide to make use of your old wood floors, make sure you get at least three bids from wood flooring refinishers. Check their references and personally take the time to look at recent jobs they've completed.

If you're not as lucky and must go to the expense of putting in all brand new wood floors,

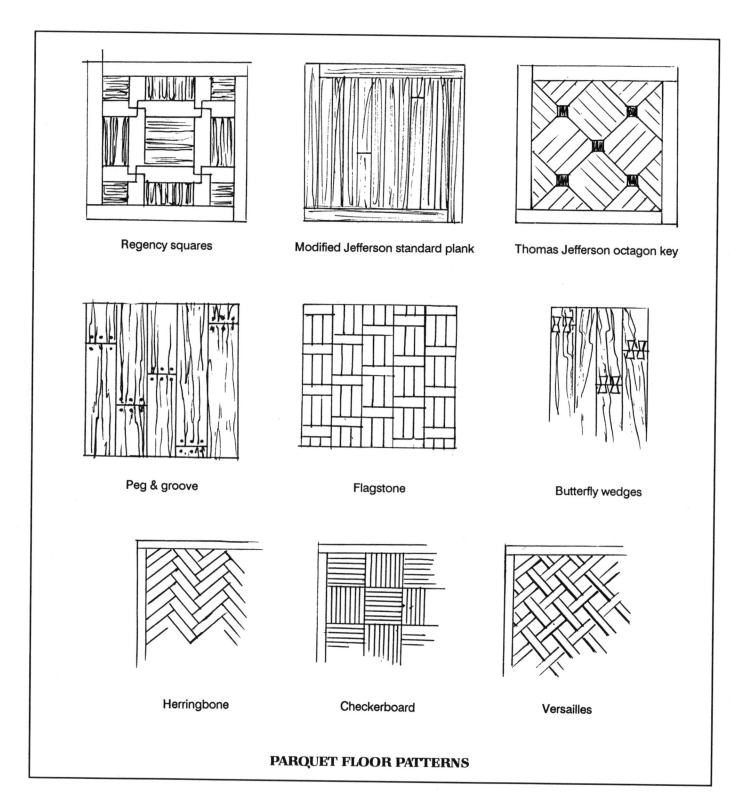

Regency squares

Modified Jefferson standard plank

Thomas Jefferson octagon key

Peg & groove

Flagstone

Butterfly wedges

Herringbone

Checkerboard

Versailles

PARQUET FLOOR PATTERNS

the good news is that your options are limitless. There are many different qualities of wood and workmanship, so research it thoroughly. If you're ready to make an investment in beauty and long wear, choose from the fine-grained hardwoods such as oak, maple, or walnut. If you'd like a more rustic look, choose a soft wood such as pine. Soft woods mark and distress easily, and look wonderful with a country decor.

Materials can be purchased in squares, blocks, and strips. Use an experienced professional who will know how to install and create any number of designs and patterns using these materials. Some manufacturers sell pre-patterned squares or other shapes in a variety of surface treatments ranging in size from eighteen inch squares to thirty-six inch squares. Choose a pattern in either a smooth, formal finish; a beveled V-groove for a stronger looking pattern; wire brushed to accentuate the texture and give a weathered look; distressed, which gives the wood the look of being aged; or pegged, where square pegs are inserted to give the wood an antique pattern. Select one or more of these treatments. These floors come unfinished and can be custom stained on the job.

A good wood floor installer can create pegged and grooved planks, checkerboards, herringbones, or planks laid on the diagonal using materials bought from a local lumber yard.

Some companies make products that stand up better in high traffic areas and are usually used in commercial installations. One company makes a solid wood flooring that is acrylic impregnated. The wood is permeated with a liquid acrylic that purportedly makes it ten times stronger than untreated wood. A vinyl-bonded wood flooring, available for homes, is made by sealing genuine wood veneers beneath permanently bonded transparent vinyl. Both of these floorings come in a variety of woods, finishes, and patterns.

Of course, if your budget is limited, you can always opt for the pre-patterned and stained wood squares that come with a cheesecloth backing. Or use the thinner wood squares that usually come prefinished with a pre-applied adhesive that you can install yourself. Shop around to see what's available and compare costs. Be cautious about laying a wood floor that looks too cheap and pre-made.

When installing a wood floor consider the thickness of the wood you're using. Some woods are very thick and will require a subflooring and/or thresholds to even out the heights to match adjoining flooring.

Use a professional to finish your floors; it's tricky and messy. She can bleach the floor, tint it with a colored water-based stain, and then seal it with a paste wax. If you want a shinier look, she can use wood-toned or colored oil-based stains and finish it with a urethane. Other finishes may need varnishes and shellacs. Discuss the look and feel you want with your floor finisher and have her prepare a sample for your approval before you let her finish the entire floor. Yes, you can use wood floors in kitchens and bathrooms if they're sealed and waxed correctly.

If you can't afford real wood floors, you'll find many vinyl copies on the market. In my opinion, these copies look like exactly what they are — cheap copies. If you're wise, you'll pass on them and choose another type of flooring.

Saving Money

If money's no object, skip this section. If you've got a tight budget like most of us, read on. There are many ways of achieving the look and quality you want without spending a small fortune.

• Know your sources. Carpeting prices and qualities vary. Bargains can be found either by buying wholesale, buying directly from a carpet mill, finding an outlet that specializes in disposing of odd lots, or locating sources of quality used carpeting. Check your city's Business-to-Business Yellow Pages and your source books. Scan your local newspapers to find ads for sales and used carpeting.

• Find bargain area rugs by shopping garage

sales, estate sales, and newspaper ads. Import stores often carry inexpensive copies of Dhurries and Oriental rugs that, when mixed artfully with finer furniture, are almost undetectable. Make your own area rug by buying a small remnant of carpeting and having the edges trimmed and bound.

• For hard surface flooring, do your homework. Comparative shopping can pay off. Once you've chosen the flooring you want, call around to get competitive bids. Check to see if your city has an outlet that specializes in odd lots of vinyl flooring that you might be able to use in smaller, less obvious areas of your home. Often, you can buy undetectable seconds and odd lots of tile directly from the manufacturer. Larger manufacturers often have yearly sales where they dispose of tiles that have been discontinued.

• Reassess what you already have before buying anything new. Old carpeting that's faded or the wrong color but still in good condition can be professionally dyed. Old tiles and wood floors can be painted to look brand new. Your money might be best spent purchasing a new area rug to throw over old flooring. Be creative.

• Don't be afraid to cover an old worn-out kitchen floor with a brand new area rug. (Make sure you use a rubber pad under it to prevent slipping.)

• Paint an old wood floor. Use one of the exciting finishes discussed in Chapter 9. Create painted marble or other faux finish borders for a new "hot" look.

• Use stone and cement floors; they're inexpensive and "in."

• Paint a zebra on your floor!

What's Hot, What's Not?

Now that we've examined your options, and I've even told you about types of flooring I wouldn't dream of putting into my worst enemy's house, let's find out what's "in" and what's "out."

• Berber carpeting is the rage right now. The larger and bulkier the loop, the better, and of course, the more expensive.

• Low cut velvet piles are still popular and widely used, with the trend being two-colored weaves in which one color seems to disappear in some lights.

• Tightly woven wool commercial carpeting is being used more and more in modern homes with a high tech feel.

• Neutral beiges and grays are here to stay.

• Dhurries in pastel colors thrown on bleached wood floors are still the rage.

• Plush velvet carved area rugs are forging ahead for more opulent rooms.

• Oriental rugs are here to stay for antique and eclectic room lovers.

• American Indian rugs are up and coming, in high demand.

• Colorful rag rugs have also been in now for a couple of years and still look great in very homey, rustic rooms.

• High tech rubber flooring with raised geometric patterns is also hot right now. Use it instead of vinyl for a more updated look.

• Tile floors are in. Use wide grout with cruder handmade tiles; use narrow grout with machine made tiles.

• Stone and cement floors are new and very hot.

• Any opulent flooring is hot. Mixing wood and marble is the hottest.

• Black and white checkerboard floors always look great. They're here to stay.

• Bleached or dark-stained hardwood floors are in. Medium and honey-colored floors are out.

• Dusty pink and forest green carpeting has seen better days.

• Vinyl flooring is great for home builders who want to cut corners and make a quick buck, but if you really want your home to look professionally decorated, choose natural materials whenever possible.

• Overly patterned vinyl flooring is really out. If you must use vinyl tiles or sheet flooring, keep it simple, using color and contrasting borders to give your room a lift.

- Indoor-outdoor carpeting is out.
- Linoleum is really out.
- Brick flooring is passé. (Anything brick is passé.) Paint all brick a mat or gloss!
- Shag carpeting is old and tacky. Throw it out!
- Different colored carpeting in different rooms, especially when they butt up against each other, is a no-no. If you can't afford to replace all the carpeting in one color, run hardwood or tile down a hallway to separate the colors.

Before You Buy

- Be sure to take a floor plan of the room along with you. Have the salesperson double check the amount of materials you will need from your plan. Always have the installer measure on the job before you order.
- If you are planning to install the flooring yourself, get complete instructions on how to install and what adhesive to use. Ask the supplier about the tools you will need and where you can get them.
- Make sure you order extra tiles or carpeting. Ask installers to leave you all leftover sheet goods.
- Make sure the supplier and/or installer will pull up your old flooring and dispose of it. Ask if there is any additional charge for this service.
- Ask about warranties and guarantees of the product. How long are they in effect?
- Ask exactly what is included in the price. For wood flooring, ask for a breakdown of the price that includes installing thresholds, staining, finishing, and sealing. For tile work, find out if the price you are quoted is per square foot or per tile. Ask if there is any additional charge for the extra labor involved in more elaborate tile designs.
- If you are using stone, ask the dealer what sealer should be used on the stone.
- Ask about continued maintenance of your flooring. Will there be any professional maintenance services required later? What products should be used? How often? What products should be avoided?

15
Choosing Your Window Coverings

One of the most frequent calls I get for consultations is a desperate client declaring, "I'm stumped. I just don't know how to cover my windows. Can you please just come over and give me some ideas?" It seems that window coverings, along with lighting, are the most difficult choices an inexperienced designer faces.

Let's analyze your window covering needs, going step by step to select the right treatments which will be both functional and visually pleasing.

First, ask yourself the following questions about the function the window covering must serve.

• Is the window covering going to be used to frame a view? Be honest, is the view worth showing off? Is it a magnificent view of mountains and canyons, a panoramic view of the city skyline, an impressive garden? If the answer to any of these questions is yes, make sure you select a window treatment that doesn't obstruct the view and can be pulled back or up to expose the view when privacy isn't necessary.

• Will you be using the room primarily in the daytime or night time? If there's no view, the blackness of the night can be cold and foreboding. You'll need a treatment that completely covers the window. If you'll be using the room in the daytime,

you'll need a treatment that lets in sufficient natural lighting. If you use the room in both day and night, you'll need a treatment that's flexible and adjustable to control light and privacy easily.

• Is the window treatment necessary for your complete privacy? If the answer is yes, you might want to consider a more permanent type of window covering, such as screens or shutters. If the answer is no, you might even want to consider having no window covering at all.

• Are the existing window sizes and shapes a problem? We'll go over a list of the major types of windows in this chapter and discuss how to overcome the difficulty of covering them.

• Are there any obstructions that create problems, such as architectural beams, columns, air conditioners, vents, or radiators?

• Does the window covering you're considering match the style and mood of the room and house? The fabrics and styles you choose should definitely reflect the formality or informality of the room.

• Is it necessary for each window covering to look the same from the outside? Yes, in the sense that the exterior of the house should look well balanced and the color of the window treatments that show on the outside should be uniform. But it's perfectly all right to use several different types of

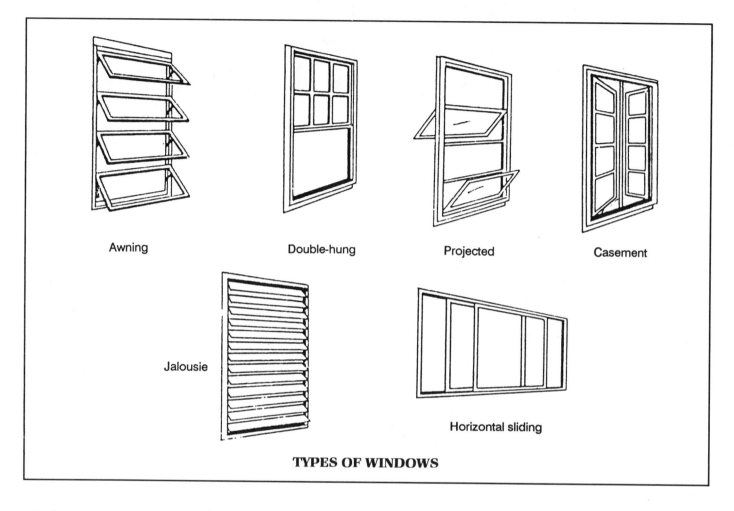

Awning   Double-hung   Projected   Casement

Jalousie

Horizontal sliding

TYPES OF WINDOWS

window coverings within the same house, as long as they relate to the house and the rooms don't look out of place, either from the inside or outside. However, it rarely if ever looks good to use different window coverings in the same room.

Windows are placed in walls for three reasons: to let in light, to ventilate a room, and to show a view. Most windows are movable, which means that the ventilation can be controlled. Fixed windows are used most frequently in commercial buildings that are centrally air conditioned. Your windows will have either metal, wood, or plastic frames. Metal frames are the strongest and don't shrink or swell. If the metal is anything other than

aluminum or stainless steel, it must be painted. Wood frames are more traditional and must be protected by paint to avoid shrinking and swelling. Plastic-framed windows are becoming increasingly popular because of the variety of finishes they now come in and their ability to withstand heat and cold.

Types of Windows

Let's go over the type of windows you're either blessed with or stuck with. We'll discuss your options — what will work, what won't.

Double-hung windows usually have two sashes. A sash is the movable part of a window or the frame that holds the panes together and can slide up or down. These types of windows are rarely put into new homes because they have many disadvantages: only one-half of the window can be opened at a time, rain can come in easily, they're difficult to clean from the inside, and they have a small, "chopped up" look.

Horizontal sliding windows work on the same premise as double-hung windows, but are placed on their sides. You'll see horizontal sliding windows with metal sliding frames used often in bedrooms of apartment buildings. These windows have the same negatives as double-hung windows. They always appear to be disproportionate to the wall and are extremely awkward to cover effectively.

Casement windows are the multi-paned windows that are hinged at one side and can swing either in or out. They can be opened or closed to adjust air circulation by a hand-controlled crank. Casement windows that swing in get in the way of furniture. Casement windows that swing out are dangerous to passersby, won't keep the rain out, and rarely can be completely waterproofed.

Projected windows look like casement windows, but are hinged at the top or the bottom. They can easily be adjusted for ventilation and do offer protection from rain and snow, but projected windows are difficult to open and close and collect dust easily.

Jalousie windows are made of narrow strips of glass or plastic-like shutters that can be adjusted easily. However, they obstruct views, are difficult to clean, and are rarely weatherproof.

Bay windows are windows set in frames which project outward from a wall and create a recess in the interior. They're usually a fixed window, but sometimes they're made with removable sections. Bay windows are generally found in more traditional homes and are wonderful for creating window seating.

Clerestory windows are windows or groups of windows placed between two roof levels that allow light into a room with very high ceilings. Usually these windows are left uncovered as they rarely affect privacy.

Skylights are windows made of reinforced glass or transparent or translucent plastic that let light in through a roof.

Garden windows are becoming increasingly popular. You'll see them most often inset over the sink area of kitchens. They protrude out to extend a room and let in more light while providing a great decorative treatment and opening up a room. Garden windows come ready made in a variety of shapes and sizes, most with fixed panes, but some are available with removable panes.

Cathedral windows are windows that have a slant at the top to follow a roof line. They meet the roof line in rooms with ceilings higher than one story.

Dormer windows are built out from a sloping roof and give air and light to a top floor room or attic.

Lunettes are half-moon shaped windows above doors or other windows.

Fanlights are semi-circular windows over doors or windows that have radiating sash bars that look like the ribs of a fan.

Types of Doors

What about exterior doors? They'll need to be covered, too. Yes, they should match the treatments you use on the windows. Let's go over what type of doors you might have to work with.

Sliding glass doors are by far the most prevalent type. Better sliding doors slide on both an overhead and floor track. These doors can be large and expansive and are widely used in modern homes as doors to dramatic backyards and patios.

Dutch doors are doors that are divided into two sections. The top half is usually made up of window panes and the bottom half is solid. Each section can be opened and closed separately.

French doors are becoming increasingly popular. Many people are tearing out their standard sliding glass doors and installing French doors to

Cartridge pleated heading with tie-back drapery

Dutch curtains

Cafe curtains

Sunburst with rosette covering a lunette and stretched curtains over French doors

Double-swag heading with cascades

Swag and floor-length cascades with sheer undercurtain

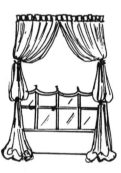

Double tiebacks, poufed and puddled with scalloped under-shade

Sunburst over double-tiebacks, poufed and puddled

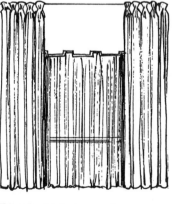

French pleated over-drapes over banded shades and sheers

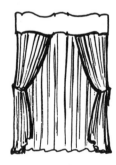

Lambrequin valance over tiebacks and sheers

TYPES OF WINDOW COVERINGS

blend with almost any decor. Basically, they're a pair of wood-framed, multi-paned doors that can open either in or out. They come ready made in a variety of styles, widths, and heights. The unfinished frames can be painted any color. Aesthetically one of the most pleasing and "in" types of doors, they do present some covering problems which we'll discuss later.

Getting itchy? Ready to make some decisions and move on with your decorating? Stop a minute and analyze the situation.

- What type of window or door will you be covering?
- What is the purpose of covering the window or door? Purely decorative? Ventilation? Showing off or blocking a view? Regulating or filtering light? Privacy? Sound absorption? Heat and cold insulation?
- What are the cost factors? Can you make some of the coverings yourself? Can you use less expensive treatments in some areas in order to cut costs? Are you willing to settle for ready-made window coverings for some of your standard size windows?
- Do the window coverings you have your heart set on match the style and decor of your home?

Read on, you'll be able to answer these questions more easily once we've gone over the many types of window coverings you have to choose from.

Curtains

Curtains are layers of lightweight fabric placed on traverse rods or stationary rods.

Sheers are very lightweight curtains. The fabric is thin and fine.

Shirred curtains are plain curtains that have been gathered across the top. They hang next to a window and are not usually placed on traverse rods.

Draw curtains can either be sheer or opaque and are hung on traverse rods.

Casement curtains are usually made out of a semi-sheer, open weave fabric and hung on traverse rods.

Stationary curtains, also called *under curtains* or *sash curtains*, are usually used under draperies and made out of very sheer fabric. They can be pulled back with either a tieback or a decorative ring.

Café curtains are double- or triple-tiered curtains that are shirred on a rod. They're usually short, window sill length, and hung with decorative rings and rods.

Ruffled tiebacks are shirred across the top and have ruffles on the edges. They're usually crisscrossed and tied back with a ruffled tieback.

Poufed curtains are gathered horizontally in several places, creating a series of puffs in the fabric. The puffs are held in place by either tiebacks, cords, or stitching to give the effect of tiers.

Stretched curtains are gathered on rods and stretched tightly from top to bottom. They're used predominantly on French doors and windows.

CURTAIN CONSTRUCTION

How your curtains are constructed and detailed is just as important as the actual types of curtains and fabrics you select. Here are some of the terms you should know in order to communicate effectively with a drapery workroom.

Valances are short, horizontal draperies usually made of a rigid material such as wood or metal or a fabric that has been stretched across the top of a window treatment for decorative purposes.

Fabric valances are made from the same, contrasting, or coordinating fabric as the curtain and are often trimmed with braiding, fringe, and/or tassels. They can be plain, pleated, or shirred, and are usually hung in the same way as the curtain itself.

Swag valances are hung in loops or curves.

Shaped valances have separate panels of fabric cut in a specific design.

Cornices are horizontal bands at the top of a window that hide the top and rods of a curtain or drapery. They're usually made from wood or metal and covered with fabric, wallpaper, or painted. You might want to use floor-length curtains with a cornice in more formal rooms.

Canopies are fabric-covered awnings. They can be used decoratively for both the inside and outside of your home.

Festoons are decorative chains or strips of fabric that loop over valance rods.

Jabots are pleated pieces of material hung decoratively either under or over the swags or sides of valances.

Lambrequins are decorative plywood frames which have been covered and trimmed with fabric and placed over the sides and tops of windows.

Curtains look best in traditional and casual rooms. Buy them ready made in standard sizes, have them custom made, or sew them yourself. No matter what route you take, make sure the curtain has a four inch hem made with a double thickness of fabric. This hem makes your curtains hang evenly.

The four correct lengths for curtains are:
1. To the window sill.
2. To the bottom of the "apron" on the window frame. (The apron is the lowest portion of the window casing located under the sill.)
3. To the floor.
4. Letting curtains "puddle" a few inches onto the floor, European style, which is very hot right now.

Draperies

Draperies are panels of medium or heavy weight fabric which have been sewn together and hung over windows. They can be lined or unlined. Drapery lining is usually made out of a plain, less expensive material. Lined draperies will hang better, look better from the exterior of the house, and block heat and light better than unlined draperies.

Decorative draperies are usually hung so they open in the center and are pulled back at either side by some type of ornamental tieback. They're usually placed on stationary rods and have some type of shirred curtain placed under them. Because decorative draperies can be made skimpier and with less fabric than draperies that draw, they're a money-saving idea for those windows that needn't be covered completely for privacy and light control. This type of drapery looks best in homes with a traditional or eclectic decor.

Tiebacks can be made out of either fabric sashes, ribbons, tapes, chains, or rings that hold draperies or curtains back at the sides.

Draw draperies can be opened and closed at will. Most often, draperies are made to open from the center and pull back to both sides. This is called a two-way draw and is correct for most types of windows. If you have corner windows, bay windows, or walls of glass with a door opening or a short wall on one side, the drapery should be a one-way draw, which means it can be drawn to one side only. Plain draw draperies work well with almost any type of decor. Although always a safe choice, they're rarely creative or professional looking.

Cascades are falls of fabric gathered at the outside corners of a drapery heading. They hang in folds of graduated lengths on each side of the window.

Pavilions are draperies that have been tied back just like the flaps of a tent.

The length of the draperies you select is determined by the type and size of the windows you're covering, the style of draperies you select, and of course, your own personal preferences. Draperies can be floor length, window sill length, or multi-tiered.

The width of your draperies will be determined by the fullness you desire, the width of the window, and how far the drapery will extend to either side as well as the width of the fabric you've selected.

For maximum fullness, use the width of the window multiplied by three, adding extra yardage for side hems, returns, and overlaps. For less than maximum fullness, use the width of the window multiplied by two.

Side hems are double one-inch hems. A return is the measurement from the rod to the wall, usually three inches. An overlap is the part of the draperies that extends over each other in the center when the draperies are closed.

Lining draperies will increase their life, add extra weight to improve the way they hang, and protect the fabric from fading and weakening from the strong rays of the sun. Lining material can either be sewn directly to the drapery or made separately and hung on a rod closer to the window. A good lining material should block out moderate heat, cold, and light. To block extremely strong sunlight, use "blackout lining" or "blackout draperies." They're made out of a special fabric which blocks most of the light and heat coming through a window.

Interlining can be used in extreme cases where a great deal of insulation against heat and cold is needed; to retain heat or cold; or to control strong light. Interlining is an inner layer of material inserted between the drapery fabric and the lining.

Facing lines the edges of draperies and gives them more body.

The drapery workroom you select will not only ask you to give them instructions for the construction of your draperies, but will also ask you what headings, pleating, and shirring you want. Be prepared.

Heading refers to the way a drapery is arranged at the top. Headings arrange the fullness of the draperies and structure the fabric into pleats, scallops, or shirring.

Shirring is the gathering of the fabric, either on the rod or along cording, to produce fullness.

Scallops are rows of curves that form a decorative edge and are sewn into a heading.

Pleats are fabric sections in flat double folds and uniform widths that are stitched or pressed into place. Single pleats are folded at evenly spaced intervals and then pressed into definite folds. Pinch pleats are first divided into three equal sections, then folded into place, stitched across the lower edge, and pressed to keep their shape. Box pleats are first divided into two equal sections. The section edges are laid together flat against the drapery and stitched across the bottom. French pleats are pinch pleats that haven't been pressed into definite folds. Accordion pleats are made with a special self-pleating material. The material is placed in the top hem of the drapery and the pleats are pushed into place manually. Tubular pleats are rows of alternating sized scallops sewn at the top of draperies. The ends of the smaller scallops are pulled together and closed with a clip to form a pleat. Special-fold pleats are extra large-sized pleats used for draperies that need to be stacked into a small area.

Hardware

Your drapery workroom will know the correct hardware needed to install the draperies or curtains you've selected. However, don't think you're finished with the details yet. You'll need to specify your preferences for decorative rods, poles, brackets, and finials.

Rods come in adjustable shapes and sizes, even bays, bows, and arches. A plain rod is used for stationary curtains or draperies.

Traverse rods have pulley mechanisms that draw the curtains or draperies.

Standard traverse rods are hollow and encase a cord and pulley system. The rods have carriers onto which drapery hooks are attached. There's one carrier for each hook. The master carrier attaches to the cord, which makes the drapery move along the rod. The rods are supported by a bracket attached to either the wall, ceiling, or window casing. Most standard traverse rods and brackets are plain white and will be hidden completely by the drapery or curtain.

Decorative traverse rods work just like standard traverse rods, but instead of carriers they have sliding rings. The draperies or curtains hang below the rod, exposing the rings and rods. Thus the rings and rods must be decorative and have an attractive finish. Decorative finials and brackets must be selected.

Motorized rods are standard traverse rods controlled by a motor to move draperies without a cord and pulley system. They're a luxury and generally only used for extremely heavy draperies or draperies in hard to reach places. Motorized rods can even be installed with remote controls.

Curtain rods are just plain smooth rods used for stationary curtains or draperies. Curtains that are hemmed at the top are slipped over the rod and fullness is created by pushing the fabric together. Like any other rods, they are mounted on brackets.

Café rods are decorative wood or metal rods with finials. They're used to hang short draperies or café curtains with rings that slip over the rods. Decorative brackets should be used.

Spring-tension rods are hollow curtain rods with springs inserted so the rods can be adjusted to fit inside window casings. The edges usually have rubber tips.

Batons are rods with handles used to open and close draperies by hand.

Carriers are the plastic or metal eyelets in a traverse track that hold the hooks in the drapery heading and allow the drapery to move along its track.

Finials are decorative wooden or metal end pieces.

Brackets are the devices attached to the wall or window casings to support rods, valances, and cornices. They're usually about three inches long and some can support up to three rods each. Multiple brackets should be used for long rods. Decorative brackets should match the style of the rods you select.

Hooks are used to attach draperies to the carriers. They're usually slipped into the hem of the heading and sewn or pinned in.

Holdbacks are the decorative pieces with hidden arms that keep draperies in place when you pull them back.

Tieback holders are the decorative pieces fastened through a tieback to hold it in place and attached to the wall. You can also use cup hooks to hold a tieback in place.

Drapery weights are thin flat, smooth pieces of metal inserted into draperies to give them weight so that they hang well.

Curtain weights serve the same purpose as drapery weights but are smaller pieces of metal hidden in a cloth strip.

Window Shades

Window shades are great used alone or in combination with curtains and draperies. They can serve a number of functions as well as being decorative. They can provide privacy, soften light, screen out light completely, control glare, insulate against cold, heat, and sound, and increase heating and air conditioning efficiency.

The negatives of window shades are that when they are pulled down from the top they block the best light from the top of the window; when they are pulled up, they often interfere with the operation of the window. Shades can also prevent outside air from circulating in and can flap annoyingly in a breeze.

Standard window shades are made from either stiffened fabric or heavy paper which has been placed on spring rollers that raise or lower. Ready-made shades for standard-sized windows can be readily purchased, but usually these shades aren't particularly up to date or attractive.

Fabric window shades can also be purchased ready made in standard sizes or custom made. The ready-made variety is an inexpensive way of covering windows, but your selection will be greatly limited. Buy ready-mades with the utmost of taste and discretion.

You'll also find shades that either pull from the top down or from the bottom up. The type you choose will depend on the type of window you are covering, the privacy you desire, and the look you want.

Custom-made fabric shades can be as expensive as draperies. There is a multitude of styles and designs to choose from and they're great for disguising the size and shape of undesirable windows.

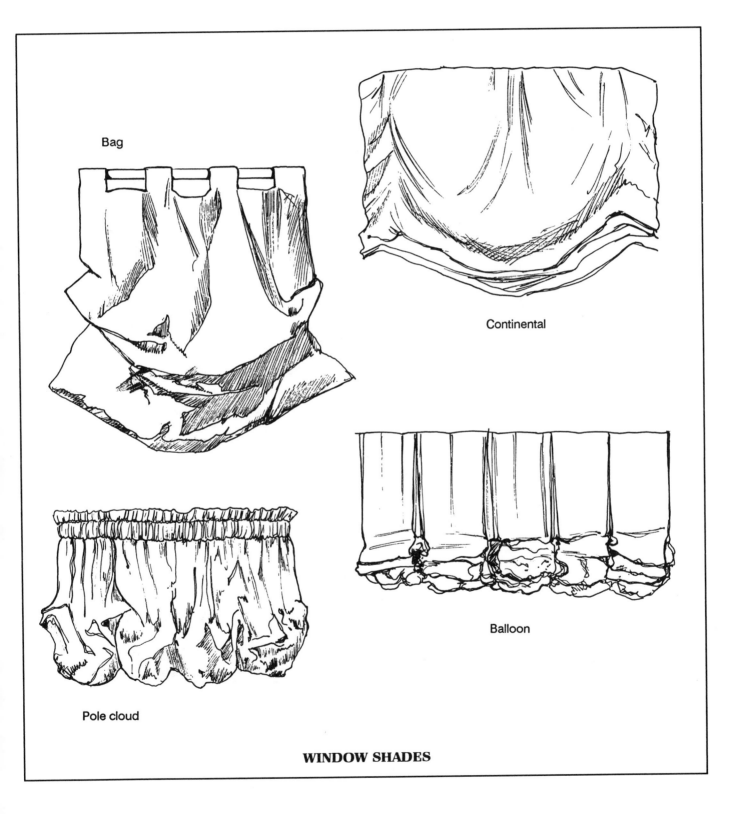

Bag

Continental

Pole cloud

Balloon

WINDOW SHADES

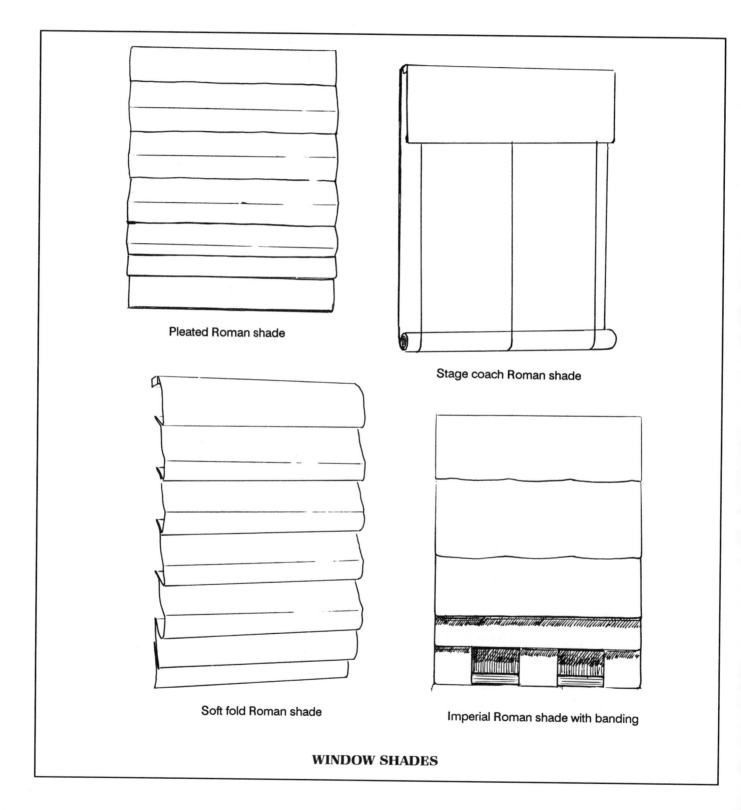

Pleated Roman shade

Stage coach Roman shade

Soft fold Roman shade

Imperial Roman shade with banding

WINDOW SHADES

For a standard window shade, use a matching or coordinating fabric from your room and have it laminated onto the shade. For a softly draped shade, use the same fabric without having it laminated.

Roman shades are made with horizontally pleated panels of fabric and raised and lowered by cords. They're a very tailored look.

Soft-fold Romans are a softer look with looser, horizontal folds of fabric.

Accordion shades are shades made with definite pleats.

Pleated Romans are plain Roman shades with horizontal seams and pleating placed midway across each wide horizontal fold.

Inverted-pleat Romans are similar to pleated Romans, but the pleats are directed to the back of the shade.

Pole shades are flat Roman shades with poles encased in fabric running horizontally in several places.

Stagecoach shades are plain Roman shades with tailored valances that roll up from the bottom without any folds or pleats.

Mini-folds are Roman shades with even folds divided by lines of fabric encased in narrow seaming. *Soft mini-folds* are similar, but narrow slats of wood covered in fabric are inserted horizontally at equal intervals.

Bag shades are stationary shades hung from an exposed fabric-covered rod by wide fabric loops. The fabric of the shade is pulled up to form a bag-like effect.

Continental shades are stationary shades in which the fabric is draped over the top rod, then the fabric of the shade is pulled up to form a horizontally draped effect.

Imperial Romans are tailored shades with uneven and slightly curved horizontal folds.

Austrian shades are curtains which have been shirred vertically. They pull up and down like any other shade.

Horizontal shades are used over horizontal windows such as skylights. They move horizontally with pulleys and cords.

Balloons are shades draped over rods. They have wide, tailored vertical folds that form a balloon-like effect when pulled up.

Clouds are shades that have been shirred over rods with decorative bands of stitching that gather the fabric. When the bottoms of the gathered fabric are pulled up, they form a cloud-like group of puffs.

Pole clouds are similar to clouds, but wider widths of fabric are gathered onto the rods to form deeper gathers. When pulled up, the cloud-like puffs are fuller than those of the clouds.

Balloons, clouds, and pole clouds are "hot." They're all fabulous to use as valances over draperies in traditional and eclectic rooms.

Select the style that best fits the decor of your room. If the room is tailored, select a tailored style; if the room is more free flowing, choose a softer, puffier look. Your drapery workroom will probably be able to make all of your curtains, draperies, and shades for you. If not, there are many companies that specialize in making custom shades, both retail and wholesale. Check your source books and the Business-to-Business Yellow Pages. Again, make sure you get several bids and check the workmanship of the company you use.

Have the company that will be making your shades measure your windows on the job. They'll be able to tell you how much fabric you'll need and will probably have a selection of stock fabrics from which to choose.

Ask whether they suggest hanging the shade inside the window frame or overlapping the frame. The answer will depend on the type of shade you select and the type of window you're covering.

Discuss any cornices or valances you might want; sketch out your ideas and find out how much extra it will cost. Don't forget to find out how much additional fabric you'll need to order for cornices and valances.

Make sure you show the person measuring for the shade the fabric you'll be using, or at least tell her the repeat. Remember, the amount of fabric you'll need is contingent on whether you use solid or patterned goods as well as the width of your fabric.

Don't forget the trimmings. Add borders, braiding, bands of decorative cloth, ribbon, tape, fringe, balls, loops, or tassels; even have a "key" or scallops cut out at the bottom of the shade. Make a detailed sketch to avoid any miscommunications and ask if you must supply the trimming or if they'll get it for you. Ask if there will be any additional costs. Specify the type of pull or decorative handle you would like fastened to the hem of the shade. Choose from a wide variety of materials, such as enamel, plastic, and metal. Use them as they are or cover them with fabric. The pulls can be tassels, rings, or drops.

Be sure all the materials you use are colorfast, washable, and waterproof.

New on the market and very "hot" are *mini-pleated shades*. They're made out of 100% polyester and come in several thicknesses. The panels of pleated fabric overlap about ¾" and the pleats are about one inch deep. They come in a variety of over eighty colors, patterns, and textures, but can also be ordered in custom colors. These pleated shades are an excellent, inexpensive solution for covering windows in more modern homes. Verosol is a trade name, but there are now many manufacturers duplicating the product. Shop around and take a look at what's available.

Blinds

Horizontal or vertical blinds come in wood, metal, or plastic. They can even be custom laminated with your own fabric. They're inexpensive and excellent for air and light control, but are difficult to keep clean.

The most popular version of the horizontal blinds has been the mini blinds. There are numerous manufacturers and minis come in a huge array of patterns, textures, and colors in both mat and gloss finishes. Mix colors within a single blind to repeat a color or design element in your room. Me-

tal minis are more popular than plastic or wood and come in a wider variety of colors.

Verticals have become increasingly popular because of their low cost and their ability to adjust light and air circulation. I use them a lot in low budget modern rooms as a pleasing background that doesn't detract from the rest of the room. The slats are wider than those of the mini blinds and they can be opened and closed easily.

Although they come in a wider range of colors in metal, I usually select plastic because the metal slats seem to clang against each other when it's breezy. Having chains placed at the bottom of the verticals helps this problem only a little. Verticals can also be laminated with any fabric; some even come with pre-made grooves for inserting laminated strips of custom fabric.

Caution! Woven fabric, macramé, embossed, and patterned verticals are passé. *Wider* horizontal metal blinds and wooden slat blinds are making a comeback, while mini blinds are on their way out.

Shutters

Shutters are always "hot," as long as they're the newer, more modern ones that have very wide slats and are either natural bleached wood or painted with a gloss paint. The old-fashioned type of narrow slatted, dark-grained shutters are "old" and dingy.

The initial cost of very good quality shutters is high. Stain grade shutters are even more expensive than paint grade shutters, and of course, wide slat shutters are the most expensive. They're a fabulous look if you can afford them and can be used in almost any style house effectively.

Don't skimp. Avoid the cheaper, ready-made shutters and splurge on a top notch professional installation. Get several bids and have a professional tell you which type of shutters will work on your windows. There are limitations depending on the depth and openings of your windows.

Shutters give solid protection from heat and cold, while allowing free control of light and air

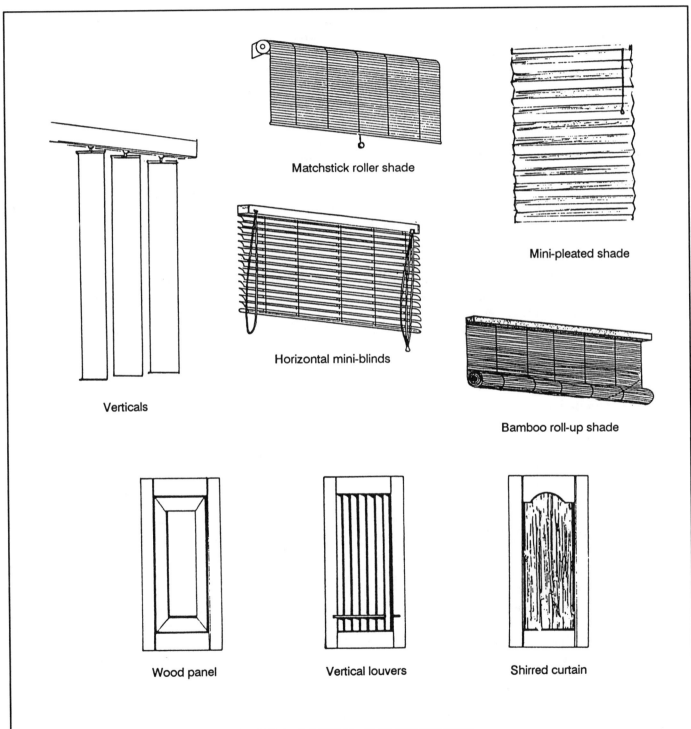

Matchstick roller shade

Mini-pleated shade

Verticals

Horizontal mini-blinds

Bamboo roll-up shade

Wood panel

Vertical louvers

Shirred curtain

BLINDS, SHADES, AND SHUTTERS

circulation. They're extremely durable, although I've seen cases of the hinges breaking if the louvers are handled too roughly. Make sure your shutters come with heavy duty hardware to avoid this problem.

Woven Shades and Bamboo Shades

Woven shades are made from narrow slats that are interwoven with yarn. Bamboo shades are made from thin slats of bamboo. Both are low cost window treatments that roll up and down with the pull of a cord. They're readily available in standard sizes and can be installed by any semi-brave do-it-yourselfer.

If you have a professional make custom woven shades, you'll be able to choose from inside mounts, outside mounts, drapery styles, angled tops, curved tops, spring roller shades, or cafés. They provide good light control, insulation against heat and cold, and privacy, and are a good money-saving idea for casual rooms.

Professional Advice

Let's discuss each type of window you might have and what your alternatives are.

If you're covering double-hung windows and your look is modern or eclectic, use horizontal blinds, soft Romans, or mini-pleated shades. You might want to add a metal or fabric covered cornice or use a simply draped fabric to frame the blinds or shades. Stay away from verticals — they won't look good on small, double-hung windows. If your room has a casual, country look, use a fresh, airy type of curtain. If your room is more elegant and traditional, use tieback draperies with sheers underneath. The window will look better if you drape from the top of the window to the floor, camouflaging the bare wall space underneath. Shutters will work if there's enough depth in the window for them to fit. Remember, you'll have to completely open the shutters in order to open and close the window.

If you're covering horizontal sliding windows and have a modern decor, use horizontal blinds from the top of the window to the bottom of the sill or verticals that extend to the floor. If your look is casual country, you might want to use a café curtain, but remember, the curtain won't block out light completely. You might want to hide a blackout shade behind the valance. If the room is more elegant, either traditional or eclectic, drape the whole window and carry the drapery treatment to the floor. Use a sheer underneath to cover the bare wall space. Shutters will work as long as the window is set in deeply enough to allow space for the shutters. In some cases, shutters can be mounted directly on the surface of the adjoining interior wall.

If you're covering casement or projected windows that swing out and your look is modern, your best options are Roman shades, blinds, or mini-pleated shades that pull up easily. If you want a more casual country look, use curtains, but remember, you'll have to reach behind the curtains every time you want to open or close the windows. For a more formal look, use draperies with or without sheers underneath, but again, you must either draw the draperies or reach under them in order to control the window. Shutters will work as long as the crank is positioned so it doesn't interfere.

If you're covering casement or projected windows that swing in, you've got big problems. Very few window coverings will work unless there is a way of setting them out far enough so that they clear the window when it's open. The best solution for this type of window is to put draperies that draw to either side when the window is open. Use sheers underneath, as long as they are on a traverse rod. If you insist on more modern fabric shades or blinds, you'll only be able to pull them down when the window is closed. Curtains will work as long as they're on traverse rods and can be pulled back easily. All window coverings will have to be pulled all the way up or all the way to the sides in order to keep the window open.

Jalousie windows allow more flexibility than casement windows for covering. Again, whatever treatment you choose, make sure the crank doesn't protrude into or interfere with the material. Use blinds and shades for a modern decor; any variation of curtains for more country looks; and draperies, with or without sheers underneath, for a more elegant look. Verticals won't look right covering jalousie windows. Feel free to use valances and cornices for added detail; they won't interfere with the window.

Bay windows need a lot of forethought. Generally, they're found in more traditional homes and look best dressed in more formal coverings. Use sections of tied-back draperies with sheers underneath. You might even want to add a cornice or valance for a cozier look. If you have a bay window but your decor is modern, blinds and mini-pleated or Roman shades made in sections will work. Keep it simple. If your home is casual country, add an upholstered window seat and have matching curtains made. They'll look best if tied back to the corners of the windows.

If you're covering clerestory windows, save your money. These windows look best left uncovered. The only exception I've ever seen is a room with wall-to-wall shutters in which the shutters extended up over the high clerestory windows but it was expensive and hard to clean.

If you must cover a skylight (which isn't usually necessary), have a custom horizontal shade made from fabric or use custom mini-pleated shades.

If you are covering a garden window (and in most cases, you shouldn't), use soft fabric shades, mini-pleated shades, or horizontal blinds. Only cover a garden window if light and privacy are a major problem.

If you're covering a cathedral window, don't. Cathedral windows, like clerestory windows, are not meant to be covered.

If you're covering a dormer window, again, stop. Dormer windows shouldn't be covered either.

If you're covering a lunette, why not use fabric gathered to create a sunburst over it, draw the gathers to the bottom, and fasten with a covered button. This is a great look for formal and eclectic rooms.

If your room is modern and you have a lunette window, why not just leave it bare? Or if you're going to shutter the window underneath, a good shutter company can make a custom shutter for the lunette.

If you're covering a fanlight, the same rule applies as for a lunette. Don't be afraid to leave it bare, it's perfectly acceptable.

If you're covering sliding glass doors, you have almost any option open to you. Follow the basic ideas for formal, casual, modern, and traditional styles. Always remember to design window coverings that allow easy opening and access in and out of the sliding glass door. Never use light curtaining over a large sliding glass door. It will always look wrong.

If you're covering Dutch doors, I hope you're country casual. Stretched curtains look best, but don't allow you to manipulate lighting easily. Cute little curtains look outdated and silly. Blinds are out; they'll clink and clank every time you open the door and are incongruous with a Dutch door. If you can live with the negatives of stretched, shirred curtains, go for them. Otherwise, fabric shades are an acceptable option. If your decor is modern, consider getting rid of the Dutch door altogether.

If you're covering French doors remember, any treatment you use must be able to pull to each side in order to allow the doors to open. Valances and cornices won't work well. Shades, blinds, Verosols, and verticals just won't work. Your only real option is a tieback drapery. Underneath the draperies you can use stretched sheers on the doors, or add sheers underneath the draperies as long as they're on a traverse rod. If your decor is modern, you might want to consider no window covering at all if privacy and light control don't present problems. If your look is country casual, you might want to use the stretched sheers alone and forgo the draperies.

Money-Saving Ideas

- If you're renting a home or apartment, use inexpensive standard size metal blinds or woven or bamboo shades. Install them yourself. If they won't work with your decor, buy ready-made sheers and drape inexpensive fabric over a top rod, tie at each side, and let the lengths of fabric fall loosely in a cascade, puddling on the floor. No need to sew or hem unless you're extra ambitious.

• Buy ready-made curtains in a plain and simple fabric, then add your own trimmings. Better yet, if you sew, make your own curtains from inexpensive fabric you've found on the remnant table of a local fabric store or on special at a fabric discount house.

• Thoroughly check the fabrics available through your drapery workroom. It will usually be less expensive to use their stocked fabric than to use your own custom fabric.

• Before you shop the more expensive fabric stores and showrooms, search discount houses and fabric outlets for large bolts of seconds or odd lots. Check your source books and Business-to-Business Yellow Pages.

• Buy bolts of plain muslin, chintz, light canvas, chiffon, voile, any fabric that drapes well. Play around with hand painting, dyeing, or tie dyeing to color coordinate with your decor. Drape the finished fabric on rods over your windows. You might want to tie the corners with a large fabric bow and create layers of puffed tiers tied with decorative cording. Let the fabric drape a few inches onto the floor for a newer, more modern look and hem the bottom one night while you're watching television.

What's Hot, What's Not?

• One-inch wide horizontal blinds are back and bigger than ever.

• Soft shades made of linen are hot.

• More opulent-looking window coverings are setting the new trend for traditional rooms.

• Fuller, free-flowing draperies are new. Feel free to layer, puddle, and tier.

• Use huge, impressive tassels and cording. Why not gold or silver?

• Use thick rods and poles covered with fabric instead of cornices and valances; it's a newer look.

• Verticals and mini blinds are always a safe and economical standby, but mini-pleated shades such as Verosols seem to be taking over the market.

• Medium to medium-lightweight fabrics have replaced the old-fashioned heavy draperies that don't flow well and just hang there.

• Wide, impressive shutters with four-inch slats are really hot. Bleach them out or paint them a gloss black or white. Try a dramatic glossy pastel . . . or even bright red!

• Naked windows are the hottest. (A great money saver and a wonderful new look.)

• Typical apartment draperies are boring and dull. If you must live with them, tie them back and add decorative trimming.

• Draperies made out of casement material are definitely out.

• Ruffled curtains that are "too cute," especially cheap ones with flimsy trimming, will look best in your trash bin.

16
Choosing Your Furniture

How many times have you heard the expression, "nothing lasts forever?" Fortunately, or unfortunately, wood is the exception. All too often we buy wood furniture expecting it to last a lifetime. It usually does, but it goes out of style long before it has lost its usefulness. My mother still has the original wood furniture she bought fifty years ago when she and my dad were first married. Although it's in perfect condition, it's outdated. Matched furniture sets went out with bubble hairdos and the Twist.

It's extremely difficult to get people like my mother to part with furniture that's out of style. They'll always declare indignantly, "How dare you suggest I get rid of that furniture, it still looks brand new. Your Dad and I bought that set when we were first married. It cost an arm and a leg when it was brand new and it's worth a small fortune now."

I usually bite my tongue. That old wood furniture set wouldn't bring more than $100 on the open market. A used furniture man would only take it if he could buy the whole lot for under $50.

So come on, let's be modern. Give up your stale ideas about conventional wood furniture and open your mind to what's newer and more exciting.

Whetting Your Appetite

• Dining tables take on a new look when the bases are made of "pickled" or lacquered wood and the tops are made of ¾" thick beveled glass.

• Some of the more modern dining tables have bases made from geometric forms: circles, squares, rectangles, semicircles, and triangles. These forms can be finished in any number of exciting ways or covered in one of the new laminates. There is a vast assortment of colors, textures, patterns, and metal finishes to choose from.

• Update an old traditional look by insetting thick glass in the top of a carved table to create a more open and spacious look. Of course, you can't add extra leaves to glass-top tables to make them larger, but be honest, how often do you really have large dinner parties anyway? Wood tables with leaves are old-fashioned and out.

• Coffee tables have taken on a new look, too. There's so much available on the market that there's no reason for you to select a table that's passé. Various solid forms and shapes, used alone or mixed and matched, are very hot right now. Have them custom made in any size, color, finish, or shape. Buy them ready made in finishes such as plastic laminate, faux stone, or coated with a polyurethane that looks almost like lacquer.

These forms and shapes are inexpensive and versatile. Use them for end tables, nightstands, table bases, or occasional tables. Top a short cylinder with a cushion and use it as an interesting seat, or top a tall geometric form with a sculpture and use it as a pedestal. Mix and match forms; use two triangles to form one coffee table.

• End tables, sofa back tables, console tables, nightstands, and dressers tend to be boring if too easy. Try to be more innovative. Ordinary end tables tend to detract from the drama of a room and create a choppy look. If an end table is absolutely necessary, try to create a concept that's completely unique. Use a section of a tree trunk sanded smooth and bleached; top it with a thick piece of glass, granite, or marble. There are many end tables available on the market that "will do," but using an interesting accessory with a "story" is much more creative. Find a large ceramic elephant or wood monkey to use as a table base; top it with a piece of glass to create your own one-of-a-kind table.

• Conventional wood coffee tables are tacky. Look for more interesting and updated designs and finishes in traditional wood furniture unless you're decorating your home in authentic period antiques.

An artist friend of mine had just bought a new home and money to decorate it was scarce. The stress of her house-warming party and the emptiness of her living room seemed to stimulate her creativity. Ten minutes before the party she remembered the large box of unpainted clay cats in her garage. (A hand-painted cat business that had never gotten off the ground.) Before the first guest arrived she had arranged the clay cats in a circle in front of her lone sofa and topped it with a circle of glass borrowed from another table. The makeshift coffee

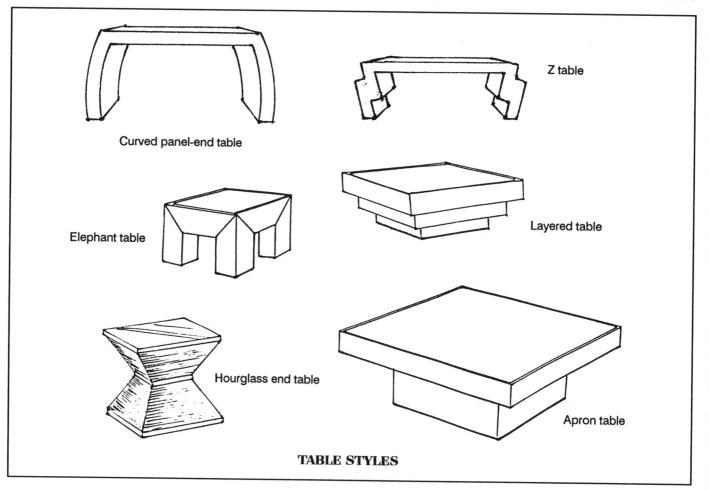

Curved panel-end table

Z table

Elephant table

Layered table

Hourglass end table

Apron table

TABLE STYLES

table remains and still looks fabulous.

- All the old stand-by sofa tables and consoles seem to look alike. Liven up a room by lacquering any boring table; make it white, black, a delicate pastel, or a bright, bold red — use any color that works well with your room.

- Shop around, you'll find a growing collection of ready-made tables designed in combinations of laminates, lacquers, faux stones mixed with glass, metals, even neon lights. Look for forms and shapes that are new and exciting.

- Conventional nightstands and dressers are passé unless, of course, as fine collector's items in a traditional home.

- Bombé chests seem to mix well with modern furniture in an eclectic room. A carved French nightstand or chest with an up-to-date finish can add an interesting touch to almost any bedroom. Use glossy lacquered finishes on small carved pieces for a new look.

- Try to find your own unique ideas for nightstands instead of just selecting what's available from the furniture store. Use a stack of three lacquered Oriental chests. Sure, you'll have to give up the utility of the drawers, but a few sacrifices must be made in the name of design and drama.

- Refinish your old boring dresser; lacquer it a bright shiny color or strip and bleach it, color washing with a delicate pastel. Better yet, throw it out. Replace it with a fabulous armoire. You'll find more and more armoire reproductions appearing on the market every day, but I prefer an antique armoire that's been restored and refinished. Have the interior customized to fit your personal storage needs.

One of the hottest armoires I've ever seen was an old inexpensive French armoire that had been lacquered white. The interior was upholstered and custom fitted with a large television swivel and elaborately divided space for stereo and videotape equipment. This look blends fabulously with almost any decor.

If your home is Italian modern, "slick" or high tech, choose a more streamlined armoire. There is a wide assortment of large lacquered and laminated pieces readily available on the market. If funds allow, have one custom made to your exact specifications.

- Steer clear of the production-line looking modern furniture sets, they're on the way out. (You know, the ones that come with matching platform beds.)

- Wood chair frames that have been custom upholstered and finished are still terrific. You'll find many different renditions and qualities of traditional reproductions; mix and match them with almost any decor. Use them as dining room chairs, desk chairs, pull-up chairs, occasional chairs, or easy chairs. Most styles are updated copies of traditional chairs, but more and more chair frame styles are being introduced. You can now find Oriental and even Egyptian frames. Buy the frames unfinished and have them custom finished and upholstered. Lacquer a Queen Anne frame black and upholster with faux zebra; "pickle" a large bergere chair and upholster it with pure white douppioni silk; or silver-leaf a frame and upholster with shiny black patent leather. Experiment with almost any combination.

- "Furniture as art" is an up and coming design concept. Look for objets d'art that perform a function.

- Mix! Create a professional look with furniture by experimenting with combinations of styles, colors, and finishes. Use goatskin finishes, pastel washes, silver and gold leaf, "crackle" finishes, lacquer, faux leather, and stencilled skins.

- Mix and match styles. Use lacquered Chippendale dining chairs with a modern glass top dining table on a stainless steel base. Or modern dining chairs fully upholstered in stark white with the old antique dining room table you inherited from Aunt Sadie.

Take the time to shop around in retail furniture stores as well as in wholesale showrooms. Browse through issues of *Architectural Digest* and other trade magazines to see what types of exciting furniture and finishes designers are using now.

Notice how they mix pieces, creating drama with surprising combinations that work. Use your imagination (or your own adaptation of a professional interior designer's work) to create your own exciting rooms.

As you shop, you'll notice that all wood furniture falls into two major categories — traditional or modern. The term "modern" describes more intellectual forms of pure design. The word "contemporary" describes the more commercial, popular interpretations of pure design.

What elements do you look for in good modern design? First, it's basic and simple; there are no tricky elements. Second, it's graceful, in proportion, and creates a feeling of harmony. Third, it's calm and beautiful. Poor modern design is usually crude, harsh, and meaningless. As you shop and browse through magazines, note who the famous furniture designers are and study their designs. These are the works of art that will become precious antiques someday.

Traditional Furniture

What elements do you look for in good traditional design? First, good traditional design will relate to one of the great style periods and will carry the stamp of authenticity. Whether you use an antique or a reproduction, a good piece has weathered the tests of taste and time.

Period furniture, synonymous with traditional furniture, can be categorized as either formal or informal. This applies to all centuries and all countries. Formal styles were developed and used by the court circles and wealthy patrons and represent the finest in styling and elegance. Informal styles are generally referred to as "provincial," and were designed by the country folk. Country carpenters used the local wood and cruder tools to create similar, but less sophisticated, furniture.

Periods of furniture design are usually associated with the particular type of wood most used at that time. Oak is usually identified with English

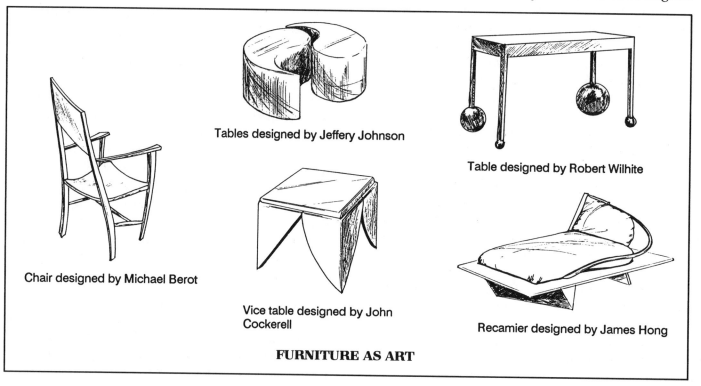

Tables designed by Jeffery Johnson

Table designed by Robert Wilhite

Chair designed by Michael Berot

Vice table designed by John Cockerell

Recamier designed by James Hong

FURNITURE AS ART

furniture made in the fifteenth and sixteenth centuries. Walnut is identified with Queen Anne furniture made in the late seventeenth century. English eighteenth century furniture, colonial and federal, is generally seen in mahogany. Pine, maple, and cherry are characteristic of early American. Before you shop, know your woods.

Wood

Alder is a lightweight hardwood. It's not very strong but resists denting and abrasion, shrinks only a little, and takes a stain well. It has a uniform grain and colors range from white to pale pinks and browns. It's used for chairs and other furniture.

Ash is hard, strong, and wears well. It can be difficult to work with and will warp. Its color is creamy white to light brown and it has a strong grain that resembles oak. It is used in furniture frames requiring strength and in exposed parts of less expensive furniture, as it's less expensive than most other hardwoods.

Beech is strong, dense, hard, and bends well. It's good for turning and polishes well, but has a tendency to warp, shrink, and develop dry rot. Its color is white or slightly reddish and it has a uniform texture similar to maple. Beech is used for flooring as well as average quality country furniture that requires strength.

Birch is a hard, heavy, and strong wood that resists shrinking and warping. Its color is usually light to dark reddish brown. It has an irregular grain but a uniform texture. It's often used in Scandinavian furniture and can be stained to look like mahogany or walnut.

Cedar is a soft, weak, and lightweight wood that resists shrinkage and decay. Red cedar repels moths. Its color is reddish brown to white and it has a close grain. Cedar is generally used for shingles, siding, porch trellises, cabinet work, and interior paneling.

Cherry is a strong, durable, medium-hard wood that carves and polishes well. Its color is light to darkish red and its grain is close. We usually associate cherry with early American and colonial furniture. It's often used as a veneer.

Cypress is a medium strong, light wood that resists decay and holds paint well. Its color is slightly reddish, yellowish and brown, or almost black, although, if exposed, it will weather to a silver gray. It's used for doors, siding, shingles, porches, and sometimes for outdoor furniture.

Elm is a hard and heavy wood. Although it's difficult to work with and tends to shrink and swell, it does bend well. It's a light grayish-brown color tinged with red or dark brown. Elm has a porous oak-like grain and is used extensively for decorative veneers. We rarely see elm used in furniture, except for the curved parts of some provincial styles.

Fir is a soft, strong, and heavy wood that has a tendency to split and will not sand or paint well. It's yellow, red, or brownish and has a coarse grain with irregular wavy patterns. It is used for low cost furniture and interior parts.

Gum is a medium-hard wood that is heavy and strong. Although it's easy to work with and takes a stain well, it does tend to shrink, swell, warp, and decay. It's commonly used for structural parts of mahogany and walnut furniture.

Mahogany is an expensive wood that's medium-hard, heavy, and strong. It's easy to work with, carves well, shrinks only a little, has a beautiful texture, and takes on a high polish easily. Its color is pale to reddish brown, but darkens with exposure to light. It has a woven grain that reflects light in many effective ways. Mahogany was the wood of choice for fine furniture in the eighteenth and nineteenth centuries. Today, it's used in expensive furniture that's either finished naturally, bleached, or stained dark.

Maple is a hard, heavy, and strong wood that resists shrinking and swelling. It has a natural luster and lends itself to a high polish. Its color is off-white to light brown and it has small, fine pores. It can be either straight grained or curly. Maple is usually associated with early American furniture, but is a good wood to use for flooring.

Oak is hard, strong, carves well, and can take

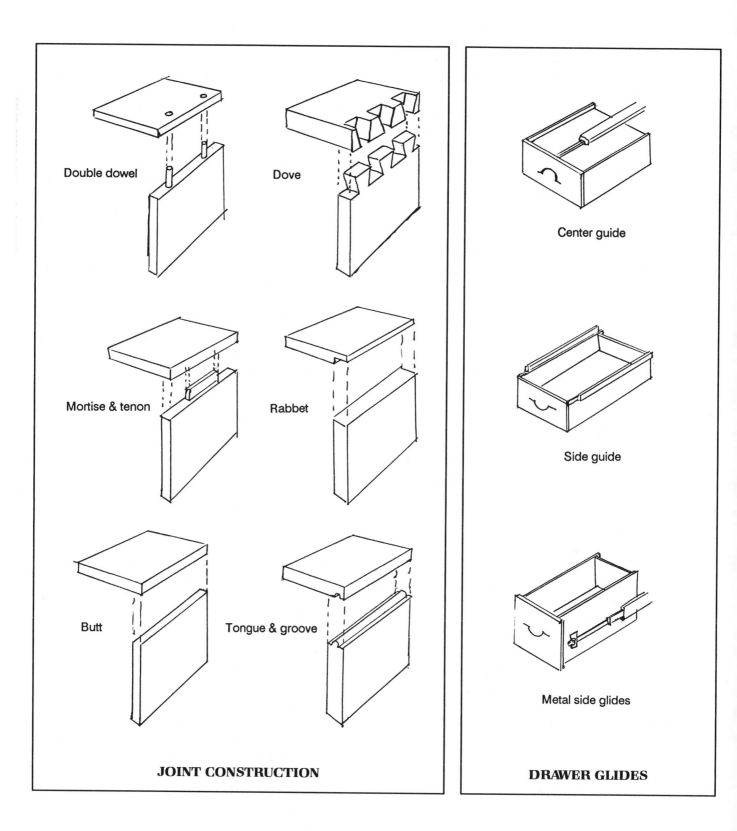

Double dowel

Dove

Mortise & tenon

Rabbet

Butt

Tongue & groove

JOINT CONSTRUCTION

Center guide

Side guide

Metal side glides

DRAWER GLIDES

a variety of finishes. Its colors range from white to pale grayish-brown, although red oaks are, of course, reddish. Oak was used extensively in the Gothic period and in the early Renaissance of northern Europe. Today, we see oak used in flooring, wall panels, and solid and veneer furniture.

Pine is a soft, light, and relatively weak wood. Although it's easy to work with, it does shrink, swell, warp, and decay easily. It takes an oil or paint finish extremely well. Pine is close grained and its color is off-white to yellow, red, and brown. We associate pine with provincial and rustic furniture as well as early Georgian. Today, pine is used as an inexpensive wood for cabinets, doors, window frames, and furniture.

Redwood is a medium-strong wood that resists rot and decay, but is soft and splinters easily. Its natural color is reddish brown, but it lightens in strong sunlight or becomes gray or blackish when allowed to weather. Its grain is either parallel, contorted, or burled, depending upon the quality. Redwood is generally used for exterior siding, garden walls, and outdoor furniture.

Rosewood is a hard, durable wood that can take a high polish. It varies greatly from a light color to a deep reddish-brown with irregular streaks of brown and black curving through it. Rosewood was used extensively for veneers and inlays in eighteenth century furniture and as solid wood for nineteenth century furniture. Its use is growing more popular in furniture today.

Teak is a heavy, durable, oily wood that's easy to work with and carves well. It takes on an excellent oil finish. Its color is straw yellow to tobacco brown with striped or mottled patterns. Teak was used widely in the Far East for carved furniture. Today, it's widely used for Scandinavian furniture because it lends itself well to sculpturing.

American walnut is a hard, heavy, strong wood that's easy to work with and resists warping. It has a natural luster and takes on an excellent finish. Its color is light to dark chocolate brown with dark, irregular streaks running through it. We associate walnut with fine furniture from the nineteenth century. Today, it's used in high quality furniture and paneling. *European walnut* is also a strong, hard, durable wood that's easy to carve and work with. It resists shrinking and warping and takes on a fine polish. It's usually fawn colored with many strong, irregular dark streaks running through it. European walnut was used in Italy, France, Spain, and England during the Queen Anne period. Today, we import European walnut to make American furniture.

Furniture Construction

The art of veneering is at least two hundred years old. Veneers are often stronger than solid wood. A veneer is wood that has been cut paper thin and applied to a core under pressure. The core may be birch, poplar, alder, or gumwood, while the veneered surface may be an exotic wood or an intricately patterned conventional wood containing swirls and wild graining. Veneers are also used for inlays and marquetry. They can be the only way of creating a beautifully patterned table or drawer front, and offer the only method of keeping large table tops from warping and cracking. Good veneer furniture has a five- or seven-ply core. Less expensive veneered furniture may only have a three-ply core made of plywood.

There are three different techniques that combine different woods along with metals, ivory, shell, and other materials. Intarsia refers to the technique in which the pieces are inlaid in solid wood. Marquetry applies to designs inlaid in veneers and then glued to a solid backing. Parquetry refers to geometric patterns, such as those we find in floors and tables.

Solid wood does have advantages: edges of table tops and chairs do not expose the "layer cake" construction of plywood, wood can be turned or carved, surfaces can be planed if they are damaged or thoroughly sanded for refinishing without fear of going through another wood, and of course, the surface cannot loosen or peel off. The major disadvantages of solid wood are its high cost and its tendency to warp, shrink, or swell.

Pieces of wood furniture such as chests, desks, and buffets are called case goods. Once the function, comfort, and aesthetics of your choice of furniture are determined, it's time to think about the construction and quality of the piece you're purchasing. Quality and construction vary. Ultimately, the strength or weakness of a piece of furniture depends on the way it was assembled and the materials used.

There are eight basic joints: butt, rabbet, doweled, splined, mortise and tenon, dovetail, tongue and groove, and lap and scarf joints. Additional strength and stability are given by the use of corner blocks held in place by screws and/or glue.

Drawers should have four dovetailed joints, be sanded smooth, and have a protective finish to keep them from swelling and shrinking. Pull out a drawer and examine the bottom. It should have small wooden blocks in each corner. There should be a center track or glide on the sides, preferably metal. There should be a dust panel between each drawer. Check the bottom of the drawer to make sure it is strong enough so that it will not sag. Drawer pulls should be firmly attached, easy to use, and have a permanent finish, as well as be consistent with the design of the piece.

Doors in cupboards and buffets should be examined to see if they fit well. They should open and close easily. The hinges should be strong enough for the weight of the door and aligned perfectly. In fine pieces, each individual pane of glass will be set in a wood frame. In less expensive pieces, small paned glass doors will be simulated by a wood or metal grille overlay.

Table tops should be checked to make sure that leaves match the table top both in wood and finish. Check to make sure any drawer-top tables are constructed and operating well.

The legs of a piece should be checked for sturdy construction. Examine the grain and the way the leg is attached and braced to the table top. Make sure the bottoms of the legs are smooth and have glides or self-leveling swivel casters. Larger pieces should be mounted on concealed casters for ease of handling.

Antiques

An antique is anything that was made in the nineteenth century or before. However, it's not a "true" antique unless it is over one hundred years old. It's a talent to be able to recognize genuine antiques, as there are so many phonies on the market. Furniture can be restored up to 40% and still be classified as an antique, but its value goes down about 50%. Even china and glass can be reproduced. Some antiques are out-and-out fakes. Others are basically old pieces that have been purposely converted to more valuable types. Some are just old pieces with more than 40% of repairs which, of course, decreases their value. Others are "married pieces" made up of several pieces of old furniture that did not originally belong together. And still others are copies that have been made at a much later date than the originals. It's common to find pieces made fifty or seventy-five years later being sold as the originals.

If you're not a serious antique collector, I suggest you just buy what you like and what works well with your home. It takes a great deal of research, reading, and shopping to become an expert on authentic antiques. However, some of the most obvious things an expert will look for are:

• The design matches the period and region the piece allegedly comes from.

• The drawer construction and wood blocks in the corners match the signs of the hand crafting of the period.

• Appearance of unfinished wood and shrinking at crucial points are clues to the age of the piece. The backs of chests and insides of drawers should have a natural coloration of aging that varies with the amount of time they have been exposed to the air.

Analyzing these details takes a lot of experience. Try detecting a phony by looking for the presence of glue or checking the turnings to see if they're handmade. If the turnings are identical, they're machine made and the piece is not authentic.

Shopping for antiques can become an interesting and rewarding hobby. Besides the many antique shops that can probably be found in your city and neighboring cities, you'll also find exciting buys at auctions, estate sales, and garage sales. Traveling to other cities and countries can also open up new sources for you.

Professional interior designers buy most of their antiques from reputable shops that stand behind the quality of their merchandise. There are also "strictly wholesale" antique outlets, usually open only to the trade. Check your city's interior designers' source books or the Business-to-Business Yellow Pages to find them.

Period Furniture

All period furniture can be divided into three main categories.

First, the Renaissance, which means "rebirth" and describes the development in Europe which started in Italy and swept over Europe. Renaissance furniture is large, heavily carved, and straight lined.

By 1715 when Louis XIV died, the Baroque era in furniture took over. It had lavish ornamentation and curves rather than straight lines. Rococo is a term that describes extreme baroque furniture which is fantastically overdecorated, gaudy, and ornate. French Rococo was at its peak during the reign of Louis XV.

The third main era of period furniture is the Neoclassic era. It swept Europe and America in the late eighteenth and early nineteenth century. Neoclassic furniture is noted for its small, slender, straight-legged pieces with flat surfaces.

Within these three main eras there are a number of periods such as Italian Renaissance, Spanish Renaissance, English Renaissance, Pilgrim, William and Mary, Queen Anne, Chippendale, Hepplewhite, Sheraton, Regency, Colonial, Federal, American Empire, Duncan Phyfe, Louis XIV, Louis XV, Louis XVI, Directoire, Empire, French Provincial, Gothic, Elizabethan, and Victorian. Since it would take an entire book just to describe and understand the furniture of each of these periods, I suggest you read one or more of the many books available on the market if you are seriously interested in learning more about antiques.

Let's move on to some of the "classics." All modern design, in some way, relates to the principles of these periods and designers. The styles and furniture of these periods, although reproduced in more updated forms, are still going strong.

Art Nouveau (1890-1905) was the first truly original style since Rococo. Art Nouveau was primarily a style of interior design that encompassed an entire home. Furniture was often built in, but freestanding chairs had tall, straight backs and lean, rectangular shapes. Other styles of Art Nouveau have stylized forms of ornamentation. Tiffany, the designer of decorative art in metal and glass best known for his lighting fixtures, combined vibrant colors and asymmetrical patterns in his stained glass.

Frank Lloyd Wright was the pioneer in modern home design. He used unpretentious materials and was influenced by Japanese architecture. He emphasized strong vertical and horizontal lines, large open spaces, unexpected light sources, and variations in ceiling heights and geometric detailing. Wright, although an architect, also designed all the furniture for his homes. Most pieces were built in, although he did design some freestanding pieces. He is known for his use of varied colors and textures of natural materials, and the way he integrated the interiors of his homes with their natural settings.

The Bauhaus (1913-33) was the German state

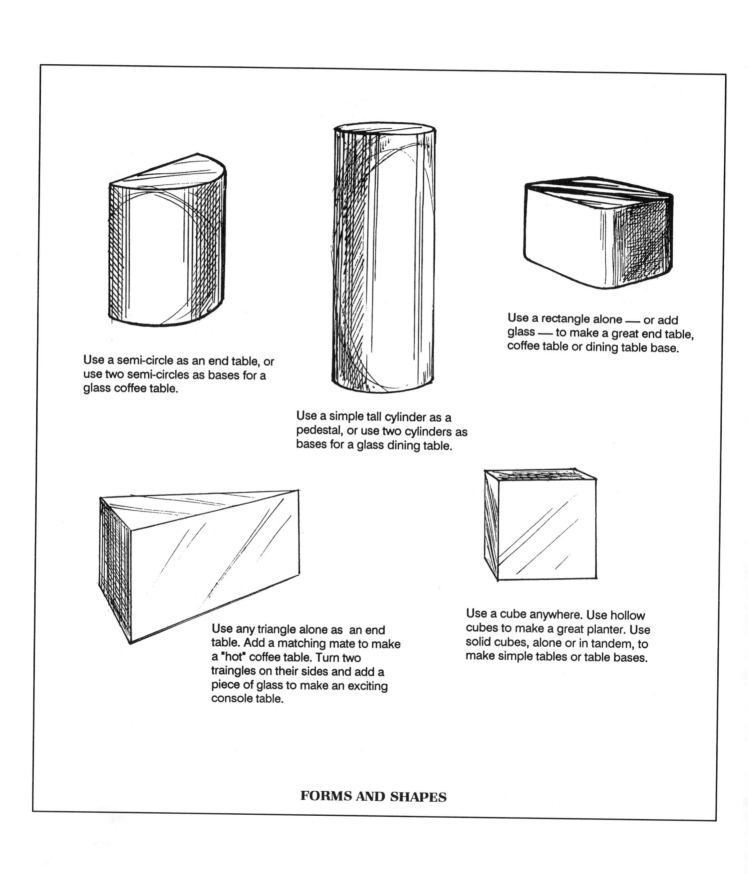

Use a semi-circle as an end table, or use two semi-circles as bases for a glass coffee table.

Use a simple tall cylinder as a pedestal, or use two cylinders as bases for a glass dining table.

Use a rectangle alone — or add glass — to make a great end table, coffee table or dining table base.

Use any triangle alone as an end table. Add a matching mate to make a "hot" coffee table. Turn two traingles on their sides and add a piece of glass to make an exciting console table.

Use a cube anywhere. Use hollow cubes to make a great planter. Use solid cubes, alone or in tandem, to make simple tables or table bases.

FORMS AND SHAPES

school of design. The chief principle was to simplify the design of any object so that no unnecessary elements would detract from the pure statement of function, material, and process of machine fabrication. Marcel Breuer, the famous Hungarian architect and designer, expressed this period by designing the well-known Breuer chair, inspired by the handlebars of a bicycle.

Ludwig Mies van der Rohe was a German architect (1886-1969) whose famous statement was, "Less is more." He is best known for his Barcelona chair.

Art Deco was the popular style of the 1920s and 1930s. It applied new materials and geometric decorations to traditional forms. It used shiny metals, glossy lacquered woods, polished stone, glass, and some of the newly invented plastics to create dynamic patterns, zigzags, thunderbolts, and sunbursts.

What's Hot, What's Not?

Whether you're turned on by the newest and hottest trends, still love and cherish the history and quality of old wood, or insist you can have the best of both worlds, here's what's happening.

- Quality is always in. If you can't afford quality, substitute creativity. Splurge on one important piece, even if you must sacrifice and leave the rest of the house empty.

- Opulent furniture is hot. More modern, casual looks are taking a back seat to elegantly furnished traditional decors.

- Eclectic furniture mixes are bigger than ever. Modern, overscaled upholstered pieces are being mixed more and more with authentic antiques.

- Overscaled anything is hot. Experiment with huge pieces in small rooms to create professional drama.

- Cleaner looking style is in. Look for high quality furniture of pure and simple design. Fabulous new finishes are replacing makeshift detailing.

- The "Michael Taylor" look is still in. Use overscaled stone furniture, sans glass tops, to make a statement.

- Fun furniture is hot. Use whimsical pieces, trompe l'oeils, and furniture as art to create cheerfully spirited rooms.

- Faux stone furniture is still in. Any faux finish will work with today's interiors. Use a finer, smoother faux stone finish; mix it with bleached wood for an even newer look.

- Art Deco is still popular. Stay away from cheap looking reproductions. Shop antique stores for the real thing.

- Parsons tables are out. They've been in long enough, haven't they?

- Oriental furniture is out. (However, Oriental accessories are very, very in.)

- Spanish furniture is definitely out and has been for over twenty years. American Indian and Southwestern looks, although enjoying great popularity right now, might soon find themselves passé.

Money-Saving Ideas

- Use commercial metal shelving anywhere. You can find it at outrageously low prices at any restaurant supply company.

- Skirt any table and add a glass top. Even use one outside for your patio. For a newer look, just knot the corners of a great decorative sheet and toss it over a round table.

- Make a table by using inexpensive wood circles attached to both ends of a press-board cube. Throw a sheet over and tie in the center. Drape it to the floor and let it "puddle."

- Use tree stumps as table bases and end tables. Sand and bleach them; add a glass top or leave them naked.

- For an inexpensive "Michael Taylor" look, use large, smooth river rocks . . . flat side up . . . as a fabulous table.
- Paint your aunt's old Victorian furniture a high gloss.
- Use glass blocks to make your own coffee table.
- Wrap an orange crate with fabric and tie with decorative cording for an almost "free" coffee table.
- Make a table base out of cardboard tubes. Glue together and paint. Add a glass top.
- Use clay pots as end tables. Paint them or leave them natural. Try using a sponged finish and adding a glass top for a more expensive look.
- Make your own faux stone table! Add the same type of coloring used for grout to any plaster, and smear it over an old wood table with a trowel. Use a comb or any other tool to create texture. Let dry. Paint with watered down paint, wipe off, and add a clear sealer.

17
Room By Room

This is almost your last chance to rethink your space. You know all the ingredients that go into each room, now it's time to blend them together in the best possible composition. The sum total of each of the elements you artfully combine will be the total look. Let's take a walk through your home, carefully analyzing the overall ambience and flow you've planned.

Foyers and Entry Halls

First impressions are important. The front door is where you welcome your guests and set the mood. Whether you're stuck with a narrow hallway or blessed with a grand entrance, the area must say "welcome." No, a bright green Astroturf mat with a daisy won't do. The first glimpse your guests have of your home should be inviting and make them feel warm and comfortable, eager to see more and make themselves at home. Even if it's just poor lonely you coming home after a harried day at the office, you should sigh pleasurably, "There's no place like home," as you walk through your own front door.

Be bold. Make your statement about color and style immediately.

Ask yourself the following questions.

Will the adjoining rooms be formal or informal?

If your home is formal, your entry should be formal. If it's traditional, you might want to use fabric-covered, even upholstered, walls and ceilings. Perhaps a fine antique mirror hung over an authentic inlaid table with a pair of crystal sconces placed on either side. The flooring might be highly polished wood with a circular Oriental rug placed over it. For a lighter, airier feeling leading into a dramatic living room, you might want to use a white-on-white wall covering blended with white floors and woodwork, then add a white console with a mirror over it. One incredible crystal chandelier will provide all the added drama you'll need.

If your home is formal and modern, feel free to make your entry breathtaking, even sexy. You might want to mirror every wall, even the ceiling, with smoked black glass, and use black marble squares on the floor. On two dramatically large lit acrylic pedestals might rest smooth, shiny, museum-quality sculptures. Lights recessed in the ceiling will add to the magical glow. Or create this same feeling in a lighter, brighter look. Go white. Use white glossy walls and floors. Light the room with a chrome ceiling that comes in squares inset with recessed lights. Add a huge, magnificent unframed modern canvas; maybe even one special chrome and white leather chair.

If your home is informal and country, your entry can be cute and casual. One good look is to use a small calico print wall covering with bleached wood floors. Add a country pine bench upholstered in matching fabric with a few contrasting throw pillows. Hang a framed mirror with coat racks over it and light the room with a wood or iron country chandelier. If you like a more rustic look, use brick or stone on the walls, and soften the effect with distressed wood floors covered with a rag rug. Add an interesting chair made from tree branches and upholstered with a heavy fabric that picks up the colors of the rag rug.

What colors will be used in the adjoining rooms?

The entry should flow easily into the adjoining rooms. Don't use any colors that will clash. Ideally, you should pick up one or more of the colors of the adjoining living room, dining room, family room, or powder room and repeat them in the entry. In more traditional homes, using colors and patterns that blend and repeat with other rooms is acceptable. In more modern rooms, a neutral color scheme with a dash of a relating color seems to work best.

How much space is there for furniture?

Obviously, you're limited by the size of your entry. It's not necessary to have seating in your entry unless the room warrants it because of its size or you can think of a real reason to have it. Usually, a table on which to place keys, mail, purses, and glasses is needed, as is a mirror to give yourself one final check before going out.

Yes, if you have a large foyer and want to add a loveseat, an armoire, a screen, a chest, a wing chair, go ahead. But some of the loveliest large entries I've seen are left open and spacious. One foyer that remains firmly in my mind had fabulous black and white squares on the floor. A large, round antique table was placed in the center, topped with a magnificent silk flower arrangement to give the room balance, drama, and color.

Another entry that I recall admiringly was completely bare. The floor was made from enormous squares of stone bordered with wood and laid on the diagonal. Dramatic trees, plants, and rocks were the only decoration other than one large abstract painting.

What type of lighting is needed?

Lighting should be friendly and welcoming, providing a subtle transition from the outside to the inside. The lighting of the entry will tell much about the character of the home and its occupants. It should be a graceful introduction into your home.

All too many times I've been in homes in which the entries are too bright and glaring. I get an overwhelming compulsion to run out as fast as possible, as I'm sure every wrinkle and flaw I possess is double magnified. If you want guests to feel at ease, light your entry with diffused light from ceiling or wall fixtures.

Will a hanging mirror or mirrored walls enhance the area?

Usually, yes. Mirrors are an excellent way to make a smaller entry look larger and to add drama and depth to an area. I was just in a restaurant in which the designer had decorated a long bare wall with French door frames filled in with panes of mirror. Each fake door was draped as though it were a real window. It gave the illusion that you were looking out into an expansive patio room rather than looking at long, blank, boring wall.

Make sure your mirrors reflect a view worthy of reflection. I've often seen people mirror walls that reflect a cluttered, messy kitchen or an unsightly closet. It's a great idea to carry a piece of mirror around the room with you, experimenting with what view or objects it will ultimately reflect if installed.

How can you make the entry look larger? Smaller?

If you're stuck with a teeny weeny entry, don't despair, there are solutions. The mirror trick won't work unless you get rid of clutter. Remember, less is more. Use minimal furniture. Add height and depth with a mirrored ceiling. Pull off door moldings and convert closet doors to flush-mount doors on a touch latch to make them disappear and give walls a smoother look. Plain, non-patterned walls and floors will make the area seem larger. Use texture instead of pattern to give the room interest. Shiny surfaces will reflect light and also give the room a larger look. Install a skylight to visually increase the room's size twofold.

If the bane of your existence is a long, narrow hallway that serves as the entry, fret no more. First, get rid of any clutter and tiny little pictures. Texture and paint the walls in a light color; you might even want to cut square or rectangular holes in the wall and build in lighting to create the feeling of more depth. Display interesting sculptures in the cutouts. Wall wash the rest of the walls with light. Change the flooring to one solid, light color, whether it is large pavers or wall-to-wall carpeting. Add a mirror at each end of the long hallway, and voilá!

If you're even more daring, cut down the wall of the hallway that divides another room. Texture and paint the new "half" wall and have lights installed inside that reflect up through glass panels. Display your favorite objets d'art on this long, dramatic divider. You might even want to cut cubicles or shelving into the bottom of the wall to show off your favorite art books.

If you feel your entry is too large, well, that's another story. Personally, I feel that no entry is too large. The drama lies in the spaciousness. However, if you insist on making it cozier and smaller, try using oversized and overstuffed furniture. Use upholstered walls and ceilings to give the room a more closed-in feeling. Area rugs will visually reduce the expanse of the floor. Darker colors, prints, and patterns will make the area seem less stark. Scattered lighting rather than overall lighting will tend to break up the room into smaller, more digestible areas.

What type of floor covering would be practical?
Any type of flooring that doesn't show dirt and wear, doesn't scuff, isn't slippery, and is easily maintainable will do. That doesn't leave you with many choices, does it?

Wood flooring is great for entries as long as it's sealed and protected well. Make sure you use the right products to give your wood floors shine. My maid once took it upon herself to polish my wood floors with spray furniture polish. I came home from work, initially delighted at the magnificent shine she had achieved. One step through the door and I slid on my rear halfway into the kitchen.

Area rugs over any hard flooring can add warmth to an entry, but make sure they're fastened in some way to the floor and are completely non-slip. Be sure any area rug you use clears the front door. There's nothing more irritating and dangerous than a rug that gets stuck or bunches up under a door all the time.

Ceramic tile and quarry tiles are also great for entries. When you select your tiles, make sure they have a porous, non-skid surface. Some tiles are too slick and slippery to be used for high traffic areas. Others are too fragile and tend to crack and chip easily. Make sure you seal your tiles properly to avoid unsightly grease and soil stains as well as scuff marks.

Vinyl is acceptable for entries only if your budget is limited. Keep it simple. Fake brick tiles and other "busy" designs tend to look tacky no matter how practical the salesperson has convinced you the flooring will be. You might want to use plain black and white vinyl squares laid in a checkerboard pattern or a solid-colored vinyl bordered in a contrasting color.

Wall-to-wall carpeting is fine for entries also. Always use the same carpeting as the adjoining rooms to create a pleasing flow. Changing types of carpeting in midstream is a definite no-no. Lower pile, tightly woven carpeting seems to wear better under the high traffic of an entry.

What elements can you add to make your guests smile and feel warm and comfortable when they see the entry for the first time?

Other than setting out a basket of $100 bills marked "take some," you can make your guests happy by making the entry as inviting and interesting as possible. Use one-of-a-kind pieces to pique their curiosity and heighten their senses. Hang a mirror to indulge their insecurities about how they appear. Use warm and flattering lighting to make them feel more attractive. Provide a convenient area for guests to hang their coats and place their hats, gloves, and purses. A wonderful idea is to have a basket or crystal bowl filled with potpourri. Yes, the aroma of a home is one of the first things a guest will notice!

What if you don't have an entry hall?

Make one. Many homes have a front door that leads directly into a living room or family room. Make your own entry by building a half wall to delineate an entry area. Use a plain or textured plaster wall with a built-in planter or build one with glass blocks. Or use a multi-paneled screen to create any shape you'd like. The screen can be Oriental, fabric upholstered, etched glass, take your pick. One great urn placed strategically on the floor in front of the screen will add even more interest. You might even want to divide the area by using a buffet or breakfront facing the front door, the unfinished back hidden by a large screen or draperies attached from the ceiling.

Living Rooms

Your living room is your personal stage. It's where you receive and entertain guests. Everything in the room makes a statement about you, your family, and your lifestyle. Whether you only use the living room for special occasions or really "live" in your living room, let's do some soul searching.

Is the room to be formal or informal?

By now you've probably pinpointed your style and are well on the way to making a final decision about your purchases. You've done your furniture plan and selected your fabrics and wall coverings. Now's the last chance to make sure what you've selected really fits your needs and lifestyle. Only you know the degree of casualness and elegance that will make you and your family feel comfortable. If you're a blue jeans and sweatshirt person, the setting of a stiff Victorian living room just seems incongruous. If you're a silk dressing gown person, country calico prints might eventually make you feel too cute.

How many are there in your family? What are their ages? Their interests?

Is the living room going to be an off limits area to your children? Woe be the day when your two year old decides to practice his finger painting on your white silk sofa. If your children have flown the nest or you plan on tying them up and keeping them in the closet, go ahead and pick delicate and sensual fabrics. But if your kids are part of your life, account for their humanness in your decorating. Choose sturdy fabrics and furniture that will withstand chocolate chip cookies and bouts of wrestling with daddy.

If your kids are past the sticky fingers stage, you might want to take the gamble and select fabrics and furnishings that are less sturdy and more what you had your heart set on. If keeping your living room perfectly neat and clean will create undue stress in your life, you might want to reconsider.

If you're lucky enough to have a family room or den for family living and your children will obey the rules you set up about going into the living room, go ahead and do anything you want. But if the living room will be the center of activity day after day, it's essential to plan for it. Provide enough comfortable seating for all family members and a number of guests; a piano for those of you who enjoy playing.

The television should be housed attractively and in a position to be easily viewed from all seating. A television placed on a metal cart with wheels is an eyesore, especially when the back can be seen from an outside window. Stereo equipment, compact disc players, speakers, and VCRs should all have their places. Use armoires or built-in cabinets to store all your electronic equipment. Books should be neatly displayed in built-in bookcases. Give your old plastic walnut-laminated bookcases to the Salvation Army, please.

Lighting, of course, should be adjustable. Ideally, you should be able to easily transform this room from the hub of family activity to an inviting and relaxing room in which to entertain your guests.

Do you have any pets?

Let's face it, not only do cats and dogs shed, they also have "accidents." If you have pets, choose fabrics that don't show fur and hair easily. Lighter, shinier fabrics will show fur and hair less than darker, more mat fabrics. Low-pile carpeting will absorb accidents more slowly than deeper pile carpeting. Beware, pet urine will stain, bleach, and damage even hardwood floors. Thoroughly check all materials you plan to use in your living room to see how "pet-proof" they really are.

How often do you entertain or have visitors? Are these visits casual or formal?

If you're a recluse, just plop one chair in the middle of your living room; it's a great way of stretching your decorating dollar. But, like most of us mortals, you probably have a neighbor or two dropping by, a few dinner parties now and then, even an occasional cocktail party. You might host your weekly poker game once a month. Plan adequate and comfortable seating for your guests. Make sure there's enough flow between pieces of furniture for visitors to get up and move around. Make sure seating is placed close enough so that guests don't have to shout across the room. Select fabrics that won't throw you into an embarrassing fit of rage if Uncle Harry accidentally spills his red wine.

What is the architecture of your house?

Your living room should not be in conflict with the basic style and architecture of your house. This doesn't mean that you can't update an old Spanish house with modern furniture, but it does mean that you can't decorate an architecturally modern house with Dutch Colonial. Some mixtures work, some don't.

The best way to learn what works and what doesn't is to study interior design magazines. Period architecture, such as Victorian or Colonial, is best left authentically furnished. Spanish and Mediterranean homes lend themselves more easily to either modern/eclectic looks or traditional. Farmhouses can be great either done in a charming, quaint country look, or modernized into an almost "art gallery" look. Ranch style homes take kindly to either a very simple modern look or a rustic look.

Architecturally modern houses appear to be the most limited and look best when decorated in the most serious modern. Bend the rule a little by using a California casual look or a Southwestern look. Classic brownstones offer a promising background for almost any style from opulent traditional to stark modern. Modern high-rise condominiums look best when done in a sophisticated decor and tend to look ridiculous when "too cute."

The best advice I can give you is to be practical without sacrificing creativity. Use all the information you've learned so far to create interesting, but usable, furniture arrangements. Play around with your furniture plan; experiment with angling furniture and using unconventional pieces in unique ways. Use colors that will flatter you and make you feel comfortable. Stay away from trendy color schemes that will look old by next year. Create your own personal and new color combinations. Make sure your living room doesn't violate any of the elements of design. Go over your plans again to check for proper balance, scale, and proportion.

Dining Rooms

Dining rooms should be planned for function and comfort. Other than these two criteria, anything goes. So throw away that old dining room set you inherited from Aunt Sophie and let's go.

What do you put on the walls?

Depends. Are you going modern, traditional, or eclectic? Is the room going to be formal or informal? The hottest wall coverings right now are Oriental murals; choose ones with pewter or muted silver backgrounds. They'll mix well with traditional wood furniture, lacquers, glass, even chrome. Painting techniques such as sponging and marbling are equally as hot and blend with almost any decor. Frame walls with large crown molding for up-to-date drama.

If your dining room is very formal, you might want to use silk-upholstered walls. If it's country, you could cover the walls with a small calico print fabric or wallpaper. If it's rustic, heavily-textured walls will look great. For opulent/traditional, you might want to use wood paneling above a chair rail, perhaps even fill in the squares with fabric or finely-beveled mirror for a more elegant look. If it's stark modern, you might just want to leave the walls plain white and display some great artwork. Mirror a wall or two to reflect an ocean view, the garden, or the city lights.

What do you put on the floors?

Again, anything goes. If you'll be using the room for everyday dining, an easily maintainable hard flooring might be the most practical. If you'll be using the room only occasionally, go ahead and use wall-to-wall carpeting or a wonderful area rug. Softer flooring will give your dining a more intimate feeling and create a quieter, more relaxed atmosphere. If you do use an area rug, make sure it's the right size. The rug should extend far enough past the chairs in order to avoid tripping and catching chair legs on the edges of the rug.

Make sure the rug is treated professionally for soil resistance. Recently I served Thanksgiving dinner on my dining room table, which sits on an expensive Dhurrie rug. I watched my ninety year old father-in-law unintentionally dropping cranberry sauce on the rug all through dinner. I cringed and bit my lips to refrain from screaming. As he had one foot out the door, I grabbed for a bowl of soap-suds and a clean rag. The bright red stains came out easily. Thank goodness I had the forethought to have the rug pre-treated for such occasions. Softer flooring will give your dining room a more intimate feeling and create a quieter, more relaxed atmosphere.

Hard flooring should be non-slip for obvious reasons. I'd hate to see you slide across the dining room floor while serving your guests a tureen of piping hot soup. Choose flooring that has good sound absorbency. There's nothing worse than a dinner interrupted by strange echoes and the clanking of heels. Ideally, if you must have hard flooring in the dining room, it should flow gracefully into the adjoining kitchen. Changing the type of flooring between the kitchen and dining room looks choppy and can even be a hazard if the different thicknesses of flooring create a gap in height.

What do you put on the windows?

Feel free to be creative and dramatic with your dining room windows, but follow the guidelines for window coverings discussed in Chapter 15.

More formal dining rooms look best with full, flowing elegant draperies. More casual dining rooms look better with less formal window treatments such as Roman shades, mini-pleated shades, horizontal blinds, verticals, shutters, or curtains. If your dining room is eclectic, choose between casual and formal window treatments. I prefer draperies because they give a warmer feel and absorb sound for quieter dining.

One great traditional or eclectic look is to attach picture frame molding to the walls, then wall upholster inside the squares or rectangles with fabric to match the draperies. To dramatize a modern room, use ceiling to floor wood-hinged panels that have been completely covered with mirror. For an eclectic room, you might just want to place a beautiful Oriental screen right in front of the window instead of draperies.

What type of furniture should you use?

I hate to be redundant, but matched dining room sets are out. Don't be afraid to mix and match modern and traditional furniture together or use several different types of wood in the same room. The size of the room and the effect you desire will dictate the size and scale of the table and chairs as well as any additional pieces, such as buffets and hutches. Play around with different furniture arrangements and review the guidelines in Chapter 5.

For a strictly modern dining room, thick ¾" glass table tops look fabulous, especially if they're beveled around the edges. Use a lacquered or faux stone pedestal for a base. If you're fighting a glass top table because you hate fingerprints and glass cleaner, I think you're sacrificing a great look for only a minor inconvenience. If you insist, use a laminated parsons table, but I warn you, parsons tables are on their way out. Be cautious about purchasing a table with a lacquered top as lacquer tends to scratch and chip easily.

Select chairs that are comfortable and pull in and out easily. Mix antique-reproduction dining chairs that have been lacquered or pickled and upholstered in a modern fabric with a glass-top pedestal table. Don't mix these types of chairs with a parsons table or a four-legged glass and chrome table — it won't work. Use either a simple upholstered dining chair or a chrome and cane chair such as the Breuer chair. One of the best looking modern dining rooms I've ever seen used high-grade commercial office chairs, complete with chrome bases and casters, placed around a chrome and glass conference table.

For a more formal, traditional dining room, select an elegant wood table with a fine patina or finely-crafted wood base with a thick glass top. Use more traditional dining chairs with a finer finish and more conventional fabric. For more country casual dining rooms, choose a bleached pine or oak table. Use ladderback chairs, perhaps with printed cushions tied neatly at each corner of the seat.

One favorite budget-stretching idea, suggested by interior designer Victoria Brucher of San Francisco, is to cover an inexpensive round press-board table with a great chintz tablecloth and top it with a ¼" thick piece of glass. This table will look great with ladderback chairs or even your old dining room chairs that have been slipcovered and skirted to the floor. You'll save enough money to be able to afford that huge Welsh dresser that will just "make" the room.

For eclectic rooms, feel free to mix and match different style chairs and tables. Be careful . . . some styles mix well, others don't. Look at magazine pictures to see what types of furniture the professionals are mixing together effectively.

You might want to add a buffet, a china closet, a hutch, a serving table, a Welsh dresser, a baker's rack, corner cupboards, or even an armoire. A stack of Oriental chests is a great idea for adding storage and drama to almost any dining room.

To make your own serving table, why not just mount a long, thick piece of glass on the wall and support it with decorative corbels? Or use a piece of bleached, lacquered, or laminated wood suspended from the wall. Just place two great urns or pieces of sculpture on either end for that professional look.

What kind of lighting should you use?

You have your choice: chandeliers, track lighting, pendants, sconces, wall brackets, ceiling spots, cupboard lighting, candlelights, picture lighting. Select the right combination to dine by. Thumb through Chapter 10 again to refresh your memory.

Hang your fixtures high enough so they don't glare in anyone's eyes, but low enough to shed light right above the dining table. Have an electrician install the wiring in the exact spot; "swagging" fixtures is totally passé.

Always install a dimmer switch to control the light level. You'll have sufficient light when you're working around the table and be able to dim it to a romantic level when you dine. Speaking of romance, don't forget the candles!

What colors should you use?

If you've read Chapter 8, you've probably already decided what colors to use. For a quick refresher, remember, dark colors will make your dining room more intimate; white, light, or neutral colors will make the room soothing and serene; bright colors will create a more festive, animated feeling.

What about tableware?

Don't set the table with old bits and pieces of chipped and cracked dishes and glasses set on frayed table linens. Invest in a good collection of coordinated tablecloths, place mats, napkins, and napkin rings. Crystal, china, and silverware should match the room and sparkle with elegance.

What about a centerpiece for the table?

Old standards, like a vase of silk flowers or a bowl of fruit, are boring. Be creative, use props. Place stalks of bamboo inside an inexpensive round goldfish bowl; add one perfect silk flower. Or use two urns, one standing upright, the other on its side. Or a set of Buddhas placed back to back. Search accessory and antique shops to stimulate your creative genius.

What if you don't have a separate dining room?

Fake it! If you have an L-shaped dining room-living room combination, you might just want to let the two rooms flow together as one for a more spacious, open feeling. If you'd like to divide the two areas, try using a screen or an open wall unit finished on both sides. Or use the same tricks with half walls and hutches as suggested for creating a separate entry.

If you have no dining room at all there's no reason you can't create an area that will work. Place a drop-leaf table against a wall; it'll convert into a dining table in a split second. Or attach a large piece of wood to the wall with a bottom hinge and a top latch. One side will be laminated and the other side will be a piece of art. When the piece of wood is flush to the wall it's a picture; when you unlatch it and pull it down, it becomes a table.

Family Rooms, Dens, and Recreation Rooms

Call them what you will, family rooms, dens, recreation rooms, rumpus rooms, basements, they're where the family gathers. These rooms will really be lived in and need to be planned and designed accordingly.

What activities will take place in this room?

Perhaps your family is a group of eager beavers. Dad likes to work on his model airplanes most weekends and evenings. Junior likes to sprawl out on the floor and organize his stamp collection. Sis works on her rock collection when she's not practicing the latest dance steps. Mom likes to quilt and sew while she's watching television. How do you please the entire clan?

Ask yourself the following questions.

1. Will the room be used for snacks and/or meals?

2. Will the room be used for music, parties?

3. Will the room be used for reading, games, crafts, television watching?

4. How much storage is necessary? Do you have an abundance of books, records, tapes, cassettes, compact disks, craft materials, sewing machine and supplies that need a neat place for storage?

5. Will the room be used primarily in the daytime or in the evening?

6. How informal do you want the room to look?

Is this room going to be the entertainment center of the house?

If you're a normal family, the focus of family togetherness includes watching television and listening to music as a group. The television will probably be the focal point of the room around which all seating is arranged. Construct a complete wall of built-in cabinets and shelving to house all of your electronic equipment. Ideally, the television should be in the center and at eye level when people are seated. Built in underneath the television should be your VCR and stereo equipment. Include room for a compact disc player even if you don't have one yet. Most of these components are only about four inches high and stack well one on top of the other. Drawers or shelving with slots to hold cassettes, discs, records, and videotapes should also be built in. On either side of the television you might want to have open shelving to display your books and any special objets d'art or trophies. Along the bottom of the built-in unit should be a series of closed cabinets where everyone can store their hobby and craft supplies. You might want to assign each family member his or her own personal section.

What type of furnishing do you select?

Sturdy and carefree! Select soil-resistant carpeting that won't mat down or show footprints easily. If you're using a hard flooring such as vinyl, tile, or wood, use an area rug over it that can be easily cleaned. Select tightly woven, heavier upholstery fabrics that wear well and resist spills and stains. If you opt for a crisper, lighter look, try using washable slipcovers that can easily pull or zip off. All table top finishes should be resistant to scratches, chipping, and staining. Shop around. You'll be surprised how many exciting products are available to meet your needs.

What colors should you use?

I warn you, you're going to have a difficult time pleasing the entire family. Your best bet is to select a neutral color scheme for this room. Add subtle dashes of color to relate and blend with the overall color scheme of your home. Avoid bold prints and patterns in this room, as they tend to create a cluttered effect and quickly look old and faded from use.

How do you make such a practical room exciting?

If your home is modern, try using plastic laminated furniture and built-ins in light neutral colors such as beige, off-white, or gray. Use heavy but smooth fabrics in darker-tone variations. Add a few red, yellow, or blue pillows for color. Use a tightly-woven commercial grade carpeting in another varying shade of the same neutral color. Paint the walls yet another shade of the same color or cover them with a simple textured vinyl wall covering.

If your home is traditional, avoid the production line wood furniture offered by the corner furniture store. Instead, search antique shops and garage sales for inexpensive pieces with character. Use comfortable, overstuffed upholstered pieces. Fabrics should be tightly woven, but soft, not stiff. Hardwood floors look great. Cover them with an inexpensive Oriental rug reproduction.

You might want to create a lighter-looking family room by using wicker, bamboo, or rattan furniture. Be careful, this type of furniture, unless particularly heavy, will wear out quickly. Choose sturdy pieces and heavier, nubby fabrics such as Haitian cotton. These rooms look best with light wall-to-wall carpeting or bleached wood floors covered with cotton area rugs.

Children's Rooms

Let's not forget personal space for our little darlings. From infancy to young adulthood, they're a major part of our lives. Children are more affected than adults by the colors and forms in their environment. Psychological studies have shown that children's surroundings stimulate their creativity and intelligence and affect their dispositions. They seem to feel more secure in smaller, cozier rooms. Children grow and change rapidly, thus their rooms should be carefully planned for adaptability.

THE NURSERY

An infant's room should be planned with plenty of play space and storage, you'll need it soon enough. You'll also need a crib and/or a bassinet, of course, plenty of drawer space, a dressing table or counter surface to use for changing diapers, shelving for displaying stuffed animal collections and other toys, as well as a comfortable chair for feeding the baby.

Most people tend to decorate their nurseries in delicate pastels such as powder blue, pink, or yellow, but children are more stimulated by bright, bold, and clear colors.

One couple I know decorated their child's room in a fantasy theme, using brightly painted plywood cutouts to create clouds, trees, and rainbows. Another couple constructed a wardrobe for their little girl that looked exactly like a fairy tale house, complete with shingle roof. They even painted shutters, curtains, and flower pots on it. There are many ingenious ways of using plywood to create decorative cutouts or even frames for beds.

Lighting should be well planned. Install good overhead lighting on a dimmer switch. You'll be able to dim the lights down easily at night for the baby to sleep, and there will be no exposed cords or wires for the baby to play with or trip over. Pre-plan at least six electrical outlets, two of them above work surfaces. Be safe. Cover them for now with plastic safety plugs that you can buy at any hardware store.

Window coverings should be simple and easy to clean. Horizontal blinds or verticals are good choices; they can filter or block the light during the baby's naps. If you use curtains, install a blackout shade behind them.

Flooring should be sensible. Choose one that's hard wearing, durable, and easy to clean. The floor will take a lot of abuse from spills, sharp toys, sitting, crawling, crayons, and paints. Your baby will eventually be spending a lot of time on the floor, playing with dolls, puzzles, building blocks, erector sets, and toy cars. Select a flooring that's not too hard or cold. Look for hard floorings with cushioned backing. Place an area rug on top of the flooring, but make sure it has a non-slip backing and is secured to the floor in some way.

Freestanding baby furniture is readily available in stores. Choose pieces that are easily washable, don't have sharp corners, and preferably are multi-functioned to grow with the needs of your baby. Many furniture companies are now making furniture that doubles as a playground, using brightly finished tubes and geometric shapes. Shop around. This might be a good place to cut expenses by buying used furniture. Children do outgrow their furniture rapidly.

For seating, if you have room, you might want to consider building platform-based twin beds strewn with pillows and set at right angles to each other in one of the corners of the room. Later, these will become the baby's bed.

You might also want to invest in a colorful cart on rollers to hold all of the baby's necessities. It can be used later for a television or stereo stand.

For baby's dressing table, you might want to build a surface that's adjustable in height. Later, it can be adapted to become a desk top.

Now's a good time to put in a whole wall of built-in cabinets and shelving to save space and plan for the inevitable toy and book collections. Plan your shelving so that there is adequate space to display stuffed animals, books, and other collections, and enough cabinet space to house less aesthetically pleasing toys and paraphernalia. You might also want to build in a section that will later house your child's personal television set and stereo equipment.

Check all wall coverings, fabrics, paints, and furniture finishes for chemical content and toxicity. Many a baby has severe reactions to the materials used in these seemingly harmless room enhancers.

ROOMS FOR TODDLERS AND PRESCHOOLERS

Safety comes first. Remove all fragile and breakable objects from the room. Double check for pointed or sharp-edged furniture. Either remove these pieces or cover the corners with plastic or cloth. Crawl around on the floor as if you were the toddler and remove all potentially dangerous objects.

Now's the time to add a blackboard, a bulletin board, and a large easel with an abundant supply of drawing paper. Toddlers and preschoolers love to draw with crayons and paint large pictures. A little forethought will deter them from practicing on the walls.

You can remove the crib and add a bed or beds now. If you opt for bunk beds, make sure they're enclosed and safe. One cute and innovative idea is to make built-in bunk beds out of wood or plastic grating painted in a bright color. It creates a playful, cage-like effect that will make a young child feel secure. Or buy tubular scaffolding complete with ladders and attachable desks you can assemble yourself. The configuration of these units can be changed around, added to, or subtracted from. Some bunk beds even come with built-in storage drawers underneath.

A large toy chest is indispensable. Children tend to jump from playing with one toy to another, leaving little scattered pieces all over the room. Cleanup time is a lot less stressful for both parents and child if the little toys and pieces can easily be thrown into one large chest. You might want to build in a toy chest under a window, complete with a liftable lid that becomes a window seat when down. Or use a large chest that doubles as a table. If there isn't adequate space in the room, consider using the closet. Large stacking boxes made from metal grating or plastic milk carton boxes will do.

ROOMS FOR EARLY SCHOOL DAYS

Once children reach about age four or five, they need a few chairs and a large work table or desk for working on their projects, drawings, and homework. If you didn't build in shelving, now might be a good time to add the type of shelving that attaches to a wall near a desk or work table for easily accessible book storage. You can make shelving yourself out of wood or buy pre-made grid shelving units that come in a variety of lengths and widths. Several companies make inexpensive free-standing laminated shelving and cabinet units. These are a dollar-stretching solution to storage and organization problems.

You might want to add another bed now for the inevitable sleep-overs. If you haven't already put in bunk beds, a trundle bed is an ingenious idea. It's a low bed placed on casters that rolls under an-

other bed. Many manufacturers make trundle beds in which the second bed is completely hidden under the main bed by a piece of wood that rolls out with the trundle bed.

ROOMS FOR PRETEENS

By now, your child is on his way to becoming a teenager. Wallpapers and fabrics that were cute when he was an infant or toddler are beginning to irritate him. Most kids this age like to think they're more grown up and would prefer a more high tech room. They seem to have definite ideas and their own personal taste about how their rooms should be decorated and organized. This is a natural process as they assert their individuality and feelings of territoriality. Their room becomes a personal retreat, a place to entertain friends, and a place to stimulate their creative processes and imagination.

It's their domain. Provide them with the essential furniture that they'll need and let them "do their thing" no matter how it upsets you. Rest assured, they'll tape their favorite posters and self-made artwork to the wallpaper. Of course, the wallpaper will peel off when you try to remove the tape. Preteens also love to display little objects on their windowsills, which almost always leaves unsightly rings and looks terrible from outside the house. Be patient.

ROOMS FOR TEENAGERS

By now your children have developed more sophisticated tastes. They will be relentless in nagging you to redecorate their rooms. You might want to give in, removing all traces of "babyishness."

Your teenager will want more lounging area for entertaining friends. If you've planned well, you can convert twin beds into serving a dual purpose as sofas. You might want to dispose of bunk beds and replace them with other sleeping and lounging units. If you've built in storage and shelving units, perhaps they can be painted an updated color. Desks and chest of drawers may be too small in scale for your teenager and will need replacement. Consider buying new furniture that will be useful as guest room furniture later on when your child goes to college or moves out and gets his own apartment.

Make sure your teenager has a large well-lit desk for schoolwork. You might want to redo the poling in the closets to accommodate the longer lengths of clothing. Consider adding portable drawers in the closet or building in more drawers. Teenagers, especially girls, tend to collect accessories that need to be put somewhere neatly.

Walls should become more sophisticated. Strip off old cute wallpaper and repaint in a plain color. Teenagers love to decorate their own walls with posters. You might want to cover hard flooring with carpeting or toss an area rug over part of the floor.

The room's window coverings have probably seen better days by now. Your teenage boy will probably insist on horizontal blinds, verticals, Roman shades, or mini-pleated shades. Your teenage girl may be more inclined to choose more feminine draperies or curtains.

The key to successfully decorating a child's room is the ability to see the space through the child's eyes. Too many young parents are overly concerned about their house guests seeing unsightly clutter in their child's room. It's understandable, but try to use good storage techniques that will keep the room neat while allowing the child some freedom of expression. Remember, adaptability and flexibility are the most important words. Your child will grow and change rapidly.

Master Bedrooms

Your personal habits and preferences will dictate how you decorate your master bedroom. Some people prefer to use their bedroom for just a place to sleep, while others "live" in their bedrooms, watching television, eating, playing cards, etc. Beyond a doubt, comfort should be the major criterion in decorating this room. Let's analyze your needs.

What activities will take place in the bedroom?
Although sleeping and other intimate activities are the obvious answers, let's be more thorough. Besides storing clothes, dressing, and putting on makeup, you might read, watch television, and listen to music. You might even need a desk to do your work or a table to do your sewing. Chances are, you're cramped for space.

Are there tricks for stretching space?
Yes! To make a room feel more spacious, use the tricks you've learned in this book. Place mirrors at right angles to the window and all along one wall. It'll make the bedroom look double its size and twice as light. Use a framed mirror as a headboard, especially if it reflects the window. Use flooring with a diagonal or geometric pattern. Repeat the same prints on beds, windows, bedspreads, and upholstery.

Use armoires or chests that blend with the color of the wall. Screens will give the illusion of more space because of their angles. Use them to hide unsightly equipment. Light colors on walls, ceilings, floors, and fabric backgrounds will make the room appear larger. Build a platform on which to place your bed to create a "two rooms in one" look. Place uplights strategically in one or two corners of the room.

To actually create more space try using multipurpose furniture such as beds with built-in storage underneath or a trunk or ottoman that serves both as storage space for extra linens and blankets and as a seat or table. Reorganize your closet; use every inch to its greatest advantage. Make a desk by using two chests of drawers set apart for adequate leg room, then covered with a glass or laminated top.

Position the bed in the center of the room, then place a desk behind it to serve as both a headboard and a desk. Build in creative shelving along the tops of walls. Use larger chests of drawers instead of nightstands for more storage. Angle your bed from the corner of the room to add drama and create more interesting space.

How do you select a style?

The master bedroom should relate to the decor of the rest of the house, of course.

If your home is basically traditional, use period furniture or antique reproductions mixed and matched eclectically. Stay away from matched bedroom sets, they're out! Fabrics should be soft, flowing, and sensual. Prints and patterns should be subtle; bold, unnerving prints and patterns might provoke you into taking sleeping pills. Lighting should be subtle. Supplement good overhead lighting on a dimmer switch with lamps. Better yet, for reading, use wall-hung lamps over your nightstands to increase table top space. Use wall-to-wall carpeting or soft, cushiony area rugs. There's nothing more uncomfortable than cold, hard flooring under your feet first thing in the morning. Window coverings should match the decor of the room. You might want to consider blackout shades or lining if light tends to seep through early in the morning.

If your home is modern, your bedroom should be too. Furniture should be sleek and simple — perhaps a mattress placed on a built-in platform. Angle it in one corner of the room and use laminated triangles for nightstands and a headboard. Or angle a simple, upholstered bed to face directly towards a view. Use track lighting on a dimmer switch for overall lighting that can be adjusted for romantic evenings. Consider uplights placed behind the bed for even more drama. Avoid the "too easy" bedroom sets widely available in furniture stores. Instead, mix and match forms and shapes as table and nightstands using, perhaps, a wall unit or lacquered armoire to store your television and stereo equipment. Window coverings should be sleek, simple, and practical. Use verticals, horizontal blinds, lacquered shutters, or mirrored panels. Mini-pleated shades won't work because too much light will shine through.

If your home is eclectic, have some fun. Maybe you'd like a four poster bed made of acrylic, wood, or brass draped with an elegant, flowing fabric. Perhaps you'd like a simple, tailored upholstered bed

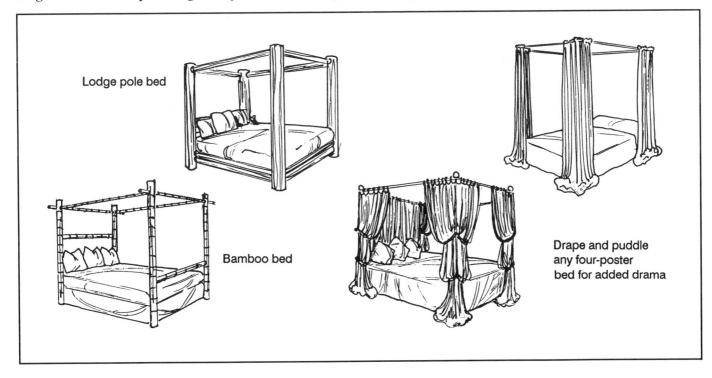

Lodge pole bed

Bamboo bed

Drape and puddle
any four-poster
bed for added drama

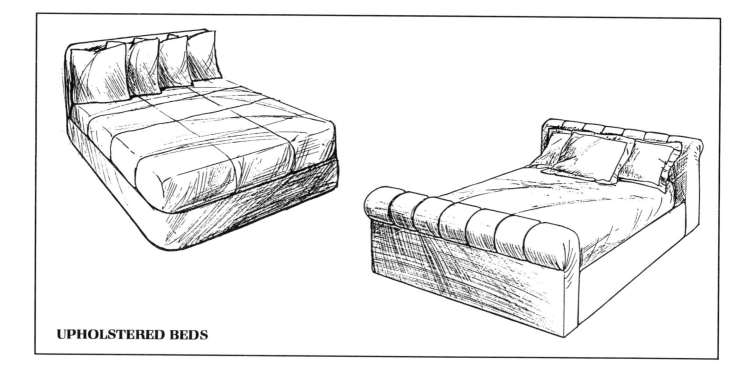

UPHOLSTERED BEDS

set against a multi-paneled Oriental screen, a luxurious fur throw tossed over the bed. Mix these looks with interestingly finished armoires. For interesting nightstands, use stacks of black Oriental chests or carved tables that have been lacquered white. Choose either wall-to-wall carpeting, a soft, plush, carved area rug, or even an Oriental rug to give the room depth and warmth. Use unusual and overscaled artwork and accessories along with provocative lighting to pull it together.

If your home is the country look, your bedroom will be cute and adorable. Use light wood and pine furniture mixed with tiny prints and plain chintzes; even combine white eyelet and lace if you're taste is ultra feminine. Feel free to decorate your bed in delicate pillow shams, duvets, and dust ruffles. If you'd like a brass or iron bed, great, but stay away from cheap-looking reproductions. Instead, find an old brass bed and have it refinished; it'll be more interesting and look more professional. Use old trunks as seating and tables and a large pine armoire to store your television and other

equipment. Cover your windows with light airy curtains, making sure you've concealed blackout shades underneath. Flooring should be soft and warm; select area rugs with subtle patterns.

If your home is California casual, be dramatic. Use glossy white or bleached four-inch wide shutters, towering trees planted in enormous baskets, oversized upholstered beds, sofas, chairs, and throw pillows. Get rid of any clutter; replace knick-knacks with one important piece of artwork. Mirror the walls and use pedestals behind the bed to hold huge sculptures, vases, or urns.

If your home is the Southwestern look, try a lodge-pole bed. (Although, unfortunately, this has been copied and overused recently.) Use nubbly, Indian fabrics in multi-pastels. Paint the walls white, add a few pieces of Southwestern art and two or three handmade drums. Toss a Dhurrie rug over light wood floors or use beige or off-white wall-to-wall Berber carpeting.

If you've always dreamt of having a "fantasy" bedroom, now's the time. Build your own four poster bed; drape it dramatically with flowing tiers of translucent fabric, tie at each corner and let it flow to a "puddle" on the floor. Use even more fabric to "tent" the ceiling or create a sunburst effect by attaching fabric to the top of each wall and gathering it at the center of the ceiling. Why not even mirror the ceiling?

Cover your windows with lace, and toss lace and satin pillows on your bed. Mix and match the same fabrics to make inexpensive skirted tables to use as nightstands. Add a few one-of-a-kind white wicker chairs with fanned backs and complete the look with a fabulous bamboo armoire.

How do you select a bed?

Very carefully. The size of the bed is dictated by the size the room will accommodate and the people who will be sleeping in the bed. The length of the bed should be six inches longer than the person sleeping on it.

Mattresses come in the following sizes:

	Width	Length
Single	30"–34"	75"
Twin (regular)	39"	75"
Twin (king or extra-long)	39"	80–84"
Full (regular)	54"	75"
Full (king or extra-long)	54"	80–84"
Queen (regular)	60"	75"
Queen (king or extra-long)	60"	80–84"
King (regular)	76"	75"
King (king or extra-long)	76"	80–84"
King (Eastern)	78"	80"
King (California)	72"	84"

Most mattresses are innerspring mattresses. They are constructed with inner coils.

An open coil mattress has flexible steel springs attached to each other and a piece of steel border wire defining the edge of the unit. Open coil construction is noted for its good recovery and is designed for one to sleep "on" the mattress, rather than "in" the mattress.

A pocketed coil unit is placed in muslin or olefin to provide strength. Each spring works independently of the others. This type of coil unit conforms more easily to the contours of the body, but is the more expensive of the two and can be highly flammable.

Stuffed mattresses are made from high grade cotton or polyester 5½" thick. The material is wrapped with a layer of ⅝" thick polyester foam, which acts as a fire retardant. They are not very durable, lose resiliency, and form lumps quickly.

Foam mattresses are generally made with polyurethane molded with a solid core and graded by density. Soft is ten to twenty pounds; medium is twenty to thirty pounds; firm or hard is thirty to forty pounds. Foams tends to recover slowly, provide less body support, and hold moisture and odors. However, foam mattresses have non-allergenic properties and are resistant to mildew and insects.

Choose your mattress carefully. Throw your inhibitions aside and lie down on it. Pay no attention to the manufacturer's grading . . . soft, medium, firm, extra firm, orthopedic, and orthopedic-type; these gradings vary from manufacturer to manufacturer. The more weight you place on the mattress, the firmer it should become. Bounce on it. There shouldn't be any annoying squeaks. Stretch out. The mattress should be at least six inches past your toes. Sit on the edge. It shouldn't feel too stiff or give too much. Check that there are enough air vents on both sides and handles for frequent turning. Forget the pattern of the ticking, you'll rarely see it. More important, it should be made out of five ounce if not eight ounce fabric and tightly woven. Avoid mattresses with buttons or tufting; they'll only make uncomfortable lumps.

The standard box spring is usually seven

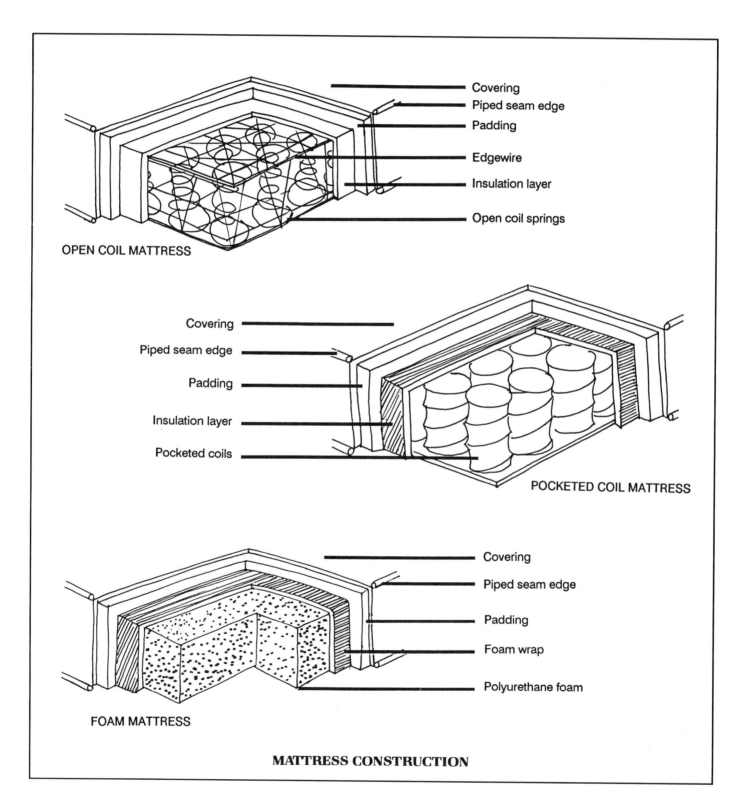

OPEN COIL MATTRESS

Covering
Piped seam edge
Padding
Edgewire
Insulation layer
Open coil springs

Covering
Piped seam edge
Padding
Insulation layer
Pocketed coils

POCKETED COIL MATTRESS

Covering
Piped seam edge
Padding
Foam wrap
Polyurethane foam

FOAM MATTRESS

MATTRESS CONSTRUCTION

inches high and comes along with the mattress as a set. It should be made of kiln-dried hardwood and have wood slats supporting each row of coils in the box along with a center brace for greater strength. The top padding should make it impossible to feel the springs inside and the ticking should be of the same fabric as the mattress.

How do you "dress" the bed?

Ready-made coordinated sets of sheets, pillowcases, pillow shams, comforters, duvets, and bedspreads are readily available in almost any department store or bed and bath shop. Shop around, some even bear the label of well-known designers such as Ralph Lauren and Laura Ashley. Be creative, use these wonderful bed linens to make matching draperies, tablecloths, and slipcovers for instant and budget-stretching decorating.

If you can't find bed linens to suit your tastes, there's no reason (except expense) why you can't have your bedding custom made. Your drapery workroom or upholsterer can either make what you want or suggest someone else to do it. Be sure to provide detailed instruction on how each piece is to be made. There are many different styles of bedspreads, comforters, and pillow covers. Specify the pattern of quilting you desire, the type of welting, the type of padding, whether the corners are to be gathered, ruffled, or tailored, and whether a cover is to have a zipper or not. For bedspreads and duvets, make sure you specify the "drop." The drop is the number of inches a bedspread or comforter extends down over the edge of the bed. In the case of a tablecloth, the drop is the number of inches the tablecloth extends from the edge of the table to the floor. Once you've given the person who is making these items for you the correct dimensions, details, drop, and pattern repeat, they'll be able to tell you how much yardage to order.

There are many different types of pillows. Down pillows are judged by bulk. Goose down, the most expensive, should weigh about 1½ pounds for a standard size 21" by 27" pillow. Duck down will weigh about twice as much because it has a tendency to pack down. Check grading labels before making any purchases. The finest down comes from Poland; processes used to make Oriental down are usually inferior. There are various combinations of feather and down; check the labels. Pillows made with better quality feathers or down will spring back quickly after pressure is applied.

Foam pillows are usually polyurethane or latex foam. They're graded soft, medium, or firm. Make sure you buy solid foam rather than shredded foam for greater comfort and wear as well as less flammability.

Dacron polyester pillows are a great alternative for those of you allergic to feathers and down. They should be filled compactly and have no lumps.

All pillows should have two covers, one to contain whatever filling you select and one to zip off and wash. Your pillowcase goes over these two covers.

Pleasant dreams.

Kitchens

Kitchens consist of many elements, both practical and aesthetic. Whether you're lucky enough to start from scratch or are just giving a facelift to an old kitchen, let's go step by step to find out how to design a well-conceived kitchen. Once you've finished this section, play around with the plan on paper to find the right solution for your space.

THE LAYOUT

A well-planned kitchen has an easy flow from the storage area to the preparation area to the cooking and serving area. These three basic areas are called work centers and should form a basic "work triangle" for maximum efficiency.

- A U-shaped kitchen has cabinets and appliances on three continuous walls or counter tops.
- An L-shaped kitchen has cabinets and appliances on two adjoining walls or counters.

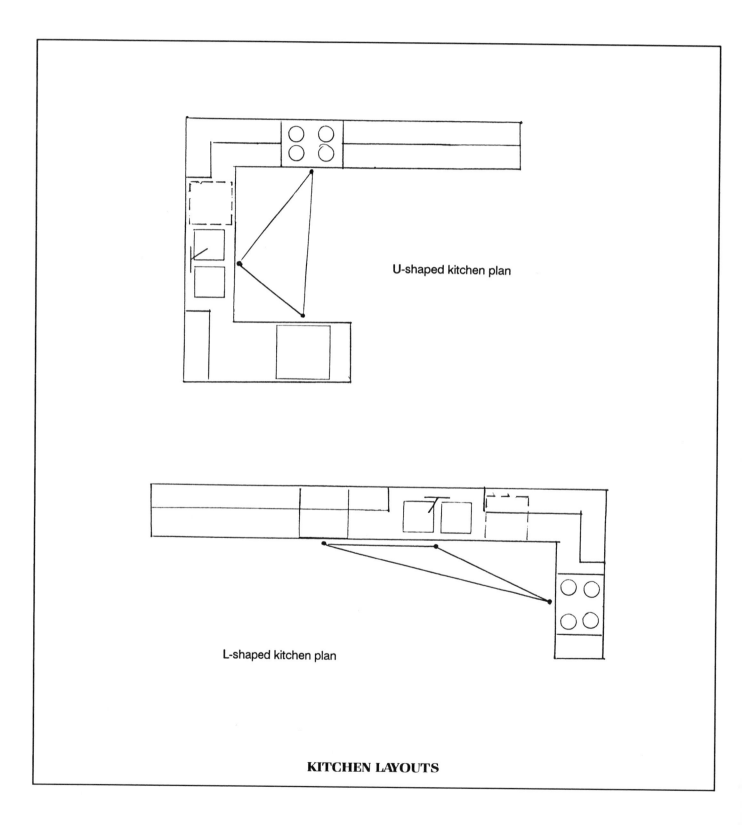

U-shaped kitchen plan

L-shaped kitchen plan

KITCHEN LAYOUTS

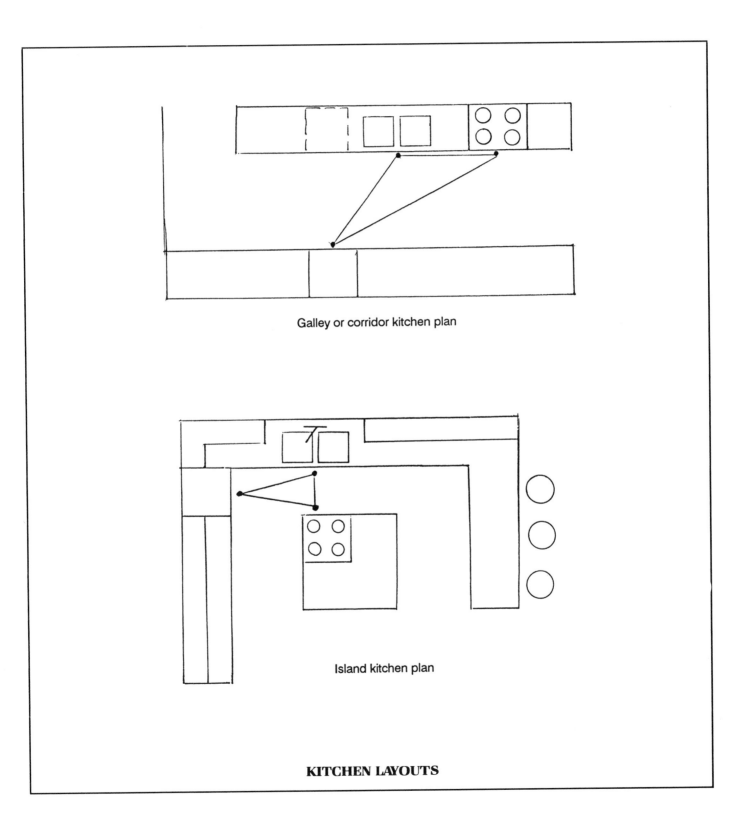

Galley or corridor kitchen plan

Island kitchen plan

KITCHEN LAYOUTS

• A galley kitchen or corridor kitchen has cabinets and appliances on opposite walls or counters.

• A one-wall kitchen has cabinets and appliances all along one wall.

• An island kitchen has an island unit which adds extra work space and storage.

• A peninsula kitchen is the same as a island kitchen, but the larger, usually rectangular, area is used to divide the kitchen from the family room or dining room.

ORGANIZING WORK CENTERS

The food storage center includes the refrigerator, freezer, and pantry. It should be located near the entry so you can unload and put away groceries easily. Allow a minimum of eighteen inches of counter space between a refrigerator and a sink. Ideally, this area should be thirty-six inches wide to use it for mixing ingredients and keeping mixing supplies such as a blender. The refrigerator door should open toward the sink and the counter.

The food preparation center includes the sink. Ideally, it should be placed between the refrigerator and range. Allow a bare minimum of twelve inches of counter space on either side. Make sure to include storage space for colanders, paring knives, salad spinners, etc. Allow adequate space for a dishwasher, trash compactor or trash container, and storage for cleaning supplies.

The cooking and serving center should be as close to the eating area as possible. Island and peninsula kitchens are great step savers between cook top and dinner table. If your cook top is on an island, allow a minimum of twelve inches on either side and at the back for pot and pan handles that may jut out. If the cook top adjoins a range, allow a minimum of twenty-one inches of work surface. Be sure the area has enough storage and counter space for coffee makers, toasters, knives, pots and pans, etc.

APPLIANCES

Refrigerators come in many sizes and have many features. The standard rule of thumb is to allow twelve cubic feet of refrigerator and freezer combined for each two-person family. Then add two cubic feet for each additional family member. However, you can adjust this figure according to your lifestyle and the amount of space you have to work with.

Choose a refrigerator by its size, its configuration of shelves and drawers, whether it is self-defrosting, whether it has a cold water and ice cube dispenser on the outside of the freezer door; some newer models even come with computerized temperature controls. If your counter space is to the left of the refrigerator, buy a right-hinged unit. If your counter space is to the right of the refrigerator, buy a left-hinged unit. Side-by-side refrigerator-freezers will always have the refrigerator door hinged on the right and the freezer door hinged on the left. If your refrigerator will be in a corner, remember, you'll only be able to open the door about ninety degrees, which might prevent you from reaching meat and vegetable bins. Most important, don't forget to measure the exact size of the existing opening allotted for the refrigerator before buying it and having it delivered. It has to fit.

For aesthetics' sake, stay away from almond or yellow-colored refrigerators, especially ones with cute little designs on them. Pass up these old colors for plain white or newer colors such as gray, black glass, or stainless steel. Do remember, though, that black and stainless steel show fingerprints easily. One company makes refrigerators that can be built in to look like part of the cabinetry or paneled with the same wall covering as your walls. They're costly, but they look great.

Sinks can be purchased in single, double, or even triple compartment models. If you don't have a dishwasher, a double-compartment sink is a necessity. Choose an extra deep sink to accommodate large pots and pans. Whether you choose a self-rimming sink or one that's set into the counter with a steel rim depends on the type of counter top you have. Sinks come in either porcelain enamel on cast iron or steel, or in stainless steel. Either choice is durable and stain resistant. Again, stay away from "old" colors; select neutrals such as white, beige, or gray.

A trash compactor should fit neatly under the counter and near the sink. Units come in standard sizes of twelve, fifteen, and eighteen inches wide.

Dishwashers come in standard widths of twenty-four inches, although recently an eighteen-inch wide model has come on the market for tighter spaces. Choose your dishwasher for its capacity and features as well as how it will coordinate with your other appliances.

Cook tops come in a variety of configurations, ranging from two burners to six burners. Some even have built-in griddles and grills and are self cleaning. Select gas or electric according to your preference and the cost of each type of energy in your area. If you select electric, look into the new flat cook tops that double as counter space when not in use. Most conventional built-in ovens come equipped with microwave ovens. Built-in units have 240 volts, while plug-in units have 110 volts. Often, convection ovens are also built in with conventional ovens. A fan circulates heated air, which speeds up the baking process and distributes the heat evenly. If you're a gourmet cook and tempted to install one of those great looking commercial units with twelve burners, be aware that they require special adaptation because they generate so much heat. Check into the extra amount of insulation, space, ventilation, and electricity or gas it might require before purchasing one.

There are two basic types of ventilating systems. The updraft type will suck the fumes up through an exhaust fan installed in an overhead cabinet or a hood. The downdraft system will draw the fumes down through the appliance cabinet and vent them to the outside. Downdraft systems don't need a hood, so they're great for island or peninsula cook tops. Check with a salesperson or your contractor to determine the right ventilating system for your kitchen. They'll be able to tell you how many cubic feet of air per minute (CFM) your situation requires.

CABINETS

If you're starting from scratch, either have custom cabinets built in by a cabinetmaker to your specifications or purchase pre-made modular units. If you're just giving your kitchen a facelift, either strip and repaint or stain your cabinets or have a carpenter install new fake fronts on them.

Custom-built cabinets are built and installed to your specifications and allow you to select any size, design, style, or finish you desire. Odd shapes, angles, and corners can be given specialized treatments. Be sure to specify both interior and exterior finishes, hardware, and any special design features.

Modular units can stretch your decorating dollar further. They come in a wide range of styles, colors, and sizes. Buy them unfinished or in finishes of stained wood, laminated, or with a European lacquer finish. The components come in three basic parts: the cupboards and shelves, the drawers and drawer fronts, and the top work surface. Wall cabinets range in height from twelve to thirty-nine inches. Widths range from nine to twenty-four inches for single-door cabinets to thirty-nine to forty-eight inches for double-door cabinets. Corner cabinets with revolving shelves are available from most manufacturers. Broom closets range from twelve to twenty-four inches deep and seven feet tall. Bottom cabinets are usually thirty-six inches from floor to top of work surface.

Installing fake fronts on existing cabinets is a great money-saving idea. A good carpenter can remove old-fashioned looking cabinet doors and install new doors in any style. I often update an old kitchen by having plain, laminated doors installed flush mount with touch latches to create an Italian-looking, high tech kitchen. If the cabinets are still in decent condition and the client is on a very strict budget, I'll have my painter strip and sand the cabinets, then either have him apply a glossy enamel or bleach and stain the cabinets, adding new pulls or knobs for a surprisingly good facelift.

Be ingenious and use every inch of space. You'll find even the pre-made modular units come with features such as swing-out corner units; open-shelved corner units; pull-out trash bins; deep drawers with wire racks for pots, pans, and lids; spice cabinets and drawers; swing-out or shallow cabinet storage; pull-out pantries; vegetable bins; pull-out food storage; knife storage; silverware storage; pull-out shelving for linens; partitioned tray storage; partitioned drawers for pot lids; half-round pull-out shelves; lazy susans; pop-up mixer shelves; even appliance garages with doors.

WORK SURFACES

Counters should be chosen for both practicality and beauty. You might even want to mix two different types of counter tops in the same kitchen. Stainless steel looks great in modern kitchens, but does scratch easily. Granite looks fabulous and performs well. It's easily maintainable and stain resistant. Marble, available in a multitude of colors, is a great surface for pastry dough, but it's porous, stains easily, and can be difficult to clean. Corian is a petroleum-based synthetic marble that can be cut or carved easily to any shape, but only comes in neutral colors.

Plastic laminate comes in a wide array of colors and patterns and resists stains, but isn't necessarily resilient against heat and scratching. Mat-finished laminates will not scratch or show fingerprints as easily as gloss-finished laminate. Butcher block is a great surface for chopping and slicing, but isn't very resistant to moisture, stains, and scorching. Tile comes in an amazing assortment of shapes, sizes, patterns, glazes, and colors that can be combined with wide or narrow tinted grout to achieve any effect. It is heat and stain resistant and easy to clean. The tile you choose should have a flat, square, and even surface so that delicate glassware

won't tumble. Check with the dealer or manufacturer to make sure the tile you select is recommended for counters.

FLOORING

Select your kitchen flooring for its look, of course, but make sure it will be easy to maintain and comfortable to walk on.

Carpeting can look good in a kitchen . . . for about one week. Spilled grease or grape juice can present a major cleanup problem. The fiber can even be melted by hot grease or flame. Use a washable area rug over old, tired kitchen flooring to give the room a new look.

Wood flooring is great for kitchens as long as it's finished with a moisture-curing urethane. Mat finishes will conceal scratches and stains better than a shiny finish. Use a hardwood such as maple rather than a soft wood like pine or fir, which won't hold up well under heavy use.

Brick and stone floors look great and can be laid in a variety of patterns. They'll last forever, wear only improving their character. However, I feel brick and stone are expensive and impractical choices for kitchen flooring. Their hard surfaces conduct noise and cold, magnify sound, and are hard on feet. If left unsealed, they'll absorb grease and stains.

Vinyl tiles and sheet goods, although the least acceptable aesthetically from a design point of view, are probably the most practical and durable choice. Some come with finishes that require no waxing and cushioning that's easy on the feet.

Ceramic floor tiles are an expensive, practical, and great looking choice, but offer no insulation against cold or noise. Unglazed tiles should be treated with a sealer for soil resistance.

Review Chapter 14 for more information and ideas.

WALLS

Choose from ceramic tile, fabric, wallpaper, paint, brick, or stone. In smaller kitchens, light colors, small patterns, and subtle textures will make the room appear more spacious. Dark colors, large patterns, and heavy textures will make the room seem smaller. A larger room can take larger, bolder wall treatments.

Vertical patterns will add visual space overhead and horizontal patterns will appear to open up the width. If you continue a pattern onto the ceiling, it will make the ceiling appear lower. Glossy wall coverings and paint tend to magnify bumps or gouges in walls or ceilings. Use mat paint, wood, laminate, or mirror to hide such unsightly marks.

CEILINGS

Enhance your kitchen and influence the mood by using interesting ceiling treatments.

Wallpaper on a ceiling can visually change the dimensions of the room. It should be coated and sealed to resist soil and grease. For more height, use a small pattern in monochromatic light colors. Use a linear pattern across the width of the room to make it appear wider.

Plaster ceilings can be smooth or heavily textured and painted any color. Use heavily-textured plaster ceilings to conceal flaws and create depth and interest in the kitchen.

Paint is the least expensive route. Remember that light colors are recessive, reflect light, and will make your kitchen seem larger. Darker colors will absorb light and make your room seem smaller, but are more dramatic and cozy. High gloss paint will increase the light reflected and show ceiling flaws and blemishes, while flat paint will do the opposite.

Metal ceilings can be used to create an embossed, turn-of-the-century look. Tin is usually used, but other metals such as copper and brass, though expensive, can be stunning. Plastic imitations are available and can be painted to look just like the real thing. Make sure they're fireproof.

Wood ceilings add warmth and intimacy to your kitchen, even if it's stark modern. The direction in which the wood is laid will emphasize either the length or width of your kitchen.

Beams will add character to your kitchen, whether you add heavy, structural beams in a rustic room or smoothly painted exposed beams and rafters in a modern kitchen. Consider using fake beams to hide unsightly ducts and lighting, making sure the size of the beams relates to the scale of your kitchen.

WINDOWS AND DOORS

Select windows that have double or even triple glazing to cut heat loss, especially if you live in a cold climate. Kitchen windows must be movable in order to ventilate and distribute air. Use greenhouse windows over kitchen sinks to extend the room, particularly if it overlooks a great view. Use sliding windows framed in wood or metal for pass-through serving counters between the kitchen and patio. Add a skylight to light up a dark and gloomy kitchen. Review Chapter 15 for more information and ideas.

Doors should be positioned correctly for the flow of traffic in and out of the kitchen. Entry doors from the outside should be made of solid wood and/or glass and be a standard width of thirty-six inches. Interior doors can be hollow core covered with wood veneer or painted, and generally come in standard widths of thirty inches or thirty-six inches. Use a pocket door for openings where a standard door would interfere with the traffic and layout. Use pocket doors that meet in the middle where there are wiring and pipes in the wall that restrict clearance.

LIGHTING

Use track lighting with floodlight bulbs to provide good overall general illumination; use spotlight bulbs to accent specific areas. Use box beams, which are hollow, surface-mounted boxes that house fluorescent tubes, for bright lighting and a beamed effect. Use fluorescent tubes mounted under wall cabinets to light the counter surface below. Use indirect lighting hidden in a beam, a soffit, or a crown molding. The light will bounce off the ceiling and create a subdued overall illumination.

Try to avoid the still available, but passé, surface-mounted lighting boxes or dropped luminous ceilings that conceal fluorescent tubes with glass or plastic panels. Tubular hanging fixtures suspended from the ceiling are hot now, as are recessed lighting fixtures built into a soffit and simple, recessed fixtures built right into the ceiling.

Whether your kitchen and budget are small, medium, or large; your style high tech, eclectic, or country; you're starting from scratch or just performing a facelift, approach the project like a professional. Acquire all the knowledge you can and plan everything on paper before proceeding. Don't hesitate to hire a professional interior designer, even a professional kitchen planner and a contractor if you need help with this difficult project.

Bathrooms

If you're completely remodeling your bathroom start with a floor plan. Experiment with interesting and efficient ways of creating new space. A new, luxurious master bath will not only uplift your spirits, but it will be a major enticement to any future prospective buyers of your home.

BATHTUBS

Bathtubs come in just about as many shapes and sizes as bodies. There are plain rectangular tubs, oval tubs, square tubs, corner tubs, round tubs, curved tubs, and old bathtubs on claw feet. There are hot tubs, jacuzzis, whirlpools, and tubs built for two people. Standard bathtubs come five feet six inches long by two feet three inches wide, but you can find tubs wider, longer, and extra deep.

Bathtubs are made from a variety of materials. The most common tubs are made from acrylic, which can be molded easily, is resistant to chipping, and keeps water hot. Acrylics do scratch easily and can be damaged by nail polish remover. Glass fiber bathtubs are made from layers of glass

fiber bonded with a polyester resin. They're stronger and more resistant than acrylic tubs and come in a wide range of colors, even metallics and pearlized. Pressed steel bathtubs have a smooth enamel coating, are lightweight, and wear well. Cast iron tubs, the most expensive, usually have porcelain enamel fused on the metal and are stain proof and easy to clean.

Create exciting bath spa areas by allowing ample space around the tub to place baskets of soap, sponges, washcloths, and trays of perfumes and dusting talcs. Even allow enough space for some lush plants if possible. Cover the surface with tile, plastic laminate, marble, granite, or even mirror. You might even want to bring the same material up over the walls and onto the ceiling. Play around with the ideas of a sunken tub, a tub on a platform, or even a tub in the center of the room.

I recently remodeled a small master bathroom for a client. The home overlooked a fabulous mountain view, but the bathroom had no windows other than two tiny slits above the counter. I left the existing cabinets and sinks, but replaced the old doors with new plastic laminate flush-mount doors and added new pulls, faucets, and handles. I gutted the rest of the bathroom and knocked out an entire wall to expose the magnificent view, then added a greenhouse window to frame the view and expand the space. Across that wall and extending in a triangular shape to the adjoining wall, I built a combination shower and bath out of tile, complete with steam unit. I mirrored all the walls, even the ceiling, and added wall-to-wall carpeting. The once small, dowdy bathroom was transformed into a luxurious showplace.

SHOWERS

If space is limited, you might want to make a combination shower-bathtub. If your bathtub area is very large and will contain the shower water, forget about a shower door or curtain altogether for a more dramatic and open feeling. If you're working with a smaller area, choose a tub enclosure made of clear shatterproof glass; it will make the room appear larger than an opaque enclosure.

If you'd prefer a separate shower area, use attractive materials such as tile or marble on the interior. Allow a bare minimum of thirty-five inches by twenty-eight inches for the shower stall. Again, use a clear glass shower door rather than the old-fashioned opaque doors that tend to look like they're coated with soap scum all the time. Consider building in a triangular seat, soap dishes, shelving for shampoos and other supplies, even installing a steam unit.

TOILETS AND BIDETS

Toilets and bidets come in a variety of styles, colors, and sizes. Buy models that match your bathtub and sink. They come in either wall-hung or pedestal models. Allow a minimum of forty-three inches by twenty-eight inches around both toilet and bidet so that they can be used comfortably. There should be a minimum of eight inches on either side and twenty-four inches in front.

I prefer toilets and bidets placed in a separate area, if possible, but experiment with your floor plan to find the ideal space.

SINKS

Ideally, you should have two sinks inset into counter tops or vanity units. Pedestal sinks, either high tech or traditional, are becoming increasingly popular. Use them for powder rooms in which extensive cabinet and counter space is not necessary. Wall-hung sinks are also popular but again, don't provide enough counter and cabinet space.

Sinks come in a wide range of colors, sizes, and shapes: oval, round, square, rectangular, corner-shaped, and shell shaped. They range in size from twelve inches wide to more than two feet six inches wide. Some are deep, some shallow. Some have lips and rest on top of a counter, others are made to be set inside a counter top. Shallow sinks or metal sinks, no matter how wonderful they might look,

tend to bounce and splash the water. Metal sinks water spot easily and are difficult to keep clean. (Hint: Make sure the holes for plumbing match the fixtures you are using.)

Shop around. There are delicately painted porcelain sinks and more rustic ceramic sinks. Many come with matching tiles, faucets, handles, knobs, pulls, towel racks, towel rings, toilet paper holders, tissue boxes, small shelves, soap dishes, and hooks. Some manufacturers even make matching wallpaper and fabric.

Choose your faucets and handles carefully. I don't recommend European-made hardware for American-made plumbing—it's generally not compatible and must be adapted by a very skilled plumber. Some faucets and handles are designed to be placed on the sink, others are made to be mounted on the counter. You'll find an overwhelming variety of styles and materials to choose from, ranging from high tech plastic to ornate brass, porcelain to shiny chrome. One of the most popular faucets on the market is a simply-designed metal faucet that distributes water just like a waterfall. There is also a faucet now that turns on and off with no handles. You just wave your hand under the faucet and the water is automatically activated and deactivated. Don't use long, goosenecked faucets made for bar sinks; they will direct water in thin streams that bounce off the sink.

Double check the compatibility of your sinks and faucets. Use only a licensed plumber to install them. There's nothing more annoying than puddled counter tops caused by improperly placed or installed faucets.

CABINETS

The same rules and suggestions apply for bathroom cabinets as for kitchen cabinets, but the standard height is usually about thirty-one inches high from the floor to the top of the counter. If you're taller or shorter than average height, you might want to raise or lower the counter while you have the opportunity.

I do suggest building in at least a small makeup counter if you're putting in new cabinets. It can be anywhere from twenty-seven inches to twenty-nine inches high. I don't suggest buying a pre-made vanity unit at the local building supply company. These units are generally cheaply made and will make your bathroom look too much like the one at the gas station.

Medicine cabinets are convenient, but most standard models are eyesores. Shop around for some of the newer models that fit neatly and flush into the wall, or have your carpenter build in a mirrored medicine cabinet that disappears into a mirrored wall.

FLOOR COVERINGS

Although I've already admitted to using wall-to-wall carpeting in bathrooms from time to time for budget reasons, I suggest you use a hard flooring with an area rug instead. Makeup and toiletry spills along with the possibility of a toilet overflow or a forgotten bath that's still running make wall-to-wall carpeting impractical.

One of my clients solved this problem by telling the carpet layers not to tack the carpeting down. As I tripped over the curling edge of the carpet, I asked him why. He shrugged, a cocky expression on his face, "So I can replace it easily." And he did. Three months later the edges had frayed and shed and we replaced the whole bathroom floor with tile.

WALLS

Of course, all wall treatments should be practical and easy to keep clean. Steam and moisture tend to peel wallpaper and paint off after a while; make sure you use the right products, the right painter, and the right wallpaper hanger. If your budget allows, cover walls with tile, plastic laminate, mirror, or marble. If you do use paint, it's "hot" to use shiny enamel or one of the special painting techniques described in Chapter 9. If you

use wallpaper, be sure it has a vinyl coating that can be wiped clean easily. If the paper you select doesn't have a vinyl coating, a protective seal can be applied after it's hung.

WINDOW COVERINGS

Look through Chapter 15 for suggestions and ideas. Be careful with the materials you select. Check to make sure they're resistant to moisture and mildew. Metal vertical and horizontal blinds tend to rust and corrode after a prolonged time in moist areas. Wood will shrink and swell with the changes in moisture and temperature.

LIGHTING

Good overall illumination is a must for a bathroom. I suggest you put all lighting on a dimmer switch, which will enable you to set the mood for a relaxing, luxurious bath. For shaving and putting on makeup, the best lighting is strip lighting (strips of bulbs placed around the mirror). You might even want to add recessed spots to accent plants and other decorative features. Don't aim lighting directly into mirrors as it will cause an extremely annoying glare.

If you're just updating your bathroom on a limited budget, there are many tricks you can use to transform your bathroom into an exciting space or a relaxing spa.

• Paint over old tiles with eggshell first, then add another coat of either epoxy paint or plain, glossy paint. For a daring, romantic bathroom, paint old yellow or green tiles black, enamel walls black, and add a patterned black and white wallpaper border around the top. Add a black area rug, a mirror or two, a few accessories, and hang some chic black and white towels.

• Paint old, dirty grout a new color.
• Paint tiles and/or grout, then add a new border of contrasting or patterned tile.
• Retile right over your old tiles. New ceramic

products on the market make it possible for you to tile right over old tile without the expense and mess of tearing out old tile.

- Have your old bathtubs, sinks, and toilets painted. Use a reputable company that specializes in this process.

- Disguise old shabby walls with sheets of plastic laminate, mirror, mirror squares, or wood.

- Refresh tired walls with vinyl or vinyl-coated wall covering or a fresh coat or two of gloss or enamel paint. Use texturing, marbling, or sponging to transform walls that have seen better days.

- Liven up boring bathrooms by painting the walls a deep, rich color. Hang interesting artwork to add drama and impact.

- Make a dark, dull room sparkle with life by painting everything white. Use inexpensive white vinyl tiles or sheetgoods and a white area rug over the old floor. Add a few frothy green plants in fresh baskets to make the room feel light and airy.

- Hide ugly plumbing and pipes under a sink by shirring fabric on thick wire and attaching it around the sink, letting it form a skirt.

- Perk up a boring powder room by installing an old sink inset into a piece of furniture. Find an old chest, perhaps with an attached mirror, at a garage sale or used furniture store; refinish or paint it.

- Add panels of mirror, large or mosaic mirrored squares, or wall-hung mirrors to visually enlarge a small bathroom.

- Ugly windows? Dress them up with new window coverings. Perhaps sleek blinds or delicately shirred curtains.

- Blah bathtub? Have it encased in fine wood, plastic laminate, marble, or mirror. Add a new backsplash and new fixtures for an even more dramatic uplift.

- Add a cute little dressing table and wicker chair. You might even want to skirt the table, pillow the chair, and dress the window with a matching or coordinating fabric.

- Replace old lighting with new. Add strips of bulbs on either side of your existing mirror.

- Hide the flooring you hate with a great area rug.

- Paint old, worn-out looking cabinets a fresh color and add new knobs and pulls.

- Replace "tacky" towel racks and rings with new, fresh, and updated ones. Add some store-bought shelving made from acrylic, wood, or plastic grids.

- Replace worn-out towels with newer, brighter ones. Or revamp old towels by sewing borders and trims over frayed edges.

18
Remembering
the Details

Often it's the details, big or little, that make the difference between a nicely decorated room and a professionally decorated room. Pre-planning decorative or architectural accoutrements for your home should be done as you select your furniture, fabrics, and wall coverings.

Molding

According to Webster's Dictionary, molding is "a decorative plane or curved strip used for ornamentation or finishing." There are innumerable companies that manufacture a complete line of wood moldings as well as other detail pieces you might need. You'll find these moldings are usually made from pine, oak, mahogany, ash, or birch. If you're going to stain your molding, be sure to select a wood that will show the wood-grain effect that you desire. If you're going to paint over the molding, save money by selecting moldings made from less expensive paint grade wood. Your painter can paint or stain the molding any color or finish after it has been installed by your carpenter. Some companies even make molding out of acrylic, mirror, metal, plastic, and various laminates.

Casings and flutings can be used as decorative trim pieces, particularly around doors and win-

dows. You'll find them in almost any style and period to match your decor. The general rule of thumb is to choose sizes that are to scale with the size of your room, however, dramatic effects can be achieved by breaking the rule and using overscaled molding. Experiment with samples of the different sizes and shapes available to add character and drama to your room.

Base moldings, or baseboards, are used around the bottom of the wall. They'll usually have a flat bottom and a curved top. Again, styles, sizes, shapes, and materials vary. I suggest you use the same base moldings throughout the entire house for unity if your home is traditional. If your home is modern, you might want to experiment with base moldings made from exciting and interesting materials in a few different rooms.

Panel molding is used to create trim for wall panels. Here's where you can really get innovative, perhaps creating wall frames from this decorative panel molding, then having the centers upholstered in a fabric to match your sofas, chairs, and/or draperies. Use carved corner blocks to create an authentic architecturally designed feeling.

Cornice moldings, crown moldings, and ceiling moldings are placed between the wall and the ceiling, usually on an angle. They can be used alone or in combination with other moldings to add interest, depth, and authenticity to a room. Use large crown moldings with faux finishes for the newest look.

Corner guards can be purchased to decoratively finish the edges of built-in counters and shelving.

Nosings are used to create decorative trim for the edges of bars, counters, and stairs.

Balusters, newel posts, and turned posts will update your old stairways and can be found in almost any design. Mix and match bottom and top rails and find finials, end scrolls, and rosettes to top them off.

Picture frame moldings can be used not only for making your own picture frames, but for creating interesting detailing for walls and doors.

Hardwood plaques can be painted or stained to create expensive looking carved detailing on walls, doors, and furniture.

Embossed moldings can be used anywhere, along with or in combination with any of the above moldings. Play around with painting and color-washing techniques to create a new look for an old wall, door, cabinet, or piece of furniture.

Corbels can be used to support shelving, beams, or fireplace mantels. You'll even find great looking corbels made out of acrylic or stone.

As I browsed through many catalogs, my imagination went wild with the creative possibilities these moldings and component pieces presented. I found catalogs that had collections of large columns and capitals to add architectural drama and carved drawer and door fronts to update old furniture and cabinets. One company even makes a complete line of unfinished forms and shapes from which you could make your own "furniture art."

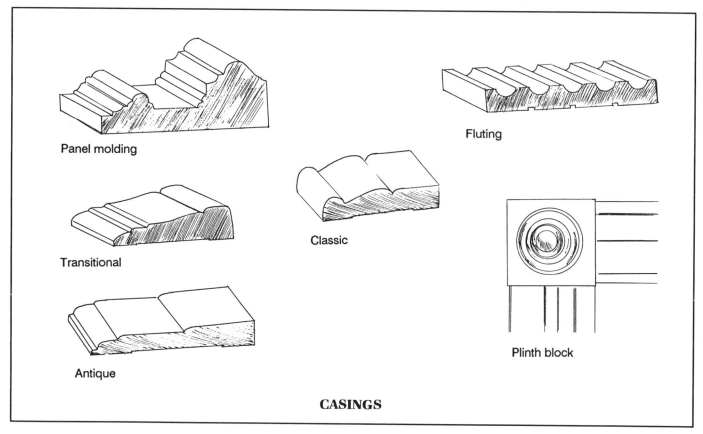

Panel molding

Fluting

Transitional

Classic

Antique

Plinth block

CASINGS

Ceilings

Ceilings tend to be the most neglected part of a home. Most people paint them, add a chandelier, then forget them. Here are some suggestions and ideas for making a ceiling an asset to any room.

• Get rid of your "cottage cheese" ceilings if possible, they're out. Sure, it's messy to have your ceilings scraped, but all your decorating efforts will be in vain if you haven't paid attention to this detail. Either look in the Yellow Pages for a company specializing in this process or ask your painter or contractor to recommend someone. If you have radiant heat, be careful, wires that run through the ceiling could be damaged by a workman who is not experienced in this procedure.

• If your budget or your look dictates that you just paint the ceiling, the rule of thumb is to paint it the same color, but a few shades lighter, than the walls. However, to make a ceiling appear lower, paint it darker. There's no rule against using painting techniques such as sponging and marbling on your ceiling. Try it.

• If your walls are wallpapered or fabric covered, you might want to use the same covering on the ceiling. This will create a warmer, cozier feeling than a plain painted ceiling, but be aware that bold patterns rarely look good on ceilings and busy patterns will make the room appear smaller and very closed in.

• Lower a ceiling with yards of fabric. Attach rods or dowels to the ceiling at equal intervals, then drape the fabric in dramatic curves over the rods.

• Create a sunburst effect with fabric on your ceiling. Attach fabric to all edges of the ceiling around the room, then pull and tie the fabric together in the center of the ceiling. Cover the center with a huge fabric-covered button.

• Heighten your ceiling by using mirror squares or small mirror mosaics that you can install yourself. Experiment with some of the new metal laminates to heighten your ceiling and create an intriguing muted glow.

• For modern rooms, consider one of the many metal lighting systems that fit flush against the ceiling. Most residential systems come in squares, but commercial systems can be used in your home. These systems can be found in narrow metal strips in which lighting can be installed at any point. Why not use these strips on an angle to heighten your ceiling, and visually enlarge the entire room?

• To lower the look of a ceiling in a modern room, use a configuration of tubular metal or enamel fixtures extended from the ceiling by invisible cables.

• For a rustic look, add a rough-sawn wood ceiling, perhaps even some fake beams. For a modern or eclectic look, take a peek in your attic. I've seen entire ceilings removed to reveal the exciting structural elements of the roof and create the illusion of double the space.

• Tack bamboo fencing on your ceiling. Paint it white or leave it natural.

• Mix and match ideas. Use a faux bois technique on wood beams that have had one too many coats of paint over the years; stripping and staining would be messy and expensive. Or add fake beams and cover them with mirror, laminate, wallpaper, fabric, or even faux stone.

• Create a sculptured ceiling by having layers of soffit installed in either a square, rectangle, circle, or oval. You might even want to have lighting inset between each layer for an indirect, moody glow.

• For children's rooms, use a mural. Why not paint your child's ceiling to look just like the sky, complete with billowy clouds?

Fireplaces

Stuck with an old fireplace you hate? Solutions range from simple and inexpensive to ornate and extravagant. Here are a few ideas to give you a gentle shove.

• Paint your used-brick fireplace; it's a newer look. Use white if you want a light and airy look. Use black if you want a more dramatic, sensual look.

• Add a new mantel. Perhaps you might want to use stained wood, lacquered wood, metal, marble,

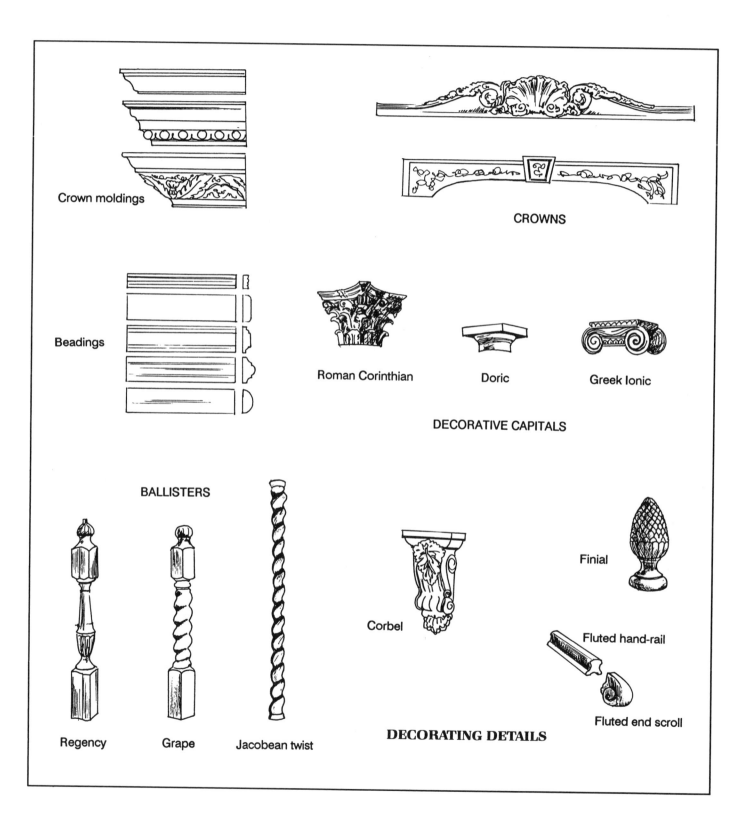

Crown moldings

CROWNS

Beadings

Roman Corinthian   Doric   Greek Ionic

DECORATIVE CAPITALS

BALLISTERS

Corbel

Finial

Fluted hand-rail

Fluted end scroll

Regency   Grape   Jacobean twist

DECORATING DETAILS

stone, mirror, or laminate. Experiment with any of the new faux finishes to stretch your decorating dollar.

• Build a frame around an existing fireplace. Make it wide or narrow, straight or curved. Use an interesting material that blends with the rest of the fireplace.

• Frame your fireplace with stainless steel, brass, copper, or brushed aluminum. Use the real thing or opt for the thinner, laminated version. Why not build a dramatic angular or curved hood that extends all the way to the ceiling?

• Update your fireplace by plastering over it, either in smooth or heavily-textured plaster. Paint it white. Leave it plain or add a mantel made of hand-painted tile or small quarry tiles.

• Have no fireplace? Add an antique or reproduction potbelly stove or a prefabricated enameled fireplace.

• Use stone to create a new fireplace. Build an entire wall of huge boulders piled to the ceiling; leave a cubbyhole to store wood. Or make the fireplace lower and add a mantel made out of rustic wood, even driftwood or a log that's been split.

• Mirror or marble the entire front of the fireplace, even extend the mirror to the ceiling. Or build a mirrored fireplace from scratch, creating depth and interest by constructing three-dimensional layers of framing.

• Add a fake front. You'll find an incredible selection of fireplace frames available, both traditional and modern. Select a delicate curved and carved French wood frame, a plain or ornate marble frame, a chunky bold stone frame, or a sleek and shiny Italian metal frame.

• Add or redo a hearth. Cover it with fabulous tiles, marble, mirror, stone, anything. Add a handmade basket filled with wood and/or a few great pillows for casual impromptu seating.

• Enhance your fireplace with a new screen. Have one custom made to fit flush or add a freestanding screen with fine brass framing and delicately etched glass.

• Accessorize your fireplace. Toss out the cheap fireplace tools you bought on sale at the local home improvement center. Replace them with a new or antique set with more character. Add a set of unique andirons to complete the look.

The treatment you select for your fireplace will be dictated by the overall scheme of your room. Whether it becomes the focal point of the room or not is determined by the architecture of your home and how you emphasize the fireplace.

Be careful. Any materials you use close to the fireplace are subject to damage from the intense heat. Make sure all materials you use, especially glass and mirror, have been tested for heat resistance.

Little Details

One of the quickest, easiest, and least expensive ways to give rooms and furniture a facelift is to replace old knobs and pulls with new and updated versions. You'll find the market is overflowing with hardware that can make or break a room. Here's a potpourri of little ideas and suggestions that will make a difference.

• Freshen up old kitchen and bathroom cabinets. For a high tech look, paint them the whitest of whites, then add new knobs and/or pulls in bright colors and interesting shapes.

For a traditional look, strip and restain old cabinets and cupboards, adding more ornate brass knobs or pulls.

For an eclectic look, paint old cabinet doors using a sponging or marbling technique; add knobs and/or pulls with a rough, crusty finish.

For a stark modern look, enamel cabinets black and add either black or shiny chrome knobs and/or pulls.

• Replace old rusty and corroded bathroom and kitchen faucets and handles with newer, fresher ones. In some cases, it's effective and cost efficient to have old faucets and handles replated.

• Make your bathroom come alive again with new towel racks and rings, soap dishes, and toilet paper holders.

- Re-grout or paint old stained and cracked grouting.

- Update old interior doors with new hardware. For more traditional rooms, pull off old knobs and escutcheon plates, repaint or stain doors, perhaps even replace old molding and trim. Either use new knobs and plates or have the old ones professionally replated with brass.

    To make a room look more modern, pull off outdated hardware and replace with shiny, new angular knobs and plates. You might even want to completely pull off all molding and trim on or around the door and have the entire door laminated or enameled in the same color as the walls for a newer look.

- Your exterior door hardware probably needs updating too. Choose a style of hardware that relates to the interior of the house, using the same colors and finishes if possible.

- Replace old cover plates over electrical outlets, telephone jacks, and television cables. If the walls are covered in wallpaper or fabric, have the plates covered too. If your walls are painted and the plates are in reasonably good condition, you might just want to paint over them to make them "disappear" and save money. If you use one of the special painting techniques, it looks best to use the same technique on the plates. If you're purchasing new plates, be sure to select a color that matches the wall. Beige or off-white plates look awful on white-white walls, as do white-white plates on beige or off-white walls.

- Basically, the same rules apply to light switch plates, although you might want to consider replacing your old switches with one of the newer types that operate by touch. Now's the time to add any dimmer switches. A picky detail, I know, but even the dimmer switch should be the right color.

- Heating and air conditioning vents can be eyesores. If yours are bent and old looking, replace them or make them "disappear" by painting them the same color as the wall or ceiling.

- Even old looking heating controls on a wall can distract the eye and destroy your efforts. Replace them with fresh, clean looking substitutes.

Detailing with Mirrors

- Pull out old tiled or laminated backsplashes in the kitchen or bathroom. Replace them with mirrored backsplashes to make the room look larger and sparkle like new. Use sandblasted glass for your backsplashes for an even hotter look.

- Cover an unsightly post or column with mirror. For a curved eyesore, cover with narrow mirrored strips from floor to ceiling.

- Hide an ugly radiator that's not in use with a great looking mirrored screen.

- Make your own expensive looking bathroom accessories by covering wood wastepaper baskets and tissue boxes with tiny mosaic mirrored tiles that come in sheets.

- Add mirror-backed acrylic or glass shelving anywhere: kitchen, bathroom, bar, even laundry room. Use acrylic corbels to support the shelving for an interesting and "expensive" look.

- Use extra large, two feet by two feet, mirrored squares with a beveled edge to cover an entire wall. Better yet, it's "hot" to use odd-shaped mirrored pieces, such as twelve inches by three feet, pieced together on a wall.

- Pull out old cracked or corroded mirrors over bathroom cabinets. Replace them with one huge sixty-inch round mirror with a beveled edge.

- Attach an empty decorative mirror frame over any mirrored wall.

- Use inexpensive mirror and acrylic baseboards to make your floor space appear much larger.

Forgotten Spaces

STAIRS

Most of us aren't blessed with winding staircases on which to make our grand entrances. Rather, we're faced with mundane stairs that need a little "oomph."

- If you have floating stairs, wrap them with carpeting. Use a low pile, dense carpeting to avoid splitting and matting.
- If you're lucky enough to have fine wooden stairs, cover them with a wide runner, then adorn each step with decorative brass stair rods. If you'd like to use a bordered runner, have one made with a darker, neutral color in the center which gets the heaviest traffic; the border can be a lighter, contrasting color. Or choose a great patterned runner to give your stairwell a personality of its own.
- Don't leave hard-surfaced stairs naked; they'll give your home a cold look and feel. Bare stairs are also unsafe and will make the clatter of heels unbearable.
- If you're in great aerobic shape, consider installing a prefabricated winding staircase to save space and heighten drama.
- Update old balusters and railings. Either replace them completely or give them a fresh new finish. Brass railings are "hot"; so are thick acrylic railings.
- Decorate the wall leading up the staircase with something a little more innovative than a grouping of family portraits. Cut holes in the wall, replaster, then use the new spaces to display your favorite objets d'art. Don't use artwork that protrudes; it's bound to end up knocked down and broken.
- Use stair landings for plants and interesting accessories.

Don't forget stair safety:
- The tread should be deep enough to accommodate the entire sole of a shoe.
- The rise, or vertical area between each tread, should be approximately five inches. Most experts suggest the total measurement of the tread and the rise be somewhere between 17 and 17½".
- Bare treads can be slippery and hazardous. Always carpet your stairs.
- If your stairway is particularly long, a landing provides an additional safety feature.
- To avoid bumping your head, there should be ample head space at the top of the stairs.

- The size and spacing of steps should be equal to prevent tripping.
- Select winding staircases only with wide treads for firm steps.
- Provide a rail on one side, if not both sides, of the staircase.
- Check the space between balusters to make sure a child's head won't get stuck between them.
- Provide adequate lighting.

CLOSETS

Use closet space to its maximum potential. If you can afford it, have a professional closet company do your organizational work for you. These companies will assess your needs and design your closets for the best possible usage. Some use wire basket modular units for shelving and drawers, others use heavy press-board units, and still others use laminated units that look like built-in furniture. I advise against the press-board units, as they must be sealed and sprayed to look good and have been known to give off toxic fumes.

ATTICS

Remember those? You might have one you've forgotten all about. Create an extra room, maybe an office, a sewing room, or a playroom. Make sure there's adequate heating and ventilation to make the room comfortable and safe.

Create your own private "home away from home," a place where you can escape to read a book or write a novel. Chances are this space will be dark and dingy, so brighten it up with colorful fabric and warm flooring. Add a desk, a worktable, a large comfortable chair, even some built-in shelving. Complete the look with good lighting and a few silk plants.

LOFTS

Lofts have made a great comeback in recent years. They're great for adding space and drama in rooms with large high ceilings. If you haven't a loft, consider the possibility of adding one. Use it as a den, library, office, sewing area, or add a large screen television and create your own movie theater.

Since a loft can almost be seen from the room below, make sure its decor relates and blends with the rest of your home. Transform it into a traditional library/study by building in fine wood bookcases. Add a plump, comfortable sofa covered in a staid plaid; toss a thick flannel throw over it for chilly nights. If there's room left over, add a small writing desk and wingback chair.

To create a modern dramatic loft, cover the floors with a low pile carpeting, perhaps light gray. Store television and stereo equipment in a built-in cabinet; use one of the new shiny grid laminates in a darker shade of gray. Add a white leather sofa and a few chrome and white leather director's chairs, one or two chrome torcheres, and even a high tech drafting table with a bright red base. Black theatrical spotlights and one large tree will top off the look.

Decorating Safety

Most states have extensive safety laws that govern the potentially flammable materials used by manufacturers. Polyurethane and polystyrene have been singled out as dangerous materials containing highly volatile gases which can make other materials burst into flame. Remember the shocking MGM Grand fire in Las Vegas? Almost everything was made of plastic, even the chandeliers.

Crib materials on the market have been known to pass rigid flammability tests and later found to be the cause of horrendous and fatal fires. All upholstery and mattress fillings should be checked for the safety of their materials. It might be a good idea to contact the Consumer Product Safety Commission and/or your state's Department of Consumer Affairs and Bureau of Home Furnishings for the most recent updates. You might also want to write to the National Fire Protection Association for a free booklet on home safety.

Most natural materials, even wood, give off some toxic gases, but plastics can give off a deadly mix of gases when they smolder or burn.

Most states have laws governing the use of smoke detectors. Since these laws are basically enforced in commercial buildings and multi-unit dwellings, it's your responsibility to make sure your home is well equipped. The Consumer Product Safety Commission recommends smoke detectors be placed on the ceiling at least twelve inches from each corner. If your home has more than one story, make sure there is at least one smoke detector on each level. If you have a hallway longer than forty feet, place a smoke detector at either end.

Whether you install battery-operated detectors or electrically-powered units, make sure you check to see if they are working every four weeks. Hold an open flame from a candle nearby; the alarm should go off within thirty seconds. Had the MGM Grand Hotel had adequate and operative smoke detectors as well as an adequate sprinkler system, the damage and loss of life would have been substantially less.

19
Accessories, Artwork, and Plants

Without accessories, artwork, and plants your rooms will be flat and dull. This is the final and one of the most important phases of your decorating project. Most interior designers tell stories about clients who had a "money's no object" attitude throughout the project, then when it came time to spend money on the finishing touches, they pulled in their purse strings and refused to cooperate. If you've followed the budgeting techniques discussed in Chapter 6, you'll be well prepared to add the finishing touches to your home.

Accessories

An accessory is anything that isn't a major furnishing. It can be either useful or purely decorative. Accessories should make a statement and relate to the style, scale, and color scheme of the room. Cheap knick-knacks and "sentimental" pieces that don't relate or add to the room are inappropriate and confusing. A collection of old, crude kitchen utensils has no place in a modern living room. In reverse, a high tech desk accessory set has no place on an antique French writing desk.

Accessorizing a room is like adding your signature, your personal finishing touch. You can "make" a room with the right selections or "break" it with the wrong ones. How can you do it right?

- Choose unique, useful accessories such as fireplace tools, clocks, candlesticks, screens, mirrors, small boxes, chests, desk accessories, accent tables, bowls, and ashtrays.
- Find one-of-a-kind decorative accessories such as artwork, sculpture, accent lighting, kitchen utensils, baskets, old books with fine bindings, arts and crafts pieces, and fascinating paperweights.
- Learn the art of arranging accessories. Don't just plop them on a table or hang them on a wall haphazardly; there must be order. Make sure they are well balanced. Consider line, shape, size, texture, theme, and color to link objects together.
- Be offbeat. Defy the rules of scale to create drama and impact. Add a lifesize plaster statue; have it standing among some plants or seated in one of your dining room chairs. Or add a huge Greek olive jar on a pedestal in a tiny entry hall; give it added depth with mirror and light.
- Avoid buyer's remorse. Select only accessories that contain one or more of the colors of your room.
- Be authentic. If your room or home is based on a particular period, choose only accessories that are from that period. Elegant crystal figurines will look ridiculous in a rustic room, as will a collection of copper pots and pans in an Italian-modern room.
- Collect objects representative of a different

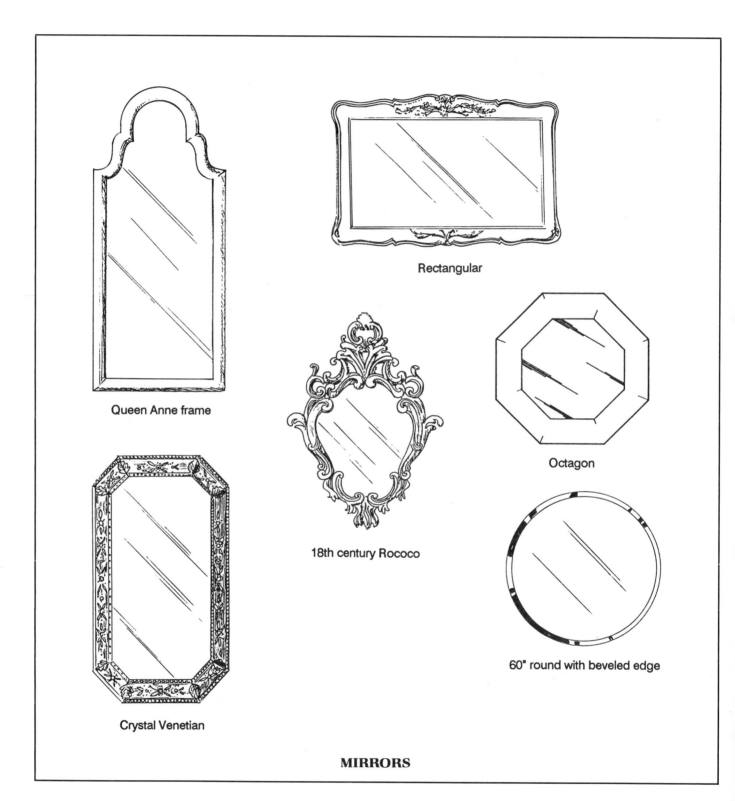

Queen Anne frame

Rectangular

18th century Rococo

Octagon

60" round with beveled edge

Crystal Venetian

MIRRORS

nationality. Start a collection of African artifacts and masks, Middle Eastern archaeological finds, Mexican handicrafts, American Indian head-dresses and drums, or Oriental objets d'art.

• Don't mix and match collections, especially within one room. A complete, well displayed collection will always look better than a hodgepodge of individual, unrelated pieces.

• Display larger pieces, such as African masks, separately. Place each piece in its own thick acrylic box, then make a larger grouping on one major wall.

• Display smaller pieces, such as a collection of tiny ivory figurines from the Orient, as a grouping. Carefully arrange each piece on the shelving inside a glass or acrylic box, varying the sizes and shapes. Place the box on an appropriate table top or shelf.

• Use accent lighting to highlight an accessory or collection and create a focal point.

• Place a collection of fascinating small objects such as shells, rocks, gems, and paperweights on your coffee table, allowing visitors to feel their textures and examine their intricacies.

• Mix a collection of tiny silver frames on a little table or a fireplace mantel. Fill them with your favorite family pictures.

• Use handmade baskets in all sizes and shapes. Fill them with flowers, fruit, firewood, magazines, or skeins of yarn. Don't hang a basket collection on the walls of your kitchen, it's boring and "out."

• Start a collection of antique clocks or mirrors. Make a powerful grouping on one large wall.

• In a country kitchen, hang copper pots and pans from a ceiling rack. Display interesting cooking utensils in a basket or ceramic pot on one of the counters. You might even want to add an antique wall-hung telephone.

• In a more modern kitchen, replace your old wood-grained plastic laminated appliances with newer, high tech models in stark white. Add a metal restaurant rack or a basket filled with gourmet food packages. Buy new, more updated tableware and perhaps one of those great streamlined stainless steel tea or coffee sets.

• In the bathroom, add a basket or fine crystal bowl filled with potpourri, decorative bars of soap, or lush hand towels. Place a huge basket of silk flowers or an oversized urn filled with bamboo stalks on the counter or floor. Collect huge, department store display-size bottles of perfume. Arrange them on the counter or show them off in a large, wall-hung acrylic box.

• Throw away that disgusting old plastic flower centerpiece in the dining room. Replace it with a dramatic vase filled with elegant silk flowers or an exciting bowl or basket brimming over with fresh fruit. You might even want to use a sculpture or a set of urns for a newer look.

• In the bedroom, add color and interest by putting extra throw pillows on the bed. Toss a fur throw on a sofa or chair. Dress up your little desk with crystal or leather accessories. Place a bowl, basket, or vase of fresh flowers on your nightstand. Add a decorative screen in one corner to make the room cozier.

• Accessorize your bookshelves in the den or office. Remove meaningless knick-knacks and replace them with "important" pieces, perhaps an antique clock you inherited from your great grandfather or a collection of well-polished silver trophies.

Artwork

Never before have so many people been "into" art. More and more galleries are popping up every day. I'm a firm believer that it's better to have no artwork and bare walls rather than fill up space with meaningless, cheap looking art. Before you rush out and spend a fortune, you should:

• Know the difference between an original piece of art and a reproduction.

• Have a knowledge of the different processes and techniques used in various forms of art.

• Read as much as you can about art, focusing on your preferences.

• Shop around. Visit museums, galleries, artists, and dealers.

• Make a decision about the forms of art that will best fit your home, taste, and budget.

"You get what you pay for" is not necessarily the rule when you buy artwork. The price is not always commensurate with the quality or value. Here's a brief lesson to get you started.

ORIGINALS

A "one-of-a-kind" is a single piece of art made without duplications by an artist. The artist, however, may decide to do another piece at another time that is almost identical.

A "one of a series" is when an artist makes the original from a stone, plate, or cut. Then, a limited number of copies are made from the original and approved by the artist. High quality small editions usually contain twenty copies, while large editions contain 150 to 200 copies. The copies are still considered "original" art. However, if the artist reproduces the same image in another medium, the work is considered a reproduction.

An "edition" refers to the creation of a series of originals by a particular process, usually by impressing an image on paper or other flat surface. The term edition also refers to a sculpture that has been duplicated using a bronze casting technique and supervised by the artist. Prints are the units of these series. Multiples are units of a larger series, perhaps 150 to 200 pieces, and are still considered originals.

OTHER PROCESSES

Original graphics are produced from various processes such as relief, intaglio, planography, stencil, and collagraphy. *Relief printing* is usually done with woodcuts or linocuts. The original is made on the surface of wood or on linoleum with a knife or sharp tool. The cut away area, called the negative area, always remains unprinted and will be the white part in the final print. The ink will stick to the raised or uncut part, called the positive area.

A *wood engraving* is made from a block of ex-

tremely hard wood, enabling the artist to achieve a white-on-white design with the pressure of the cut on the paper.

Intaglio printing, much like engraving, is done nowadays with alloys and copper. The artist etches by using a metal plate coated with an acid-resistant substance, drawing his design on this ground with a sharp needle. The needle will remove the ground and expose the plate surface. The plate is put into an acid bath where exposed parts will be etched, or eaten away, and produce a depressed line. When ink is applied, it will settle in the etched areas. The plate is placed on damp paper and passed through a roller press, forcing the paper into the etched areas to receive the ink. Etched areas will appear as black or colored areas in the final prints, while areas left untouched will appear white.

Drypoint, similar to intaglio, is when etching is done at an angle, which throws up a burr. The burr tends to break off after a small number of prints are made, thus there are usually a very limited number of prints in drypoint editions.

Mezzotint is similar to drypoint, but the final image is produced by selectively removing some of the burrs.

Aquatints are etchings with a tonal background. Small flecks of rosin are dropped on the plate, then heated until the powdery substance melts and creates an acid resist, allowing the acid to etch between the melted specks.

Collagraphy involves building up the printing surface instead of cutting it to produce a relief.

Serigraphy, or *silk screening*, is much different than intaglio or relief and is often used on fabric as well as paper. A tightly stretched screen made of close-meshed silk or nylon is used. The artist blocks out the area to be left unprinted by filling the mesh with varnish or applying a paper stencil to the screen, leaving a positive image. The printer forces the color through the screen to ink the paper or fabric placed below.

Lithography is printing from a plane surface by use of a chemical process. Machine-fed lithographs use a thin metal sheet stretched around a cylinder on a rotary press operating at a high speed. An edition of 200 to 500 pieces can be created in an hour, but a certain amount of control and quality is lost in this high speed process. Many artists prefer to use the slower, hand-printing techniques involving a printer and sponger, which takes an entire day to produce fifty high quality prints. When the faster machine method is used, one edge and one side must be trimmed to provide a guide for the feeding operation. When buying a lithograph, check the edges. One trimmed edge is a sign that production shortcuts have been made and the piece is not finely hand printed.

Signing and numbering prints to establish originality has been a standard practice of artists since 1960. The artist's signature will appear in pencil at the lower right edge of the margin. The number of the print and the size of the edition will appear at the lower left-hand corner of the margin as a fraction. The upper number is the number of the print and the lower number represents the size of the edition. Old and valuable prints do not meet these standards. In order to avoid being taken, I suggest you educate yourself, buy only from reputable dealers, and employ an expert's advice if there's any doubt.

If you're not a serious collector, it's best to choose artwork because you love it and it looks great in your room. Don't bet on the fact that it will increase in value . . . experts have revealed that 80 to 90% of art actually decreases in value. Just buy it and enjoy it!

HANGING YOUR ART

As a general rule, hang your artwork at seated eye level. Use non-glare glass if it doesn't detract from the art. Use overhead spots about twenty-four inches from the wall in rooms with an eight to nine foot ceiling; thirty inches from the wall in rooms with a nine to ten foot ceiling; and thirty-six inches from the wall in rooms with a ten to eleven foot ceiling. Experiment with different types of bulbs to bring out or soften tones.

• Use pieces that are taller than they are wide or a grouping that follows a vertical line to give your room a lift.

• Allow 8½″ of space between a table and the bottom of the frame of a large piece of art.

• Two pictures of identical size look best when hung one above the other. If you insist on hanging them side by side, add a third picture of a different size.

• Hang three pictures of the same size side by side.

• If you want to hang two matching pictures of different sizes, hang the larger of the two on the top.

• Don't stair-step pictures on the wall.

• Pre-plan an entire grouping on paper first. Use large sheets of wrapping paper to trace the frames and mark the correct spots for nails. When you're satisfied with the arrangement, tape the paper to the wall and place nails right through the paper.

• For extra drama, use overscaled pieces of art that cover an entire wall.

• Don't use one or two small pictures on a large wall. Save them to fill in smaller spaces or make a complete grouping.

• Mark your nail spot with an X of masking tape to avoid crumbling paint and plaster.

Hot tip: For the newest look, don't hang a large canvas, just rest it against a wall.

Plants and Flowers

Use a simple, strategically placed plant to create a focal point or a mass of dense foliage to let the outside flow into your interior. Plants will give your room life. Play some soothing music for them and watch them grow.

• Hot, sunny windows? Use cacti or other succulents. Plants with colorful foliage such as coleus will thrive with hours of sunshine. Geraniums and citrus trees will also fare well.

• Moderately cool east and north windows? Use

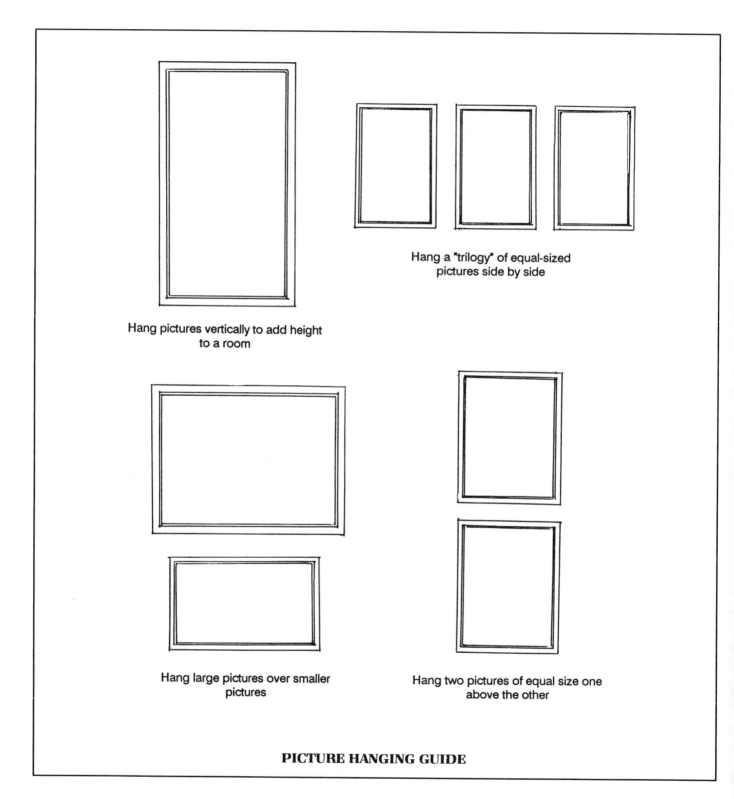

Hang pictures vertically to add height
to a room

Hang a "trilogy" of equal-sized
pictures side by side

Hang large pictures over smaller
pictures

Hang two pictures of equal size one
above the other

PICTURE HANGING GUIDE

begonias, African violets, or the right variety of orchids. Plain or variegated ivy or philodendrons will do great.

- Low light areas far from a window? Use philodendrons, rubber trees, and ferns.
- Bathrooms? Warm and moist rooms are ideal for lush ferns and many tropical plants.
- No light? Use a high quality silk plant. It might not grow, but it won't die.

SMALL PLANTS

Place them in baskets, ceramic pottery, an old copper tea kettle, a wooden box, anything. Give them a cozy home by nestling them in moss.

- Decorate your garden window with a dense foliage of small plants. Use matching planters throughout to avoid a hodgepodge look. Or display a collection of interesting cactus in terra cotta pots.
- Jazz up an odd corner with an exotic plant placed on a tall, thin pedestal.
- Add drama to your bookshelves by adding a few small plants.
- Use two larger matching plants on either side of your fireplace. Place them in large baskets or metal firewood bins.
- Create a tropical spa by framing your bathtub with lush green ferns. Or add a plant on the bathroom counter to perk up a dull room.
- Hang a plant in the bathroom, kitchen, or on a balcony for that "garden look." Use wire baskets filled with moss rather than those old macramé holders that were so popular in the '60s.
- Place a delicate plant on your nightstand for color and companionship.
- Decorate your entry hall with an assortment of plants in various shapes and sizes placed on the floor. Frame them with large rocks and boulders. Have one plant sitting on a bleached tree stump.
- Add a row of lacy plants in baskets on the bottom shelf of your country pine hutch.
- Dramatize a wide staircase by placing matching plants on each stair.
- Set off a wide, arched opening to a room with dramatic matching plants on either side.
- Use one magnificently rounded cactus stuffed in a terra cotta pot as an accessory for California casual and Southwestern rooms.
- To save money, shop garage sales. Many people sell their mature plants before they move. Give an old plant a new container and a little tender loving care; adopt it as part of your family.
- Remove damaged or dead leaves as soon as you spot them. There's nothing that ruins a room's look faster than an unkempt plant or tree (other than a dead plant or tree).

TREES

Use live trees to add height and drama to almost any room. There is an amazing number of species available that will flourish indoors. You'll find them sold at indoor plant shops and home improvement centers, even on street corners in some cities. Interior designers usually buy their plants and trees from a wholesale warehouse at about a 50% savings. Check your Business-to-Business Yellow Pages to find a wholesale source in your city.

If you've got cold feet and a "black thumb," you might want to consider using a professional plant service. These services will recommend specific trees and plants for the different lighting levels in your home. They'll select and deliver new healthy plants and trees to your home, carefully arranging them in the containers of your choice. Most plant services will purchase baskets and planters for you and give you detailed instructions on how to care for your new foliage.

If you're still apprehensive about taking care of live plants and trees, most plant services will maintain your foliage on a regular basis for a monthly fee. They'll take full responsibility for any plants or trees that might die or develop a disease and replace them at no additional charge.

Here are some suggestions to start you on your way.

- Before shopping, always use your furniture

plan to figure out how many and what size trees (and plants) you will need.

• Always buy your plants and trees from a reputable company. There are inferior and diseased plants on the market.

• Know what kind of lighting the plant or tree will be exposed to before going shopping. Have the salesperson suggest appropriate species and give you detailed instructions for care.

• Measure and note ceiling heights before going shopping. Buy trees that are at least six inches, if not more, from the ceiling to allow for growth.

• To make rooms look more unified and professional, use the same variety of tree throughout the room. Vary height and fullness to add balance.

• Use matching planters throughout each room. Give your trees a permanent home and a more finished look by using moss and/or smaller plants to fill in the top of the planter.

• Use delicate trees for delicate rooms, heavier leafed trees for rooms with a larger scale. The size and style of container used should relate to the size and type of tree and create a pleasing composition.

• Defy the rules of scale and use a huge tree or two in a small room to heighten drama and give the room a cozy look. However, don't use short or skimpy trees in very large rooms, you'll only end up with a "dwarfed" look.

• Ficus trees appear to be the most available and least expensive trees around. Use them anywhere there's lots of strong sunlight. Buy them tall and full, group them, or use one magnificent ficus alone to fill in a corner.

• Use dracaenas for areas that receive medium light. One great trick of the trade is to combine two or more dracaenas together in one container for a fuller, more dramatic and expensive look.

• Use rubber trees for low light areas.

• Kentia palms are "hot" but expensive. Owning a Kentia is like owning an original piece of art. Use one of the less costly varieties of palms to give a spacious, well-lit room a delicate, tropical look.

• Use bird-of-paradise trees with expansive, dramatic "elephant ear" leaves to add height and drama to rooms with very high ceilings.

• For dark areas that are crying out for a tree, consider using a fake. There are many authentic looking silk trees on the market; some machine made, some hand tied. You can even have a custom tree made to the exact size you need. Of course, hand-tied silk trees look better, but they're more costly than production-made versions.

Fresh flowers add the final personal touch to a room. Keeping up baskets and vases of flowers throughout your home may seem extravagant and time consuming, but the effect is well worth it. They'll breathe life and color into your home. Add a fresh bouquet of flowers anywhere, turn on some soothing music, and feel your stress fade away.

Professional tip: Remove old, dead orchid blooms from still green plants; replace with a fresh silk orchid.

20
Avoiding Decorating Mistakes

Decorating is much like driving a car. If you do it defensively and always assume the other guy is incompetent, you'll greatly reduce your risk of accidents. Every interior designer I've questioned about mistakes over the years has replied, "Who, me? Make mistakes? Oh, never!" This is a tongue-in-cheek answer, of course, and is always accompanied by laughter and a few confessions.

Unfortunately, hindsight is always better than foresight. Since each step of decorating your home is a new experience, how could you possibly recognize a potential calamity before it happens? Experience is the best teacher. Once I've encountered a decorating mistake, I'll take every precaution to avoid making that same mistake again.

Here's a complete set of guidelines. They're based on my many years of experience and my growing number of gray hairs.

The Basic Rules

Rule 1. Never, ever, assume anyone knows what they're doing or is telling the truth. This might seem negative and drastic, but the best defense is a good offense.

Rule 2. Pre-plan! Always make a furniture plan and a budget worksheet before purchasing anything.

Rule 3. Always assume items you order will arrive late.

Rule 4. Always assume items you order will be the wrong color, the wrong size, defective, or damaged.

Rule 5. Check, double check, and triple check every detail. PUT EVERYTHING IN WRITING!

Words to the Wise

• Don't take educated guesses. When in doubt about using a particular product, ask questions and gather all the information you can before purchasing.

• If the proportion, scale, and balance of a room are wrong, everything's wrong. Learn the basics of design.

• If you're confused or lack self confidence, don't be afraid to consult an expert. Hire an interior designer, a kitchen designer, an architect, a lighting consultant, a color consultant, a contractor, or a plant service. It'll save time and money in the long run.

• Don't be penny wise and dollar foolish. Use good budget-saving ideas instead of inferior products.

• Don't be stubborn about using a cherished piece if it won't ultimately work with your decor.

• Don't add insult to injury by designing a room around a piece you just bought last year, perhaps under a friend's misguided influence. Admit the piece is ugly and you hate it. Don't browbeat yourself for having wasted money . . . just forget it and move on before you waste more money.

• Don't defy the architecture of your home, it won't work. Either completely remodel your home to another style or work within the existing scope your home suggests.

• Certain rooms cry out to be decorated a certain way. Listen to them.

• Ignore friends and neighbors who try to coerce you into using their Uncle Harry to paint your rooms or build your cabinets. Rest assured, Uncle Harry will turn out to be an out-of-work car salesman who uses the "earn while you learn" technique between visits to the unemployment office.

• Do insist upon using only licensed and bonded workmen in your home. Use only workmen who are referred by reliable sources and conduct business professionally. Check at least three references to confirm honesty and reliability. Check craftsmanship with your own eyes. Never assume a workman is good because he's expensive or busy; these are not necessarily valid indicators of skill.

• Make a purchase order in duplicate for every item you order. Retain the original, attaching it to the corresponding copy of the sales slip or contract. Give the store, showroom, upholsterer, drapery workroom, or factory your duplicate copy. The purchase order should be numbered and clearly state:

Date the item was ordered
Date the item is due
Terms of payment
Method of shipping
Method of delivery
An accurate name and description of the item or items ordered
Manufacturer's style name, number, and color
Exact dimensions of the piece
Price

Any additional freight or delivery charges
Your initial deposit upon ordering
The balance due.

• Before ordering fabrics or wall coverings, always request a "cutting for approval" to make sure the dye lot or color run you will receive will be acceptable. Ask if the goods are in stock or on back order. Ask exactly when you can expect to receive the goods.

• Snip small cuttings off of the original samples of fabric or wallpaper. Attach a cutting to both copies of the purchase order.

• Before ordering a fabric that's in stock, ask if the goods are in one piece. Many fabric companies will ship odd lengths of leftover yardage, making it difficult, if not impossible, for your upholsterer or drapery workroom to use the fabric.

• Before ordering wallpaper, make sure a professional wallpaper hanger has quoted you the correct number of rolls or yardage to buy. Make sure you are both clear about the width of the wallpaper and its repeat. Are you all in agreement about the word "roll"? Is it a single roll, a double roll, or a triple roll you're ordering?

• Follow through. Call to inquire about orders periodically, if only to make sure your order doesn't get lost in the shuffle. If the salesperson informs you of a major delay, begin your nagging, whining, and threatening techniques immediately. Be relentless until your order is safely delivered.

• Use only licensed and insured delivery companies. Assume even the most professional delivery service will scratch a piece of furniture, crack a piece of glass, or get grease stains on your new sofa. Don't panic. A reputable company will take care of any repairs for you.

• Supervise! Make sure all workmen are performing their tasks according to your plans. If you catch a mistake early enough, it can usually be corrected. If you can't be there to supervise, hire a contractor you'd trust with your life.

• Pre-test any and all materials. Test every sample you will be using by inflicting the same abuse it might eventually be subjected to over the course of years. Show no mercy — burn it, scratch it, trample it, crumple it, spill red wine on it.

• Shop till you drop. Take the time and energy to be thorough. There's nothing more upsetting than finding the perfect item after you've already compromised and purchased the "wrong" item. Use interior design magazines and source books to save steps and locate sources.

• Don't fight with your furniture plan. If a piece of furniture you'd like to buy just won't fit, no matter how you angle it or squeeze it, give up. If it doesn't work on paper, it won't work in the room.

• Don't order any custom-installed built-ins from your own measurements. Have the professional who will be installing them take his own measurements. This relieves you of all responsibility for mistakes.

• Shop competitively. Don't assume the same item will be the same price in every store or showroom. Prices will vary greatly.

• Don't cast your budget in stone. Allow yourself enough cushioning for adjustments and mistakes.

• Don't purchase bargains just because you can't resist them. Make sure they work or they're not a bargain.

• Avoid trendy color schemes; they'll look tired quickly.

• Always give your paint a color test by applying a good-sized sample on the wall where it's to be used. Don't paint an entire room until the paint has dried and the color is acceptable in both natural and artificial lighting.

• Use a professional licensed electrician to install all lighting and electrical outlets.

• Buy your lighting fixtures from a reputable store or showroom. Ask the salesperson if the fixture comes with any additional parts that might be needed. Order the right bulbs when you order the fixture. You'll waste time and money if the electrician shows but he doesn't have the correct parts to install your lighting.

• Make sure you have checked and double checked all measurements on drawings you'll be providing to your custom furniture makers. Put every detail in writing on the drawing and the purchase order. The slightest mistake or oversight could result in a fiasco. For double insurance, instruct the custom furniture maker to stop working and call you immediately if he notices any oddities or discrepancies in your dimensions.

• To insure your custom-made upholstered pieces will be usable, compare measurements from similar ready-made pieces that are comfortable. Check to make sure the seat is deep enough after you've added those extra pillows.

• Some materials don't hold up well in moist and damp climates such as the beach. Have flooring, especially wood flooring, installed by a professional who knows the correct subflooring and sealer to use for your climate.

• Avoid brass accessories in salt air climates. They'll darken and pit within weeks.

• Don't overlook flooring thicknesses. Use padding, subflooring, or thresholds to alleviate floor height discrepancies between rooms.

• Don't skimp at the end with cheap artwork and accessories. Wait, if you must, until your bank account has recovered. Splurge on one expensive piece rather than several cheaper pieces.

• Pay attention to each and every small detail, from the stitching on a throw pillow to the way the joint is connected on your new molding. It's these tiny details that make the difference.

Whew! We did it. So much to learn, so little time. By now you probably know more about decorating than most professional interior designers. Use the Decorating Dictionary at the back of this book to refresh your memory from time to time. Congratulations, you're on your own now!

Decorating Dictionary

Antiques

ANTIQUES — According to the United States Customs Law, anything over 100 years old.

ANTIQUES — Furniture that has been painted, stained, and distressed to create a worn, mellow look that comes with aging.

BALL AND CLAW — A Chinese motif in which a dragon's claw is clutching a pearl. It was used in English furniture, but changed to an eagle's claw by eighteenth century American designers.

BIEDERMEIER — A neoclassic style of furniture from nineteenth century Austria.

CABRIOLE LEG — A gracefully curved leg with a rounded knee. It was used by furniture makers of the eighteenth century in England and the United States.

CHINOISERIE — Any Chinese decoration, but especially pieces done in eighteenth century England and Italy.

CHIPPENDALE, THOMAS — A well-known English cabinetmaker whose style became famous in 1754 with the publication of his book on English furniture.

COLONIAL — Furniture made from 1700-81.

COUNTRY — A basic style, an expression of the "back to basics" movement that swept the country in the 1970s.

DIRECTOIRE — The period following the French Revolution noted for its simple, classic furniture. It was the transitional furniture between the Neoclassicism of Louis XVI and Napoleon's Empire style.

DIRECTORY — The period when American furniture makers, especially Duncan Phyfe, were influenced by French Directoire.

EARLY AMERICAN — Maple, oak, or pine furniture used by the settlers in the New World (1608-1720). It was the provincial version of seventeenth century English styles.

EMPIRE — Napoleon's style. American Empire includes classic motifs from Greece, Rome, and Egypt.

FEDERAL — Elegant, classic furniture. It was prevalent in the United States after the Revolution (1781-1830), and greatly influenced by England and France.

GEORGIAN — Furniture made during the period of all four King Georges of England (1715-1830).

HEPPLEWHITE, GEORGE — A well-known English cabinetmaker who produced dignified and refined furniture from the mid to late eighteenth century.

LOUIS XIV (1643-1715) — Furniture period known for its grandiose, gilded, and baroque qualities.

LOUIS XV (1715-74) — Furniture with rococo, delicately curved styles.

LOUIS XVI (1774-93) — Furniture known for straight lines and classic motifs.

MISSION — Simple, dark oak furniture named for the Spanish missions prevalent in early California.

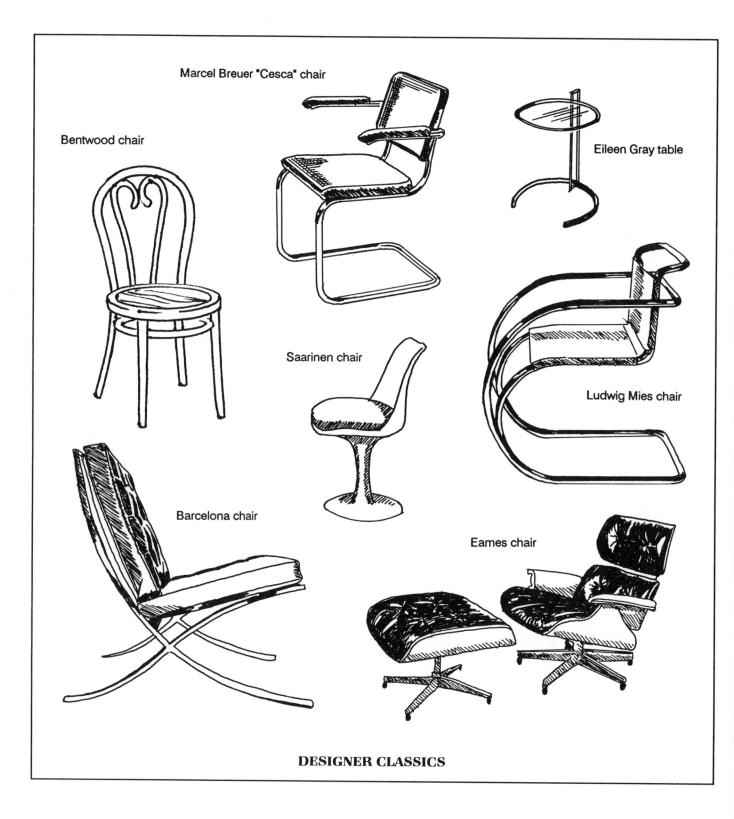

Marcel Breuer "Cesca" chair

Bentwood chair

Eileen Gray table

Saarinen chair

Ludwig Mies chair

Barcelona chair

Eames chair

DESIGNER CLASSICS

NEOCLASSIC — "New classic." It refers to the revival of any classic form.

PATINA — The soft, mellow finish found on furniture and metal. A true patina is caused by age and use.

PHYFE, DUNCAN — A Scottish-born furniture designer who worked in New York from 1790-1847.

POST MODERN — "After modern." It refers to a return to the use of classic forms and furnishings that were used before "form follows function" furniture became popular in the twentieth century.

PROVINCIAL — Furniture made in the provinces that copied the styles of the sophisticated cities.

QUEEN ANNE (1701-14) — This period is known for its graceful furniture.

REGENCY — The English form of neoclassicism that swept the design world from 1780-1820.

REPRODUCTION — An authentic copy of an antique.

SHAKER — Simply designed furniture made by the Shakers, a religious sect in the United States, during the eighteenth and nineteenth centuries.

SHERATON, THOMAS — A famous English furniture designer (1751-1806) known for his straight-lined furniture.

SLEIGH BED — A term used for a nineteenth century American bed. It has a rolled headboard and footboard that make it look like a sleigh.

VICTORIAN — The period of Queen Victoria's reign in England (1837-1901). The furniture was stiff, formal, and ornate.

WILLIAM AND MARY — An English period (1689-1702). French influence replaced Dutch baroque, and furniture became lighter and less ornate.

Architecture and Construction

ATRIUM PLAN — An architectural plan in which all of the major rooms open directly on a central courtyard.

BAUHAUS — The famous German school of design founded by Walter Gropius in 1919. It had a profound influence on all furniture today.

BEAM — The horizontal member of a structure's support that rests on vertical posts, usually a heavy timber or metal bar.

BI-NUCLEAR PLAN — An architectural plan that divides a home into two wings, usually one for group living and one for bedrooms.

BOARD AND BATTEN CONSTRUCTION — A type of wall construction in which wide, vertical boards are sealed by narrow strips of wood, called battens.

CAVITY WALL CONSTRUCTION — A construction technique that allows hollow space within a wall to leave room for pipes, wiring, and insulation.

CLOSED PLAN — An architectural plan that divides the interior space of a home into separate, distinct rooms.

CONDUCTION — A heating system in which radiators circulating hot water or steam warm the air in an enclosure.

CONTEMPORARY — Architecture made of today's materials in the "form follows function" theory of modern architecture.

CONVECTION — A heating system where air warmed in a furnace is blown out through registers.

COVE CEILING — A ceiling which is rounded where it meets the wall.

BASEBOARD — The molding covering the wall at the point where it meets the floor.

BEARING WALL — A thick wall that carries the weight of the roof to the foundation.

CANTILEVER — A projection from the wall.

CHAIR RAIL — The molding placed on the wall at the approximate height of the back of a chair.

CORBEL — An architectural member that projects from a wall and supports weight.

CROWN MOLDING — The molding that goes around a room at the point where the wall meets the ceiling.

DADO — The wall area between the chair rail and the baseboard.

DOME — A hemisphere or inverted cup, the rotation of an arch on its axis.

DOORS — See complete list in Chapter 15.

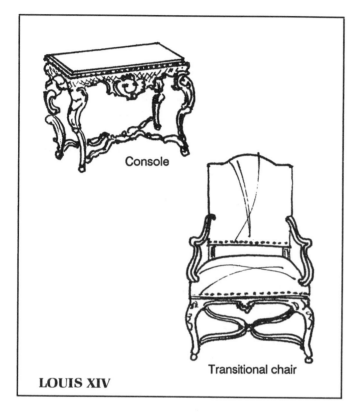

Console

Transitional chair

LOUIS XIV

GEODESIC DOME — A dome composed of small modules based on a triangle.

GLASS BLOCKS — Hollow, brick-like forms of glass that come in a variety of shapes and sizes and are set together with mortar.

GYPSUM BOARD — Also known as wallboard, plasterboard, or drywall. Its thin layers of plaster-like material are used for interior walls.

HOLLOW-CORE DOOR — A door that is hollow inside, as opposed to a door made of solid wood.

INSULATION — The prevention, by use of certain materials, of the transfer of electricity, cold, heat, or sound from the outside of a structure to the inside. It also refers to the type of material used.

LATH — The wood or metal framework of a structure that supports other materials, such as tiles and plaster.

LOFT — A raised platform or projecting balcony.

MANSARD ROOF — A roof sloped in two planes, the lower being steeper.

MASONRY — The use of bricks, tiles, concrete blocks, or glass blocks joined together with mortar. It also refers to the construction of a wall with plaster or concrete.

DOUBLE GLAZING — The process of providing windows with two thin sheets of glass that are hermetically sealed together and trap air between them. It provides extremely good cold insulation.

DROPPED CEILING — The portion of a ceiling lowered below its actual functional level or below other sections of the ceiling.

ELL — A right-angled building extension.

FACADE — The exterior, usually the front, of a building.

FLUSH MOUNT DOOR — A door that fits flush to a wall or cabinet. There are no gaps, hardware, or moldings that can be seen.

FOYER — An entry or entrance hall.

GABLE — The vertical triangular end of a building from cornice or eaves to ridge.

GABLED ROOF — A double-pitched roof that comes to a point and forms a triangle.

Console

Side chair

Bergère

LOUIS XV

MODERN — An approach to architecture that lets the function dictate the form. There is emphasis on the materials used and no unnecessary frills.

MORTAR — Cement, lime, or plaster combined with sand and water.

OPEN PLAN — An architectural plan with very few fixed partitions or walls.

PEDIMENT — A triangular space forming the gable of a low-pitched roof in classic architecture.

PLASTER — A paste, usually made of lime, sand, and water, which hardens when dry.

POST — The vertical member that supports horizontal beams.

POST AND LINTEL — A structural system in architecture in which beams, or lintels, are placed horizontally across upright posts.

RADIANT HEAT — Heating which is transmitted by radiant electrical panels, usually placed in the ceiling.

RANCH STYLE — A type of one-story house, usually with an open plan and a low-pitched roof.

SASH — The window frame that holds the panes of glass; the movable part of a window.

SHED CEILING — A single-sloped, lean-to type of ceiling.

SHINGLE — A thin slab of wood or other material laid in overlapping rows to form a siding or roof covering.

SITE — The actual space on which a house is constructed.

SOFFIT — The underside of a part of a building, such as an overhang or a staircase.

SPLIT LEVEL — A house in which the floor level of one portion lies about midway between floors of an adjoining two-story section.

SPUR WALL — A freestanding wall that projects from an adjoining wall at one end.

STUCCO — A weather-resistant plaster used for exteriors.

TOUCH LATCH — A type of hardware used on flush-mount doors. This type of hardware allows the door to open and close by touch so that no pulls, handles, or knobs are necessary.

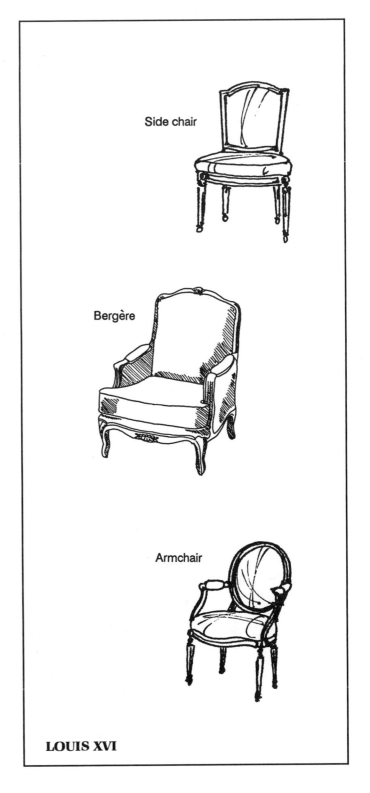

Side chair

Bergère

Armchair

LOUIS XVI

TRUSS — A structural form consisting of rigid bars or beams arranged in a system of triangles joined at their apexes.

WAINSCOT — Interior wood paneling that reaches only part way up a wall.

WINDOWS — See complete list in Chapter 15.

WING — A portion of a building that extends from a major central area.

Art

ABSTRACT — Non-objective. A recognizable form has been simplified or distorted in some way.

ABSTRACT EXPRESSIONISM — An art style that emphasizes non-objective form and energetic activity. It's also called "New York School" and "Action Painting."

ACRYLIC — Rigid, clear, and transparent plastic in solid form. It's used as a binder for pigments used in painting.

AQUATINT — Used in print making. A porous ground of resin is applied to a plate, then dipped in stages into an acid bath, which then creates a range of values.

ASSEMBLAGE — A piece of art created by combining different objects or fragments of objects.

BAS RELIEF — A sculpture in which the figures are attached to the background and project slightly out from it.

BINDER — The substance used in paints that causes the pigment particles to hold together.

CALLIGRAPHY — The art of decorative writing.

CARTOON — A drawing made to scale on paper. It is used to transfer designs as a basis for painting, mosaic, or tapestry.

CASEIN — A painting medium in which the pigment is bound with milk curd.

CASTING — The process of making a liquid substance into a specific shape by pouring it into a mold and letting it harden.

COLLAGE — A two-dimensional piece of art in which pieces of paper, cloth, or any other material are pasted together to create a design.

COLLAGRAPH — A print made from a collage.

CONCEPTUAL ART — Art that depends on the concept of the artist.

CONTENT — The subject matter of a piece of art.

CUBISM — An art style, characterized by flattened

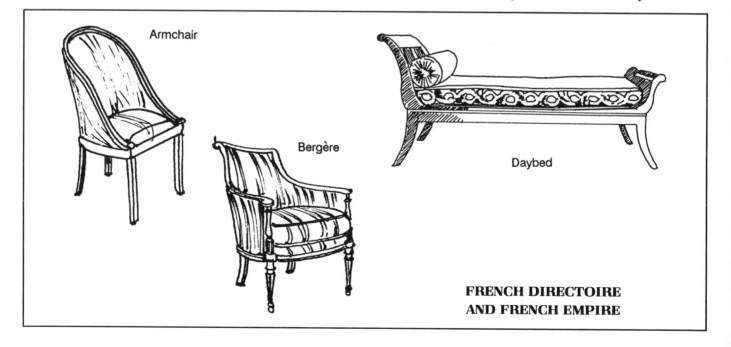

Armchair

Bergère

Daybed

FRENCH DIRECTOIRE AND FRENCH EMPIRE

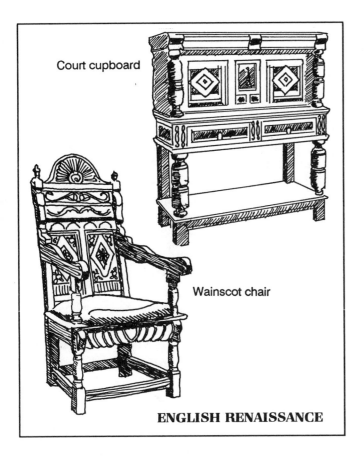

Court cupboard

Wainscot chair

ENGLISH RENAISSANCE

pictorial space and figure/ground ambiguity. It was developed by Picasso and Braque in the early 1900s.

ENAMELING — The art of creating designs in colored, glassy materials which are fused to metals.

ENGRAVING — A printing technique in which an image is created by scratching into a metal plate with a sharp tool. Ink is placed in the depressions and the paper is forced to make an impression.

ETCHING — A printing process in which acid acts as the cutting agent. A metal plate is coated with acid resist, scratched away in printing areas, then dipped in acid.

EXPRESSIONISM — An art movement of the early twentieth century. It emphasized the artist's emotional response through color and symbolic imagery.

FAUVISM — An art movement originating in France in the early 1900s. It was characterized by the unconventional use of bright, contrasting colors for structural and expressive effects.

FIGURE-GROUND — A term referring to the relationship of a form to its background.

FRESCO — A painting medium used for murals. The paint is applied to a ground of wet plaster.

GESSO — A mixture of white pigment, glue, and plaster or gypsum used as a ground for tempera paint.

GLAZE — A glassy coating fired onto ceramics. It also applies to the layer of paint applied to canvas to achieve translucency or luminosity.

GOUACHE — Opaque watercolor paint. The binder is gum arabic and a paste of zinc oxide.

GRAPHIC — The art of drawing or writing. Graphic design usually means design for advertising, books, magazines, and packaging.

GROUND — The material applied to prepare for a drawing or painting medium. It also means the background of a picture.

HAUT RELIEF — Sculpture in which the forms project from a background to a great depth.

ICONOGRAPHY — The "story" behind a piece of artwork.

IMPRESSIONISM — An art style that originated in France in the 1870s. Artists focused on painting effects of light, shade, and color that occur in nature.

INTAGLIO — A depressed image that is created by carving, cutting, or incising.

LITHOGRAPHY — A flat surface printmaking technique based on the use of grease and water.

LUMINAL ART — Art in which light is an element.

MACRAME — A construction technique in which form is produced by knotting strands of fiber in varied patterns.

MEDIUM — The material used for a piece of art.

MIMIMAL ART — An art style of the mid-twentieth century. It is noted for its contour or geometric shapes, flat surfaces, and pure, undiluted colors.

MONOPRINT — A one-of-a-kind print. It is made by transferring an image drawn on plate, usually glass, to paper.

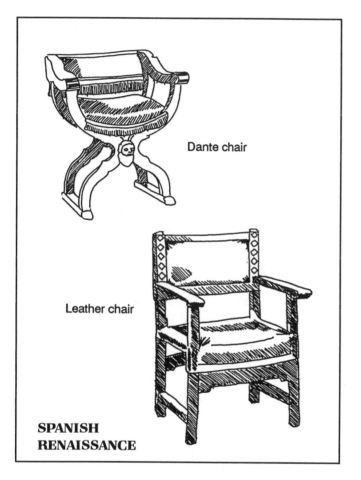

Dante chair

Leather chair

SPANISH RENAISSANCE

MOSAIC — An art form in which pieces of glass or ceramic tile are fitted together and glued to form a design.

OP ART — An art style of the mid-twentieth century which used optical illusions, a sense of vibration, and afterimages.

PALETTE — The range of colors used for a painting. It also refers to the surface on which an artist mixes paint.

PHOTOREALISM — An art style of the mid-twentieth century in which objects or people are depicted with photographic accuracy.

PIGMENT — The fine powder used to color paints and dyes.

POINTILLISM — The technique of applying tiny dots of color to canvas.

POP ART — An art style of the mid-1950s. Its subject matter is generally popular, mass-produced symbols.

PRINT — An impression made on paper from a master plate, stone, or block created by an artist.

RELIEF — A printmaking process in which portions of the image to be printed are raised above the surface of the plate or block. It can also refer to any raised image.

RELIEF SCULPTURE — Sculpture attached to a background.

SECCO — A method of painting in which color is applied to dry plaster walls.

SERIALISM — Sculpture, photography, or painting in which each individual work is part of a continuum.

SERIGRAPHY — A printmaking process that uses stencils and screens.

SILK SCREEEN — A printmaking process where the image is transferred to paper or cloth by forcing ink through fine silk screens in which nonprinted areas are prevented from taking color.

SUPPORT — The material to which the drawing or painting material is applied, such as the canvas.

SURREALISM — An art movement of the early twentieth century. It emphasized intuitive and nonrational relationships and symbols occurring in dreams.

TAPESTRY — A type of weaving where the weft yarn carries the design and shows on the surface of the fabric in specific design areas.

TEMPERA — A painting medium. The pigment is bound together with egg yolk or with animal or vegetable glue.

WATERCOLOR — A painting medium. The binder is gum arabic.

Color

ACHROMATIC — Having no color. A neutral, such as black, white, or gray, is achromatic.

ADVANCING COLORS — Warm colors, such as red, yellow, and orange, that make surfaces appear closer.

AFTERIMAGE — When the retina of the eye becomes fatigued after viewing a hue for any sustained length of time, causing the complementary color to be seen.

ANALOGOUS COLOR SCHEME — Groups of colors related in hue or neighbors on the color wheel.

COLD-WARM CONTRAST — A sensation of temperature within the visual realm of color sensation.

COMPLEMENTARY COLOR SCHEMES — Strong and bold color combinations developed by using two hues directly opposite each other on the color wheel.

COMPLEMENTARY CONTRAST — When the pigments of two complementary colors are mixed together, making a neutral gray-black.

CONTRAST OF EXTENSION — The proportion in which we use colors.

CONTRAST OF HUE — Exemplified by the triad color scheme of red, yellow, and blue.

COOL COLORS — Blue, green, and violet, or any color that has blue added.

GRAY SCALE — The series of value gradations between black and white.

HUE — Color, pure and undiluted.

INTENSITY — The strength of a color, weak or strong.

INTERMEDIATE COLORS — These lie midway between the primary and secondary colors of which they are products.

IRIDESCENCE — The rainbow effect caused as a material or surface reflects the light of all the hues of the spectrum.

LUMINOSITY — The actual or illusionary effect of giving off light.

LUSTER — The glow of reflected light.

MONOCHROMATIC — A color scheme of all one color, or various shades of all one color.

NEUTRAL — Colors such as white, beige, gray, and brown.

NORMAL VALUE — The value of a color when in its pure, unmixed state.

PRIMARY COLORS — Red, blue, and yellow from which all other colors are derived.

RECEDING COLORS — Cool colors, such as blue, green, and violet, that make objects appear smaller or further away.

RELATED COLORS — Colors that are analogous or monochromatic.

SECONDARY COLORS — Orange, green, and violet. They are made by mixing equal parts of two primary colors.

SHADES — Hues with black added.

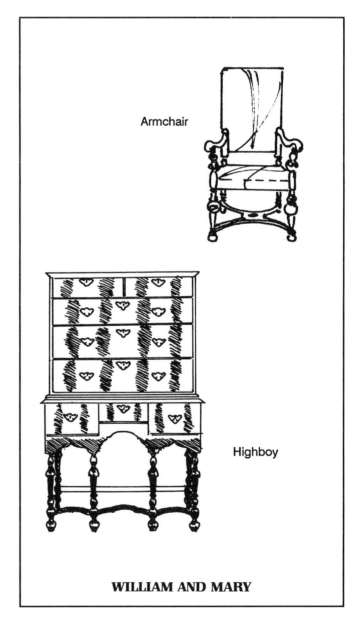

Armchair

Highboy

WILLIAM AND MARY

SIMULTANEOUS CONTRAST — The tendency of complementary colors to intensify each other when placed side by side.

TERTIARY — Colors made by mixing equal parts of a secondary color with a primary color, such as red-orange, yellow-green, and red-violet.

TINTS — Hues with white added.

TONES — Hues with gray added.

VALUE — The darkness or lightness of a color.

WARM COLORS — Red, yellow, and orange, or any color to which yellow has been added.

Fabrics

ABRASION — Friction wearing away the surface of a fabric.

ABRASION RESISTANCE — How resistant a fabric is to surface wear.

ABSORBENCY — The quality of a fabric to absorb and retain moisture.

ACETATES — Manmade soft, lustrous fabrics that drape well. They resist fading, mildew, and wrinkles, but usually must be dry cleaned.

ACRYLICS — Soft manmade chemical fibers that drape well and are hand washable, but darken in prolonged exposure to sunlight.

BLEEDING — When excess dyes run as fabrics are being washed.

BLENDING — Two or more fibers are combed together prior to the spinning process.

BONDING — When a face fabric is joined with adhesive to a backing fabric or when fibers are adhesively joined to each other.

BULK YARNS — Yarns that have been increased in their mass, bulk, or size, but not in weight or length.

CANDLE — Describes how a fabric looks when it is held up to a light, or how the light actually comes through the fabric.

CARDING — The process of separating fibers from each other and laying them in a parallel, thin web.

CASEMENT — A general fabric term used to describe a variety of materials, weaves, and fibers used for draperies and curtains.

CELLULOSE — A fiber-like substance derived from the cell walls of plants.

COCOON — The case spun by the silkworm which is the source of silk filament.

COLORFAST — Describes how well a fabric retains its color with washing and prolonged exposure to sunlight.

COMBING — A fabric process that creates fine, smooth yarns by eliminating short fibers.

COUNT — A term used for the number of threads or yarns per square inch of fabric.

CROCKING — When a color from a fabric can be transferred to another surface when rubbed. It is caused by using the wrong dye or poor dyeing techniques.

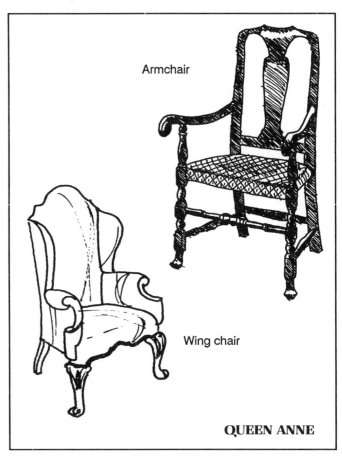

Armchair

Wing chair

QUEEN ANNE

CUT PILE — Fabric with an extra set of warp or filling threads that form a pile which is cut in designs.

DENIER — The international measure used to determine the weight of silk or some synthetic fibers. The lower the number, the finer the weight; the higher the number, the heavier and stronger the weight.

DRAPABILITY — How a fabric falls into graceful folds when it is hung.

DYEABILITY — How well a fabric will take a dye.

ELASTICITY — How easily a fabric will return to its original strength after it has been stretched.

EMBOSSING — Passing a fabric between hot engraved rollers to create a raised design.

FABRICS — See complete list in Chapter 11.

FACE — The side of the fabric that's meant to be shown and has the better appearance.

FADING — The tendency of fabrics to change or fade from smoke, soot, fumes, or sunlight.

FELTING — When fibers mat down when exposed to heat, abrasion, or moisture.

FIBERGLASS FABRICS — Easily washable and dry quickly and wrinkle free. They resist moths, mildew, heat, sun, wrinkling, and fire. But they fade easily and are difficult to sew.

FILLING YARN — The crosswise yarn in a woven fabric.

FINISH — Any way a fabric is treated to give it a special effect, such as luster, softness, or waterproofing.

FLAMEPROOF — The fabric will not burn when subjected to open flames. It doesn't mean the fabric won't melt when exposed to extreme heat.

FLAME RESISTANT OR FIRE RESISTANT — The fabric will not burn rapidly when subjected to open flame.

FLAME RETARDANT OR FIRE RETARDANT — The fabric will extinguish itself when subjected to open flame.

GENERIC — A general class or group of fibers; not a trademark.

GRAIN — Surface quality of a fabric achieved by the lengthwise and crosswise yarns.

GRAY GOODS — Fabrics that have been woven, but not solution dyed. They will be dyed, printed, or finished by another processor.

GROUND — The background of a fabric surrounding its design.

HEAT SENSITIVITY — How a fabric softens, shrinks, melts, or discolors when exposed to heat.

HEAT SET — A process used to help fabric retain its size, shape, pleats, and/or color.

INSULATION — Gives a fabric thermal qualities. Either one side is coated with metal or a plastic foam is bonded to the back of the fabric.

JACQUARD LOOM — A loom used for complicated patterns.

LAMINATION — Joining two or more layers of materials together by bonding, resins, or adhesives.

LIGHTFAST — Fabrics that are resistant to fading from strong sun exposure.

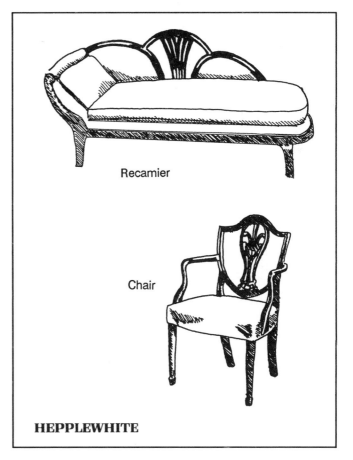

Recamier

Chair

HEPPLEWHITE

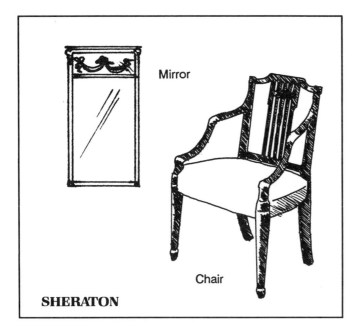

SHERATON

LOFTED YARNS — Yarns with an increased bulk and thickness, but no increase in weight.

LOOM — The machine used to weave cloth with thread and yarns.

MAT — The dull, lusterless quality of the surface of a fabric.

MERCERIZING — A finish applied to cotton and some synthetics to add strength, luster, and absorbency.

MILIUM — The insulating material used to line draperies.

MODACRYLICS — Fabrics that drape well, are flame resistant, spot and stain resistant, and retain their whiteness in prolonged exposure to sunlight.

NAP — The soft, downy surface of a fabric that can be raised with brushing.

NYLONS — Wrinkle resistant fabrics that dye well and clean easily, but are weakened by strong sunlight.

PELLON — A trade name, now used generically for inner facings or inner linings.

OPAQUE — Any material that cannot be seen through.

PERMANENT PLEATING — A process used on polyesters and polyester blends to make them shed wrinkles and retain pleats.

PIECE GOODS — Fabric sold by the yard in retail stores.

PILLING — The balls or tangled fibers that form on fabric surfaces from abrasion.

PLUSH — A high pile, exaggerated form of velvet.

PLY — The number of yarns twisted together to form a single strand.

POLYESTERS — When heat set, they are durable, wrinkle resistant, and retain creases. They are washable and don't easily deteriorate in strong sunlight.

PRESHRUNK — A fabric that has gone through a shrinkage process before it is sold. Legally, the manufacturer must inform you of the percentage of any additional shrinkage that may occur.

RAYONS — The first manmade fiber. They are soft and dye and drape well, are wrinkle and heat resistant, but will burn quickly.

REPEAT — The distance in inches on a patterned fabric for the design to recur. It can be any number of inches.

REPELLENCY — Soil repellent fabrics resist soil and stains. Water repellent fabrics resist water stains. Oil repellent fabrics resist grease and oil stains.

RESILIENCY - The ability of fibers or fabrics to spring back after they've been crushed or wrinkled.

SARAN — A fabric that drapes well, dyes easily, and is wrinkle and fire resistant. It retains its strength and is not affected by sunlight.

SCOTCHGARD — Trademark for a process used to make fabrics soil resistant.

SECONDS — Flawed goods that are still usable.

SHUTTLE — The tool used in weaving to carry the filling thread back and forth between the warp threads.

SHUTTLELESS LOOM — A loom that uses air jets or water jets instead of a shuttle. They are faster than conventional looms.

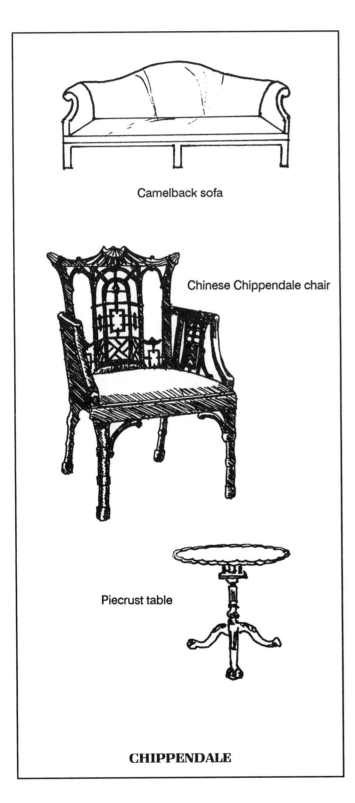

Camelback sofa

Chinese Chippendale chair

Piecrust table

CHIPPENDALE

SLUB YARNS — Yarns with irregular diameters by error or nature. Slub yarns can be purposely created for some desired fabric effects.

SOLUTION-DYED FABRICS — Fabrics made from fibers that were dyed before they were spun.

SPUN YARN — Yarn made up of short lengths of yarns or staple fibers that are twisted together in continuous lengths.

STABILITY — How a fabric retains its shape and size after it has been washed or dry cleaned.

STATIC ELECTRICITY — The electricity generated by the friction of one fabric against another or a fabric against any other object.

TENSILE STRENGTH — How strong a fabric or yarn is.

TEXTILES — A term referring to woven fabrics.

THERMOPLASTIC — A term meaning that a material will soften when heat is applied, and harden when heat is removed.

TRADE NEWS — Trademarks and brand names of products of particular manufacturers. These names are registered and patented.

TRANSLUCENT — Any material that is semi-clear and can be seen through.

URETHANE LAMINATES — Thin layers of backing, usually ⅛ inch thick, attached to the back of lighter weight fabrics to give body and add insulation.

WARP — The lengthwise yarn in woven fabrics.

WICKING — A quality that allows water to travel quickly through a fabric. It means that the moisture is retained in the fibers of the fabric.

YARNS — Fibers twisted in continuous strands and used for woven and knitted fabrics.

ZEPEL — A protection process that makes a fabric resistant to oil and grease stains as well as water repellent.

Floor Coverings

ABOVE GRADE — Wood or concrete floors suspended above a full or partial basement.

AREA RUG — A small rug used to set off a specific or special area.

ASPHALT TILE — The least expensive tile.

BELOW GRADE — A concrete floor placed below ground level, such as a basement floor.

BERBER — A rug or carpet made from undyed off-white wool yarn. It is flat woven, usually in a horizontal ribbed effect.

BROADLOOM — A carpet woven on a broad loom; the term is not to be confused with a standard of quality.

DHURRIE RUGS — Flat reversible rugs with geometric patterns in soft colors, usually woven by hand in India. New Dhurrie rugs are made of wool, while a Dhurrie rug over fifty years old is made of cotton and is considered an antique.

GAUGE — The thickness of tiles or sheet goods.

KILIM RUGS — Flat, reversible rugs with floral or geometric motifs in bold colors. Most Kilims are woven by hand from fine wool and are different from Dhurries in that their weave is much finer and their designs more intricate.

LINOLITE — Linoleum that is much thicker and usually used for commercial installations.

NAVAJO RUGS — American Indian rugs, similar to Dhurries, woven now in a wide variety of colors and geometric designs.

ON GRADE — A concrete slab placed at ground level, either directly on the earth or on a gravel fill.

ORIENTAL RUGS — Rugs handmade in the Middle East or Far East. They come from a district or town, for which they are named, within six major groups: Persian, Bokhara, Turkish, Caucasian, Chinese, and Indian.

RAG RUGS — Dating back before the American Colonies, when recycled cloth was made into strips of fabric, then woven together with cotton or linen warp threads.

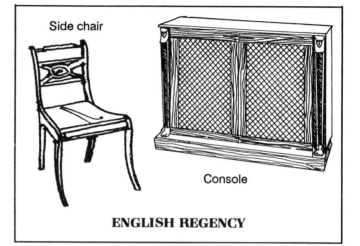

Side chair

Console

ENGLISH REGENCY

RUBBER TILE — Available in tile or sheet form in a variety of strong colors, sizes, and patterns.

RYA RUGS — Handwoven in Scandinavia, they are shag rugs that blend a deep pile with a flat weave and are available in a wide range of colors.

TERRAZZO — A mixture of broken stone and cement which has been highly polished.

VINYL — Available in both tile and sheet form in many colors, patterns, and styles.

Furniture

APRON — The exposed wood frame around the seat rail of a chair or the side of a table.

ARMOIRE — A tall cabinet with two doors. While armoires were originally made in France for the purpose of storing tools, armoires are now made in almost any country and for any purpose.

BACHELOR'S CHEST — A small chest of drawers.

BAMBOO — Furniture made from treelike tropical grass with woody, jointed, and often hollow stems.

BANQUETTES — Long, upholstered seats built in along a wall. They are usually for dining room seating.

BARCELONA CHAIR — The classic leather chair on an X-shaped steel support. It was designed by architect Ludwig Mies Van der Rohe, and introduced in 1929 in Barcelona, Spain.

BENTWOOD — Furniture made from wood, bent and shaped under steam and pressure. Michael Thonet, an Austrian furniture designer, is famous for his bentwood chairs.

BERGERE CHAIR — A wide, wood-framed upholstered armchair.

BLOCK FRONT — A term referring mostly to desks, chests, and secretaries with fronts made of thick boards cut in a series of curves.

BLOND — Light-finished furniture that has been bleached and finished anywhere from eggshell white to a very light brown.

BOMBE — A type of chest that bulges out in the front.

BOW BACK CHAIR — A chair that has an archer's bow-shaped back and arms formed by another bow extending around the back.

BRACKET FOOT — A simple, square foot formed by two pieces of wood angled together at the corner.

BREAKFRONT — A tall storage unit that has a lower cabinet topped with glass-enclosed shelving.

BROKEN PEDIMENT — The triangular pediment at the top of a piece of furniture. It is often filled with a decorative ornament.

BREUER, MARCEL — A famous furniture designer from the Bauhaus school, known for his metal furniture. He emphasized simplicity and function.

CAMELBACK — An upholstered chair or sofa with a back and top curved like a camel's hump.

CANE — The flexible rattan used for woven chair seats and backs, as well as for cabinet doors.

CANOPY BED — A tall, four poster bed with a fabric canopy.

CESCA CHAIR — A famous chair designed by Marcel Breuer. It is a still-popular tubular steel chair with a cane seat and back.

CHAISE LONGUE — An elongated chair for lounging.

CHINA CABINET — A buffet topped with shelves, often enclosed with glass, used to display china and crystal.

CLUB CHAIR — An easy chair that is comfortable and upholstered.

COFFEE TABLE — Any table, usually low, used in front of seating for the purpose of serving beverages and hors d'oeuvres.

COUCH — A sofa.

COMB BACK CHAIR — A chair with a braced back and a top rail shaped like a comb.

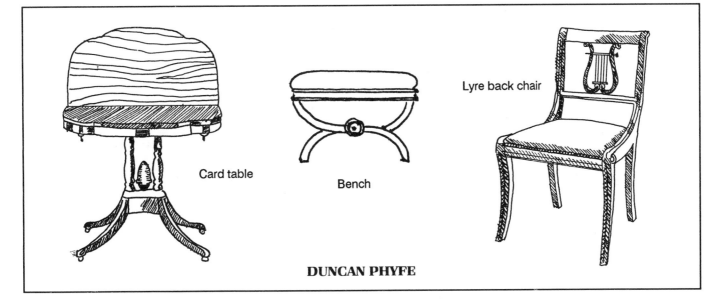

Card table

Bench

Lyre back chair

DUNCAN PHYFE

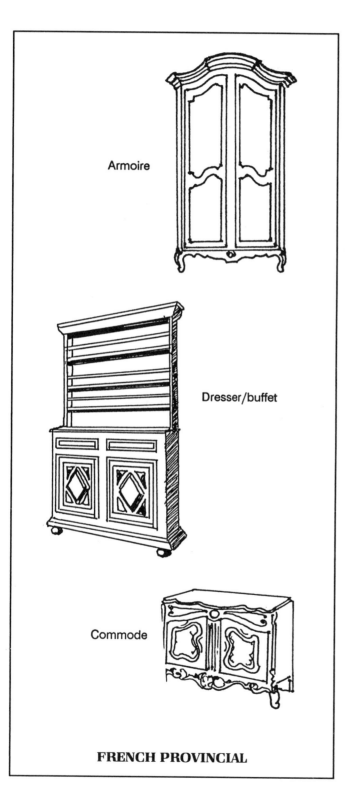

Armoire

Dresser/buffet

Commode

FRENCH PROVINCIAL

CONSOLE — A table used against a wall. It is usually supported by legs in the front only. Often used in entry halls or as a serving table in the dining room.

CUBE — A little box used as a small table. They can be made or found in almost any size and material.

CUPBOARD — Another term for a china cabinet.

DAVENPORT — A large sofa named after a nineteenth century manufacturer.

DIRECTOR'S CHAIRS — Made famous by Hollywood directors. They are wood or metal armchairs with canvas sling seats and backs. They can be folded flat.

DROP LEAF TABLE — A table with hinged leaves that can be raised to extend the top area.

EAMES, CHARLES — A twentieth century designer famous for his classic contour lounge chair made of molded plywood and leather.

ETAGERE — French term for freestanding or hanging shelves.

FAUTEUIL — French term for an upholstered armchair with the arms left un-upholstered.

GATELEG TABLE — A drop leaf table with legs that swing like a gate to support the leaves when they are open.

GRAIN — The natural pattern that a piece of wood displays when it is cut.

HIGHBOY — A tall chest of drawers mounted on a long-legged commode or lowboy.

HITCHCOCK CHAIR — A painted and stenciled chair. The original Hitchcock Chairs were made by Lambert Hitchcock in Connecticut in the early nineteenth century.

HUTCH — A low chest or cupboard used for storage and topped with open shelving.

KAS — Large Dutch cupboards with paintings or carvings.

KILN DRIED — Wood that has had moisture extracted in a heated chamber to reduce potential warping.

LADDERBACK CHAIRS — Chairs with a series of ladder-like horizontal supports on the back.

LINGERIE CHEST — A tall, narrow chest with seven drawers, one for each day of the week. Also called a Semanier.

LOUNGE — A backless sofa with a headrest at one end.

LOVESEAT — A small sofa that is no longer than sixty-six inches.

LOWBOY — A low chest of drawers placed on long legs.

INLAYS — Designs made in furniture or flooring by inserting pieces of wood, metal, or ivory.

LOOSE CUSHIONED BACK — A chair or sofa with loose or removable back cushions.

MARQUETRY — Inlays where the entire surface creates an overall pattern, such as herringbone.

MIES VAN DER ROHE, LUDWIG — A well-known architect of the twentieth century, famous for his clean-lined modern furniture. His most famous piece is the Barcelona Chair.

MODULAR FURNITURE — Furniture that comes in standard-sized components that can be combined easily to suit different needs.

NEST OF TABLES — A group of tables in graduated sizes that fit one over the other.

OTTOMAN — A low upholstered seat; armless and backless.

PARSONS TABLE — Also called a T-square table. A simple, squared off table.

PEDESTAL — The center support for a table top. The term is also used to describe the rectangular freestanding piece that holds sculptures and other objets d'art.

PULL-UP CHAIR — An occasional armchair that is pulled up when needed.

RATTAN — Furniture made from a climbing palm with long, slender tough stems.

RECAMIER — A chaise longue that has one end higher than the other.

SADDLE SEATS — Upholstered or solid wood seats of chairs that have been scooped out.

SAARINEN, EERO — A well-known architect from Finland who is known for his famous pedestal chairs and tables made out of sculptured plastic.

SCANDINAVIAN MODERN — A style of furniture that is simple and has no ornament. It is usually made from teak.

SECRETARY — A desk with a drop front writing surface. It generally has drawers below and shelves above.

SELF-COVERED SEAT DECK — Matching fabric used on the surface of the seat where the cushions are placed instead of muslin.

SEMANIER — A tall chest with seven drawers, also called a lingerie chest.

SETTEE — A bench with an upholstered seat and a wood or upholstered back. It is no longer than sixty-six inches.

SHIELD BACK CHAIR — A chair with a back shaped like an open shield.

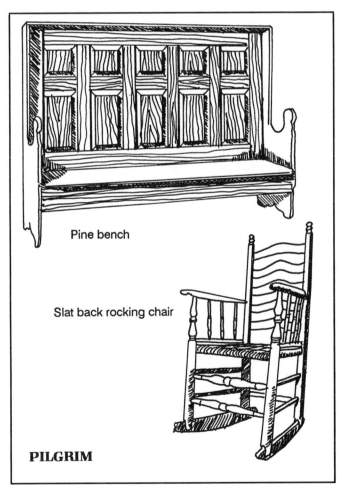

Pine bench

Slat back rocking chair

PILGRIM

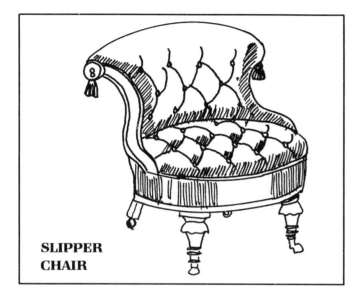

SLIPPER CHAIR

SIDE CHAIRS — Either straight chairs or dining room chairs without arms.

SIDEBOARD — A piece of dining room furniture that has compartments and shelves for holding articles of table service.

SLEEPER — A sofa bed.

SLIPPER CHAIR — A low armless upholstered chair. It was originally designed for people to sit on when putting on their shoes.

SLIP SEATS — The removable, padded seats of side or arm chairs fastened underneath with four screws.

SOFA — A seating unit, generally a minimum of fifty-two inches long, with upholstered seat and back and fixed arms. A standard sofa is eighty-four inches long.

SOFA BED — A sofa that opens into a single, double, or queen-sized bed.

SOFA TABLE — A long, narrow table used in back of a sofa.

SPLAT — The term used for the vertical support on a chair back.

SPRING EDGE — The seat springs are extended to the front of the seat deck for added comfort.

STRETCHERS — The rods that link the legs of a chair together. They can be side stretchers or cross stretchers.

TAILORED EDGE — Term meaning that the springs do not edge the seat platform.

TALLBOY — A tall chest of drawers, often made in two sections.

TRESTLE TABLE — A long table supported by uprights at each end and attached to a heavy horizontal stretcher.

TUB CHAIR — A chair with a rounded back.

UPHOLSTERED SEAT — Any chair that has been made with the full upholstering process.

WICKER — Furniture made from thin, flexible twigs that have been woven together.

WINDSOR CHAIR — An all wood chair that originated in Windsor, England. The colonists revised the chair with bow and comb backs.

WING CHAIR — An upholstered chair with a high back and projecting sides.

Hardware

BAIL HANDLE — A looped drawer pull.

BRASSES — A general name for all cabinet hardware.

DROP HANDLE — Either a pear- or teardrop-shaped pull.

ESCUTCHEON — A metal shield framing a keyhole to protect the wood from being scratched.

MOUNTS — Another general name for all cabinet hardware.

Lighting

ACCENT LIGHTING — Lighting for mood, not utility; spot lighting.

AMBIENT LIGHT — General illumination.

AIMING ANGLE — The angle from which light falls onto a surface.

BALLAST — The electrical device that supplies the proper current to start and operate a lamp.

BUILLOTTE LAMPS — Lamps with tole, silver, or bronze shades and bases, named after an eighteenth century card game. They have either one, two, or three candles and shallow opaque shades.

CANDLEPOWER — The intensity of light from a source in a specific direction.

CHROMATICITY — The degree of warmth or coolness of the color of light from a particular source.

CONTROLS — The switches and dimmers.

CORNICES — Decorative horizontal ornaments placed at the ceiling line or over a window. They can be used to conceal fluorescent lighting tubes or to cast light down onto draperies.

COVES — Over-sized cornices used on high walls to hide fluorescent lighting tubes or cast light down onto draperies. Coves will throw light up and reflect it off of the ceiling.

DIRECT LIGHTING — Lighting that shines directly on the object to be illuminated.

FINIALS — The decorative ornaments that screw into the harps or center sockets of the shades of lamps.

FIXTURES — Permanently-mounted electrical installations that hold bulbs or tubes.

FOOTCANDLE — A measure of light uniformly produced by one candle onto a surface one square foot in area from one foot away.

FRAME-MOUNTED PICTURE LIGHTS — Small clip-on lamps used for lighting important pictures.

GIRANDOLES — Sconces with back plates made of mirror.

GROUND LIGHT — Light reflected from the ground.

HARD WIRING — Built-in wiring.

HARPS — The looped wires that fit around a bulb and hold a lamp shade.

HOUSING — The part of a fixture surrounding the bulb.

ILLUMINANCE — The light that is produced.

INDIRECT LIGHTING — Lighting reflected on ceilings, walls, and other surfaces to give a soft overall illumination.

KILOWATT HOUR — The measure of electrical energy consumed. One kilowatt is equal to 1000 watts for one hour.

LOW VOLTAGE LIGHTING — Lighting that operates at 5.5 or twelve volts, not the standard 120 volts.

LUMEN — A measure of light produced by a light source.

PANEL LIGHTS — Recessed reflector boxes covered by frosted glass panels or metal grids that are set into a ceiling.

PAR LAMP — A floodlight.

SCONCES — Lighting fixtures with a back plate attached to a wall. They can hold candles or be wired electrically. They are also called wall lights or wall brackets.

SEMI-INDIRECT LIGHTING — A combination of indirect and direct lighting.

SKYLIGHT — Lighting reflected from the sky and clouds.

SOCKETS — The threaded recesses into which bulbs are screwed.

TASK LIGHT — Work light.

TORCHERES — Freestanding floor lamps. They can also be called candle stands or floor lamps.

UNIFORM LIGHTING — The same amount of light throughout a space.

Tableware

BOHEMIAN GLASS — A fine cut glass with diamond engravings.

BOROSILICATE GLASS — Glass used for cooking. The addition of boric oxide makes it heat resistant.

CASED GLASS — Also called overlay glass. It is made by coating crystal or milk glass with colored glass to form a pattern.

COUPE SHAPE — A plate that has no rim or indented center.

CRYSTAL — Originally used by the French to describe flint glass. It comes from the Greek word, charice.

CUT GLASS — Glass with patterns on the surface achieved by machine or hand.

DELFT — Earthenware with a colored tin glaze, originally from Delft, Holland.

ENGRAVED GLASS — Glass with patterns made on a wheel or by a diamond point.

ETCHED GLASS — Glass with a shallow, lacy pattern that has been etched with acid.

FLINT GLASS — An obsolete term for lead crystal.

GLAZES — The coating of glass that gives a surface its brilliance.

JASPER WARE — Made by Wedgwood in the late eighteenth century. It is black unglazed stoneware with classic decorations.

LALIQUE GLASS — Heavy, decorative French glassware.

LATTICINIO GLASS — Venetian glass which has thin, slightly swirling lines of milk glass alternating with crystal.

LOWESTOFT — A soft porcelain decorated with Chinese patterns on a blue enamel underglaze. It was originally made in Lowestoft, England.

LUSTER — The shiny surface film on porcelain or pottery made by firing metallic pigments.

MAJOLICA — Vividly colored decorative pottery with a tin glaze. It is made in Italy or Spain.

MILK GLASS — An opaque white glass.

OPEN STOCK — A pattern to be kept in a manufacturer's line for a stated number of years or for an unlimited time.

ORREFORS — High quality Swedish glassware.

PONTIL MARK — The scar left on blown glass when the iron removes the glass from the blowpipe.

PYROCERAM — A cross between glass and ceramics that has great strength but looks like china.

QUEEN'S WARE — A fine cream-colored earthenware made by Wedgwood.

RELIEF DECORATIONS — Raised patterns.

RIM SHAPE — The standard form for a plate. It has a depressed center section bordered by a two inch rim or flange.

SANDWICH GLASS — A specific manufacturer from Cape Cod, known for its pressed glass and cut, engraved, and molded tableware.

SGRAFFITO — A type of plate decoration achieved by scratching through slip to a different colored body.

SILVER PLATE — A hard, white metal that has been coated with silver by the process of electroplating.

SLIP — Clay that has been thinned and poured over another clay to color or decorate it.

STERLING SILVER — It must legally contain 92.5% pure silver. Copper is added to harden the silver and increase its wearing ability.

STEUBEN GLASS — Fine American crystal known for its great quality and beauty.

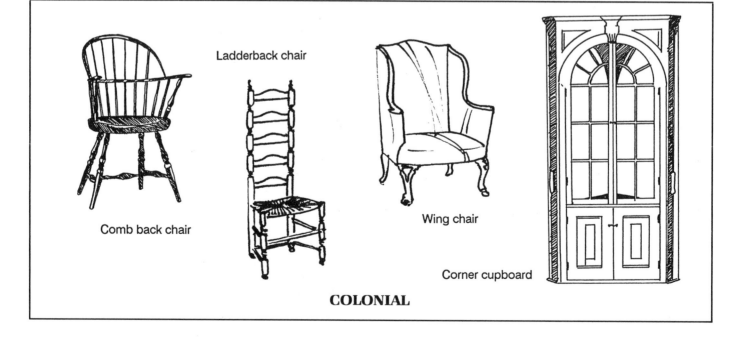

Comb back chair

Ladderback chair

Wing chair

Corner cupboard

COLONIAL

TIFFANY GLASS — Opalescent glassware that appeared in the beginning of the twentieth century.

UNDERGLAZES — Colors applied before a glaze is put on and fired.

VENETIAL GLASS — Known for its thinness and unique shapes and colors. It is a delicate, clear blown glassware from the eleventh century.

WATERFORD — An eighteenth century Irish glass. It is characterized by a geometric crosshatch cut and a low stem.

Wall Coverings

ADHESIVES — Natural or synthetic pastes for applying wall coverings.

BLANK STOCK — The material used as a base under wallpaper to provide a smooth or slightly textured surface so that the wall will look smooth and even.

BOLT — A term referring to the amount of yardage in a single, double, or triple roll of wallpaper.

BUTTED SEAMS — The edges of panels of wallpaper that butt up together with no overlap to form a neat, flat seam.

CELLULOSE PASTE — An adhesive used to hang natural wall coverings such as silk and linen. It is non-staining and odorless.

CHINOISERIE — French scenic wallpapers done with Oriental themes.

COLOR DECK — Another name for color fan; the fan of color samples you can get from a paint store.

COLOR RUN — The numbered dye lot of a particular run in which all inks and backgrounds are a consistent color. Use this number to reorder any additional paper.

COLOR WAY — The particular combination of colors in a wall covering. Most wall coverings come in a variety of color ways.

CORNICE — A decorative molding used to finish the top of a wall.

DOCUMENTARY — A wallpaper design from a given period, usually before the turn of the century. A documentary should have a seal or statement that it is an authentic pattern used in that period.

DOUBLE ROLL — A double length of one wallpaper roll, sold only as a double roll. It is usually sixteen yards long.

DYE LOT — The color run.

EMBOSSING — A design with a raised effect impressed on a wall covering.

FAUX BOIS — A decorative finish that looks like wood and is achieved with paint.

FLOCKED PAPER — Originally created to imitate Italian cut velvet. It is made by printing a pattern on paper with glue or adhesive and sprinkling finely chopped fibers onto the glue while still wet.

GLAZE — The transparent coat of paint used to change the look of a base coat.

GROUND — The background that the wall covering has been printed or embossed on. Some wallpapers can be ordered with custom grounds in the color or texture of your choice.

HOT SPOTS — These occur when wall plaster is not perfectly mixed. Concentrated spots of lime form on the wall, creating areas where wallpaper will not adhere.

MARBLING — An imitation marble finish achieved with paint.

MAT — A paint finish that is flat, with no shine or luster.

MATCH — The pattern repeat. There are small arrows or signs on the wallpaper to tell your wallpaper hanger where the match is to be made.

PATTERN REPEAT — The length of paper a particular pattern takes to repeat itself. The exact repeat will be noted on the back of the sample and on the paper itself.

PLUMB LINE — The term used by paperhangers and carpenters for a straight line. They will use a professional level or a weighted string dropped from the ceiling to find the plumb line.

PRE-PASTED — Wall coverings that have been pre-treated with an adhesive prior to packaging. This adhesive must be activated by another step.

PRE-TRIMMED — Wall coverings that have had their edges trimmed prior to packaging. Most wallpapers are not pre-trimmed.

PRIMER — A preparation coating applied to walls to seal them before hanging a wall covering.

RAILROADING — Hanging wallpaper horizontally instead of vertically. It is sometimes done to economize on the number of rolls.

REPEAT — The designer's way of saying "pattern repeat."

ROLL — The unit in which wallpaper is sold. Most American wallpaper rolls contain thirty-six square feet, untrimmed.

SEALER — Another word for "primer."

SEAM — The place where two strips of wallpaper butt up against each other.

SEAM ROLLER — The tool used to flatten seams.

SINGLE ROLL — A roll of wallpaper that is usually about eight yards long and will cover approximately thirty square feet of space.

SIZING — Used to prepare a wall for better adhesion. It is similar to priming or sealing.

SPATTERING — A decorative paint finish that gives walls a lightly flecked appearance.

STRIP — The length of wall covering that is cut to fit the height of the wall.

STRIPPABLE WALL COVERINGS — These can be removed from a wall without steaming or scraping.

TROMPE L'OEIL — Anything that fools the eye. It can be a wallpaper or painting effect.

VINYL COATED — A thin layer of vinyl has been applied to the top of a regular paper, making it more stain and moisture resistant.

WALL COVERINGS — See complete list in Chapter 12.

WALLPAPERS — See complete list in Chapter 12.

WATER TRAY — A tray in which to soak pre-pasted wallpaper.

Window Coverings

APRON — The lower portion of the window casing under the sill.

AUSTRIAN SHADE — A vertically shirred curtain with pull cords.

BARREL PLEATS — Tubular pleats evenly spaced across the top of a drapery.

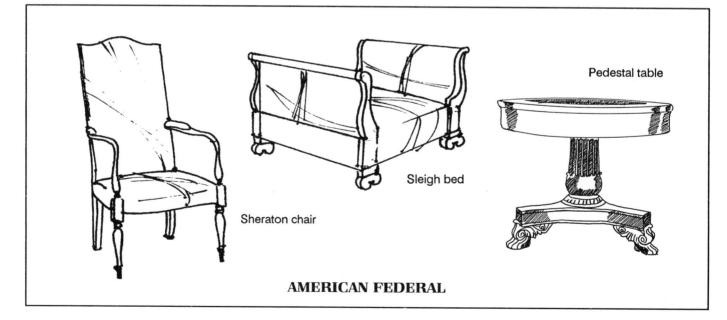

Sheraton chair

Sleigh bed

Pedestal table

AMERICAN FEDERAL

BATON — The rod and handle used to open and close draperies by hand.

BOTTOM-UP SHADE — A shade placed on a spring roller that is mounted at the bottom of a window and can be pulled up to close.

BOX PLEATS — Pleats, sewn and pressed flat, spaced evenly across the top of draperies.

BRACKETS — Hardware that attaches to the wall or window casing and supports rods, cornices, and valances.

BUCKRAM — Plainly woven jute cloth used to line draperies and valances to give them more weight.

CANOPY — A fabric covered awning used over indoor or outdoor windows.

CARRIERS — The metal or plastic eyelets on a traverse rod that hold the hooks and move the drapery on the track.

CARTRIDGE PLEATING — Barrel pleating.

CASCADE — The decorative material that falls in folds of graduated lengths at the outside corners of drapery headings.

CURTAINS — See complete list in Chapter 15.

FACING — Lining used on the edges of draperies to give them more body.

FESTOONS — The decorative chains or strips of material that loop over a valance pole or rod.

FINIAL — The decorative end piece used for curtain rods or tops of cornices.

FLOOR PULLEY — A spring tension device used with a traverse rod to take up the slack in the rope.

FRENCH PLEATING — Fabric that is gathered and stitched together in small folds at even intervals.

HARDWARE — A general term for all the accessories necessary to operate windows: pulls, locks, weights, rods, brackets, holdbacks, hooks, rings, carriers, finials, clips.

INSTALLATION — Installing rods and other hardware as well as hanging any window coverings.

JABOT — The pleated piece of material which hangs under or over the sides of a valance.

LAMBREQUIN — A covered plywood drapery frame over the top and/or sides of window.

OPAQUE — Impenetrable by light, as in lined draperies.

OVERDRAPERIES — The outer and most decorative draperies around a window.

OVERLAP — The center closing where two drapery panels overlap each other.

PAVILIONS — Draperies tied back like the flaps of a tent.

PELMET — A cornice or valance that hides the drapery rod. It is usually shaped out of wire.

PINCH PLEATS — Evenly spaced pleats that are pinched or squeezed together, then tacked at the pinched point.

PLEATING TAPE — The tape attached to the back of the drapery heading in which the hooks are placed for hanging.

PUDDLE — Designer term for fabric that flows onto a floor and creates a "puddled" effect.

PULL — The draw on a traverse drapery.

RETURNS — The brackets that hold cornices and rods out from the wall.

SASH — The movable part of a window or the frame that holds the panes together.

SHADES — See complete list in Chapter 15.

SHEERS — Fine, delicate, transparent curtains.

SHIRRING — The gathering of fabric in parallel rows.

STATIONARY — Curtains or draperies hung in a fixed position.

SWAG — To drape fabric at the top of a window, over the drapery headings, and have it catch up at the ends.

TABS — Decorative pieces of fabric through which the rod is inserted instead of a pocket.

TACKED — Sewn.

TIER — One of a series of rows of fabric placed one above another.

TRACK — A rod with carriers to move draperies that are suspended by hooks from the carriers.

TRAVERSE — Drapery or curtain rods that can be opened or closed by pulling a cord.

WINDOWS — See complete list in Chapter 15.

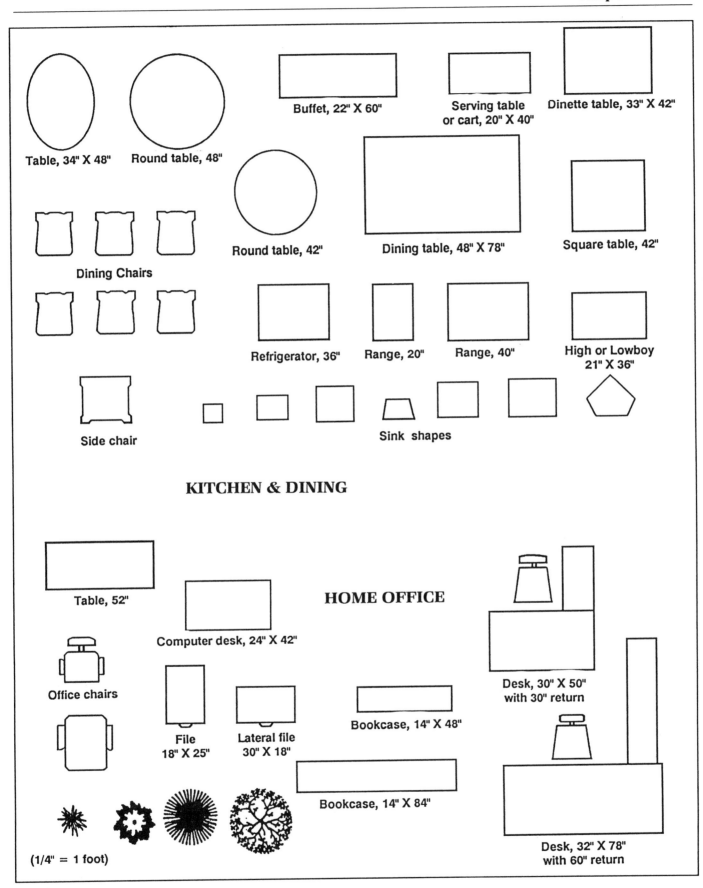

Table, 34" X 48"

Round table, 48"

Buffet, 22" X 60"

Serving table or cart, 20" X 40"

Dinette table, 33" X 42"

Round table, 42"

Dining table, 48" X 78"

Square table, 42"

Dining Chairs

Refrigerator, 36"

Range, 20"

Range, 40"

High or Lowboy 21" X 36"

Side chair

Sink shapes

KITCHEN & DINING

Table, 52"

Computer desk, 24" X 42"

HOME OFFICE

Office chairs

File 18" X 25"

Lateral file 30" X 18"

Bookcase, 14" X 48"

Desk, 30" X 50" with 30" return

Bookcase, 14" X 84"

(1/4" = 1 foot)

Desk, 32" X 78" with 60" return

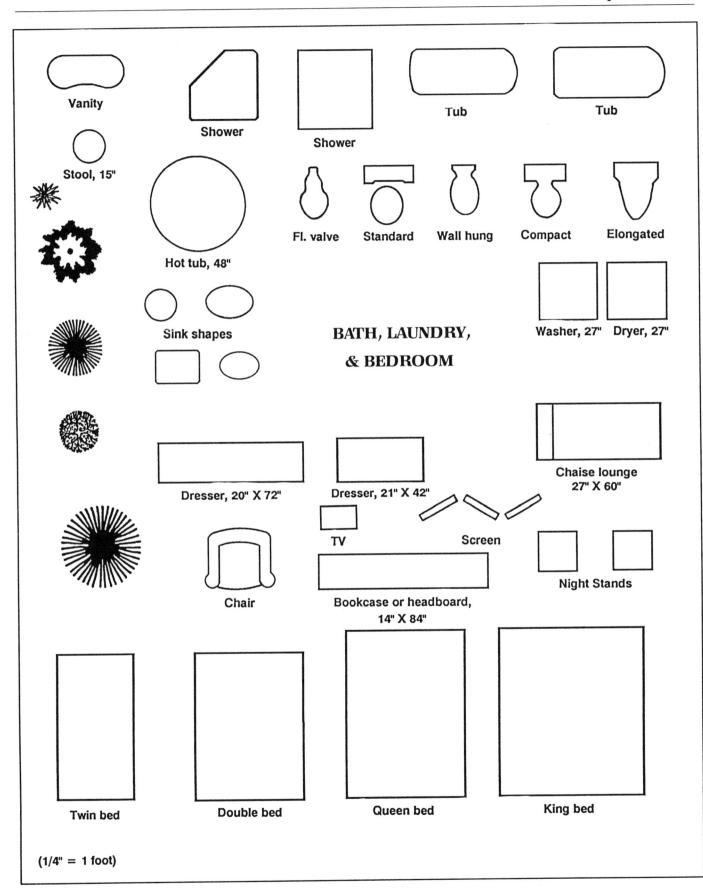

Vanity

Shower

Shower

Tub

Tub

Stool, 15"

Fl. valve

Standard

Wall hung

Compact

Elongated

Hot tub, 48"

Washer, 27"   Dryer, 27"

Sink shapes

**BATH, LAUNDRY,
& BEDROOM**

Chaise lounge
27" X 60"

Dresser, 20" X 72"

Dresser, 21" X 42"

TV

Screen

Night Stands

Chair

Bookcase or headboard,
14" X 84"

Twin bed

Double bed

Queen bed

King bed

(1/4" = 1 foot)

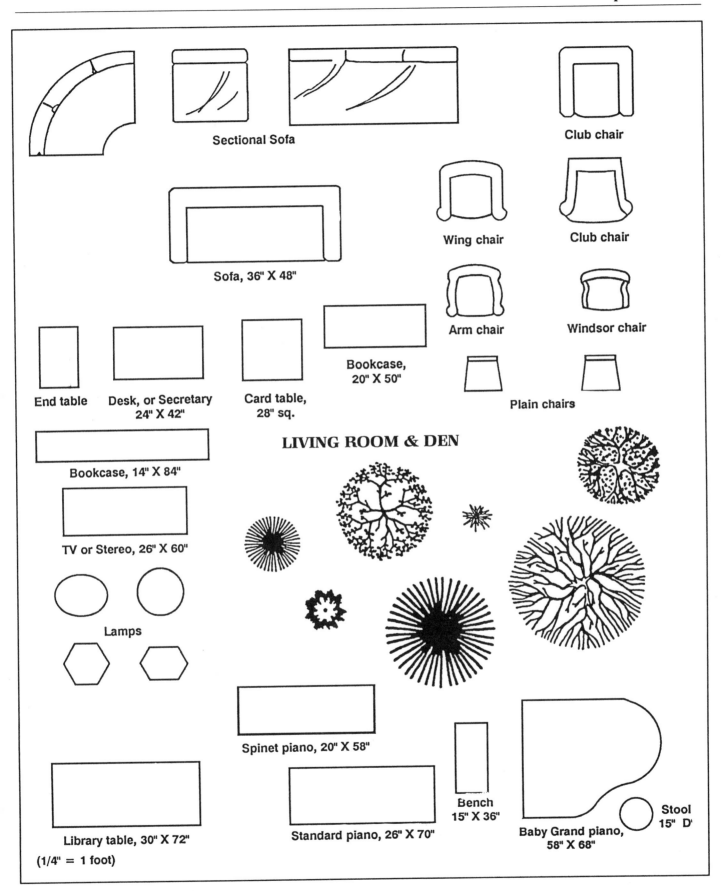

Sectional Sofa

Club chair

Wing chair

Club chair

Sofa, 36" X 48"

Arm chair

Windsor chair

End table

Desk, or Secretary
24" X 42"

Card table,
28" sq.

Bookcase,
20" X 50"

Plain chairs

Bookcase, 14" X 84"

LIVING ROOM & DEN

TV or Stereo, 26" X 60"

Lamps

Spinet piano, 20" X 58"

Library table, 30" X 72"

Standard piano, 26" X 70"

Bench
15" X 36"

Baby Grand piano,
58" X 68"

Stool
15" D'

(1/4" = 1 foot)

Index